Wolf Schmid

Narratology

An Introduction

De Gruyter

Translated by Alexander Starritt

ISBN 978-3-11-022631-7
e-ISBN 978-3-11-022632-4

Library of Congress Cataloging-in-Publication Data

Schmid, Wolf.
  [Narratologiia. English]
  Narratology : an introduction / by Wolf Schmid.
      p. cm.
  Includes bibliographical references and index.
  English translation of: Elemente der Narratologie, which is a German translation and expansion of the Russian work Narratologija (Moscow 2003).
  ISBN 978-3-11-0226321-7 (alk. paper)
  1. Narration (Rhetoric)   I. Title.
  PN212.S3413   2010
  808–dc22

                                                    2010008423

Bibliographic information published by the Deutsche Nationalbibliothek

The Deutsche Nationalbibliothek lists this publication in the Deutsche Nationalbibliografie; detailed bibliographic data are available in the Internet at http://dnb.d-nb.de.

© 2010 Walter de Gruyter GmbH & Co. KG, Berlin/New York

Printing: AZ Druck und Datentechnik GmbH, Kempten
∞ Printed on acid-free paper

Printed in Germany

www.degruyter.com

Contents

Preface IX

I. Features of narrative in fiction
   1. Narrativity and eventfulness.. 1
      a) The classical and structuralist concepts of narrativity 1
      b) Narration and description.. 5
      c) Mediated and mimetic narrative texts............................. 6
      d) Events and eventfulness 8
      e) Tellability 13
      f) Eventfulness, interpretation, and context 13
      g) Historicity of eventfulness..................................... 16
      h) Temporal and non-temporal linking............................... 18
   2. Fictionality... 21
      a) Fiction and mimesis... 21
      b) The controversy about fictionality 23
      c) Characteristic features of fictionality 25
      d) Representation of other people's inner worlds 27
      e) The fictive world 29
      f) Author communication and narrative communication................ 32

II. The entities in a narrative work
   1. Model of communication levels...................................... 34
   2. The abstract author.. 36
      a) Concrete and abstract entities 36
      b) History of the abstract author concept 37
      c) Critique of the abstract author concept 40
      d) For and against the abstract author 42
      e) Two attempts to split the abstract author 44
      f) Sketch of a systematic definition............................... 48
   3. The abstract reader.. 51
      a) The abstract reader as an attribute of the abstract author..... 51
      b) History of the abstract reader concept 52
      c) Definition of the abstract reader............................... 54
      d) Presumed addressee and ideal recipient.......................... 55
      e) Critique of the ideal recipient concept......................... 56

4. The fictive narrator... 57
   a) Explicit and implicit representation of the narrator 58
   b) Individuality and anthropomorphism of the narrator.......... 60
   c) The narrator's markedness 61
   d) Abstract author or narrator?................................ 65
   e) Typologies of the narrator.................................. 66
   f) Primary, secondary, and tertiary narrators.................... 67
   g) Diegetic and non-diegetic narrators......................... 68
   h) Types of diegetic narrators 74
   i) Narrating and narrated self................................. 76
5. The fictive reader 78
   a) Fictive addressee and fictive recipient 78
   b) Fictive and abstract reader 80
   c) Explicit and implicit representation of the fictive reader 81
   d) Narration with a sidelong glance at the fictive reader
      (*A Raw Youth*).. 84
   e) Dialogic narrative monologue 87

III. Point of view
1. Theories of point of view, perspective, and focalization 89
   a) F. K. Stanzel... 90
   b) G. Genette and M. Bal 91
   c) B. A. Uspensky, J. Lintvelt, and Sh. Rimmon.................. 95
2. A model of narrative point of view 99
   a) The happenings as the object of point of view 99
   b) Comprehension and representation.......................... 99
   c) The parameters of point of view............................. 100
   d) Narratorial and figural point of view 105
   e) Point of view in diegetic narrative ("The Shot")............... 107
   f) Narratorial and figural manifestations in the five parameters of
      point of view 109
   g) Compact and diffuse points of view 116
   h) On the methods of analysis: three central questions........... 117

IV. Narrator's text and characters' text
1. The two components of the narrative text 118
   a) Narrator's discourse and characters' discourse................. 118
   b) The characters' discourse in the narrative text 118
   c) Narrator's discourse and narrator's text, characters' discourse
      and characters' text 120
2. Ornamental prose and *skaz*..................................... 122
   a) Ornamental prose.. 122

	b) The *skaz*: definitions	129
	c) The *skaz*: history of research (B. Eikhenbaum, Yu. Tynyanov, V. Vinogradov, M. Bakhtin)	130
	d) Characterizing and ornamental *skaz*	132
	e) Features of characterizing *skaz*	133
	f) Ornamental *skaz*	135
3.	The interference of narrator's text and characters' text	137
	a) The structure of text interference	137
	b) The opposition of the texts and their features	139
	c) The pure texts and the neutralization of oppositions	143
	d) Text interference as a transformation of the characters' text	145
	e) Direct discourse and direct interior monologue	148
	f) Quoted figural designation	152
	g) Indirect representation of speech, thought, and perception	153
	h) Autonomous indirect discourse	155
	i) Free indirect discourse (FID): definition	156
	j) FID in German, English, French, and Russian	158
	k) Free indirect perception	162
	l) Free indirect monologue	163
	m) FID in diegetic narration	165
	n) Figurally colored narration (FCN)	166
	o) Functions of text interference	168
	p) Ambiguity and bi-textuality	170

V. Narrative constitution: happenings—story—narrative—presentation of the narrative

1.	"Fabula" and "sujet" in Russian formalism	175
	a) Models of narrative constitution	175
	b) V. Shklovsky	176
	c) M. Petrovsky	179
	d) L. Vygotsky	181
	e) B. Tomashevsky	184
2.	The overcoming of formalist reductionism	186
	a) "Histoire" and "discours" in French structuralism	186
	b) Three-tier models	188
3.	The four narrative tiers	190
	a) The ideal genetic model	190
	b) The location of point of view	194
	c) From the happenings to the story	195
	d) Selection and point of view	197
	e) Compression and expansion	199
	f) The non-selected	204

  g) From the story to the narrative 205
  h) The composition of the narrative and point of view 207
  i) From the narrative to its presentation 208
  j) An ideal genetic model of point of view 209
  k) Discourse happenings and discourse story 211
  l) The semiotic model 212
  m) The correlation of the tiers in verbal art 214
Conclusion 216
Works cited 221
Glossary and index of narratological terms 243
Index of authors and narratives 251

Preface

The present book is based on my Russian-language *Narratologiya* (Moscow 2003, 2nd ed. 2008) and its German equivalent, *Elemente der Narratologie* (Berlin/New York 2005, 2nd ed. 2008). This English edition has been revised and extended in response to reactions to the Russian and German versions.

That the book initially appeared in Russian and in Russia was due to the fact that modern narratology owes many of its categories to the essential ideas of Russian theorists and schools. Particular mention must be made here of the proponents of Russian formalism (Viktor Shklovsky, Boris Tomashevsky, Yury Tynyanov, Roman Jakobson), theorists such as Vladimir Propp, Mikhail Bakhtin, Valentin Voloshinov, and the members of the so-called Moscow-Tartu school, such as Yury Lotman and Boris Uspensky. *Narratologiya* was intended to familiarize the Russian reader with recent developments in a theory that is ultimately of Russian origin, and to illuminate the theoretical potential, not yet fully realized in its own country, of the Russian contribution. The decision to make the Russian *Narratologiya* accessible to the West was based on the consideration that the contribution made by Russia (and other Slavic countries) to the theory of narrative, no matter how much attention was paid to it by the nascent discipline of narratology in the 1960s and 1970s,[1] demanded an even more comprehensive appraisal.[2]

However, the focus of the present book—including its English version—is not so much on the history as on a systematic approach to the theory. Historical surveys of some key concepts serve primarily to describe the corresponding phenomena. In contrast to the Russian title *Narratologiya*, which was designed to introduce an as yet not established term to the motherland of formalism and structuralism, and thus present the discipline, the titles chosen for the West and its elaborated narratological context, *Elemente der Narratologie* and *Narratology. An Introduction*, signal that the approach adopted is aimed at fundamentals, and is not exhaustive.

After an exposition of the features of narration in fiction, the book concentrates on elements taken, on the one hand, from the study of perspective (the communication structure and entities of a narrative work, narrative point of view, relationship between narrator's text and characters' text) and,

---

1 Cf. Todorov 1966, 1971a, 1971b.
2 On the influence of Slavic schools on narratology cf. Schmid (ed. 2009a; 2009b).

on the other, from the study of the *sujet* (narrativity and eventfulness, narrative transformations of happenings). Issues about the anthropological conditions and pragmatics of narration are not presented, or are touched on at most. Also omitted are the nature of narratology, the relevance of its tools for related disciplines and the question of so-called "new narratologies."[3] Center stage in the book is taken by constitutive structures of fictional narrative texts. As a result, it can be seen as a theory of the narrative work, oriented in a particular way on the Slavic origins of research into narrative.

In the English version, a number of examples from Russian literature have been replaced with examples from Anglophone literatures.

For the research of English translations and for editorial help with the production of the manuscript, I am grateful to Maciej Grzenkowicz. My thanks go also to Elizabeth Everard, for help with proof-reading.

Abbreviations of Literary Sources

Augustine = Saint Augustine: *Confessions*. Ed. by M. P. Foley. Tr. by F. J. Sheed. Indianapolis 2007.
Chekhov, S = *Anton Chekhov's Short Stories. Texts of the stories, backgrounds, criticism*. Selected and ed. by Ralph E. Matlaw. New York 1979.
Chekhov, PSS = Anton P. Chekhov: *Polnoe sobranie sochinenii i pisem v 30 t. Sochineniya v 18 t*. Moskva 1974–82. Vol. VIII.
Coetzee, MP = John M. Coetzee: *The Master of Petersburg*. London 1999.
Dostoevsky, BK = Fyodor Mikhailovich Dostoevsky: *The Brothers Karamazov*. Tr. by Constance Garnett. Chicago 1952.
Dostoevsky, D = Fyodor Dostoevsky: "The Double. A Petersburg Poem." In F. D., *The Eternal Husband and Other Stories*. Tr. by Constance Garnett. London [1917], 138–284.
Dostoevsky, EH = Fyodor Dostoevsky: "The Eternal Husband." In F. D., *The Eternal Husband and Other Stories*. Tr. by Constance Garnett. London [1917], 1–137.
Dostoevsky, GS = Fyodor Dostoevsky: "A Gentle Spirit." In F. D., *The Eternal Husband and Other Stories*. Tr. by Constance Garnett. London [1917], 285–323.
Dostoevsky, MP = Fyodor Dostoyevsky: "Mr Prokharchin." In F. D., *Poor Folk and Other Stories*. Tr. by D. McDuff. London 1988, 215–48.

---

3   For the first area, cf. the anthology produced by the first colloquium of the Hamburg Research Group "Narratology," *What is Narratology? Questions and Answers Regarding the Status of a Theory* (Kindt/Müller [eds.] 2003); an answer to the question of narratology outside the limits of literary study is sought by the anthology of the second colloquium, *Narratology beyond Literary Criticism* (Meister [ed.] 2005); on the question of multiple narratologies and "new narratologies," cf. the anthology from David Herman (ed. 1999) and Ansgar Nünning's contribution to the first colloquium (Nünning 2003).

Dostoevsky, NU = Fyodor Dostoevsky: *Notes from the Underground and The Gambler.* Tr. by J. Kentish. Oxford UP 1991.
Dostoevsky, P = Fyodor Dostoevsky: *The Possessed.* Tr. by A. R. MacAndrew. New York 1962.
Dostoevsky, PSS = Dostoevsky, Fyodor M.: *Polnoe sobranie sochinenii v 30 t.* Leningrad 1972-90.
Dostoevsky, RY = Fyodor Dostoevsky: *A Raw Youth.* Tr. by Constance Garnett (= The novels of Fyodor Dostoevsky, volume VII). London 1916.
Feuchtwanger, JK = Lion Feuchtwanger: *Der jüdische Krieg* (= Gesammelte Werke in Einzelbänden. 2). Berlin 1998.
Feuchtwanger, Josephus = Lion Feuchtwanger: *Josephus. A Historical Romance.* Tr. by W. & E. Muir. London 1932.
Flaubert, MB = Gustave Flaubert: *Madame Bovary.* Paris 1972.
Gogol, O = Nikolay Gogol: "The Overcoat." In N. G., *The Overcoat and Other Short Stories.* Tr. by I. F. Hapgood. Mineola, NY, 1992, 79-102.
Gogol, VE = Nikolay Vasilevich Gogol: "Village Evenings near Dikanka." In N. V. G., *Village Evenings near Dikanka and Mirgorod.* Tr. by Christopher English. Oxford/New York 1994, 1-216.
Joyce, Ul. = James Joyce: *Ulysses.* 7th impr. London 1955.
Karamzin, SP = Nikolay M. Karamzin: *Selected Prose.* Tr. by H. M. Nebel. Evanston 1969.
Mann, RH = Thomas Mann: *Royal Highness.* Tr. by A. C. Curtis. London 1940.
Nabokov, KQK = Vladimir Nabokov: *King, Queen, Knave.* London 1968.
Nabokov, TS = Vladimir Nabokov: "Torpid Smoke." In V. N., *Collected Stories.* London 2001, 396-400.
Pushkin, EO = Alexander Pushkin: *Eugene Onegin. A Novel in Verse.* Tr. by Vladimir Nabokov, Vol. I. Princeton UP 1990.
Pushkin, Prose = Alexander Pushkin: *Complete Prose Fiction.* Tr. by Paul Debreczeny. Stanford 1983.
Rilke, Weise = Rainer Maria Rilke: *Die Weise von Liebe und Tod.* Frankfurt a. M. 1974.
Rilke, Lay = Rainer Maria Rilke: *The Lay of Love and Death of Cornet Christopher Rilke.* Tr. by L. Phillips & S. Schimanski. London 1948.
Solzhenitsyn, OD = Alexander Solzhenitsyn: *One Day in the Life of Ivan Denisovich.* Tr. by Ralph Parker. London 1963.
Tolstoy, AK = Leo Tolstoy: *Anna Karenina.* Ed. and introd. by L. J. Kent & N. Berberova. The Constance Garnett Translation revised by the editors. New York 1965.
Tolstoy, PSS = L. N. Tolstoy: *Polnoe sobranie sochinenii v 91 t.* Moskva 1936-64.
Tolstoy, Sebastopol = Leo Tolstoy: "Sebastopol in December." In L. T., *The Sebastopol Sketches.* Tr. by D. McDuff. London 1986, 39-58.
Tolstoy, Strider = Leo Tolstoy: *Strider: the Story of a Horse.* Tr. by Louise and Aylmer Maude. http://great-authors.albertarose.org/leo_tolstoy/strider/
Tolstoy, WaP = Leo Tolstoy: *War and Peace.* Tr. by Constance Garnett. New York [n.d., ca. 1936].
Turgenev, A = Ivan Sergeevich Turgenev: "Asya." In I. T., *First Love, and Other Stories.* Tr. by Richard Freeborn. Oxford 1999.

Woolf, L = Virginia Woolf: *To the Lighthouse*. 9th impr.. London 1951.
Woolf, W = Virginia Woolf: *The Waves*. Oxford UP 1992.
Zamyatin, Cave = Yevgeny Zamyatin: "The Cave." In Y. Z., *The Dragon and Other Stories*. Tr. by M. Ginsburg. Harmondsworth 1983, 140–49.
Zoshchenko, LA = Mikhail Zoshchenko: "The Lady Aristocrat." Tr. by H. McLean. In *Mass Culture in Soviet Russia: Tales, Poems, Songs, Movies, Plays, and Folklore, 1917–1953*. Ed. by J. Von Geldern, R. Stites. Indiana UP 1995, 54–56.

Russian names and titles

In the text the established English transcription of some Russian words, names, and titles has been retained. Russian names ending in *-ii* and *-yi* are spelled with *-y* (*Dostoevsky* rathe than *Dostoevskii*). The soft sign is omitted in proper names and titles in the English text (*Gogol* rather than *Gogol'*).

I. Features of narrative in fiction

1. Narrativity and eventfulness

a) The classical and structuralist concepts of narrativity

Two distinct concepts of narrativity can be identified in the study of literature. The first became established in classical narrative theory, particularly in the works of German critics, long before the term *narratology* was introduced to describe it. In this tradition those texts were regarded as narrative which contained specific features of communication. Narration was bound to the presence of a mediating authority, the narrator, and contrasted with the direct presentation of events in drama. The existence of such a mediator between the author and the narrated world was the defining feature of narrativity in classical narrative theory. The nature of narration is revealed in the refraction of the narrated reality through the prism of the narrator. This paradigm provides the background for the argument of Käte Friedemann (1910), student of Oskar Walzel and the founder of classical German narrative theory, when she compares the immediate presentation of reality in drama with the mediation that takes place in narrative:

> "Real" in the dramatic sense is an action that is occurring now, which we witness and in the development of which into the future we participate. "Real" in the epic sense, however, is not primarily the narrated action, but the narration itself. (Friedemann 1910, 25)

With these words, Friedemann openly distances herself from the views of Friedrich Spielhagen (1883, 1898). In the name of the quest for objectivity, he demands that epic authors renounce the use of a subjective narrating authority: that means, however, that he demands—Käte Friedemann supposes—nothing other than "dramatic illusion":

> [The narrator] symbolizes the epistemological conception familiar to us since Kant that we do not grasp the world as it is in itself, but rather as it has passed through the medium of an observing mind. (Friedemann 1910, 26)

Many theories of the more recent past have continued to describe the distinctive nature of narrative in terms of a mediation process. Franz Stanzel, for example, begins his *Theory of Narrative* (Stanzel 1979; tr. 1984), in which he summarizes his earlier works (Stanzel 1955, 1964) against the background of new theoretical horizons, by reaffirming mediacy (*Mittelbarkeit*) as the defining characteristic of narrative texts. He thereby renews the status of a property that he had previously invoked as the indispensable defining feature of narration in the introduction to his *Narrative Situations in the Novel* (Stanzel 1955; tr. 1971).

The second concept of narrativity was developed in the structuralist study of narrative, for which Tzvetan Todorov (1969) coined the term *narratology*. In structuralism, the defining characteristic of narrative is not a feature of discourse or communication but rather a feature of what is narrated. Texts that we describe as narrative in the structuralist sense of the word contrast with descriptive texts in that they contain a temporal structure and represent changes of state.

The classical concept restricts narrativity to the domain of verbal communication, covering only those works containing a narrating authority, or mediator, including purely descriptive sketches and travel reports, while excluding all lyric, dramatic, and cinematic texts. The structuralist concept, on the other hand, can apply to a representation in any medium, but excludes representations whose referents do not have a temporal structure and consequently do not contain any changes of state. Thus, drama and lyric poetry are also narrative, in so far as changes of state are portrayed in them.

It might seem as if we have to choose one concept or the other, but practical experience with texts makes clear that, in fact, neither is completely satisfactory—the two concepts are either counterintuitive or insufficiently differentiated. As a result of these shortcomings, a mixed concept has emerged in literary criticism, and it is this hybrid notion that the present chapter is intended to describe and systematize.

To begin with, we must note that the concept of narrative has two basic meanings, one broad and one narrow. They will be terminologically distinguished at a later stage.

The broader concept of narrative refers to representations that contain a change of state (or of situation). In the context of this definition, a state is to be understood as a set of properties pertaining to an agent or an external situation at a particular point in time. We can distinguish internal and external states on the basis of whether the represented features are linked to the inner life of the agent or to elements of the external situation. (A state can, of course, be a combination of features of external situation and internal properties of an agent.)

The minimal condition of narrativity is that at least one change of state must be represented. Edward Morgan Forster's famous example of a minimal story is still too extensive. Forster (1927) coined the example: "The king died and then the queen died." Gérard Genette (1983; tr. 1988, 20) pointed out that, for a minimal story, it is sufficient to have the simple "The king died."[1] The changes of state and their circumstances do not need to be explicitly represented. For narrativity, it is sufficient that the change is implied, for example through the representation of two mutually contrasting states.

The change of state that constitutes narrativity implies at least the following:

(1) A temporal structure with at least two states, the initial situation and the final situation (the king alive and the king dead).
(2) The equivalence of the initial and final situations, that is, the presence of a similarity and a contrast between the states, or, more precisely, the identity and difference of the properties of those states (being alive and being dead form a classical equivalence).[2]
(3) Both states, and the change that takes place between them, must concern one and the same acting or suffering subject (in our case this is the poor king).[3]

Some theorists have gone a step further and postulated that, in addition to the relationship of temporal sequentiality, there is also some kind of motivational relationship between the states or situations. One of the earliest of these theorists is Boris Tomashevsky, associated with the Russian formalists, who in his *Theory of Literature* (1925; tr. 1965a, 66) contrasts narrative works with descriptive works and calls the former "works with a fabula"[4]; he stipulates that they must be bound together by temporal *and* causal connections.

The requirement that there must be more than just a temporal connection between the states has been repeatedly proposed in different guises.

---

1 Forster's definition of the minimal story and Genette's undercutting of it are discussed from a cognitivist perspective by Meister 2003, 23–26.
2 Complete identity of the properties would mean that there would not be a change of state at all, while absolute difference would prevent a change of state from occurring because the situations at the beginning and end of a change must be comparable by having something in common.
3 Wolf-Dieter Stempel (1973) identifies the following set of requirements for the minimal narrative sequence: the subject affected by the transformation must be identical; the contents of the narrative statement must be compatible; there must be a contrast between the predicates; and the facts must stand in chronological order. Prince (1973b) posits a more differentiated catalog of requirements for narrativity, which is itself reformulated by Titzmann (1992, 2003).
4 Unfortunately, in L. T. Lemon and M. J. Reis's anthology (1965), which was authoritative in the reception of Russian formalists in the English-speaking world, the key formalist terms *fabula* and *sujet* (cf. Schmid 2009c, 1–2) were translated with *story* and *plot*, which made them appear to be equivalents of Forster's (1927) well-known terms. The equation of the entirely different dichotomies *fabula* vs. *sujet* und *story* vs. *plot* led to not inconsiderable terminological confusion. Clarity in the classification of the four terms was provided first by Sternberg (1974, 8–14; 1976), Volek (1977) and García Landa (1998, 32–60).

But, nonetheless, the minimal definition of narrativity can and should be formulated in such a way that it does not require the presence of an additional (e.g. causal) connection between the states. After all, only rarely do literary texts contain an explicitly expressed causality. For the most part, the cause of a change of state is open and must be "determined" (Ingarden 1931; tr. 1973a, 246) or "concretized" (Ingarden 1937; 1973b, 50) by the reader. Even if the reader of a story encounters a passage that is so explicit that it can only be read in a single, unambiguous manner, it is still the case that the reader must interpret it in order for the relations of cause and effect to be concretized. Moreover, in many works there are actually a number of very different possible explanations for a single change of state.[5]

Martinez/Scheffel (1999, 111–18), discussing the three types of "motivation"[6]—the causal, the eschatological (in texts with a mythical world view), and finally, (following Tomashevsky 1925) the compositional or esthetic motivation, which is not part of the represented world—, come to this conclusion: even when causal links are not explained in the text, they are nonetheless existent in the narrated world, and are concretized by the reader. However, a motivation of this sort, existent in the text and only to be more or less adequately analyzed by the reader, should not be taken as the rule. On the question of whether represented states are causally related, it is not seldom that literature keeps the reader in a state of irresolvable uncertainty.

As readers, we tend to see a causal connection between states that follow one another temporally.[7] But this does not mean that the connections we infer are actually contained in the text, nor that they explain its logic. Causality and other forms of motivation, which are the concerns of interpretation, need not be present, in any case, in a minimal definition of narrativity. A text is already narrative if it contains only temporal connections.[8]

---

5   Ambiguous motivation which underlies an action and the causality of events should not be misinterpreted as a property unique to post-realistic poetics. In Alexander Pushkin's pre-realist prose, above all in the *Tales of Belkin* (1830), the reasons for the heroes' actions are enigmatic and can be read in any number of ways (see Schmid 1991).

6   Cf. already Martinez 1996, 13–36.

7   On the logic of *Post hoc ergo propter hoc* ("After this, therefore because of this"), which Aristotle (*Sophistical refutations* 167b, 168a; *Rhetoric* 1401b) called into question, cf. now Pier 2007.

8   The Hamburg Research Group "Narratology" has discussed the question of whether the category of point of view, or perspective, should be included in the definition of narrativity; I believe that it should not. The presence of an implicit perspective is not unique to narration but is really a property of all modes of representation. Any representation of reality presupposes the selection, naming, and evaluation of certain elements of what takes place; and this inherently entails the presence of perspective. In other words, every representation of reality has its own particular perceptual, spatial, temporal, axiological, and linguistic point of view (see below, III.2).

1. Narrativity and eventfulness

Many, but by no means all structuralist definitions concur in stating that narrative texts in the broader sense described above narrate a story. *Story* itself has a variety of meanings—Prince's *Dictionary of Narratology* (Prince 1987) distinguishes five definitions of the concept. For our purposes, we shall take *story* as referring to the content of narrative (as opposed to discourse). What is the relationship between story and change of state? How many changes of state are needed to make a story? The difference between change of state and story is not a quantitative one, the difference between them lies in their extensions—the changes of state form a subset of the story. As well as represented changes of state, which are *dynamic* elements, a story includes *static* elements, which are the states or situations themselves, the settings and the agents or patients within them. Thus, by necessity, the presentation of a story combines *narrative* and *descriptive* modes.

b) Narration and description

Descriptive texts are the opposite of texts which are narrative in the broader sense discussed above. Descriptive texts represent states: they describe conditions, draw pictures or portraits, portray social milieus, or categorize natural and social phenomena. They represent a single moment in time and a single state of affairs. Description is also found in texts which represent more than one state of affairs if those states of affairs lack the double bond of similarity and contrast or are not connected to a single identical agent or element of setting.

Despite the clear theoretical contrast between the narrative and the descriptive text, the boundaries between them are fluid, and deciding the category of a given text is often a matter of interpretation. As has been shown above, a descriptive component is necessarily present in all narration—it is impossible to represent the initial and final states of a change without employing a certain amount of description. Conversely, any description can employ narrative means in order to foreground particular aspects of a situation. Thus, whether a text is descriptive or narrative in nature depends not on the quantity of the static or dynamic segments in it, but on the function which they have in the overall context of the work. This functionality can assume a distinctly hybrid character. For most texts, the nearest we can get to a definitive classification is identifying the dominance of one of the two modes, which itself is a matter of interpretation. When a text includes no more than the description of, say, two situations, it can be interpreted equally as descriptive or narrative. (The latter, of course, presupposes that there is an equivalence between the two situations.) The reader who treats such a text as a narrative will focus on difference, on what is inconstant in the elements of the text, and thereby read a change of state into it.

Conversely, the reader who understands the text as a description will treat the differences between the situations as differences between equally representative views of one and the same phenomenon and concentrate on what the different elements have in common.

Tomashevsky includes works of travel writing in the class of descriptive texts "if the account is only about the sights and not about the personal adventures of the travelers" (Tomashevsky 1925; tr. 1965, 66). However, a description of travel can become a narrative without explicitly thematizing the traveler's internal state; this can happen when a transformation inside the seeing figure becomes apparent from the selection of what is seen. In such cases, it is clear that we are dealing with an implicit narrative structure in which the different states, and the change in the seeing subject which can explain them are indirectly suggested by indices or symptoms in the description.

In general, we can assume that a tendency towards narrativity develops in descriptive texts if and when a describing authority makes itself apparent in them. Certainly, the resultant narrativity is related not to what is described but rather to the presence that describes and the way in which it does so. The changes that take place in this case are related not to the *diegesis*[9] but to the *exegesis*[10]; they are changes in the consciousness of the describing authority and constitute a story located on the level of discourse, a "discourse story" (*Erzählgeschichte*, as used in Schmid 1982).

c) Mediated and mimetic narrative texts

I propose that a text is narrative in the narrower sense of the word if it both denotes a story and, implicitly or explicitly, represents the mediating authority (narrator) behind this story. This narrower definition immediately excludes that subset of texts which represent a transformation without the

---

9   *Diegesis* (from Greek διηγήσις 'narration') is taken here to denote the narrated world or storyworld. The adjective *diegetic* means 'belonging to the narrated world'. In narratology, *diegesis* has a different meaning than in classical rhetoric (cf. Weimar 1997). For Plato, the term denotes 'pure narration' in contrast with 'representation' (mimesis) of the hero's speech. The new diegesis concept was introduced by Etienne Souriau (1951), a theoretist of film narration, who uses *diégèse* to denote the world represented in a work of art. Genette (1972; tr. 1988, 17) defines *diégèse* as the "spatio-temporal universe designated by the narrative" and the corresponding adjective *diégétique* as "that which has reference or belongs to the story."

10 The term *exegesis* (from Greek ἐξήγησις, 'analysis', 'explanation'), which appears as a synonym for *narratio* in the Latin grammarian Diomedes's *Ars* (4th century P.D.), refers to the level of narration and of the narrator's comments, explanations, reflections and metanarrative remarks that accompany a story.

1. Narrativity and eventfulness

mediation of a narrator. These include dramas, films, comic strips, ballets, pantomimes, narrative paintings, and so on.

The least complicated terminological way to represent our findings is to refer to narrative in the broader sense simply as "narrative," while narrative in the narrower sense can be sensibly referred to with the term "mediated."

The theory presented in this book refers to those texts in which the classical concept of narrativity coincides with the structuralist one. Its subject matter will therefore be literary texts that present a story and thereby represent, more or less explicitly, the mediating authority of a narrator. (This certainly does not mean that most of the categories handled cannot be applied to narrative texts in the broader sense.)

The typology of texts is illustrated in the following diagram (the mass of mediated narrative texts on which the present book concentrates has been emphasized with a double border; the remaining text types, discursive, edifying, didactic etc. texts, are not further differentiated):

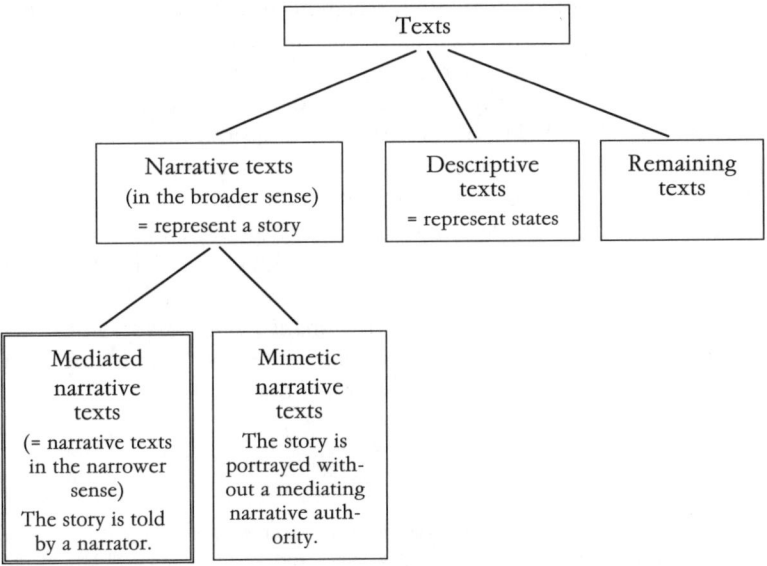

This diagram is a modification of Seymour Chatman's well-known model (Chatman 1990, 115), in which narrative texts are subdivided into "diegetic texts, recounting an event with the mediation of a narrator," and "mimetic texts, enacting the event without a mediation."[11]

---

11   The words *diegetic* and *mimetic* are meant here in the sense used by Plato, whose *Republic* (III, 392d) distinguishes between *diegesis* (= pure narration) and *mimesis* (= imitation of the

d) Events and eventfulness

Literary theory must do more than just register the presence of changes of state. Even the shortest of stories, not to speak of novels on the scale of Tolstoy's *War and Peace*, will represent a vast number of changes. Nor is it enough to distinguish various types of change such as natural, actional, interactional, and mental ones (the categories proposed in Doležel 1978). Instead, we require categories which will allow us to distinguish between the countless natural, actional, and mental changes—from thunderclap to victory in battle to a hero's moral conversion or psychological transformation—that take place in a storyworld, according to their importance.

I suggest, therefore, that we should employ a concept that has enjoyed widespread use in literary theory: the *event* (German *Ereignis*, Russian *sobytie*) (cf. Schmid 2003b; 2007a; 2009a; Hühn 2009). In all three languages, English, German, and Russian, an event is a special occurrence, something which is not part of everyday routine. The term *event* is used here in the sense of the "unprecedented incident" ("ereignete unerhörte Begebenheit") with which Goethe defined the material of the novella,[12] or in the sense of Yury Lotman's various concepts such as the "shifting of a persona across the borders of a semantic field," the "meaningful departure from the norm" (Lotman 1970; tr. 1977, 233-34), or the "crossing of a prohibition boundary" (Lotman 1973a; tr. 1976, 66). This border can be topographical, or else pragmatic, ethical, psychological, or cognitive. Lotman uses topological terms as the basis for his definition, but he stresses the normative relevance of the definition by pointing out that normative values tend to be described using spatial images and oppositions. Thus, Lotman's spatial semantics should be understood as a metaphor for non-spatial, normative values. An event consists of a deviation from the normative regularity applying in a given narrative world and preserving the order of that world.[13]

---

characters' discourse). The dichotomy between *diegesis* and *mimesis* appears in English-speaking narratology in the tradition of Henry James and Percy Lubbock (1921) in the contradistinction of *telling* and *showing*.

12   Words spoken to Eckermann, 25 January 1827.

13   Lotman contrasts "sujet texts" with "sujetless" or "mythological texts," which do not relate new developments in a changing world but represent the cyclical iterations and isomorphisms of a closed cosmos, the order of which is fundamentally affirmed by the text. For Lotman, the modern "sujet text" is the result of the interaction of the two typologically primary text types (Lotman 1973b). Lotman's event categories are taken up and further developed, in the sense of a formalisation, by Renner 1983 and Titzmann 2003. Critical of Lotman's hermeneutic model and Renner's attempted inductive application: Meister 2003, 91-95.

1. Narrativity and eventfulness

Every event is a change of state, but not every change of state constitutes an event. The event, therefore, has to be defined as a change of state that fulfills certain conditions.

The first basic requirement of the event, I propose, is that its associated change of state must be *real* (real, that is, in the framework of the fictional world). It follows that changes of state which are wished for, imagined, or dreamed are not events. However, the real acts of wishing, imagining, or dreaming can qualify as events.

Resultativity, the second requirement of the event, is a correlate of the event's reality. The change of state that constitutes an event is neither inchoative (begun), nor conative (attempted), nor durative (confined to an ongoing process). Rather, it must be resultative in that it reaches completion in the narrative world of the text.

Reality and resultativity are necessary conditions of an event in the strict sense. However, it is clear that these requirements alone are not sufficient to turn a change of state into an event, for they can both be fulfilled by trivial changes of state in a storyworld.

In the following pages, I shall describe five features which I believe a change of state must display if it is to be described as an event. These features are listed in a hierarchical order because of their different levels of importance. If a change of state is to be called an event, it must display the first two features in the hierarchy to at least some degree. The five features are gradational and can be realized to varying degrees (unlike binary features, which are either unambiguously present or absent). This means that events can have varying levels of eventfulness. There is not a fixed universal threshold of eventfulness which a change of state must cross in order to become an event; conversely, we cannot specify a minimum level of eventfulness below which events cannot exist. Instead, the amount of eventfulness needed to turn a change of state into an event is dependent on the influence of contextual factors (see below, I.1.f).

The five features which have a key role in determining the level of eventfulness in a change of state are not derived from a prototypical perfect event, as it exists, for example, in Dostoevsky's or Tolstoy's novels. Instead, my five features are based on a reduced form of the event in the poetics of Anton Chekhov. By examining these shortcomings, we can identify more accurate features of eventfulness.

1. *Relevance.* The first condition of eventfulness is that the change of state must be relevant. Eventfulness increases to the degree to which the change of state is felt to be an essential part of the storyworld in which it occurs. Changes that are trivial (in terms of the axioms which underlie the storyworld) do not give rise to eventfulness and thus, in this respect, do not produce events.

The idea of relevance is, of course, a relative one, as Chekhov illustrates in a story with the narratologically promising title "An Event." The story is, apparently, about nothing more than how a cat gives birth and Nero, an enormous dog, eats all the kittens. But, in Chekhov's hands, it illustrates the subjectivity which can influence how we evaluate relevance. The birth of the kittens is a happening of great significance for the little children Vanya and Nina. Then, while the adults readily accept Nero's eating the kittens and feel nothing more than surprise at the dog's insatiable appetite, the children feel that the world has come to an end.

Generally speaking, the criticism of the event in Chekhov's "eventless" stories tends to undermine the apparently self-evident place of relevance in realism by showing how the evaluation of relevance depends on the subject and its physical and psychological state.

2. *Unpredictability*. Eventfulness increases in proportion to the extent to which a change of state deviates from the doxa of the narrative (i.e. what is generally expected in a storyworld). This does not mean that the event must rest, as Lotman suggests, on the breach of a norm or the violation of a prohibition. Instead, the essence of the event lies in the fact that it breaks with expectations. A highly eventful change is paradoxical in the literal sense of the word: it is not what we expect.[14] *Doxa* refers to the narrative world and its protagonists and is not equivalent to the reader's *script* (what the reader expects in the action on the basis of certain patterns in literature or the real world). A change of state that comes as a surprise to the protagonists in a storyworld can be perfectly predictable for an expert reader if it is a genre characteristic. It follows that the reader's script concerning the course of a work and the protagonists' expectations concerning the course of their lives must be treated as distinct and separate notions.

A change of state that can be seen to follow the normal rules of a storyworld is predictable and thus will have a low level of eventfulness, even if it is of great importance to the individual protagonists involved in it. If a bride marries her groom, it is not, strictly speaking, eventful. But it is likely to be surprising for everyone involved, including the bride herself, if, as in Chekhov's story "The Betrothed," she dumps her prospective husband just before the wedding, after all the arrangements and plans have been made. If this happens, the failure to marry is far more eventful than the expected marriage would have been.

Another of Chekhov's marriage stories, "The Teacher of Literature," illustrates how unpredictability is not a constant feature but can change during the course of a narrative. Masha Shelestova seems unattainable to Nikitin, the teacher of literature, and declaring his love for her means gather-

---

14 Aristotle defines paradox as that which contradicts general expectation (*Rhetoric* 1412a 27).

1. Narrativity and eventfulness

ing all his courage and taking a truly heroic step, for it seems completely impossible to him that he will ever be able to marry his sweetheart. The reader, on the other hand, can tell from Masha's behavior that she is not likely to resist the proposal with any great conviction; and, after the hero takes the decisive step, he must himself recognize that what he supposed to be a border crossing was actually a perfectly normal act that everyone expected.

Relevance and unpredictability are the primary criteria underlying the continuum of eventfulness. A change of state must meet both of these requirements to a minimum degree, if not more, if it is to be perceived as an event. We can then go on to consider several additional, less crucial requirements.

3. *Persistence.* The eventfulness of a change of state is in direct proportion to its consequences for the thought and action of the affected subject in the framework of the storyworld. A lack of persistence can be observed in Chekhov's "The Teacher of Literature." After Nikitin's dream of being united with his beloved Masha Shelestova becomes reality against all his expectations, he enters into the untroubled life of the petite bourgeoisie, where he is forced to realize that his marriage was hardly the surprising event for which he took it and was really a perfectly reasonable outcome of his regular visits to the Shelestovs' household. This sobering realization results in the desire to leave the secure world of his quiet and happy married life and break out into another world, "to work himself at some factory or big workshop, to address big audiences, to write, to publish, to raise a stir, to exhaust himself, to suffer…" (Chekhov, S, 126). At the end of the story, however, when Nikitin confides in his diary and complains of the triviality which surrounds him, confronting the urge that "I must escape from here, I must escape today, or I shall go out of my mind!" (Chekhov, S, 128), his entire mental change seems to be exhausted in the writing of the diary. There is considerable doubt—as in many of Chekhov's breakout stories—about the persistence of the change in mental state.

Chekhov frequently disguises the lack of persistence in his stories by bringing them to an end before the stories of the characters themselves have ended. Interpreters who transform the potential of the open ending into reality are imbuing the change of state with a resultativity and persistence which are not present in the construction of the story itself.

4. *Irreversibility.* Eventfulness increases with the irreversibility of the new condition which arises from a change of state. That is to say, the more improbable it is that the original condition can be restored, the greater the level of eventfulness. In the case of "rethinking" (the mental event that was of such concern to the Russian realists), an insight must be gained that ex-

cludes any return to earlier ways of thinking. An example of irreversible events is provided by the chain of conversions that runs through Dostoevsky's *The Brothers Karamazov*. None of the converted persons could conceivably return to their godless initial position in future.

Chekhov's narratives cast doubt on every aspect of the idea that there can be irreversible mental states and decisions to act. In none of his works is the certainty about a character's definite border crossing more precarious than in "The Betrothed." A shadow is cast over the finality of the bride's escape by the fact that it is Alexander who persuades her not to marry. Alexander, who perpetually calls on women to break their bonds, is as much subject to a repetitive cycle as Andrey Andreich, the bridegroom who is forever playing the violin and, as his name shows, nothing more than his father's son. Will the bride really be able to escape the circle of her old existence, or will she be drawn back into it by the force of repetition that rules the world she is trying to leave? This contentious question is raised by the famous final sentence that Chekhov made ambiguous by modifying the final draft to include the phrase "as she supposed": "She went upstairs to pack, and the next morning she said good-bye to her family, and left the town, gay and full of spirits—as she supposed, forever." (Chekhov, S, 263)

5. *Non-Iterativity*. Repeated changes of the same kind, especially if they involve the same characters, represent a low level of eventfulness, even if they are both relevant and unpredictable with respect to these characters. Chekhov demonstrates this with the marriages in "Darling" and the concomitant radical changes of state in Olya Plemyannikova, the heroine of the story. The complete reformulation of her basic values to fit in with the world of her husbands seems to be an event in her first marriage, but repetition shows it to be the unchanging emptiness of a vampire's existence.

The eventfulness of "The Betrothed" is undermined by the fact that the breakout of the title heroine occurs in a context of negative iterations which envelop the female characters, the mother and the grandmother, just as much as they do the groom and the mentor. Perhaps the journey of the former bride to Petersburg, her return home, and the—"as she supposed"— ultimate breakout "forever" are nothing more than the beginning of a new cycle.

When it represents iteration, narration approaches the mode of description; it is anything but coincidental, therefore, that descriptive genres show a strong preference for treating iterative occurrences and actions.

e) Tellability

There is another term which has recently often been used in connection with eventfulness: *tellability*. This term, introduced by William Labov (1972), designates something that is *worth* telling, the *noteworthiness* of a story (cf. Baroni 2009). In a narrative with a high degree of eventfulness the eventfulness will, as a rule, coincide with tellability. In narratives with low eventfulness or no eventfulness at all, tellability can stem from the absence of an event that the reader might have expected. Though the non-expectedness of a change of state is an important prerequisite for an event, the non-fulfillment of an expectation is not, as such, an event. But it can be the point of a narrative. This can be seen from *Tales of the Little Quarter,* a collection of stories by the nineteenth-century Czech writer Jan Neruda. In one of them "How Mister Vorel Broke in His Meerschaum Pipe" the hero attempts to establish a new grocery somewhere in the Little Quarter of Prague where there has never been a shop before. Lotman would have called this a "shifting of a persona across the borders of a semantic field" or the "crossing of a prohibition boundary." The grocer's border crossing, i.e. his attempt to establish a new grocery where there has never been a shop before is doomed to fail because of the reluctance of the established bourgeoisie to accept change in their lives. The boycott of the new shop leads to the border violator's bankruptcy and eventual suicide. The death of the grocer is therefore not completely unexpected for reader and narrative world. It is a somewhat foreseeable consequence of what precedes it and is therefore a change with a relatively low degree of eventfulness. The actually tellable element in this story is the failure of an intended border crossing or the lethal consequences of a completed border crossing. The whole collection of stories in *Tales of the Little Quarter* is devoted to the uneventfulness of this microcosm, to the impenetrability of its borders. This is symbolized by the oft-mentioned city walls that enclose the Little Quarter (for details: Schmid 1994).

f) Eventfulness, interpretation, and context

A range of objections to this catalog of features for gradable eventfulness has been raised in the discussions of the Hamburg Research Group "Narratology."

The first significant objection concerns the lack of homogeneity in the five criteria of eventfulness. Although I have attempted to formulate the criteria in such a way that homogeneity exists between them, a certain amount of disparity is inevitable because of the fact that we are dealing with different components of eventfulness. However, any concerns that this disparity may raise are surely outweighed by the fact that the feature set has been compiled on the basis of empirical evidence. Moreover, it acquires a certain compensatory homogeneity because all the features were deliberately derived from one particular kind of narration, Chekhov's post-realist narration and its critical discourse on the event concept.

A second key objection holds that the features I have introduced involve interpretation and thus have no place in narratology, which, like the study of metrics, for example, is concerned with objective description rather than interpretation. It cannot be denied that the features I have described above are subject to the influence of interpretation. This is only a problem, however, if we subscribe to the belief that interpretation is avoidable in the first place. The fact of the matter is that there is little merit in the dichotomy between objective description and subjective interpretation. To take the example of metrics again, interpretation is not as remote from this subject as many critics would have us believe. Deciding, for example, whether a given verse form should be described as syllabotonic or purely tonic is, in many ways, a question of interpretation. Narratology must not confine itself to providing analytical tools which can supply objective descriptions that are free from presuppositions and independent of interpretation; we have little to gain by making that our aim. To give just one example, the narrator entity, when it is not explicitly presented as an anthropomorphic figure but semantically dependent on symptoms in the text, is heavily dependent on interpretation. The controversy that surrounded free indirect discourse in the 1910s shows how rich in presuppositions the models of description that we employ can be.[15] Even the basic task of *recognizing* a change of state is, more often than not, heavily dependent on interpretation, either because the explicit properties of the initial and final states are not equivalent and thus require suppositions which make them comparable, or because the difference between the states is not unambiguous. In Chekhov's late story "The Lady with the Dog," for example, critics are bitterly divided over whether the change in inner state diagnosed by both hero and narrator (the hero's conversion from a cynic into a truly loving man) ever takes place at all.

The first two features which largely determine the degree of eventfulness, namely relevance and unpredictability, are particularly dependant on interpretation. This dependency has two facets: (1) reference to textual entities and (2) context-sensitivity (cf. Schmid 2009a).

Let us start by examining the first facet: it is not only the characters in a storyworld who can evaluate the relevance and unpredictability of a change of state in different ways, as was demonstrated with Chekhov's tale "An Event," but the narrator and implied semantic entities such as the abstract

---

15 The discussions in the e-mail list of the International Society for the Study of Narrative show that these controversies have not come to an end yet.

1. Narrativity and eventfulness

author and the abstract reader, can also evaluate the relevance and unpredictability of a narrated change of state in different ways. Moreover, we need to take account of the fact that real readers can have individual concepts of relevance and unpredictability that do not conform with those of the fictive and implied entities.

As we have seen, relevance and unpredictability are heavily dependent on the subject evaluating the change of state. Each of the depicted, narrating and reading entities is a subject on his or her own and has his or her own social and axiological context, which determines his or her norms and expectations.

Now to the second facet: the assessment of relevance and unpredictability is heavily context-sensitive. But what is context anyway? What does it mean to be context-sensitive? At least four meanings of *context* can be distinguished.

1. First, *context* means the system of the general social norms and values of the author's time or of the time depicted in a work. The force of social perspectives on literature in the 1970s, however, led to a tremendous overestimation of the relevance of reconstructing the social context of the author's epoch or of the epoch of the storyworld. To understand the eventfulness of *Madame Bovary*, there is no need to study the social order of France or the curriculum of French convent schools or the state of medical science at the time. It is clear that Emma's expectations of happiness have been spoilt by reading too many bad romance novels, and that Bovary is a poor surgeon. It is a happy truth that literary works provide, more or less overtly, information about the norms and values in terms of which their eventfulness should be understood. This is the reason why we can understand medieval narratives without having studied the social norms of the time depicted.

2. More specifically, *context* means the individual social norms, ideologies etc. that are attributed to the depicted, narrating and implied sending and receiving entities of a narrative. The intersection of contexts in a narrative is a challenge to the real reader. S/he cannot simply immerse him or herself in the depicted world and take the position of a hero but is, on the contrary, invited to check the relevance and unpredictability of a change of state against the background of the different axiological contexts.

3. Also very important is the reconstruction of another context, that is to say the *concept of the event* in different genres and literary movements in a given period. Genres and movements are characterized by certain concepts of what is eventful. In Russian literature of the 1830s, for example, epic poetry developed event concepts quite different from those of contemporary narrative prose, and late romanticism allowed for forms of border crossing different from those of contemporary early realism. To understand eventfulness,

it is necessary to know the event code of the genre and movement in question.

4. Considerably important but often underestimated is the *intertextual* context. I have already pointed out that a change of state that comes as a surprise to a character may be not surprising at all to well-read readers because they are prepared by pretexts. On the other hand eventfulness may emerge in view of the pretexts. Let me give an example. In Pushkin's novella "The Stationmaster" the titular hero drinks himself to death through grief at the presumed ruin of his daughter who, as it seems to him or as he wants to believe, was abducted by a young hussar. But, after her father's death, the daughter seems to have made her fortune. The changes to both father and daughter emerge as highly surprising, and thus eventful, when perceived against the background of pretexts. The daughter's happiness contradicts the sad fate of all the poor Lizas, Marfas and Mashas, the peasant heroines of Russian sentimental literature, who having been seduced by young noblemen eventually drown themselves in the village ponds. The father's behavior contradicts the generosity of the father in the Parable of the Prodigal Son, a pretext that is presented by four illustrations adorning the walls of the Russian stationmaster's humble room. Instead of patiently waiting for his presumably prodigal daughter, the father, the real prodigal, drinks himself to death (details in Schmid 1991, 103-70; Russ. 1996a, 94-152).

Following Viktor Shklovsky (1919, 50-51), it can in general be said that literature is perceived against the background of preceding literature rather than against the background of real life. This is why the intertextual context is so important.

g) Historicity of eventfulness

Where, then, lies the usefulness of the category of eventfulness? Eventfulness is a culture-specific and historically changing phenomenon of narrative representation. The category is therefore particularly important when it comes to dealing with problems of cultural typology and the history of literature and thought. Let us examine some examples of different concepts of eventfulness in Russian literature.

In Old Russian literature, i.e. Russian literature up to the seventeenth century, which was strongly influenced by religious thought, eventfulness does not present itself as a positive quality. There is little unpredictability in hagiography, the leading genre of the time. Of course, hagiographical texts as a rule represent changes of state, and they often culminate in miracles. Miracles are, however, not genuinely surprising and unforeseeable in this textual world, as they follow holy models and affirm the Christian world order. Essentially, the hagiographical world does not admit fundamental surprises.

Eventfulness in our modern sense of something really unpredictable appears in Russia only in some "secular tales" of the seventeenth century which were influenced by western European novellas of the Renaissance. These secular tales tell of morally dubious heroes and their border crossings, which ultimately go unpunished, in contrast to the pattern of religious tales. The hero in "The Tale of Frol Skobeev," for example, is able to rise in society and marry the daughter of a dignitary whom he has cunningly seduced earlier, all without the prospect of worldly retribution.

This phase of secular narrative, of course, was never more than an episode; it was not returned to in the subsequent development of Russian literature. In the eighteenth century, the classical concept of literature pushed eventful narration aside. The classical episteme is defined by the idea of order and seeks to classify all phenomena. This leads to the predominance of description over narration. Varying predications are not the basis of changes but characterize things in terms of their nature and possibilities, both of which serve to predetermine development as something essentially non-contingent (cf. Dehne 2006, 56–78). This means that eventfulness in the modern sense is impossible, since the unpredictability and border crossing that are its constituent features have no positive place in the eighteenth century's image of the world.

Eventfulness gained the upper hand only with the prose of sentimentalism and romanticism around 1800. The event was increasingly modeled as a change in the mental state of a character. This development culminated in the realist novels, in which, of course, a variety of event concepts are deployed. In Ivan Turgenev's novels, people are portrayed as basically unchangeable (cf. Markovich 1975); Tolstoy and Dostoevsky, on the other hand, give form to mental processes that have been described as cases of insight, illumination, and sudden understanding. The realist event concept culminates in Rodion Raskolnikov's "resurrection" in *Crime and Punishment*, the sudden understanding of the meaning of life gained by Konstantin Levin in *Anna Karenina* and by Pierre Bezukhov in *War and Peace*, as well as in the Karamazov brothers' final acknowledgement of guilt. It should, however, be remembered that in both authors, the internal change is linked with transcendental forces. Clear enough in Tolstoy, this is clearer still in Dostoevsky, who uses the saint's life as a model when crafting the chain reaction of conversions in *The Brothers Karamazov* (cf. Schmid 2005b; 2007c). It is not accidental that the story of the first conversion, namely that of Markel, Zosima's atheist brother, is told in the language of hagiography. This reflects Dostoevsky's attempt to reconcile hagiography and realism, to write a realistic *vita,* and thus move realism to a "higher level."

While the novels of the two realists show people who have the capacity to undergo fundamental transformations and transcend the boundaries of morality and the logic of personality, Chekhov's post-realist narratives place a major question mark over the eventfulness of the world and the ability of people to change. Chekhov's narration is centered on interrogating the idea of a mental event, an existential or social insight, an emotional switch, or an ethical/practical reorientation. As an event does not occur, the tellability of the stories lies in how they represent its prevention, in how they illustrate the reasons that lead to the intention of change and prevent it from being realized. Chekhov's post-realist poetics thrive on the fact that tellability and eventfulness are no longer congruent. Consider, for example, the famous play *The Three Sisters*. The heroines, who lead an unfulfilled life in rural Russia, seek a fundamental change, as expressed in the repeated phrase "to Moscow, to Moscow." The tellability of the play lies in the impossibility of crossing the topographical, occupational, existential, and, last but not least, characterological borders involved.

Socialist realism appears at first glance to have been a development in which eventfulness thrived. The conversion of the doubter or miscreant into a liberator of the people who supports the right side in the struggle was one of the most popular scripts in this kind of literature. On closer examination, however, this way of thinking, with its similarities to salvation history, turned out to limit the possibility of border crossings just as much as the Church literature of the Middle Ages.

In the literature of post-communist Russia, the picture is extremely varied. In the neo-realist, neo-mythic, and postmodern movements, the eventful stories of high realism are continued, are transposed into mythic iteration, or have their illusory nature exposed. In all cases, though, event and eventfulness are useful narratological categories that can help us describe even the narrative structures and thought that define the most modern literature.

h) Temporal and non-temporal linking

Besides the *temporal* linking of elements, which forms the basis of narrativity, there is also—entirely different—*non-temporal* linking. One of its essential forms is *equivalence*. Equivalence means identity of elements in reference to a particular feature. This feature, the *tertium comparationis*, is a feature contained in the work, a characteristic that connects two or more passages or elements in a non-temporal way.

Equivalence comprises two types of relation: *similarity* and *contrast*. They have in common that the elements they link are identical in at least one feature and not identical in another. The similarity of two elements *A* and *B* implies, beside their identity in a feature *x*, their non-identity in a feature *y*. And the contrast of *A* and *B* presupposes the comparability of these elements. This can be given in that *A* and *B*, which are non-identical in a feature *c*, are connected by a common feature *d*. The comparability of oppositional elements is, however, also always founded on an identity at a deeper level, insofar as the contrast (for example of *man* vs. *woman* or *birth* vs. *death*) is neutralized in a more abstract, deeper-lying generic feature (here: *person* or *life's borders*). Similarity and contrast can therefore be represented as bundles of identities and non-identities concerning those features actualized by the story.

Whether an equivalence appears as similarity or contrast is not decided by the number of identities and non-identities, but solely by the position that the corresponding features take in the story's hierarchy. The hierarchization which the features experience in the story can be very dynamic. When the story emphasizes a feature *x* in which two elements *A* and *B* are identical, the equivalence of *A* and *B* appears as a similarity. In another phase of the story, a feature *y* can be highlighted. If the elements *A* and *B* are non-identical in *y*, the equivalence appears as a contrast, regardless of in how many other, non-actualized features *A* and *B* coincide.

Naturally, the highlighting of specific features and the assignment of equivalences is a matter of interpretation. Although the equivalences do characterize and reciprocally determine one another, their identification and integration into a semantic thread remains an action performed by the reader. The actualization of potential equivalences contained in the work will only ever be partial. This partialness is not based on just the number of equivalences, but also on their multiple relatability, which produces new results from each different analytical perspective. Of all the equivalences and equivalence relations available, the reader will only ever select the one that corresponds to the meaning s/he expects. Reception reduces the complexity of the work in that it selects those relations that become identifiable as meaningful within its particular horizon. In reading and interpreting, we therefore draw a thread through the thematic and formal equivalences and the thematic features that can be actualized in them, and necessarily disregard an abundance of other features and equivalences.

Equivalence is a principle that, according to the one who first described it, the Russian formalist and linguist Roman Jakobson (1960), is constitutive of poetry, but also occurs, by all means, in narrative prose; albeit not so strongly in the areas of prosody, metrics, grammar and lexis, but rather in larger thematic structures:

> [...] in prose, semantic units differing in extent play the primary role in organizing parallel structures. In this case, the parallelism of units connected by similarity, contrast, or contiguity actively influences the composition of the plot, the

characterization of the subjects and objects of the action, and the sequence of themes in the narrative. (Jakobson/Pomorska 1980; tr. 1983, 107)

In narrative prose, two basic types of equivalence can be distinguished with regard to basic features (cf. more detailed: Schmid 1992b). The first type is based on an actualized thematic feature, a property or a narrative function which links elements of the story (situations, characters and actions). This *thematic* bracketing is the primary form of equivalence in prose. It represents the basic relation in the construction of meaning, the axis of crystallization upon which all further, non-thematic equivalences semantically condense.

The second type, secondary in prose, is *formal* equivalence. It is not based on a thematic feature, but is dependent on the identity or non-identity of two passages in terms of one of the devices that constitute the narrative.

In the developmental stages of a literature in which the poetic dominates, narrative prose tends to broaden the equivalence principle beyond its domain—thematic units—to euphonic, rhythmic and syntactic textual structures. In such prose, non-temporal linking is not merely attendant, but constitutive.

This is the case, for example, in "lyrical," "poetic," or "rhythmized" prose, widespread in the literatures of post-realist modernism. In Russia, this prose, which is known as "ornamental," gained great significance between 1890 and 1930 and, at the time, dominated the entirety of narrative literature (see below, IV.2.a). The ornamentalism of Russian modernism is, however, not merely a stylistic, but a structural phenomenon, which manifests itself as fully in the narrative text as in the narrated story. The equivalences overlay both the linguistic syntagma of the narrative text, where they lead to rhythmizing and sound repetition, and also the thematic sequence of the story, onto the temporal sequence of which they place a network of non-temporal concatenation. In extreme ornamental prose, the narrativity is so weakened that there is no longer any story whatsoever being told. The temporal links are then merely embryonic and no longer align the happenings into the continuous line of a story. The unity of the work is instead provided by the, as it were, simultaneously given equivalences or their (in Joseph Frank's [1945] sense) "spatial form."

But what form does the coexistence of temporal and non-temporal links take in traditional or only slightly ornamental prose? Equivalence produces, against the sequentiality of the story, a simultaneity of elements which are often distant from one another not only on the syntagmatic axis of the text, but also on the time axis of the story. In this way, equivalence competes with temporal links such as sequentiality and causality. These cannot be transformed into equivalences. Being before or after, being cause or effect; these are ontological designations of a completely different nature to being equivalent. The categorical difference between temporal and non-temporal linking cannot be dissolved.

But in what hierarchical relationship do the two basic forms of linking now find themselves? The reader will, with every story, be prepared primarily for the temporal links and their logic. The ascription of meaning in the reading of narrative texts aims to identify changes to the initial situation, as well as the logic that underpins them. Not only the determining causes, but even the changes themselves are only rarely described explicitly and reliably, and must therefore usually be reconstructed. In their reconstruction, the reader will draw on equivalences. This is because, in many cases, it is only non-temporal linking that brings temporal changes and their logic to the surface. Thus, in many stories, the event is not explicitly unfolded through each and every step, but only implied by the contrast of the initial and final situations. Temporal links can be identified via the interplay of the non-temporal links. An example of this is provided by the late stories of Chekhov which model the life stories of their titular heroes as a chain of equivalent episodes: "The Grasshopper," "Ionych," "Darling," "The Lady with the Dog," "The Betrothed." Whether there is a fully-fledged event here, i.e. a far reaching change to someone's situation, or whether the same thing merely repeats itself, can only be decided by registering the concealed similarities and contrasts between the episodes. Temporal links therefore remain fundamental in a narrative work. They are the aim of the reconstructive ascription of meaning, but it is often only as a result of non-temporal links that they reach a form accessible to reconstruction.

2. Fictionality

a) Fiction and mimesis

In what way does narration in a work of art differ from everyday narration in, for example, anecdotes; the news via print, radio and television; police reports, or the account of a sports reporter?

One of the basic features of an artistic narrative text is its *fictionality*, i.e. the state that the world represented in it is *fictive*. To explain the use of this term: the term *fictional* characterizes the text; the term *fictive* denotes, by contrast, the status of what is represented in the fictional text.[16] A novel is fictional, the world it portrays fictive. Fictional texts are, as a rule, not fictive, but real (unless they appear in the fictive world of another fictional

---

16   On this terminology, cf., for instance, Gabriel 1991, 136; Rühling 1996, 29; Zipfel 2001, 19.

text). Where the fictive is contrasted with the real, the opposite of the fictional is the *factual* (cf. Genette 1990).

The term fictive, derived from Lat. *fingere* ('to shape,' 'to form,' 'to fashion,' 'to represent artistically,' 'to imagine,' 'to contrive,' 'to fabricate,' 'to pretend'), denotes objects that have been thought up but are presented as real. As a result, the concept of fictiveness entails an element of the deceptive, the treacherous, which is hinted at in German everyday usage in such phrases as *fiktive Ehe* (sham marriage), *fiktive Rechnung* (a fraudulent bill) and appears in words such as *fingiert* (faked; *ein fingierter Unfall*: a faked accident) and *Finte* (feint; via Ital. *la finta* from Lat. *fingere*). Literary fiction is, however, a simulation without a negative character, a pretense in which the element of lying and deception is expunged. It is for this reason that the fictive should not be too closely linked to the concept of appearance, something tended towards by those theorists who explain fiction with an "as-if-structure."[17] Fiction should rather be understood as the representation of a distinct, autonomous, inner-literary reality.

This type of conception is closely connected with the theory of mimesis, as presented by Aristotle, albeit not entirely explicitly, in his *Poetics*. The Aristotelian concept of mimesis should not be reduced to imitation of something that already exists, an idea the Renaissance, classicism and realism tended towards. As well as the semantic element of mimicking something that already exists, which is undoubtedly still found in Aristotle's use of the term he borrows from Plato (cf. Sörbom 1966, 176), the *Poetics* is, as a whole, infused with the idea of a mimesis that does not mean reproduction or imitation, but *representation* of something that is not already existent, which is constituted for the first time in the mimesis.[18] In Aristotle's treatise, the "representation of the action" (μίμησις πράξεως) is equated with the

---

17 Fiction as an "as-if-structure" originates with Hans Vaihinger's philosophy of "As If" (1911), and is still encountered in recent explications of fiction, such as John Searle's speech act theory (1975), in which the category of "pretending" plays a central role (see below).

18 On Aristotelian *mimesis* as a term that does not only, and not primarily, denote 'imitation' (as does Plato's *mimesis* in chapter 10 of the *Republic*) but also and predominantly 'representation', cf. Koller 1954; Hamburger 1957, 6–10; 1973, 10–14; Weidlé 1963; Kohl 1977, 28–39. An overview of the semantic aspects and pragmatic implications of the verb μιμεῖσθαι, not explicated in the *Poetics*, in pre-Platonic, Platonic and Aristotelian usage is given by Neschke 1980, 76–89. The equivalence of Aristotle's *mimesis* and today's conception of fiction is pointed out by Hamburger 1957; Genette 1991; tr. 1993d, 6–9; Gebauer & Wulf 1992, 81–84. Dupont-Roc & Lallot (1980) translate *mimesis* with *représentation*. Paul Ricœur (1983, 55–84), who, in light of the double meaning of the term, always renders *mimesis* with *imitation ou représentation*, underlines that the *représentation* does not have the character of a copy, of a doubling of the *présence*, but should rather be understood as an *activité mimétique*. The correlation of Aristotelian terms with those of modern semiotics is discussed by García Landa (1998, 22–32).

2. Fictionality

"myth" (μῦθος), a term—best rendered as (narrated) "story"—which Aristotle defines as the "joining together of happenings" (σύνθησις—or σύστασις—τῶν πραγμάτων; 1450a, 5, 15). It can be recognized from Aristotle's analyses that he does not see the value of mimesis in similarity with an extra-literary reality, but in just such a "joining together of happenings," which is suitable for eliciting the desired effect in the recipient. In the case of tragedy, the most valuable form of mimesis—according to Aristotle—, this consists of "effecting through pity and fear the proper purgation of such emotions" (1449b, 27-28).

Aristotle, who goes beyond the Platonic teaching that artistic representation is third rate, the imitation of an imitation,[19] not only awards mimesis—which he understands as "making" (ποίησις) (cf. Hamburger 1957, 7-8; 1973, 11) or as construction (Zuckerkandl 1958, 233)—primacy (cf. Else 1957, 322), but also establishes its cognitive function (cf. Boyd 1968, 24) and therefore its value. In contrast to the historian, who narrates what has happened, what, for example, Alcibiades has said and done, it is the poet's task to report "what could happen and what would be possible according to necessity or probability" (1451a, 36-38). The poet's subject-matter is therefore not "what has really happened" (τὰ γενόμενα), but the "possible" (τὰ δυνατά). This is why fictional poetry is "more philosophical and more meaningful than history" (1451b, 5-6).

Fiction, understood as mimesis in the Aristotelian sense, is an artistic construction of a possible reality. Insofar as it represents not specific existing or previous actions, agents and worlds, but possible ones, this construction is paradigmatic.

b) The controversy about fictionality

In recent decades, the theory of fictionality has been the subject of fierce debates between ontology, semantics, expression theory, speech act theory, pragmatics and other disciplines.[20] A disagreement arose, and continues, pri-

---

19 According to Plato, works of art, in so far as they imitate objects in the visible world, which are, in turn, imitations of the higher world of ideas, are merely "at the third remove from truth" (τρίτον τι ἀπὸ τῆς ἀληθείας; *Republic*, X 597e).

20 Compare the overviews from the standpoint of pragmatics in Hoops 1979 and Zipfel 2001 and from the anti-mimetic position of the possible worlds theory in Doležel 1998, 1-28. It is not entirely clear, however, why Doležel reduces the entire "mimetic doctrine" since Socrates, Plato and Aristotle to the imitation of "actual prototypes" (1998, 6-10). To Aristotle, the founding father of this school of thought, who—as we have seen—emphasized not the imitative but the constructive component of mimesis, not the reality but the possibility of what is represented (cf. also Doležel 1990, 34), the reductionism of the "one-

primarily on the question of whether the specific status of literature should be determined in consideration of the ontology of the objects represented, or of the pragmatics of the representing discourse. These alternatives correspond to two schools of thought in the current debate (cf. Rühling 1996). In the study of literature and in philosophical esthetics, the specific feature of literature is usually treated as an ontological problem of the fictivity of the objects represented. As part of the linguistic turn in the humanities, and under the predominance of analytical philosophy, a method is spreading that, in place of the objects' character of being, puts the special features of the discourse on center stage and investigates the semantics and pragmatics of fictional communication.[21] For a while, John Searle's (1975) speech act theory enjoyed particular esteem. It holds that the author of a fictional text makes statements that only have the form of statements, but are in reality—because they do not fulfill the conditions of statements—merely pretended statements. The creation of apparent "illocutionary" speech acts,[22] which the author does not perform "seriously"; this contradiction is, for Searle, the core of fictionality.

Serious objections were raised to Searle's pretense theory soon after its formulation. One of these applies to the author's intention, implied in Searle's theory, to present something that is not meant seriously. Searle certainly makes clear that, of the two meanings that *to pretend* could have, he does not mean the one associated with deceit, but the one associated with an "as if" action, and that, in the author's pretending, there is not the smallest intention of deceit. But it has been repeatedly doubted whether the "as if" model, which necessarily suggests something inauthentic, adequately describes the author's mimetic activity. So, Dorrit Cohn (1989, 5–6) asks in a polemic against Barbara Herrnstein Smith (1978, 30) whether Tolstoy, in the tale "The Death of Ivan Ilyich" really "is pretending to be writing a biography." She argues that, in reality, Tolstoy is not pretending anything, but actually performs an act he means seriously, namely conveying to his reader a fictional tale about the death of a fictive person.[23]

---

world-frame" would have been completely alien. In reality, Doležel's theory of fictionality within the framework of the possible worlds concept is not so far removed from Aristotle.

21 On overview of the discussions on the fictionality of literature from the perspective of analytical philosophy is given by Lamarque & Olsen 1994; Thürnau 1994.

22 "Illocution" in John Austin's (1962) speech act theory is the action completed by a speaker in a particular context with the help of utterances, for example, promising, judging etc. While the content of the speech act can be true or false, the illocution is, dependant on extra-linguistic circumstances, successful or unsuccessful.

23 Cf. already Félix Martínez Bonati's (1981, 157–59) criticism of Richard Ohmann's (1971) similar theory of fiction as "quasi-speech-acts" and of the activity of the author as "pretending." Critical overviews of the newer pretense theories are provided by Crittenden 1991, 45–52; Zipfel 2001, 187–95.

2. Fictionality

Another criticism of the theory of the author's pretended illocutionary acts is leveled at Searle's claim that the only authority that can determine the fictionality of a work is its author:[24] "what makes [a text] a work of fiction is, so to speak, the illocutionary stance that the author takes toward it, and that stance is a matter of the complex illocutionary intentions that the author has when he writes" (Searle 1975, 325). To which Genette (1989; tr. 1993b, 53) retorts, using Searle's own words against him: "For it may be the case, most fortunately, and contrary to the rules of illocution, that 'whether or not a [text] is literature is for the readers to decide.'"

The polemic shows that, in the debate on the status of literature, even the authority that decides fictionality is disputed. According to Käte Hamburger (1957, 21–72; 1968, 56–111; 1973, 55–231), it is the text that determines fictionality. For her, fictionality is an objective property manifested in individual "symptoms" of the text. According to Searle, it is—as we have seen—exclusively the intention of the author that decides. For a third group of theorists, fictionality is a relative and pragmatic category. Whether a text is read as fictional, in their opinion, is the result of the de facto assignment of a function by the recipients, an assignment that depends on the historical and social context of the reader and the dominant conceptions of what is real in that context.

c) Characteristic features of fictionality

There is disagreement not least on the question of whether fictional texts are distinguished by certain distinctive features. The discussion was opened up in the 1950s by Käte Hamburger who, in a series of works (1951; 1953; 1955; 1957), argued for the uniqueness of the "fictional or mimetic genre," in which she included third-person narrative, drama and film, but from which she excluded not only lyric poetry but also first-person narrative. The fictional genre was to distinguish itself from the second basic type of literature, the "lyrical or existential genre,"[25] by a range of "symptoms." Named were:

(1) The epic preterite loses its grammatical function of designating what is past. This is shown in the possibility of connecting the past tense of a verb with a deictic future adverb (of the type *Tomorrow was Christmas*),

---

24 Another point of criticism often made against Searle is the failure to distinguish between author and narrator; cf., for example, Martínez Bonati 1980; Hempfer 1990.
25 This second main genre and, with that, the entire binarism of the genre system was dispensed with in the second edition (Hamburger 1968; tr. 1973), in which first person narrative features as merely a "special form."

and leads to the detemporalization of grammatical time in fiction generally.
(2) That which is narrated is referred not to a real I-Origo, i.e. a real genuine "statement-subject," but rather to fictive I-Origines,[26] i.e. to one or more of the characters represented.
(3) The use of verbs of inner action in reference to third-persons (of the type *Napoleon thought...*) without motivation from a source of information.

Hamburger's theses immediately encountered varied criticism. The debate centered primarily on the question of the epic preterite.[27] The main objection was that the features named and all signs of the detemporalization of the epic preterite and the a-temporality of fiction could be attributed to the German free indirect discourse in which the narrator's and the characters' points of view merge. So, in *Tomorrow was Christmas*, the use of the preterite *was* refers to the narrator's point of view, and the deictic adverb of time *tomorrow*, by contrast, to the perspective of the character for whom, at this point in the action, Christmas will be on the next day. It is no coincidence that all the examples Hamburger adduces comprise the structure of free indirect discourse. However, this model of a narratorial rendering of a character's internal speech is in no way limited to third-person narrative, as Hamburger still postulates in the second, considerably altered, edition of her *Logic of Literature* (1968; tr. 1973), but is also regularly encountered in so-called first-person narrative (see below, IV.3.m).

For many theorists, the whole structure of characteristic features of fiction collapsed with the refutation of the main argument. For Searle, for example, "there is no textual property that will identify a stretch of discourse as a work of fiction" (1975, 327). Theorists who consider fictionality a rela-

---

26 The central concept of the "I-Origo" in Hamburger's theory, or—more specifically—the "Origo of the Here-Now-I system," which goes back to a term derived from geometry by Karl Brugmann (1904) and Karl Bühler (1934), "designates the originary point occupied by the I (the experience- or statement-I), i.e., the Origo of the system of temporal and spatial coordinates which coincides or is identical with the Here and Now" (Hamburger 1968; tr. 1973, 67).

27 The most important positions in the controversy are: Seidler 1952/53; Koziol 1956; Stanzel 1959; Rasch 1961; Busch 1962; Lockemann 1965; Horálek 1970; Bronzwaer 1970, 42–46; Zimmermann 1971; Anderegg 1973, 48–52; Weimar 1974; Petersen 1977. Genette is particularly noteworthy, because, already in his *Discours du récit* (1972; tr. 1980, 220), he admires in Hamburger's thesis of the a-temporality of the epic preterite ("this extreme and strongly contested position") "a certain hyperbolic truth." In his comparison of Searle and Hamburger, Genette (1990; tr. 1993c, 82–83) not only pays tribute to the latter—whom he later (1991; tr. 1993d, 8) described as "the most brilliant representative of neo-Aristotelian poetics of our time"—despite all the criticism of her one-sidedness, but also views her extremes and mistakes with barely concealed sympathy.

tive, pragmatic category point to the existence of particular, not necessarily categorical, "orientation signals" (Weinrich 1975, 525) or "meta-communicative" as well as "contextual signals" of fiction (Martinez/Scheffel 1999, 15). In the first of these, Weinrich includes the conscious withholding of particular circumstances of place or time, and the negative introduction, as it is encountered, for example, in the "disorientating" first sentence of Max Frisch's *Stiller*: "I am not Stiller." The function of *meta-communicative* signals is performed by "paratexts" (Genette 1987; cf. also Moenninghof 1996) such as the title and subtitle, prefaces, dedications and so on, which indicate the fictionality of the work more or less explicitly. A *contextual* signal is, for instance, the publication of a work in a particular imprint or a particular series. Lastly, *metafictional* signals must be taken into account, contained in texts that thematize their own provenance, their status (possibly even their fictionality), the desired reception and so on (Martinez/Scheffel 1999, 16).

A comprehensive summary of "signs pointing to the fictionality of fiction" has been undertaken by Michel Riffaterre (1990, 29–30). This slightly unsystematic attempt, which is, in some places, open to attack, has been discussed, corrected and systematized by Frank Zipfel in his explication of fiction signals on the levels of story and discourse (2001, 232–47). Of all the direct and indirect signals of fictivity and fictionality—which are dependant on varying conditions and have varying effects as signals—summarized by Zipfel, the most relevant, least dependant on particular conditions and most unambiguous seems to be that placed in the foreground by Käte Hamburger. Although her attempt to stand fictionality on the firm ground of objective textual characteristic features is now generally seen as having failed,[28] the *Logic of Literature* remains an astute introduction to fiction as the creation of other people's subjectivity.

d) Representation of other people's inner worlds

Käte Hamburger is, in any case, right that fiction distinguishes itself from all other types of text by allowing us direct access to other people's inner worlds: "Epic fiction is the sole epistemological instance where the I-

---

28   However, there are exceptions. Against Searle, and supporting Hamburger, Dorrit Cohn (1990; 1995) claims an "absolute difference" between fiction and non-fiction and the existence of criteria of fictionality: 1. In fiction, there is no historical happening, no "referential level" on which the historian builds his story. 2. The omniscient or freely inventing author of a novel can portray the world through the eyes of a character who lives in this world without himself narrating. 3. In novels, a "splitting of voice [namely between author and narrator] can be recognized, which destabilizes the meaning of what is said" (1995, 110). The possibility of a distinction between fictional and factual texts on the basis of narratological criteria is discussed by Genette 1990 and Löschnigg 1999.

originarity (or subjectivity) of a third-person *qua* third-person can be portrayed" (Hamburger 1968; tr. 1973, 83). Although this "characteristic feature" occasionally also appears in non-fictional texts, as was always asserted against Hamburger, it is nonetheless far more characteristic of fictional than of factual texts. The use, neither commented nor justified, of verbs of inner action (*Napoleon thought*...) is only possible in factual texts when a mere assumption on the part of the author is signaled, or when a source for this knowledge can be assumed. But, in factual texts, it is much rarer, far less natural, not so matter-of-course and not so naïve as in, for example, Tolstoy's *War and Peace*. Let us examine only a brief extract, in which the omniscient narrator of this novel presents, without any explanation or foundation, Napoleon's innermost feelings during the Battle of Borodino in the form of an interior monologue:

> Napoleon was experiencing the bitter feeling of a lucky gambler, who, after recklessly staking his money and always winning, suddenly finds, precisely when he has carefully reckoned up all contingencies, that the more he considers his course, the more certain he is of losing. [...] In his former battles he had only considered the possibilities of success, now an immense number of unlucky chances presented themselves, and he expected them all. Yes, it was like a nightmare, when a man dreams that an assailant is attacking him, and in his dream he lifts up his arm and deals a blow with a force at his assailant that he knows must crush him, and feels that his arm falls limp and powerless as a rag, and the horror of inevitable death comes upon him in his helplessness. (Tolstoy, WaP, 757–59)

In a factual, historical text, presenting the inner life of a statesman in this way would be unthinkable and would not be accepted. There are no sources even imaginable that would allow the historian to employ corresponding speculation. The omniscience of the author is a privilege and a mark of fiction, for in reality it is not knowledge, but free invention (Cohn 1995, 109).[29] In fiction, we can get to know other people in their inner lives, and form a reliable image of their innermost feelings, something which, in life, where, even with friends and spouses, we are reliant on signs and their uncertain interpretation, is ultimately denied us.

Compare E. M. Forster's (1927, 46–47, 61) classic analysis of access to the consciousnesses of characters of a novel:

---

29 Genette has already, in his comparison of fictional and factual narration, alluded to this situation: "one's guesses are unerring only in the case of something that one is in the process of inventing" (Genette 1990; tr. 1993c, 65). Alongside direct access to the characters' subjectivity, Genette also claims the opposite position as a feature of fictional texts, which he calls *focalisation externe* and which consists in forcibly objective narration, in the absence of any encroachment on the characters' subjectivity.

2. Fictionality

[…] people in a novel can be understood completely […]. And this is why they often seem more definite than characters in history, or even our own friends; we have been told all about them that can be told; even if they are imperfect or unreal they do not contain any secrets, whereas our friends do and must, mutual secrecy being one of the conditions of life upon this globe. […] We cannot understand each other, except in a rough and ready way; we cannot reveal ourselves even when we want to; what we call intimacy is only a makeshift; perfect knowledge is an illusion. But in the novel we can know people perfectly, and, apart from the general pleasure of reading, we can find here a compensation for their dimness in life. In this direction fiction is truer than history, because it goes beyond the evidence, and each of us knows from his own experience that there is something beyond the evidence, and even if the novelist has not got it correctly, well—he has tried.

The natural staging of someone else's inner world is certainly one of the reasons for the anthropological and cultural significance of fiction. The reader can step outside of himself or herself and not only lead someone else's life but slip into someone else's subjectivity and tentatively play out someone else's perceptions and ambitions. No conversation and no psychological document can offer so much alterity. Only immersion in the inner world of the fictive other gives a person the possibility of forming a notion of his or her own identity. The price for the playing out a foreign subjectivity is that everything has been thought out and remains oriented on the representing author, his knowledge of the world, the power of his imagination.[30]

Käte Hamburger's emphasis on the representation of the hero's inner world as an objective characteristic feature of fictionality corresponds entirely to the Aristotelian conception of mimesis as the "making" (ποίησις) of acting people.

e) The fictive world

No generally accepted theory of fiction has yet emerged from the discussions mentioned, but, despite all the divergence on theoretical approaches and models, a certain practical consensus is nonetheless becoming apparent on the main characteristics of literary fictionality and fictivity. In the following, a basic model will be sketched that covers the common ground of different positions, and should largely be able to provide the basis for a consensus.

---

30 On the cathartic effect of the identification of the reader with foreign interiority, cf. also Aage Hansen-Löve's (1987, 11) explications of the reader, "who, 'in foreign clothes,' 'recuperates' from his or her own consciousness's claim to totality."

Being fictive means being represented only. Literary fiction is a representation of a world which implies no direct relationship between what is represented and a real extra-literary world. Fiction consists in making, in the construction of an invented, possible world.[31] For mimesis, the creator of the represented world can take and combine elements from differing worlds. The thematic entities that appear as elements in the fictive world can be familiar from the real world, can figure in varying discourses of the corresponding culture, be descended from older or foreign cultures or exist only in the imagination. Regardless of origin, all thematic entities become fictive by appearing in a fictional work.

The referential signifiers of the fictional text do not refer to particular extra-textual referents, but only to inner-textual denotata of the represented world. In other words, the "transposition" (*Hinausversetzung*) of inner-textual referents into the real ontic sphere (Ingarden 1931; tr. 1973a, 161–62), which is characteristic of factual texts, does not take place in fictional literature.[32] Thus arises "a paradoxical function of pseudoreference, or of denotation without denotata" (Genette 1991; tr. 1993d, 25). However, the absence of a direct relationship between text and extra-textual world does not, in any way, mean that the fictive world is irrelevant for the reader or, indeed, even that it is less relevant than the real world. On the contrary, the fictive world can attain the highest significance for the reader. The reader can engage with the innertextual referents, e.g. characters and their actions, as with real, individual, concrete entities,[33] even when s/he is aware of their fictivity. Which reader would not sympathize with Anna Karenina's unfortunate end, or would not follow, with the greatest interest, Konstantin Levin's search for the meaning of life?[34]

---

31 On the intersection of the theories of fictionality and of possible worlds, cf. Pavel 1986; Doležel 1998, 1–28.

32 According to the phenomenologically influenced ontological theory of the Polish philosopher Roman Ingarden (1931; tr. 1973a), literature is distinguished from non-literature by a special type of statements that Ingarden calls "quasi-judgments" (*Quasi-Urteile*). The difference from real judgments consists in that their objects exist only as "purely intentional" (*rein intentional*) and are not "transposed into the real ontic sphere."

33 On the individuality of fictive characters cf. Martínez Bonati 1981, 24.

34 In order to characterize artistic narration, it is necessary, but not sufficient, to refer to the feature of fictionality. Being fictional and being artistic are not identical. There are fictional narrative texts that do not belong in the sphere of literature, e.g. stories that serve as examples in an academic or didactic work, textual examples in a mathematics book, advertising and so on. Artistic narration distinguishes itself also through a second feature, estheticity, more specifically: the esthetic function of the work in which the narration appears as a component of the represented world. What relevance does estheticity have for narrative structure and narratology? For the esthetic function for which art is predestined to actually become effective, the narration must develop qualities that elicit the esthetic approach in its recipients. Of course, this does not mean that the narrator must narrate

2. Fictionality

So, what is fictive in a fictional work? The answer is: the entire represented world and all its parts: situations, characters, actions. Fictive objects do not differ from real ones through any kind of thematic or formal features, but only through a characteristic that cannot be observed in them themselves: that they do not exist in the real world.[35] Non-existence in the real world is not in doubt as long as openly invented characters are meant, such as Natasha Rostova and Pierre Bezukhov in *War and Peace*. But what about the historical figures that appear in the novel, such as Napoleon or Kutuzov? These are only quasi-historical figures. Tolstoy's Napoleon is not a reproduction of the real historical figure but a mimesis of Napoleon, i.e. the construction of a possible Napoleon. Much of what is narrated about Napoleon in the novel—one need only think of the hero's deliberations in the face of the imminent defeat at Borodino quoted above—cannot, after all, be documented in any source and will not be found in any history book. In *War and Peace*, Napoleon and Kutuzov are no less fictive than Natasha Rostova and Pierre Bezukhov.

The characters' fictive status is evident when they are endowed with characteristics which must be invented and which could not be demonstrated in any historical source. But even if the author of a historical novel adhered strictly to the documented historical facts (which would rule out any representation of psychological motivation), all his heroes, however closely they resemble historical figures, would still be unavoidably fictive. Merely the fact that the quasi-historical figures live in the same world as the overtly invented ones makes them fictive. The Napoleon and the Kutuzov who could have encountered Natasha Rostova and Pierre Bezukhov have never existed in the real world.

The fictiveness of the characters makes the *situations* in which they find themselves equally fictive, and also the *actions* in which they participate.

Also fictive in the fictional work is *place*. This is clear in the case of Skotoprigonevsk, the setting, marked on no map of Russia, of *The Brothers*

"beautifully." The carrier of the esthetic intention is, after all, not the narrator, but the author portraying him or her and his or her narration or—as one wishes—the text. The narration must rather be formed in such a way that it does not only carry thematic information, but also that its form itself becomes meaningful. Fictionality and estheticity are two separate features of the art of narration, independent of one another. But they influence the work's reception in similar ways. Estheticity determines, like fictionality, an isolation of the text, a transcending of external reference, the weakening of the direct relationship to extra-literary reality (cf. Mukařovský 1938). To compensate for the loss of external reference, both qualities guide attention onto the work itself, its structure, its internal reference. With this further feature, we, admittedly, reach the sphere of esthetics in general, which is not specific to narration.

35 This conclusion does not contradict, by any means, the existence, explicated above, of particular textual, contextual, metatextual etc. markers of fictionality.

Karamazov. But the places that have a concrete equivalent in reality are also fictive. The Moscow in which the heroes of *War and Peace* live, the Borodino at which Andrey Bolkonsky is injured, cannot be found on a historical map of Russia. Neither Moscow nor Borodino nor any other setting in the novel denotes a point on the spatial axis of the real space-time coordinate system. On the real spatial axis, we find only the Moscow and the Borodino in which a Natasha Rostova or an Andrey Bolkonsky have never existed.

Lastly *time* as represented in fiction is also fictive. This is evident in utopian or dystopian works. George Orwell's *Nineteen Eighty-Four* long served as an example. But, as the year denoted in the title dawned, it was no longer sufficient for a simple proof of the fictivity of fictional time to point to real time. Although the fictivity of time became less obvious, it continued regardless.

In a fictional work, all the thematic elements of the narrated world are therefore fictive: people, places, times, actions, speeches, thoughts, conflicts and so on. Against the explication of a "mixed-bag conception," widespread in theories of fictionality, according to which real objects (real people, places or times) can appear alongside fictive objects, it will be assumed here that (1) the fictive world of the narrative work has a homogenous ontology, that all objects represented in it, regardless of how closely they can be associated with real objects, are fundamentally fictive, and (2) that there are no gradations of fictivity.[36]

f) Author communication and narrative communication

The *narrated world* is the world created by the narrator. The *represented world* created by the author is not limited to the narrated world. The represented world includes the narrator, his or her addressee and the narration itself. The narrator, the listener or reader whom the narrator assumes and

---

[36] Similar positions are argued by Rudolf Haller (1986) und Lubomír Doležel (1989, 230-31). That they paid too high a price for the unity of description, namely the counterintuitive levelling of differences significant in textual analysis, is put forward by Zipfel (2001, 95). Zipfel himself distinguishes for the supposedly real objects in fiction between "real objects" ("immigrant objects" in Parsons 1980, 51) and "pseudo-real objects" ("surrogate objects" in Pavel 1986, 29): the former deviate less "significantly" from their real equivalents, and form "points of contact between the fictive story and the real world" (Zipfel 2001, 100). The advantage and necessity of this distinction are not apparent. Neither can "deviation" of, say, a character from a historical prototype be established without any further explanation, nor is it of any importance for the reading experience of the average reader. Must one pursue studies in Russian and French history before reading *War and Peace*? Zipfel awakes the suspicion that he secretly wants to introduce a gradation of the fictive, which he, at other points in his book, rightly calls problematic (Zipfel 2001, 294).

2. Fictionality

the act of narration are represented in the fictional work and are fictive entities. Therefore a narrative work does just narrate, but represents an act of narration. The art of narrative is structurally characterized by the doubling of the communication system: the *narrator's communication* in which the narrated world is created is part of the fictive represented world, which is the object of the real *author's communication*[37].

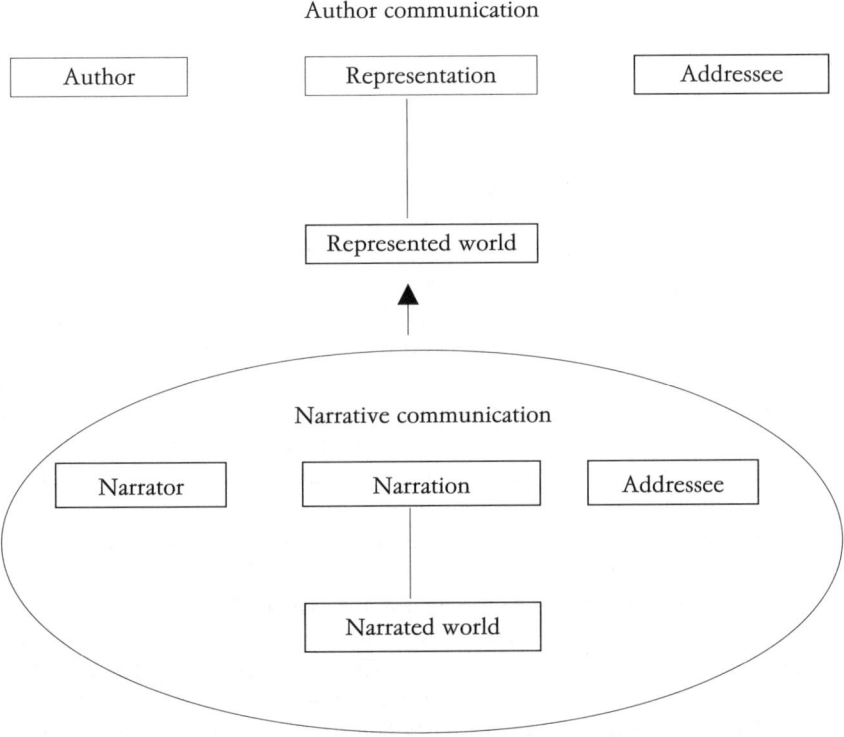

The doubling of the communication system

---

37 The phrasing of the "communicated communication," with which Janik (1973, 12) characterizes narrative work, abbreviates the actual content a little: what is directly communicated is not the narrative communication but rather the represented world in which this is contained (cf. Schmid 1974a).

II. The entities in a narrative work

1. Model of communication levels

The narrative work, which, as we have established, does not narrate but, *represents* a narration, encompasses a minimum of two levels of communication: *author communication* and *narrative communication*. To these two levels, which are constitutive of a narrative work, a third, facultative level can be added: *character communication*. This is the case when a narrated character acts as a speaking or narrating entity.

On each of these three levels, we can distinguish a transmitting and a receiving side. There is a considerable ambivalence in the concept of the recipient, something often neglected in communication models. The recipient can be divided into two entities, which differ *functionally* or *intensionally*, even when they coincide *materially* or *extensionally*: into the *addressee* and the *recipient*. The addressee is the receiver presumed or intended by the transmitter, the one to whom the transmitter sends his message, whom he had in mind as the presumed or desired receiver while writing; the recipient is the factual receiver, of whom the transmitter possibly—and, in the case of literature, as a rule—has only a general mental picture. The necessity of a distinction of this sort is clear: if, for example, a letter is not read by the person who was the intended addressee, but by someone else into whose hands it happens to fall, inconvenience may arise.

The communication levels and entities in a narrative work have been sketched in various models since the start of the 1970s. Here, I will take up my own model (Schmid 1973, 20-30; 1974a), which has subsequently been used as the basis for textual analyses and has been discussed, modified and developed in theoretical works.[1] Janik (1973) published a model at the same time as my own, and for this reason I could not take it into account at that time.[2] Moreover, important works by Polish narrative theorists were not yet accessible to me, particularly Okopień-Sławińska 1971 and Bartoszyński 1971.[3] Naturally, I now present my model in modified form, in which the

---

[1] For example Link 1976, 25; Kahrmann/Reiß/Schluchter 1977, 40; Hoek 1981, 257; Lintvelt 1979; 1981; Díaz Arenas 1986, 25, 44; Weststeijn 1991; Paschen 1991, 14-22.
[2] Cf. then, however, the review Schmid 1974a and Janik's reply 1985, 70-73.
[3] Cf. the systematization and further development of the Polish models by Rolf Fieguth (1973, 186; 1975, 16; 1996, 59).

1. Model of communication levels

published criticism has been taken into account (cf. Schmid 1986). The diagram of communication levels will be presented first, followed by a discussion of the individual, level-specific entities.

Model of communication levels

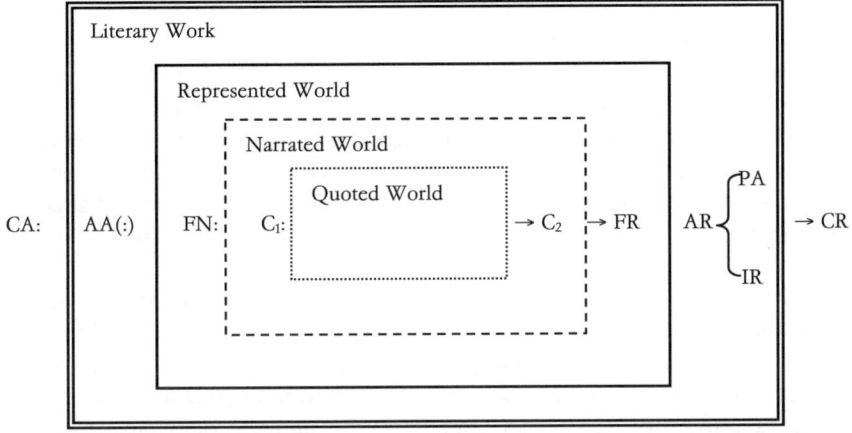

Explanation

CA = concrete author
AA = abstract author
FN = fictive narrator
: = produces
C_1, C_2 = characters
→ = addressed to

FR = fictive reader (narrataire)
AR = abstract reader
PA = presumed addressee
IR = ideal recipient
CR = concrete reader

2. The abstract author

a) Concrete and abstract entities

Let us begin with the level and those entities that are constitutive of, but not exclusive to, narrative work: author communication, between author and reader. In each linguistic communication, the two entities appear in two modes, as concrete and abstract entities.

The *concrete author*, the real historical figure, the creator of the work, is not a part of the work, but exists independently. Leo Tolstoy would have existed even if he had never put pen to paper. The *concrete reader* equally exists outside and independently of the work. To be specific, this is not one reader, but the unending mass of all people, who, in some place and at some time, have been or will yet be recipients of the work (cf. the model of external communication in Schmid 1973, 22).

Although author and reader, in their concrete mode, are not part of the work, they are nonetheless present in a particular way. Any given linguistic expression contains an implicit picture of its creator and also of its addressee. To demonstrate, a quick thought experiment: imagine we are sitting in a university lecture hall and hear, through the door, an unknown person speaking to someone. Without seeing the speaker or the listener, we will involuntarily form an impression of the speaker based on what we hear: his or her sex, age, mood, function at the university, perhaps even, if the speech is long enough and touches on the relevant subjects, his or her way of thinking. And we will also form a mental picture of his or her interlocutor even if s/he remains silent throughout, or, more specifically, not of the interlocutor himself but of the image which the speaker has of him or her, i.e. of the *presumed addressee*. From what the speaker says, we try to divine whom s/he has in front of him or her or whom s/he believes the other is, a man or a woman, a student or a teacher, an acquaintance or a stranger, what knowledge s/he assumes on the part of the other, what personal relationship s/he has, or wants to have, with him or her.

The image of the transmitter contained in every utterance is based on the linguistic function that Karl Bühler, in his "Model of language as organon," first called "profession" (*Kundgabe*) (1918/20), then later (1934; tr. 1990, 35) "expression" (*Ausdruck*).[4] By that, he means the involuntary, unintended expression of self by the speaker, which takes place in every speech action. The word as a sign is not functioning as a "symbol," representing objects and states of affairs but rather as a "symptom" (*Anzeichen, indicium*) by virtue of its dependence on the sender, whose inner states it expresses"

---

4 Description and modification of Bühler's theory by Kainz 1941. Overview of various extensions to a theory of linguistic functions in Schmid 1974b, 384–86.

(Bühler 1934; tr. 1990, 35). In the following, I will use the term "indexical sign" or, going back to Charles S. Peirce (1931–58), "index," to denote this indirect mode of self-expression with involuntary, unintended, nonarbitrary, natural signs.

What applies to any linguistic expression can also be related to a literary work as a whole. In it, the author is expressed through symptoms, indexical signs. The result of this semiotic act is, however, not the concrete author, but rather the image of the creator as s/he shows himself in his or her creative acts. This image, which has a two-fold, objective and subjective, foundation, i.e. is contained in the work and is reconstructed by the reader, is what I call the *abstract author* (latest Schmid 2009b).

b) History of the abstract author concept

Before defining this entity more precisely, we must first cast a quick glance over the history of the concept. The first to develop the concept systematically, using the corresponding term of the "author's image" (*obraz avtora*), was Viktor Vinogradov in his book on artistic prose (1930).[5] In 1927, when he first conceived of the term "author's image", calling it "image of the writer" (*obraz pisatelya*), Vinogradov wrote to his wife:

> My thoughts are captivated entirely by the author's image. It shines through in any work of art. In the fabric of the words, in the techniques of depiction, we sense its form. This is not the person, the "real," extra-literary Tolstoy, Dostoevsky. It is a specific role-playing form of the author. In every distinctive characteristic, the author's image takes on individual traits, but its structure is nonetheless not determined by the psychological character of the author, but by the author's esthetic-metaphysical attitudes. It is entirely possible for them to remain unconscious, if the author has no particular intellectual and artistic culture, but they must exist [...]. The entire question consists in how to reconstruct this author's image on the basis of the author's works. In this, I definitely exclude the help of any biographical information. (Quoted by Chudakov 1992, 239)

In a late work, which appeared only posthumously, Vinogradov (1971, 118) defined the author's image in the following way:

> The author's image is not simply the subject of the discourse. It is usually not even named in the structure of the work. It is the concentrated embodiment of the work's essence, unifying the entire system of the characters' linguistic structures in their correlation with the narrator or narrators, and thus constituting the ideal-stylistic center, the focus of the entire work.

---

5   On the emergence of the theory of the author in the West and in Russia, cf. Rymar'/Skobelev 1994, 11–59. On the development of the concept "author's image" by Vinogradov: Chudakov 1992, 237–43. On the various contents that Vinogradov gives the term: Lichachev 1971; Ivanchikova 1985. On the Russian author concepts cf. now also Gölz 2009.

When Vinogradov then adds that, in the forms of the *skaz* style, widespread in Russian literature, which is narrated in a strong symptom-rich way by an entity clearly dissociated from the author (cf. IV.2), the "author's image does not usually coincide with the [personified] narrator," he indirectly concedes that an author's image could possibly coincide with a neutral narrator. A lack of consistency in the distinction between abstract author and narrator is characteristic of Vinogradov's entire work.

As Russian literary study began to free itself from the pressure of Marxist demands at the end of the 1950s, the idea of the author within the text was taken up and further developed in the works of Boris Korman (cf. Rymar'/Skobelev 1994, 60–102). Drawing on Vinogradov's concept of the "author's image" and supported by Bakhtin's theory of the dialogic interaction of differing "evaluative positions" in the work, Korman developed a method which he named "systemically subject-based," in which the investigation of the author as the "consciousness of the work" took center stage. Korman's approach differs from the theory of his predecessors in two essential ways. In Vinogradov's writings, the author's image is described stylistically and presented as the product obtained when the different styles brought into play in a work are drawn together; Korman, on the other hand, concentrates primarily on the relations between the various centers of consciousness in the work. Whereas Bakhtin's interest in the problem of the author's image is primarily philosophical and esthetic in nature, Korman's deliberations are dominated by poetics (Rymar'/Skobelev 1994, 62–63, 72–73). For Korman, the author within the work—whom he calls the "conceived author"—is realized "in the correlation of all the constituent textual elements of the work in question with its subjects of speech, i.e. those subjects to whom the text is attributed, and the subjects of consciousness, i.e. those subjects whose consciousnesses are expressed in the text" (Korman 1977, 120). In Korman's *Experimental Dictionary*, we then find the following definition of the "author as subject of consciousness":

> The author is the *subject* (the bearer) of *consciousness*, the expression of which the entire work is. The author conceived in this way must above all be distinguished from the biographical author, the person who really exists or has existed. The correlation of the biographical author and the author as subject of consciousness, the expression of which the work is, is, in principle, the same as the correlation of life experiences and artwork in general: guided by a certain perception of reality and based on certain normative and cognitive opinions, the real, biographical author (the writer) produces, with the help of imagination, selection and the processing of life experiences, the artistic (conceived) author. To the alterity of this author, his mediation, is owed the entire artistic phenomenon, the entirety of literary work. (Korman 1981, 174; emphases in the original)

2. The abstract author

Important ideas on the theory of the author within the work were contributed by Czech structuralism. Jan Mukařovský (1937) referred at an early date to the author in the work as an "abstract subject that, contained in the structure of the work, is merely a point from which it is possible to survey the entire work at a glance." In any given work, Mukařovský adds, it is possible to find indications pointing to the presence of this abstract subject, which must never be identified with an actual individual such as the author or the recipient: "in its abstraction [the subject of the work] merely makes it possible to project these personalities into the internal structure of the work" (Mukařovský 1937).

Taking his teacher's ideas as his starting point, the second-generation Czech structuralist Miroslav Červenka (1969 [1978, 169-71]) suggested that the "subject of the work," or "personality"—the entity that Mukařovský called the "abstract subject"—is the "signified," the "esthetic object" of the literary work, the work itself being treated as an index in the Peircean sense. For Červenka, the "personality" thus defined embodies the principle by which all the semantic levels of the work are dynamically united, without suppressing the inner richness and personal color that points back to the concrete author (cf. Stempel 1978, XLIX-LIII).

Polish research on the subject of the work begins with Janusz Sławiński (1966; 1967), whose writings reflect the ideas of Vinogradov and Mukařovský. Sławiński himself calls Vinogradov's "author's image" the "subject of the creative acts" or the "maker of the rules of speech." Edward Balcerzan (1968) uses the term "internal author" to refer to the same entity. Particularly significant is Aleksandra Okopień-Sławińska's article on "personal relations" (1971), which, through the mediacy of Rolf Fieguth, exercised a not inconsiderable influence on Western models of narrative communication. In Okopień-Sławińska's five-level schema of roles in literary communication, two extra-textual transmitting entities appear: (1) the "author" (in Fieguth's complementary definition [1975, 16]: "the author in all his life roles"), (2) "the transmitter of the work (the maker of the rules, the subject of the creative act)" (in Fieguth: "the maker of the literary rules, from which the rules of the individual work are selected and combined; the author in the role of a producer of literature").[6] These two extra-textual hypostases of the author are contrasted with an entity within the work, which Okopień-Sławińska calls the "subject of the work" and which Fieguth defines as "subject of the rules of speech in the whole work; subject of the use of literary rules for this work." The distinction between two extra-textual communica-

---

6   In a later work, Fieguth (1996, 59) uses the example of the novel to distinguish as many as three manifestations of the transmitter that transcend the work: (1) the author as historical person, (2) the author as novelist, (3) the author as creator of a concrete novel.

tion levels is, however, problematic from a systematic perspective insofar as complications arise in the correlation of the roles of the concrete author to the entities on the receiving side. Moreover, it is, from a pragmatic perspective, not particularly helpful for textual analysis.

In Western narratology, the concept of the *implied author* is widespread,[7] as developed by the American literary scholar and member of the *Chicago School* Wayne C. Booth (1961) in connection with his conceptualization of the *unreliable narrator*, i.e. a manifest axiological dissociation of the narrator from the value horizon of the work.[8] In opposition to the demand for objectivity made of the author since Flaubert, i.e. to be neutral, dispassionate and *impassible*, Booth underlines the unavoidable subjectivity of the author:

> As he writes, [the real author] creates not simply an ideal, impersonal "man in general," but an implied version of "himself" that is different from the implied authors we meet in other men's works. [...] the picture the reader gets of his presence is one of the author's most important effects. However impersonal he may try to be, his reader will inevitably construct a picture of the [author] who writes in this manner [...] (Booth 1961, 70-71)[9]

Since then, Booth's approach has often been taken up and refined (cf. esp. Iser 1972; Chatman 1978 [1986, 147-49]; Rimmon-Kenan 1983, 86-87). In varying dependency on Booth, equivalent terms have also been introduced: Eco (1979) discusses the "model author" as an interpretative hypothesis of the empirical reader, and Antony Easthope (1983, 30-72), drawing on the linguist Émile Benveniste, introduces the term "subject of enunciation."

c) Critique of the abstract author concept

In Western theoretical discussions, the terms "abstract" or "implied" author have not been met with unconditional acceptance although they are, in practice, widely used for analysis. The rejection of the conception of an author entity contained in the work developed as part of a general mistrust of the author, which can be observed in Western literary study from the 1940s onwards (cf. Jannidis et al. 1999, 11-15).

---

7   In German theory, the English *implied* has, as a rule, been simplified to *implizit*, which ontologizes the reception-oriented term.
8   On the intention and context of Booth's term cf. Kindt/Müller 1999; 2006a; 2006b.
9   These words have been interpreted in terms of an "image of the self" intentionally produced by the author, and an irresolvable contradiction has been seen between this definition and the explication by Booth of the *implied author* as an inference by the reader (Kindt/Müller 2006b, 167-68). The intentional production of an image of the author is, however, probably not meant by Booth's imprecise formulation. Booth, rather, aims at the involuntary and unavoidable indexical co-representation of every creator in his product. As a result, the accusation of inconsistency can be dropped.

2. The abstract author

An influential factor in this development was criticism of the so-called *intentional fallacy*, formulated by the New Critics William Wimsatt and Monroe Beardsley (1946). The "fallacy," according to the critics, consists in the belief in the relevance to interpretation of the author's explanations of his or her intention, or of other biographical information. It is not the author's intention that should be the object of interpretation, but rather the literary text, which has already become independent of the author in its creation and no longer belongs to him or her. Therefore, no extra-textual information was seen as relevant to interpretation; the only valid principle was that of *internal evidence*. Booth, who, at that point, clearly shared the criticism of the intentional fallacy in principle, attempted to use the concept of the implied author to overcome the rigid immanentism and autonomist doctrine of New Criticism, which—as Booth complained (1968, 112–13)—ruled out, as part of a fight against all kinds of fallacies and heresies, not only the author (*intentional fallacy*) but also the audience (*affective fallacy*), the "world of ideas and beliefs" (*didactic heresy*), even the "narrative interest" (*heresy of plot*) itself. The mediating concept of authorship within the work offered the possibility of discussing the meaning and intention of a work without falling under suspicion of having committed the notorious heresies.[10]

A still influential critique of the author as the object of literary study was formulated in French post-structuralism under the slogan "The Death of the Author."[11] Julia Kristeva (1967), drawing on Mikhail Bakhtin's concept of "dialogicity," which she interpreted as *intertextualité* (with which she introduced the concept into literary study), replaced the author as the generating principle of the work with the conception of an active text that creates itself in reaction to other texts, which it absorbs and transforms. One year later, Roland Barthes (1968) announced "La mort de l'auteur." Whereas, for Kristeva, the author appears as merely the *enchaînement* of the discourses, Barthes reduces his or her function to the combination of discourses: "[T]he text is a tissue of citations, resulting from the thousand sources of culture. [...] [T]he writer can only imitate a gesture forever anterior, never original; his only power is to combine the different kinds of writing" (Barthes 1968; tr. 1977, 146). According to Barthes, it is not the author

---

10 It was, of all things, the compromising nature of the implied author concept, which connected the stern autonomism of New Criticism with the acceptance of an authorial presence in the work, which later became the object of criticism; cf. Juhl 1980, 203; Lanser 1981, 50; Polletta 1984, 111; Nünning 1993, 16–17; Kindt/Müller 1999, 279–80.

11 On criticism of the rejection of author-oriented categories cf. the collections *Avtor i tekst* (Markovich/Schmid [eds.] 1996)—in which esp. Evdokimova 1996 and Freise 1996—and *Rückkehr des Autors* (Jannidis et al. [eds.] 1999).

who speaks in the artwork, but the language, the text, which is organized according to the cultural codes of its time.

Finally, the idea of authorship was discredited in Michel Foucault's essay *Qu'est-ce qu'un auteur?* (1969). The author, according to Foucault, is a historical concept outlived by modernity, one which has served merely the regulation and disciplining of how literature is handled.

The post-structuralists' "anti-author Philippics" (Ilyin 1996b) met with only a limited response in Russia. This may be connected with the fact that a practical ethicism dominated in classical Russian literature, which still shapes the cultural mentality, and which attached the greatest importance to personality and authorship. This ethical tendency is also shown in the esthetic thinking of Mikhail Bakhtin. It was no accident that the young philosopher, in his first publication, a concealed polemic against formalism, set against the Opoyaz motto *Art as Device* his own formula *Art and Responsibility* (Bakhtin 1919).[12]

d) For and against the abstract author

An intense controversy has broken out over the concept of the implied author and its equivalents. A categorical and general verdict on the concepts of the implied author and reader is expressed by Hempfer (1977, 10): both entities "seem to be not only theoretically useless but also to confuse the actually fundamental distinction, namely that of innertextual and extratextual speech position." Zipfel (2001, 120) reaches a similarly summary judgement, dismissing the concept of the implied author as "narratologically superfluous," "hopelessly vague" and "terminologically imprecise." Against the incorporation of the implied author into a model of communication levels, in particular, a range of arguments has been put forward:

(1) In contrast to the narrator, the implied author is not a pragmatic entity in the narrative work, but rather a semantic dimension of the text (Nünning 1989, 33; 1993, 9).

(2) The implied author is no more than a construction formed by the reader (Rimmon-Kenan 1983, 86; Toolan 1988, 78), which should not be personified (Nünning 1989, 31–32).

(3) The implied author is not a participant in a communication (Rimmon-Kenan 1983, 88), as modeled, despite all warnings against an overly anthropomorphic conception, by Seymour Chatman (1978, 151) (cf. Nünning 1993, 7–8).

---

12 Cf. Todorov 1997. On Bakhtin's conception of authorship and responsibility cf. Freise 1993, 177–220.

2. The abstract author

(4) Insofar as it denotes not a structural but a semantic phenomenon, the term "implied author" does not belong in the poetics of narration, but in the poetics of interpretation (Diengott 1993, 189).

(5) The methodology of reconstruction is also questionable. Booth and those who have since used the concept have not demonstrated how one moves from a text to its implied author (Kindt/Müller 2006b, 167–68).

The arguments listed are all completely sound but do not deliver an adequate justification for excluding the implied author from narratology. It is no accident that many critics use this concept despite all objections. This is clearly because no term has been found that better expresses the presence of the inferred authorial element in a work. On the one hand, the term denotes the semantic center of the work, which exists independently of any declarations by the author, the point at which all creative lines in the work converge. On the other hand, the term points, behind the abstract principle of the semantic unification of all elements, to a creative entity, whose — conscious or unconscious — intention is realized in the work.

It is also telling that those critics who have argued for the relinquishment of the implied author category have, as yet, offered only partially convincing alternatives. Nünning suggests replacing this "terminologically imprecise," "theoretically inadequate" and practically unusable term with the "entirety of all formal and structural relations of a text" (Nünning 1989, 36). Chatman (1990, 74–89) argues (despite having criticized five of Booth's key definitions from the perspective of anti-intentionalism) in line with his chapter title *In Defense of the Implied Author* and recommends to readers made uneasy by the term *implied author* a series of surrogates to choose from: "text implication," "text instance," "text design" or simply "text intent." And Kindt/Müller (1999, 285–86) reach the conclusion that it is wise to replace the term "implicit author" simply with the term "author," which would, of course, call down the well-known anti-intentionalist objections, or, if a non-intentionalist conception is to be clung to, to refer to "text intention" (whereby a metonymic shift from producer to product must be accepted, as a text has no intentions).

The ambiguous attitude of many theorists towards the concept of the implied author is illuminated by the example of Gérard Genette. The theorist who, in his *Narrative Discourse*, believed that he could cope perfectly well without the implied author, something which elicited justified criticism,[13] dedicated an entire chapter of *Narrative Discourse Revisited* to the ignored entity, under the title *Implied Author, Implied Reader?* (1983; tr. 1988, 135–54). The laborious argumentation against the "'complete' table" of enti-

---

13 Cf. e.g. Rimmon (1976, 58) and Bronzwaer (1978, 3).

ties[14] leads to a conclusion in no way disadvantageous for the implied author. Genette first states that the *auteur impliqué*, since not specific to the *récit*, is not a valid object of narratology. But the question—"is the implied author a necessary and (therefore) valid agent between the narrator and the real author?" (1983; tr. 1988, 139), he answers ambivalently: "As an actual agent, obviously not: a narrative of fiction is produced fictively by its narrator and actually by its (real) author" (ibid.). But it is conceivable as an *ideal agent*. Genette completely accepts the abstract author as the *idea of the author*, an expression he finds more appropriate than *image of the author*: "The implied author is everything the text lets us know about the author" (1983; tr. 1988, 148). But one must not, according to Genette's concluding warning, make of the idea of the author a *narrative agent*. With that, Genette is not so far from the exponents of the "'complete' table," none of whom intended to transform the abstract author into a *narrative agent*.

e) Two attempts to split the abstract author

The Dutch narratologist Mieke Bal has emerged as an embittered opponent of Booth's *implied author* and my abstract author. For her, this superfluous concept is responsible for the false isolation of the author from the ideology of his or her work:

> It promised something which [...] it has not been able to deliver: it promised to account for the ideology of the text. This would have made it possible to condemn a text without condemning its author and vice versa—a very attractive proposition to the autonomists of the '60s. (Bal 1981, 42)

In light of this rebuke, it is surprising that Bal, in the Dutch edition of her *Narratology* (1978, 125), actually suggests a division of this entity. She differentiates between *impliciete auteur* and *abstracte auteur* and separates them schematically in the following way:

impliciete auteur ⇒ TEKST ⇒ abstracte auteur

While the author's first hypostasis—in line with Bronzwaer's (1978) ostensibly wider term—is understood as the "technical, overarching entity, which calls all other entities into being and is responsible for the construction of the entire narrative text," the second author entity, corresponding to the definitions by Booth and Schmid, is conceived of as the embodiment of the "total meaning structure" of the text, though not as the "producer of meanings" but as the "result of semantic analyses" (Bal 1978, 124-25). For Bal, both figures remain outside the remit of narratology.

---

14 Genette refers here to Schmid (1973, 20-30), Bronzwaer (1978, 10), Chatman (1978, 151), Hoek (1981, 257-58) and Lintvelt (1981, 13-33).

2. The abstract author

The Amsterdam Slavist Willem Weststeijn (1984) also proposes a division of our abstract entity. However, he undertakes this quite differently than does Bal. He differentiates between *implied author* and *author in the text*. The former is understood as the text's "governing consciousness," as "something 'complete' (a set of implicit norms, the technical instance responsible for the entire structure of the text)." The latter is "a more fragmentary notion," which only appears in individual lexical signs or in the ideas expressed by characters. Whereas the "implied author" changes from text to text, the "author in the text" remains more or less constant (Weststeijn 1984, 562).

Neither of the two divisions seems meaningful. The two author figures Bal distinguishes reveal themselves, upon closer inspection, to be nothing other than two sides of one and the same entity. The terminological intensions "producer" and "result" merely define this entity, which remains extensionally identical, from two different perspectives. As the "producer" of textual meanings (it should actually be: as the image of the "producer" within the text), the abstract author appears in the sphere of production esthetics; the "result" of precisely these textual meanings is the abstract author from the perspective of reception esthetics. In other words: the abstract author is the image of the author that the concrete reader forms by unifying all the meanings of a work. The image itself is the "result" of the semantic activity of the reader; its content, however, what it represents, is the "producer" in both Bal's "technical" and "ideological" senses. Bal's diagram, in which the *impliciete auteur* as "producer" is placed before the text, and the *abstracte auteur* as "result" subordinated to it, therefore does not model two separate entities, but only a change of perspective.

Weststeijn's dichotomy throws up certain problems from both narratological and hermeneutical perspectives, which will be countered with the following theses (which will lead us beyond the debate with Weststeijn to the problem of the relationship between concrete and abstract author):

1. Weststeijn's opposition of *implied author* and *author in the text* is problematic insofar as the former is fundamentally nothing other than the—well-understood—author in the text, i.e. the author as s/he is realized and manifested in his or her text, and not only in individual sections which are accentuated or conspicuous to the reader, but in the entire text; not only in thematic material (in key scenes, commentary by the narrator, or characters' speech) but in the text's entirety, including all its devices.

2. The "œuvre author," who remains constant throughout his or her works, is not the real author in himself, but equally an implied entity inferred by the reader, or more specifically: a stereotype, such as the typical Tolstoy, at which Yury Tynyanov's (1927b; tr. 1971, 75) concept of the "literary person-

ality"[15] or Booth's (1979, 270) "career author" is aimed.[16] But it must not be overlooked that the œuvre author is no less a (re-)construction than the abstract author of a single work, and also depends to no lesser a degree on interpretation. There are also more general author stereotypes, which refer not to a single work or an œuvre, but to literary schools, stylistic movements, epochs and genres.

3. Beyond individual reconstructions, there are, of course, also stereotypes of a single-work or œuvre author that are typical of a specific period. For example, the images early Soviet reception constructed of Dostoevsky's œuvre or of the *Brothers Karamazov* are extremely different from the stereotypes which dominated at the end of the 19th century, and also from those widespread in later years in non-socialist reading societies, and, again, from the stereotypical Dostoevsky image cultivated by contemporary Russian readers.

4. The individual readers' abstract authors are incorporated in a period's typical stereotype of a single work or œuvre only to the degree that they are subject to the doxa of their period and their social context. Individually and independently receiving readers play only a minor part in the doxic image of an author, but they can, however, insofar as they articulate their analysis publicly, initiate new receptions and thus constitute new author images typical of their period and context.

5. Weststeijn is, of course, right to say that many works formulate ideas on the level of the narrator or the characters, behind which one supposes to hear the voice of the concrete author directly. The inference about the concrete author is then indeed an interpretation based on knowledge of the work and the life of the author. Differing information necessarily determines different images of the real author and leads to different hermeneutical results. Weststeijn's *author in the text* is therefore—just as *the implied author*—a hermeneutical construct, which competes with the constructs of other readers.

6. Of course, it is by no means rare for an author to place his or her own opinions, which can be deduced biographically, in the mouths of the work's fictive entities. In that process, the words and ideas which seem to represent the real author necessarily become fictionalized. By virtue of their fictivity, their being represented, these word and ideas are unavoidably objectivized and relativized, and thereby forfeit the privileges of their authorial origin.

7. It is possible for an author to experiment with his or her ideas through fictionalization and thus subject them to questioning. One need only think of the speaker in Dostoevsky's *Notes from the Underground* or of Pozdnyshev,

---

15   Cf. Rymar'/Skobelev 1994, 39–42.
16   Cf. Chatman 1990, 87–89.

2. The abstract author

the narrating protagonist in Tolstoy's *Kreutzer Sonata*—both undoubtedly mouthpieces for their authors, who compromise their own ideologies and those of their author in the course of the stories they narrate. These are certainly two extreme cases, but they illustrate the principle: the fragmentary *author in the text*, as conceived by Weststeijn, is nothing other than a fictive figure endowed with certain characteristics of the author, subject to competition with other characters and their perspectives.[17]

8. In such cases, an author can make a *sujet* out of his or her ideological, personal or intellectual tensions and conflicts. This narrativization of conflicts experienced internally by the author is encountered often; nevertheless, the reversal of this process, the reduction of a narrated story to its author's mental structures, is problematic in literary study and is an acceptable hermeneutical discipline only as a verified aspect of psychology.

9. The objectivizing of the author in the fictive characters of his or her work is not a rare phenomenon. Lermontov's Pechorin, from *A Hero of Our Time*, the autobiographical layout of which is so clear that the fictive author of the novel's preface thinks it necessary to ironically distance himself from it, is the obvious example of the author objectivizing himself. The entanglement of the author as protagonist in a *sujet*, which, according to its own strict logic, objectivizes the hero, is naturally not free of auto-reflexivity in the real world. One need only think of Tolstoy's later narratives "The Devil" or "Father Sergius," the heroes of which openly struggle with the author's weaknesses.

10. Authors sometimes perform experiments with themselves by endowing a fictive character with their own characteristics. In Russian literature, there is a series of heroes who serve their authors as tools of self-recognition and also as means in the struggle with themselves. All these conclusions, of course, remain within the confines of biographical speculation. And why should this be barred? It is thoroughly legitimate for a reader to develop an interest in the struggle of various authors with themselves and find, in this conflict, stimulus for the further understanding of himself. Of course, the internal struggles of the author are not a subject for narratology.

---

17   This is somewhat different when the concrete author appears in the narrated world, as happens with Vladimir Nabokov for the first time in his novel *King, Queen, Knave* (ch. 12 and 13): the hero, Franz, observes a foreign couple speaking in a language he doesn't know, speaking about him, he believes, and even naming him. Franz gets the feeling "that this damned happy foreigner hastening to the beach with his tanned, pale-haired, lovely companion, knew absolutely everything about his predicament and perhaps pitied, not without some derision, an honest young man who had been seduced and appropriated by an older woman who, despite her fine dresses and face lotions, resembled a large white toad" (Nabokov, KQK, 259). This crossing of the border between the fictive and the real world is the classic narrative paradox that Genette (1972, 244) names "métalepse."

f) Sketch of a systematic definition

Let us now undertake an attempt at a systematic definition of the abstract author. A basis for consensus should be provided by the definition of the abstract author as the correlate of all indexical signs in a text that point to the author. These signs delineate both an ideological position and an esthetic conception. "Abstract" does not mean "fictive." The abstract author is not a represented entity, nor an intentional creation of the concrete author,[18] and is categorically distinguished in this way from the narrator, who is always—whether explicitly or implicitly—a represented entity.

The abstract author exists on a different level of the work from the narrator; s/he embodies the principle of representation of a narrator and the entire represented world. S/he has no voice, no text.[19] His or her text consists of the entire text on all levels, the entire work in its artificiality and composition.[20] His or her position encompasses both ideological and esthetic norms. The abstract author is only the anthropomorphic hypostasis of all creative acts, the personified intention of the work.

The abstract author is real but not concrete. S/he exists in the work only virtually, indicated by the traces left in the work by the acts of creation, and requires concretization by the reader. S/he therefore has a double existence: on one hand, s/he is objectively given in the text, as a virtual schema of the symptoms; on the other, s/he depends for his or her configuration on the

---

18 Therefore, the critical question that Bakhtin (1992, 296) poses of Vinogradov's concept of the "author's image"— "When and to what degree is the intention of the author [...] to create an author's image"—must be seen as the attempt at a reduction of this concept, to which Bakhtin had an ambivalent relationship, ad absurdum. Bakhtin's basic acceptance of an author entity within the text is, however, indicated in the following definition: "Every utterance [...] has its author, whom we hear in the very utterance as its creator. Of the real author, as he exists outside the utterance, we can know absolutely nothing at all" (Bakhtin 1963; tr. 1984, 184).

19 Mikhail Bakhtin appears to have misunderstood my concept of the abstract author in this sense. In his excerpt, largely written in German, of my review of B. A. Uspensky's (1970) *Poetics of Composition* (Schmid 1971), which, prepared in 1971, has now been published (Bakhtin 2002a), he poses the question, concerning the various names of Dmitry Karamazov in Dostoevsky's novel ("Dmitry Karamazov," "Dmitry Fyodorovich," "Mitya," "Miten'ka," "Brother Dmitry"): "What would be his name in the language of the 'abstract author' (perhaps it would be as official as a birth certificate 'Dmitry Fyodorovich Karamazov')? Does the 'abstract author' have his own language (a code)?" (Bakhtin 2002a, 418). Lyudmila Gogotishvili (2002, 661), the commentator in the Bakhtinian workbook, states that Bakhtin, although he "weakly" problematizes the existence of the author's own words, principally advances the position, in the other fragments of the workbook, that the author has no speech of his or her own. But that was precisely my position in the Uspensky review.

20 Cf. in this context Peter Hühn's (1995, 5) concept of the "subject of composition," which draws on Easthope's (1983) "subject of enunciation."

2. The abstract author

actualizing, subjective acts of reading, understanding and interpretation. In other words: the abstract author is a construct of the reader's, on the basis of his or her reading of the work. The emphasis cannot be placed solely on "construct," something the proponents of constructivism tend towards. The process of construction must, if it is to find more than its own preconceptions, focus on the symptoms contained in the text, the objectivity of which fundamentally limits the freedom of interpretation. Therefore, it would be better to use, instead of "construct," "reconstruction."

The abstract author is insolubly bound to the work, and forms its indexical signified. Every work has its own abstract author. Insofar as different readers can concretize the abstract author differently and as this can even vary for one individual reader from one reading to the next, it is not only every work and every reader, but actually every reading that corresponds to a separate abstract author.

The abstract author can be determined from two sides, from the work and from the standpoint of the concrete author. From the former perspective, the abstract author is the hypostasis of the construction principle shaping the work. From the latter, it is the trace of the concrete author in the work, his or her representative within it. The relationship between the abstract and concrete authors, however, should not be understood in terms of reflection or reproduction, which is what is misleading about the term "author's image." Nor can the representative within the work be modeled as the mouthpiece of the concrete author, something suggested by the term "implicit author."

As we have seen, it is not unusual for authors to experiment with their views in their works and to test their own convictions. Many authors realize possibilities in their work which must remain unrealized in life, and take up positions which, for whatever reasons, they would not want to, or be able to, propose in real life. In ideological respects, the abstract author can be more radical and less compromising than the concrete author ever has been in reality, or—phrased more carefully—than we imagine him or her as having been, based on the available historical sources.

This sort of radicalization of the abstract author is typical of Tolstoy's later work. As is well known from the work of biographers, the later Tolstoy was far less convinced by some of his own ideas than his abstract authors were, who embodied only a dimension of Tolstoy's thinking and took it to an extreme.

The opposite relationship also exists: the abstract author can go significantly beyond the more or less ideologically limited concrete author in terms of their intellectual horizons. An example of this is Dostoevsky, who, in his later novels, developed an astonishing understanding for ideologies which he, as an essayist, strongly opposed.

Dostoevsky's last novel demonstrates another phenomenon, the splitting of the abstract author. On the ideological level, the abstract author of the *Brothers Karamazov* pursues the goals of theodicy. Simultaneously, a contradictory meaning is realized in the novel, which reveals that theodicy entails a violation of the self for the author, despite his desperately wanting to believe (cf. Schmid 1996b). A struggle between two ideological positions is played out, a fluctuation between for and against. The abstract author appears in doubled form: affirming (Dostoevsky I) and doubting (Dostoevsky II).

This all certainly begs the question of why a semantic entity that is neither a pragmatic entity nor a specific component of the narrative work should be included in a model of communication levels at all. Should one not be content with the author and narrator, something counseled, as mentioned above, by some narratologists?

Rimmon-Kenan (1976, 58) ascertains that: "Without the implied author it is difficult to analyze the 'norms' of the text, especially when they differ from those of the narrator." Bronzwaer (1978, 3), similarly, states that:

> We need an instance that calls the extradiegetic narrator into existence, which is responsible for him in the same way as he is responsible for the diegesis [...] The scope of narrative theory excludes the writer but includes the implied author. [...] It is therefore at the implied author that a theory of narrative can, and must, begin.

Another advantage of the concept is mentioned by Chatman (1990, 76): "positing an implied author inhibits the overhasty assumption that the reader has direct access through the fictional text to the real author's intentions and ideology."

The concept of the abstract author is particularly useful in textual interpretation because it helps describe the layered process by which meaning is generated. The existence of the abstract author, who is not part of the represented world but nonetheless part of the work, puts the narrator, who often appears as master of the situation and seems to have control over the semantic order of the work, in proper perspective. The presence of the abstract author in a model of communication highlights the fact that narrators, their texts, and the meanings expressed in them are all represented. These meanings take on their ultimate (in terms of the work) semantic intention only on the level of the abstract author, whose presence in the work, above the characters and the narrator and their associated levels of meaning, establishes a semantic level arching over the whole work: the authorial level.

The conferring of meaning by the author corresponds to the basic hierarchical relations indicated in the diagram of communication levels: in the production of characters' speech by the narrator, the figural signs and meanings become, as signifiers, part of the more complex signs of the narratorial

2. The abstract author

level, and aid the realization of the narrator's intended meaning. A comparable relationship exists between narrator and author. The signs built up in the narration—partly by the integration of the figural signs—are, in turn, used by the author to express his or her intended meaning. Everything articulated by the characters and the narrator expresses character- or narrator-oriented content and, in that, contributes to the expression of the author's intended meaning. The relationship between the meaning creating activities of the characters, narrator and author, analogous to the matryoshka-doll structure of narrative communication, can be schematically represented in the following way:

$$C: \quad \underbrace{Sa_C \Leftrightarrow Se_C}$$
$$N: \quad S_C \in \underbrace{Sa_N \times \Leftrightarrow Se_N}$$
$$A: \quad S_N \in Sa_A \Leftrightarrow Se_A$$

The diagram is to be read like this: the signs (S, *signes*), created by the interdependence ($\Leftrightarrow$) of signifier (Sa, *signifiants*) and signified (Se, *signifiés*) on the level of the characters (C), belong ($\in$) to the mass of signifiers on the level of the narrator (Sa_N), which, for their part, are in a state of interdependency ($\Leftrightarrow$) with the signifiers of this level (Se_N). A corresponding relationship exists between the level of the narrator and the level of the author (A). The signs constituted on the level of the narrator (S_N), partly through the integration of signs on the character level, become part of the mass of signifiers (Sa_A), which are expressed by the authorial meaning (Se_A).

3. The abstract reader

a) The abstract reader as an attribute of the abstract author

On the receiving side of our diagram of communication levels, the abstract reader is drawn in opposite the abstract author. Naturally, there is no contact whatsoever between these two abstract figures, which are, after all, not pragmatic communicative entities, but semantic reconstructions. This suggests a deceptive symmetry: if the abstract author (AA) is a reconstruction of the concrete author (CA) by the concrete reader (CR), then, one might be tempted to conclude, the abstract reader (AR) is the concrete reader as imagined by the concrete author. This arrangement would be represented in the following diagram, in which the arrows symbolize the acts of reconstruction and the ovals the reconstructions themselves:

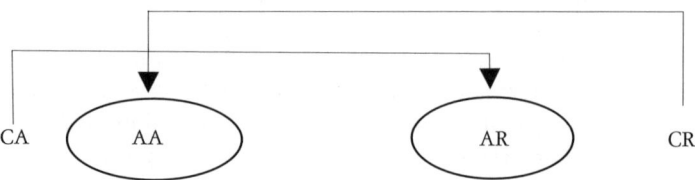

The actual state of affairs is, of course, more complicated. It is not the concrete author, about whose intentions we know very little, but rather the work s/he has created or his or her abstract author that bears the projection of the reader's image. The visualization of the counterpart is one of the characteristics that the reconstructing concrete reader attributes to the abstract author. Consequently, the abstract reader depends no less on individual explication, i.e. on the reading and understanding of the text by the concrete reader, than does the abstract author. Therefore, we must correct the diagram in the following way:

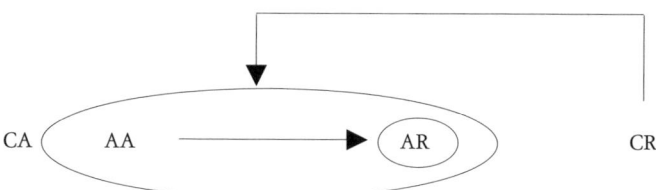

b) History of the abstract reader concept

There is a range of older conceptions of the abstract reader. In Booth (1961), the *implied reader* appears as a counterpart of the *implied author*. In the Slavic area, which has made significant contributions to the study of communication in literary work, hardly noticed in the West, the text's addressee was first systematically described by the Polish literary scholar Michał Głowiński (1967), and labeled the "virtual recipient." This entity was not a pragmatic entity, but a role prepared by the text. The most important question for Głowiński was, therefore, "how the structure of the poetical work configures the role of the addressee." Głowiński already made a distinction between the addressee of the author and the addressee of the lyrical "I" or the narrator, and distinguished two basic types for the former, the differentiation of which he justified with differing presentations of the work's meaning: the

3. The abstract reader   53

"passive reader," who needs to take on only the meaning obvious in the work, and the "active reader," who needs to reconstruct the meaning encrypted in specific techniques.[21]

Miroslav Červenka (1969, 174-75) characterizes the "addressee's personality," by which he means the abstract reader, with the statement that:

> If the subject of the work was the correlate of the totality of the acts of creative choice, then the overall meaning of the work's addressee is the totality of the interpretive abilities required: the ability to use the same codes and develop their material analogously to the creative activity of the speaker, the ability to transform the potentiality of the work into an esthetic object.

In Russia, Boris Korman (1977, 127) contrasted the "author as bearer of the work's concept" with the corresponding entity of the "reader as postulated addressee, ideal principle of reception": "The method of reception is the process of transforming the real reader into the ideal, conceived reader."[22]

The investigation of reader roles was deepened and concretized in the sphere of literary history in the works of Wolfgang Iser (1972; tr. 1974; 1976; tr. 1978). With his term "impliziter Leser" ("implied reader" in the English editions), which was not entirely unambiguously defined in its extension, and which fluctuated between the addressee of the work and the addressee of the narration, Iser describes a structure in the text:

> [The implied reader] embodies all those predispositions necessary for a literary work to exercise its effect—predispositions laid down, not by an empirical outside reality, but by the text itself. [...] The concept of the implied reader is therefore a textual structure anticipating the presence of a recipient without necessarily defining him [...] Thus the concept of the implied reader designates a network of response-inviting structures, which impel the reader to grasp the text. (Iser 1976; tr. 1978, 34)

A clear differentiation of the text's addressees was introduced by Gunter Grimm (1977, 38-39) who placed, alongside Wolff's (1971) and Link's (1976) "intended" reader (the author's "objective"), an "imagined" reader ("the conception that the author has of his actual readership") and a "conceived" reader ("the construction of a reader oriented on the text").

c) Definition of the abstract reader

Although the terms mentioned refer to the image of the reader contained in the text, their practical application activates different facets and functions of the abstract reader. In many cases, the ontological and structural status of

---

21   More exhaustive and on other positions in the Polish history of the concept: Schmid 2007b, 172-73.
22   Rymar' and Skobelev (1994, 119-21) also use the term "conceived reader."

the entity denoted remains unclear. It is not rare for the term to fluctuate between denoting the addressee of the author (i.e. the work) and the addressee of the narrator. For this reason, it seems sensible to render the content of the term and its domain of use more precisely.

It must first be emphasized that the abstract reader never coincides with the fictive reader, the narratee, i.e. the addressee of the narrator. A coincidence of this sort is assumed by Genette (1972, 266) who identifies the "extradiegetic narratee," i.e. the addressee to whom an "extradiegetic narrator" addresses himself, with the implied reader. Genette, in *Narrative Discourse Revisited* (1983; tr. 1988, 138), embraces this coincidence as a small simplifying measure "to the delight of our master Ockham." But this economy is only possible on the basis of Genette's system, in which the extradiegetic narrator does not appear as a fictive entity and takes the place of the absent abstract author. Genette (1983; tr. 1988, 132-33) states that: "the extradiegetic narrator merges totally with the author, whom I shall not call 'implied,' as people too often do, but rather entirely explicit and declared."

Of course, the more closely the fictive narrator is associated with the abstract author, the more difficult it is to separate clearly the ideological positions of the fictive and abstract reader. However, their difference remains absolutely in force. The border between the fictive world, to which every narrator belongs, no matter how neutrally, objectively or "Olympic" s/he is constituted, and reality, to which, for all his virtuality, the abstract reader belongs, cannot be crossed—unless in some narrative paradox.

What is meant here by the abstract reader are the contents of the image of the recipient that the author had while writing, or—more accurately—the contents of the author's image of the recipient that is fixed in the text by specific indexical signs.

An "intended reader"—in the terminology of Link (1976, 28) or Grimm (1977, 38-39)—who is not fixed in the text, but exists merely in the imagination of the concrete author, and who can be reconstructed only with the latter's statements or extra-textual information, is not a part of the work. This sort of reader belongs exclusively to the sphere of the concrete author, in whose intention he or she exists.

d) Presumed addressee and ideal recipient

Two hypostases of the (re-)constructed abstract reader must be distinguished on the basis of the functions they can be thought to have.[23] First, the abstract reader can be seen as a *presumed, postulated addressee* to whom the work is directed and whose linguistic codes, ideological norms, and es-

---

23   Cf. Schmid (1974a, 407) and thereafter Lintvelt (1981, 18); Ilyin (1996c).

3. The abstract reader

thetic ideas must be taken into account if the work is to be understood. In this function, the abstract reader is the bearer of the codes and norms presumed in the readership. For example, the addressee of Dostoevsky's later novels is conceptualized as a reader who can not only read Russian and knows how to read a novel, but also has a command of all the language's registers, possesses a developed sense for the stylistic expression of evaluative positions, has at his or her disposal a good knowledge of Russian literature, a high inter-textual competence, knows the dominant philosophical positions of the century, has an overview of the history of ideas in Europe and is familiar with the social discourses of the period.

Of course, an author can make mistakes in the norms and abilities assumed in the readership. S/he can be mistaken in the philosophical majority position of his or her contemporaries, s/he can overestimate the ability of his or her readers to decode metaphorical statements or assume too high an understanding of esthetic innovation. It is not unusual for an author to fail in addressing the intended public as a result of being mistaken about the language, the values and norms of his or her public, or of being unable to encode his or her message correspondingly.

Second, the abstract reader functions as an image of the *ideal recipient* who understands the work in a way that optimally matches its structure, and who adopts the interpretive position and esthetic standpoint put forward by the work. The attitude of the ideal reader, his or her relation to the norms and values of the fictive entities, are thus entirely specified by the work, though it must be noted that this is not the result of the concrete author's intentions, but of the acts of creation objectivized in the work. If contradictory evaluative positions are found in a hierarchy in the work, the ideal recipient will identify with the entity that is highest in this hierarchy. If the position of the entity at the top of the hierarchy is relativized, the ideal reader will identify with it only insofar as that is allowed by the overall meaning of the work. The position of the ideal recipient is thus entirely predetermined by the work; the degree of ideological certainty, however, varies from author to author. Whereas those works with a message demand a specific response, the spectrum of readings permitted by the work is wider with experimental or questioning authors. With Leo Tolstoy, the spectrum of positions permitted by the work is undoubtedly narrower than, for example, with Anton Chekhov.

The difference between the two functions, the presumed addressee and the ideal recipient, is all the more relevant the more specific the work's ideology is, the more it calls for a way of thinking that does not correspond to the doxa. In Tolstoy's later work, the ideal reader is clearly very distant from the presumed addressee. Whereas the latter is conceptualized with very general characteristics—such as command of the Russian language, knowledge of the social norms of the late 19th century and the ability to read a literary work—the former is distinguished by a series of specific idiosyncrasies and Tolstoyan evaluative positions.

e) Critique of the ideal recipient concept

The conception of the abstract reader presented here (as put forward in Schmid 1973; 1974a) has encountered objections. However, criticism has not called for the division of the entity into the presumed addressee and the ideal recipient, but the supposed responsibility of the concrete reader—as the executor of the intended reception—for the reading sketched in the ideal reader. So, Jaap Lintvelt (1981, 18) charges my definition with incapacitating the concrete reader:

> Schmid's definitions imply that a "text is supposed to program its own reading." In this kind of conception, reading would be limited to "a (subjective) recording of an arrangement of meaning that pre-exists the reading itself [...]" As such, Schmid fails to indicate that the concrete reader [...] can also carry out other readings which do not necessarily correspond to the abstract reader's, supposedly "ideal," reception.

Jan van der Eng (1984, 126–27) also argues in favor of according the concrete reader more freedom and creative involvement in the formation of meaning than is envisioned in my concept of the abstract reader. The individual recipient—according to this critic—not only has the freedom to concretize and deepen the interpretative, emotional and cognitive contents of the work in his or her own way, but also, by projecting these contents onto new realities, onto philosophical, religious and psychological developments, brings new aspects of meaning to light, which were neither manifested nor intended in the work.

In his workbooks of the 1960s and 1970s, Mikhail Bakhtin already expressed criticism of the concept of the ideal recipient formed in the literary study of the time:

> Naturally, it is not the empirical listener and not the psychological idea, the image of the listener in the soul of the author. It is rather an abstract ideal construction. It is the counterpart of an equally abstract ideal author. In this conception, the ideal listener is a mirror image equivalent of the author, which duplicates him or her. (Bakhtin 2002b, 427)

Lyudmila Gogotishvili (2002, 674), the commentator on Bakhtin's workbooks, suspects that these words contain a critical allusion to my review of B. A. Uspensky's (1970) *Poetics of Composition* (Schmid 1971), which Bakhtin excerpted shortly after its publication (2002a). The review argued that the abstract reader as ideal recipient mirrors changes in the author's position and does not, as Uspensky had postulated of the reader in general, remain trapped in inertia (Schmid 1971, 132). Bakhtin advanced the argument that the ideal reader conceptualized in this way does not contribute anything of himself, anything new, to the work and that he lacks "otherness" (*drugost'*), which is a pre-requisite of the author's "surplus" (*izbytok*) (Bakhtin 2002b, 427–28).

The conception of the abstract reader as ideal recipient naturally does not postulate an obligatory ideal meaning prescribed in the work, which the concrete reader must merely grasp correctly. It is in no way to be doubted that the contributory creative action of the recipient can have dimensions and take directions not laid out in the work, nor that readings that miss the reception sketched in the work, or even intentionally reject it, can widen the work's meaning. But it must be emphasized that every work contains, to a greater or lesser degree of ambiguity, signs pointing towards its ideal reading. Only in rare cases does this ideal reading consist of a concrete ascription of meaning. As a rule, the ideal reception constitutes a spectrum of varying breadth, of functional attitudes, individual concretizations and subjective ascriptions of meaning. In extreme cases, the ideal reading can exist precisely as a contradiction to a pre-prepared attitude and an obvious meaning, if an author demands of his or her reader the rebuttal of evaluative positions suggested by the narrator.

To postulate the ideal recipient as an image more or less clearly implicit in the work does not mean, in any way, the constraint of the concrete reader's freedom, nor the forming of any kind of pre-suppositions on the legitimacy of the meanings actually assigned to the work.

4. The fictive narrator

Mediated narratives differentiate themselves from mimetic ones in that the real communication, which encompasses author, represented world and addressee, is, as it were, repeated in the represented world, as the arrangement of fictive narrator, narrated world and fictive addressee. Let us first examine the transmitting entity of represented narrative communication, the fictive narrator.

a) Explicit and implicit representation of the narrator

Two modes can be distinguished for representation of the narrator: the *explicit* and the *implicit*. Explicit representation is based on the narrator presenting himself. The narrator may name himself, describe himself as the narrative voice, tell his life story, and present his philosophy. Explicit representation is, of course, not dependent on the narrator describing himself exhaustively. Simply the use of the first person is a—albeit reduced—form of presenting oneself. Whereas explicit representation is facultative, implicit representation is, by its very nature, obligatory. Explicit representation builds on the implicit, but the implicit can also function without an explicit superstructure.

Implicit representation is based on the narrative text's symptoms or indexes. These signs are founded on the expression function of language mentioned above (Bühler 1918/1920; 1934). All the actions that constitute narration participate in the indexical representation of the narrator. Particularly significant are the indexical signs created in the following ways:

(1) Selection of elements (characters, situations, plots, also speech, thoughts, consciousnesses) from the "happenings" as the narrative material for the creation of a story (cf. below, V).
(2) Concretizing and detailing of the selected elements with definite properties.
(3) Composition of the narrative text, i.e. juxtaposition and the placing of the selected elements in a certain order.
(4) Presentation of the narrative in more or less lexically, syntactically and grammatically marked language.
(5) Evaluation of the selected elements (this can be implicit in the four actions mentioned above, or be provided explicitly).
(6) All kinds of "intrusions" by the narrator, i.e. reflections, comments, generalizations directed at the narrated story, the narration or at the narrator him or herself.

The implicitly provided image of the narrator is the result of the interaction of the six symptoms mentioned. The relevance of each of these techniques is not identical in every work. Whereas the narrator could be indicated in one work through the actions of selection, concretization and composition of the elements, in another s/he could be indicated primarily by stylistic means, or, in a third, his or her image could be based on explicit and implicit value judgements, comments, reflections and so on.

The indexes contained in the narration can indicate narratorial characteristics of various types and dimensions:

(1) Mode and form of narration (spoken or written, spontaneity or carefully prepared narration, colloquialisms or rhetoric).
(2) Narrative competence (omniscience, ability to see into the consciousness of the characters, omnipresence or absence of such abilities).
(3) Social status and origin.

4. The fictive narrator

(4) Geographical origin (presence or absence of regionalisms and dialect).
(5) Education and intellectual horizons.
(6) Worldview.

The implicitly represented narrator is a construct formed from the narrative text's symptoms. Strictly speaking, it is no more than the bearer of the indexed characteristics.

To obviate anthropomorphism and psychologizing, Roland Barthes (1966; tr. 2004, 82) called the narrator a "paper being." For the same reasons, Käte Hamburger (1968; tr. 1973, 134–94) replaced the term "narrator" (a "metaphorical pseudo-definition") with the concept of the "fluctuating narrative function," which could be manifested in various forms: as narrating discourse, as monologue or dialogue of the characters or as free indirect discourse. But these kinds of depersonalization of the narrator concept do not, in most cases, correspond to our perception of the narrative text and the entity reconstructed behind it. As a rule, the reader does not perceive the narrator as an abstract function, but as a subject that is inevitably equipped with particular anthropomorphic characteristics of thought and speech. It is precisely this perceived subject status of the narrator that is presumably responsible for the resistance of the concept to any attempt at replacing or dissolving it.

In the history of the narrator concept's use, what has been emphasized from the beginning is the prismatic function, which—in Käte Friedemann's words, (1910, 26) quoted above—prevents us from grasping "the world as it is in itself, but rather as it has passed through the medium of an observing mind."

This "observing mind" should certainly not be identified as a living person equipped with the abilities expected of one. The narrator can be constituted as a superhuman, omniscient and omnipresent entity, or also reduced to the humblest of abilities. However s/he is equipped, the narrator is perceived as a subject that is characterized by a particular view of the world, by a perspective that is manifested, at the very least, in the selection of particular elements from the "happenings" and the non-selection of others.

The narrator can also be constituted as inconsistent and variable. That can be seen in Dostoevsky's *Brothers Karamazov*. Large parts of the novel are narrated by an omnipresent, omniscient, impersonal entity capable of looking into the deepest secrets of each character's consciousness. But, at certain points, often at particularly important ones (e.g. the "Author's Foreword"), this narrator is transformed into a chronicler with restricted knowledge, who, as it initially appears, narrates naively and artlessly, and reports all sorts of superfluous things. This variation in the image of the narrator correlates to the degree of the narrator's markedness, whose presence in the novel is sometimes strongly perceived, sometimes completely forgotten.[24]

b) Individuality and anthropomorphism of the narrator

The narrator can possess the well-developed traits of an individual, but can also be the impersonal bearer of an (e.g. ironic) evaluative stance without possessing any individual characteristics whatsoever. The problem of the narrator's individuality does not coincide with that of his or her human nature. The narrating entity can have personal characteristics without being a person. This is the case when the narrator is omnipresent and omniscient and thereby withdraws from the spatial and temporal determinacy of the human perspective. The omnipresent and omniscient narrator is a godlike entity, with a perspective that is traditionally denoted "Olympic" (Shipley [ed.] 1964, 439–40). On the other hand, the narrator can be less than a person: an animal, a plant, an object. The classic example of a narrating animal is the *Asinus aureus* of Lucius Apuleius, a novel that, like the parallel Greek text by Lucian of Samosata (*Lucius or The Ass*) draws on the Greek *Metamorphoses* of Lukios of Patrai. In all these texts, the narrator takes the form of a donkey, into which he is transformed because of his curiosity. In more recent European literature, there are countless examples of narrating animals. This tradition developed under the influence of fairy tales and fables. One literary model is *The Dialogue of the Dogs* (from Cervantes' cycle of *Exemplary Novels*), in which the dog Berganza tells his friend, the dog Cipión, the story of his life. This conversation is taken up again in *News of the Latest Fortunes of the Hound Berganza* by E. T. A. Hoffmann (who also provided another classic example of narrating animals in *The Life and Opinions of Tomcat Murr*. This line can be followed through to Kafka's *Investigations of a Dog* and *A Report to an Academy*, in which a humanized ape describes his former life as a primate.

Animal narrators are not particularly "unreliable",[25] but, on the contrary, prove themselves to be keen observers of the human world, and often serve the authors as means of *defamiliarization*. A good example of this is *Strider: The Story of a Horse* by Leo Tolstoy, in which an old gelding, who conveys

---

24 On the fluctuating image of the narrator in the *Brothers Karamazov* cf. Matlaw 1957; Busch 1962; Meijer 1971; Schmid 1981.

25 The, not entirely clear, concept of the "unreliable narrator" was created by W. C. Booth (1961). According to his definition, we are dealing with an unreliable narrator when the norms of the narrator and of the implied author do not coincide. According to newer definitions in light of cognitive theory, the yardstick of unreliability cannot be the implied author, but only the concrete reader (cf. Nünning 1998; Nünning [ed.] 1998a; Nünning 1999). For an overview of unreliability concepts cf. Shen 2010.

4. The fictive narrator

his experiences of people to the younger horses, appears as the mouthpiece of an author critical of human conventions:

> The words "*my* horse" applied to me, a live horse, seemed to me as strange as to say "my land," "my air," or "my water." But those words had an enormous effect on me. I thought of them constantly and only after long and varied relations with men did I at last understand the meaning they attach to these strange words, which indicate that men are guided in life not by deeds but by words. They like not so much to do or abstain from doing anything, as to be able to apply conventional words to different objects. Such words, considered very important among them, are *my* and *mine*, which they apply to various things, creatures or objects: even to land, people, and horses. They have agreed that of any given thing only one person may use the word *mine*, and he who in this game of theirs may use that conventional word about the greatest number of things is considered the happiest. (Tolstoy, Strider, Ch. 6)

An interesting example of a narrating non-human is provided by *Flatland. A Romance of Many Dimensions* (1884) by Edwin A. Abbott.[26] In it, the narrator is a geometric shape: a humble square, resident of Flatland, who describes not only normal life in the circumstances of a two-dimensional world but also three trips to foreign worlds. In a kind of vision, he first visits Lineland, the king of which is the longest line and in which every line is condemned forever to look at its neighbour. After that, he travels to Pointland, a world without dimensions, whose inhabitant believes himself to be the only being in existence, the all-powerful god. Even more interesting, however, is the journey to a world with three dimensions. Having returned from there to Flatland, the square attempts to convince his countrymen of the existence of a three-dimensional world. In vain, for the circles, the rulers of Flatland, declare him mad and incarcerate him. In all these cases, the narrator, however little similarity to a human he appears to have, is perceived as a subject characterized by a particular view of the world.

c) The narrator's markedness

Does a narrator exist in every narrative work? Is it meaningful to speak of a narrator when a narrative text demonstrates no individual characteristics of a fictive speaker or writer other than the ability to narrate a story? Differing answers have been given to these questions and these can be classified, following Marie-Laure Ryan (1981), as three basic positions.

The adherents of the first position see no fundamental difference between a strongly marked and an extremely impersonal, objective narrator.

---

26 For the reference to Abbott, I thank Wilhelm Schernus, member of the Hamburg Research Group "Narratology."

This position is characteristic of Francophone narratologists, who work from the assumption there is no narration entirely without a narrator (cf. Ilyin 1996a).

The second position, which stands in the tradition of Lubbock (1921) and Friedman (1955) and is more widespread in Anglophone narratology, emphasizes, by contrast, the difference between "personal" and "impersonal" narration. The latter is present in the "omniscient narration" of the classic novels of the 19th century and in the "anonymous narrative voice" of some 20th century narratives, such as those of Henry James and Ernest Hemingway. One adherent of this thesis that there need not be a narrator in a narrative work, Seymour Chatman (1978, 34, 254), regards the impersonal narration in Hemingway's works, where the narrative text is reduced to the presentation of facts, as *nonnarration*, in which, paradoxically, a *nonnarrator* narrates. Between the *nonnarrator* and the *overt narrator* stands, according to Chatman, the *covert narrator*. Many adherents of this position orientate themselves on texts where the perspectives are consistently bound to characters. In their view, the narratorial element is entirely absent in, for instance, free indirect discourse. The adherents of this position believe that the task of narrating in these narratives without a narrator is fulfilled by the characters or an abstract "narrative function" (Hamburger 1957; 1968; Banfield 1973; 1978a; 1978b; 1983).

The third position, which M.-L. Ryan herself supports, is a weak interpretation of the concept of the nonnarrated narration, i.e. it consists of a compromise between the first and second positions: "In this perspective the concept of narrator is a logical necessity of all fictions, but it has no psychological foundation in the impersonal case" (Ryan 1981, 519). Whereas the first position sees the impersonal narrator as an individual, but unknown being, and the second position questions his or her logical necessity, s/he is, according to the third position "an abstract construct deprived of a human dimension."

The first position seems the most plausible to me. There are three reasons why I cannot accept the compromise suggested by Ryan:

1. Ryan confuses the problem of the narrator's personality and individuality with that of his or her markedness. A narrator can be strongly marked without having a personal identity. The markedness of the narrator is based on the indexical signs present in the text; his or her individuality presupposes the convergence of all symptomatic lines in a homogenous, psychologically plausible image. In ornamental prose, for example, it is not unusual to come across strongly marked narrative entities that remain entirely abstract and non-individual, because the narrative text's symptoms do not reveal a conclusive image of a personality.

4. The fictive narrator

2. The dichotomic treatment of markedness is hardly acceptable. This characteristic cannot be reduced to two limits such as "individuality" and "abstraction" or "objectivity." It forms a continuum that stretches between the maximum and minimum presence of indexical signs. The minimum presence will certainly never be zero. Ultimately, even the Hemingway type (Chatman's *nonnarration*) does not manage entirely without certain symptoms of a mediative entity, which shows itself in the selection, contrasting and ordering of the narrated elements (even if they are only the characters' speeches). As for language, it must be questioned whether the forced dryness of the Hemingway narrative does not also constitute a specific feature, signaling a particular type of narrator.

3. Ryan (1981, 523) presents a position inspired by Searle's Speech Act Theory, namely that, in impersonal narration, the relationship between the "substitute speaker" (i.e. the narrator) and the "actual speaker" (the author) is so close that the reader does not need to reconstruct the narrator as an autonomous consciousness standing between author and character. This position seems to me to be an oversimplification of the facts. It is not unusual for minimally marked, apparently objective narrators, consistently narrating from the perspective of the characters, to leave traces of a different emphasis, a superior axiological determination, in the reproduction of interior monologue, i.e. signs of their additional judgment contradicting that of the character. Signifiers of this evaluative position are the selection, concretization, combination and linguistic realization of individual segments of the character's text.

A change in accentuation of the character's words by an otherwise entirely objective narrator can be seen in Dostoevsky's story *The Eternal Husband*. The beginning of the story is made up almost entirely of fragments of the characters' text, which are presented partly in veiled form with the help of free indirect discourse or figurally colored narration, and partly by quoted figural designation (on the terms cf. below, ch. IV):

> The summer had come and, contrary to expectations, Velchaninov remained in Petersburg. The trip he had planned to the south of Russia had fallen through, and the end of his ease was not in sight. This case—a lawsuit concerning an estate—had taken a very unfortunate turn. Three months earlier it had appeared to be quite straightforward, almost impossible to contest; but suddenly everything was changed. "And, in fact, everything has changed for the worse!" Velchaninov began frequently and resentfully repeating that phrase to himself. [...] His flat was near the Grand Theatre; he had only recently taken it, and it, too, was a failure. "Everything is a failure!" he thought. His hypochondria increased every day; but he had for a long past been subject to hypochondria. (Dostoevsky, EH, 1; tr. slightly revised)

Many of the explanations put forward by the apparently objective narrator ("The trip he had planned to the south of Russia had fallen through"—"And, in fact, everything has changed for the worse!"—"[the flat], too, was a failure"—"His hypochondria increased every day; but he had for a long past been subject to hypochondria") prove, in context, not only to be taken from the character's consciousness but also to be not entirely justified. The motivations cited are, in each case, contradicted by the real causal connection of motives, something which becomes increasingly apparent during the course of the narrative (cf. Schmid 1968). The "pseudo-objective" explanations[27] emanating from the protagonist's consciousness are ironically accentuated by the narrator, who thereby indicates his own evaluative position, which is not explicit in the text. Subsequently, the ironic accentuation is shown in the frequent quoted figural designation:

> [Velchaninov] was a man whose life had been full and varied, he was by no means young, thirty-eight or even thirty-nine, and his "old age," as he expressed it himself, had come upon him "quite unexpectedly" [...] What really happened was that certain incidents in his past, even in his distant past, began suddenly, and God knows why, to come more and more frequently back to his mind, but they came back in quite a peculiar way. [...] Suddenly, for instance, apropos of nothing, he remembered the forgotten, utterly forgotten, figure of a harmless, grey-headed and absurd old clerk [...] And now when, apropos of nothing, Velchaninov remembered how the poor old man had sobbed and hidden his face in his hands like a child, it suddenly seemed to him as though he had never forgotten it. (Dostoevsky, EH, 1–5)

Here, the narrator's evaluative position is realized almost exclusively in the material of the character's consciousness and speech. But it exists nonetheless as the implicitly represented position of a subject autonomous in the fictive world.

To provide an answer to the question posed at the beginning of the section: a narrative text always contains symptoms, no matter how weak they may be. Therefore, we can proceed on the assumption that a more or less clearly marked narrator is represented in every narrative work.[28]

---

27 Cf. in this context Leo Spitzer's (1923a) terms "pseudo-objective motivation" and "pseudo-objective speech." Spitzer shows how, in Charles-Louis Philippe's novel about pimps and whores, *Bubu de Montparnasse*, countless explanations that appear as the speech of the narrator actually render the opinion of the narrated characters.

28 In my Dostoevsky book (Schmid 1973, 26), I still granted the possibility of a complete absence of symptoms and, consequently, of a narrative without a narrator, something which rightly attracted criticism (cf. de Haard 1979, 98; Harweg 1979, 112–13; Lintvelt 1981, 26; Penzkofer 1984, 29).

4. The fictive narrator

d) Abstract author or narrator?

If the indexical signs contained in a narrative text can express both the author and the narrator, every example begs the question of to which of the two entities the sign should be applied. This is a hermeneutical problem, which can be answered only with very general remarks.

The representation of a story and of a narrator to present it are a matter for the author. In each of these acts, all indexes point to the author as the entity ultimately responsible for them. The selection of the elements of the "happenings," their combination into a story, their evaluation and naming are operations that fall into the ambit of the narrator, who reveals himself in them.

In the characters' text, it is primarily the speaking, thinking or perceiving character that expresses him or herself. However, there is a narratorial component contained in every manifestation of the characters' text (see below, IV.1). The narrator is, after all, represented as the entity that selects the characters' words, thoughts and perceptions and—at least in the case of indirect or free indirect discourse—renders them more or less narratorially.

All acts that reveal the character and the narrator naturally also function ultimately as indexes for the author, whose creation the two fictive entities are. But the narrative process does not achieve an indexical function for the author directly and immediately, but rather with a certain refraction or displacement, which we have already taken into account in the model of the semantic hierarchy. The expression of the author position is served not only by the narrator position itself, but also by the interrelation between the expression and contents of the narrator's text. The level of narratorial expression is, for its part, founded on, amongst other things, the interrelation between expression and contents in the characters' text.

Lastly, it must be clarified that there is a crucial difference between the abstract author and the narrator in the intentionality of their indexical presence. The indexical signs that reveal the narrator are intended. The author uses them to represent the narrator. The indexical signs pointing to the author, however, are, as a rule, not intended, but emerge involuntarily in the creative process. The author does not usually intend to represent him or herself. The indication of the author is, as a rule, just as involuntary as the self-expression of any given speaker. However, as every speaker can consciously stylize him or herself in his or her speech acts, it is also possible that an author wants to communicate a particular "image" of him or herself in the work.

e) Typologies of the narrator

At first, the typology of the narrator and his or her perspective stood at the center of narratological interest. Typologies competed with one another to attain the highest degree of differentiation. Whereas Percy Lubbock (1921) differentiated only four types of narrator or perspective and Norman Friedman (1955) reached eight, Wilhelm Füger (1972) managed to find twelve types (cf. the overview by Lintvelt 1981, 111–76). However, the systems of such highly differentiated typologies are not always convincing and their usefulness is in no way evident. They often confuse the type of narrator with the type of perspective and define the underlying criteria only imprecisely. Moreover, not all types gained by the combination of factors are documented in the literature. All three of these failings can be seen in Füger's typology, which, however, suffers most from the ambivalence of the *external vs. internal position*-dichotomy of the narrator. In the same way as Erwin Leibfried (1970, 245–48), from whom this opposition was borrowed, Füger mixes two categories: (1) the presence of the narrator in the narrated story and (2) the narrator's perspective.[29]

As a schema that can have merely heuristic meaning, a typology of the narrator must be simple and may be based on only the most elementary criteria, without striving for an exhaustive picture of the phenomenon being modeled. The following criteria and types can serve as the foundation for such a typology of the narrator (in which the category of perspective must remain unexamined):

Criteria	*Types of Narrator*
Mode of representation	explicit – implicit
Diegetic status	diegetic – non-diegetic
Hierarchy	primary – secondary – tertiary
Degree of markedness	strongly marked – weakly marked
Personality	personal – impersonal
Homogeneity of symptoms	compact – diffuse
Evaluative position	objective – subjective

---

29 This ambivalence is conditioned by the fact that both Leibfried and Füger use the term *narrator* in a very wide sense, namely as the term for the "center of orientation," which can be the narrator as well as the perceiving character, the "reflector" (one of Henry James' terms). It is self-evident that such a wide conception of the key term limits the clarity of the typology based on it.

4. The fictive narrator

Ability	omniscient – limited knowledge
Spatial fixing	omnipresent – fixed in a specific place
Access to characters' consciousnesses	expressed – not expressed
Reliability	unreliable – reliable

f) Primary, secondary, and tertiary narrators

Based on the level to which the narrator is assigned in the case of a frame narrative, we differentiate between the *primary* narrator (the narrator of the *frame story*), the *secondary* narrator (the narrator of the *inner story*, who appears as a character in the frame story), the *tertiary* narrator (the narrator of an inner story of second degree, who appears as a character in the first inner story), and so on.[30]

Examples of all three types can be found in Pushkin's "The Stationmaster." The primary narrator is the sentimental traveler, who reports on three encounters at a Russian post station. The stationmaster, Samson Vyrin, is a secondary narrator, who tells the traveler the story of the alleged kidnap of his daughter Dunya, as is the one-eyed son of the brewer's wife, who describes Dunya's visit to her father's grave to the traveler. Two characters appear in Vyrin's inner story as tertiary narrators, the German doctor, who admits his secret agreement with the hussar to the father, and the coachman, who reports both Dunya's tears and her obvious consent to the drive to Saint Petersburg.

The attributes *primary*, *secondary* and *tertiary* should, of course, be understood only in the technical sense as levels of embedding, the degree of framing, and in no way as an axiological hierarchy. The secondary narrator of the tales in *One Thousand and One Nights*, Scheherazade, attracts substantially more interest than the primary narrator, as does also the narrating horse in Tolstoy's *Strider: The Story of a Horse*. Indeed, the function of the primary narrator in frame narratives is often limited to merely providing a motivation for the inner story.

---

30 These terms were introduced by Bertil Romberg (1962, 63). To me, they seem more plausible than Genette's (1972; tr. 1980, 227-31) complicated and conceptually problematic terminology ("extradiegetic," "diegetic" or "intradiegetic", and "metadiegetic"). The latter denotes, for Genette, not a narration *about* a narration, but rather the third level of framing, the narration of a narrator who appears in an inner story and, as a narrator, presents an inner story of second degree. Genette later (1983, 61) defended the unmotivated *meta-* against entirely justified criticism (Bal 1977a, 24, 35; 1981; Rimmon 1983, 92, 140). On the preference for the traditional terminology cf. also Jahn/Nünning 1994, 286-87.

What is narrated in the secondary narration (i.e. by a character of the frame narrative) forms a world which I suggest naming the *quoted world* because a character's discourse functions as a quotation in the primary narrator's discourse. The quoted nature of the inner story can be actualized in various ways: through stylistic alignment of the secondary discourse on the discourse of the primary narrator, through the latter's comments, and particularly in that the latter uses the secondary narrative for his or her own purposes. (On the problems of the stylistic embedding of characters' discourse or the discourse of the secondary narrator, see below IV.1.b.)

In many cases, a secondary narrative disentangles itself from the framing situation and bursts its motivation. This can be seen, for example, in Dostoevsky's novel *A Raw Youth*. The secondary narrator's, Makar Dolgoruky's, narrative about the salesman Skotoboynikov, consisting of more than eleven pages, decisively goes beyond the limits of what could be expected from the primary narrator, the young man Arkady Dolgoruky, in terms of the ability to reproduce other persons' idiolects. The narrative is presented in a strongly stylized archaic-folksy *skaz*, which mirrors Makar's religious world.

g) Diegetic and non-diegetic narrators

One important distinction is that between *diegetic* and *non-diegetic* narrators. These terms should replace the traditional, terminologically problematic dichotomy of "first-person" and "third-person narrator." The new opposition describes the presence of the narrator on both levels of the represented world, the level of the narrated world, or diegesis, and the level of narration, or exegesis.

A narrator is diegetic if he belongs to the diegesis, if, accordingly, he narrates about himself—or, more specifically, about his previous self—as a character in the narrated story. The diegetic narrator appears on two levels: in both the exegesis, the narration, and the diegesis, the narrated story. The non-diegetic narrator, on the other hand, belongs only to the exegesis and does not narrate about himself as a character in the diegesis, instead narrating exclusively about other people.[31]

---

31 Taking classical usage as her starting point, Elena Paducheva (1996, 203) calls the non-diegetic narrator "exegetic." But the dichotomy introduced by her of *exegetic vs. diegetic* narrator does not model the asymmetry of the two types satisfactorily. The diegetic narrator would actually have to be called the "exegetic-diegetic" narrator, insofar as s/he is present on both levels. Since belonging to the exegesis is not a distinctive feature but is, on the contrary, default, the dichotomy of binary features diegetic vs. non-diegetic is preferred here.

4. The fictive narrator

Diegetic narrators can be broken down into two entities differentiated by level and function, the *narrating* and the *narrated* self,[32] whereas non-diegetic narrators are limited to one level and function.

	Diegetic narrator	*Non-diegetic narrator*
Exegesis	+ (narrating self)	+
Diegesis	+ (narrated self)	–

To say, as E. Paducheva (1996, 203) does, that the diegetic narrator "steps inside the inner world of the text," can be accepted only with certain caveats. The narrator, as the narrating entity, remains outside the "inner" (better: narrated) world. It is only the narrator's "previous" self that appears in the narrated world.

Lubomír Doležel's (1973a, 7) comment that the narrator is sometimes "identical" with one of the characters is also in need of correction. The narrator is not identical with the character as a narrator, as narrating self, but only as the narrated self. Nor can Doležel's conclusion be accepted, that, in the transformation of the narrator into one of those participating in the action, the character assumes functions characteristic of the narrator, namely "representation" and "control," neutralizing the opposition of narrator and character. Here, Doležel mixes functional and material viewpoints. The narrator, as bearer of the narrative function, becomes a character only when s/he is narrated by a narrator of a higher degree, and a character can become a narrator only when s/he functions as a secondary narrator.

The dichotomy *diegetic* vs. *non-diegetic* corresponds essentially to the opposition "homodiegetic" vs. "heterodiegetic," introduced by Genette (1972) and now widely accepted. But Genette's terminology, which demands an attentive reader and a disciplined user, is problematic in its system and its terminology. What is actually "the same" and "different" in the *homo*-diegetic and *hetero*-diegetic narrator? Moreover, the prefixes can be easily confused with *extra*-, *intra*- and *meta*-, which denote the degree of framing, the primariness, secondariness and tertiariness of the narrator.[33] The following

---

32 In German theory, the narrated self (das *erzählte* Ich) is often called the *experiencing* self (das *erlebende* Ich) (cf. Spitzer 1928a, 471 and, independently of him, Stanzel 1955, 61–62). However, the functional attribute *narrated* must be preferred to the psychological attribute *experiencing*.

33 The diegetic narrator could be called "intra-diegetic," insofar as s/he appears in the diegesis as narrated self, and the non-diegetic narrator "extra-diegetic," since s/he remains outside the diegesis. But such a designation would cause complete chaos, because in Genette's terminology *intra*- and *extra*- denote other phenomena.

table is included for Genettists and provides information about the correlation of the terms:

Genette's Terminology	Suggested Terminology
extradiegetic-heterodiegetic narrator	primary non-diegetic narrator
extradiegetic-homodiegetic narrator	primary diegetic narrator
intradiegetic-heterodiegetic narrator	secondary non-diegetic narrator
intradiegetic-homodiegetic narrator	secondary diegetic narrator
metadiegetic-heterodiegetic narrator	tertiary non-diegetic narrator
metadiegetic-homodiegetic narrator	tertiary diegetic narrator

As mentioned above, the opposition of *diegetic* vs. *non-diegetic* is intended to replace the traditional but problematic dichotomy of *first-person* vs. *third-person* narrator. It is not particularly sensible to base a typology of the narrator on personal pronouns, since every narration fundamentally originates from a "first person," even if the grammatical form is not expressed. It is not the personal pronoun itself, but its frame of reference that is crucial: when the *I* applies only to the act of narration, the narrator is non-diegetic, but when it relates also to the narrated world, s/he is diegetic:

Type of narrator	Domain of the first person
non-diegetic	I $\Rightarrow$ exegesis
diegetic	I $\Rightarrow$ exegesis + diegesis

It is perfectly possible for first-person forms to be absent from non-diegetic narration.[34] That does not mean that the narrator is entirely absent. S/he can judge what is narrated, make comments etc., without mentioning him or herself. The first person can also be absent from diegetic narration. The diegetic narrator can report on him or herself in the third person and use his or her own name, as Caesar does in *De Bello gallico*. There are many examples in Russian literature of diegetic narration without the first person, which, as in Ivan Bunin's tale "The Well of Days," are motivated by the fact that the narrator regards his previous self as a different person. In the autobiographical trilogy *Khlynovsk* by Kuzma Petrov-Vodkin, the narrator even describes his own birth (on both cases cf. N. Kozhevnikova 1994, 18).

A special case exists when a narrator who initially appears to be non-diegetic suddenly proves to be diegetic. In Vladimir Nabokov's tale "Torpid

---

34 The dichotomy *diegetic* vs. *non-diegetic* is also used here for narration.

4. The fictive narrator 71

Smoke," which initially appears to be presented by a non-diegetic narrator, individual, unmotivated first-person forms, appearing as if by chance, reveal that the "long-limbed flat-chested youth with a pince-nez" is none other than the narrator himself:

> On his way out of the dining room he noticed his father turn his whole torso in his chair to face the wall clock as if it had said something, and then begin turning back—but there the door I was closing closed, and I did not see that bit to the end. (Nabokov, TS, 400)

The opposite phenomenon can be observed in Nabokov's novel *The Eye*: after his "suicide," the narrator uses the first person exclusively for the narrating self whereas the narrated self, which survived, features only as "Smurov," whose identity with the narrator is not immediately guessed by the reader.

The extreme case of a diegetic narrator to whom no direct reference is made in either the diegesis or the exegesis forms the narrative entity in Alain Robbe-Grillet's *La Jalousie*. Despite radical omission of the narrated self and the complete absence of any self-thematization on the part of the narrating self, the impression emerges in this *nouveau roman* that a jealous man is reporting the possible infidelity of his wife and her relationship with a mutual friend of theirs. The presence of the narrated self is indicated solely by the arrangement of the objects observed: there are three chairs round the table, three places set etc. The narrated self appears merely as the one who could take the third place at the table. And the narrating self is indicated exclusively by the extremely objective, technical description of the objects, the exaggerated and needlessly precise observation of which suggests the suppressed emotions of the observer.

This kind of narrator, who conceals his identity with the narrated character, is sometimes encountered in detective stories, in which the narrating self is the detective and the narrated self the suspect. In post-modernist literature, it is not unusual for the *veiled diegetic narrative* to broach the general question of a person's identity. One model is Jorge Luis Borges' short story "The Shape of the Sword," whose narrator admits that, in reality, he is himself the repulsive informer about whom he had hitherto spoken with contempt in the third person (cf. Genette 1972, 255).

When personal pronouns are omitted as a criterion for a typology of the narrator, where does the *second-person narrative*, which appears in many typologies as a variant of the first person (e.g. Füger 1972, 271), belong?[35] Depending on whether the narrator appears only in the exegesis or also in the

---

35 Variants of second-person narration are examined by Korte 1987 and Fludernik 1993b; 1994.

diegesis, s/he is non-diegetic or diegetic. To take a well-known example of a second-person narrative, Leo Tolstoy's sketch "Sebastopol in December":

> As you step inside, you enter the large chamber of the Assembly Hall. No sooner have you opened the door then you are assailed without warning by the sight and smell of about forty or fifty amputees and critically wounded, some of them on camp beds, but most of them lying on the floor. Ignore the sensation that makes you hesitate at the threshold of the chamber—it is not a pleasant situation—make your way forward and do not be ashamed to have come, as it were, to observe the sufferers, do not be embarrassed to go up to them and talk to them [...] (Tolstoy, Sebastopol, 44–45)

This narrator can be considered either diegetic or non-diegetic. If one identifies the present "you" of the fictive reader with the previous self of the narrator, who, masked by the second person, gives his own opinions, one will assume that one is dealing with a diegetic narrator. If one does not make this identification, one will consider the narrator non-diegetic.

There are three dichotomies with which—though they appear similar and are often lumped together—the opposition of *diegetic* vs. *non-diegetic* does not coincide:

1. The opposition *diegetic* vs. *non-diegetic* is categorically different from the dichotomy *explicit* vs. *implicit*. The non-diegetic narrator should not be identified with the implicit narrator, as is done by Paducheva (1996, 203), who works from the assumption that the non-diegetic (in her terminology: "exegetic") narrator "is a narrator, who does not name himself." The non-diegetic narrator *can* be represented exclusively by implication and that is often the case, but he can also appear explicitly, that is, by naming and describing himself as the narrating self. At the beginning of modern narration, both Western European and Russian literature were dominated by the explicit non-diegetic narrator, who spoke extensively about himself and directed himself at the "dear" reader. Almost all of the sentimentalist Nikolay Karamzin's narrators belong to this type. The tale "Natalie, the Boyar's Daughter" (1792) begins in the following way:

> Who does not love those times when Russians were Russians, when they were attired in their own dress, walked in their own way, lived according to their own customs, spoke in their own language and from their hearts, that is, they spoke as they thought? At least I love those times [...] (Karamzin, SP, 73)

On the other hand, the diegetic narrator is not necessarily explicit, as is shown by the example of third-person diegetic narration given above.

2. The dichotomy *diegetic* vs. *non-diegetic* does not coincide with the opposition *personal* vs. *impersonal*. The latter was brought into the debate by Jürgen Petersen (1977, 176), who works from the assumption that the third-person narrator is distinguished from the first-person narrator principally by the

4. The fictive narrator

absence of "personality." Similarly, Stanzel (1979, 119–24) ascribes to both the narrating and narrated self in the first-person novel a certain "corporeality." Doubtless, non-diegetic narration has tended towards a minimization of the narrator's personality ever since the advent of realism, towards a reduction to merely a position from which value judgments are made. In pre-realist narration, by contrast, the non-diegetic narrator is, as a rule, equipped with personal characteristics. Examples of this can also be found in Karamzin's tales: at the start of "Poor Liza" (1792), for instance, a narrator appears who characterizes himself as a sensitive rambler and nature lover:

> Perhaps none of the inhabitants of Moscow knows the environs of the town as well as I because no one frequents the fields more than I, no one wanders, without plan, without aim more than I—where the eyes lead—through the meadows and groves, over the hills and plains. Every summer I find new, pleasant sites or new beauties in the old.
> But most pleasant of all for me is that place over which rise the gloomy, gothic towers of the Si-nov Monastery. (Karamzin, SP, 53)

On the other hand, the diegetic narrator as narrating self is not necessarily more personal or subjective than the non-diegetic narrator. The diegetic narrator can also be reduced to an impersonal voice, if the emphasis is on the narrated self.

3. The suggested distinctions do not touch on the problem of perspective. The mixing up of two categories, of the participation of the narrator in diegesis and of perspective, is an error often encountered in the common typologies. The best known example is Stanzel's (1964; 1979) "typological circle of narrative situations," in which the "authorial" and "figural" "narrative situations" are placed alongside the "first-person narrative situation." Whereas the first two narrative situations differ in their perspective, the third is defined exclusively by the presence of the narrator in the narrated story. Regardless of the numerous objections made against his system (e.g. Leibfried 1970, 246; Schmid 1973, 28; Cohn 1981; Petersen 1981; Breuer 1998), Stanzel never accepted the argument that he was mixing two criteria and that two perspectives could be differentiated for the "first-person narrative situation," one "authorial" and one "figural."

Whereas Hamburger makes the opposition *diegetic* vs. *non-diegetic* the foundation of her unconventional genre typology ("fictional or mimetic" vs. "lyrical or existential" genre), many narratologists doubt its relevance. Booth (1961, 150), for example, considers this dichotomy overestimated. This is, however, contradicted by the practice of literary production. Stanzel (1979, 114–16) provides examples in which authors change a novel that has already been begun from one form to the other on the basis of artistic considerations, from the non-diegetic to the diegetic (Gottfried Keller's *Green Henry*) and the reverse, from the diegetic to the non-diegetic (Franz Kafka's *The Castle*).

Dostoevsky's notebooks for *A Raw Youth* are enlightening in this context. After long vacillation between the two forms, as is documented in the notebooks (cf. Schmid 2005a, 92–94), Dostoevsky decided on a diegetic narrator. The decisive factors were that "first-person" narration was "more original" and demanded "more love, more artistry." The author saw the main drawback of this form as being that the "main ideas of the novel" could not be "naturally and fully" expressed by a twenty-year-old narrator.

h) Types of diegetic narrators

The narrated self can be present in the diegesis to varying degrees and can participate in the story with differing functions. Genette (1972, 253–54) distinguishes two tiers of presence, assuming that the "narrator" (actually: the narrated self) cannot be a normal character. According to Genette, the character in the storyworld is either the protagonist (in which case, it is an "autodiegetic" narrator, e.g. *Gil Blas* by Lesage) or an observer and witness (Conan-Doyle's Doctor Watson). Susan Lanser (1981, 160), who follows Genette's terminology, has produced a detailed schema that envisions five levels of participation in diegesis and of distance from the "heterodiegetic" (i.e. non-diegetic) narrator. This schema is not only theoretically acceptable but demonstrates its suitability in practical analysis. By translating the Genettist terms, we obtain the following result:

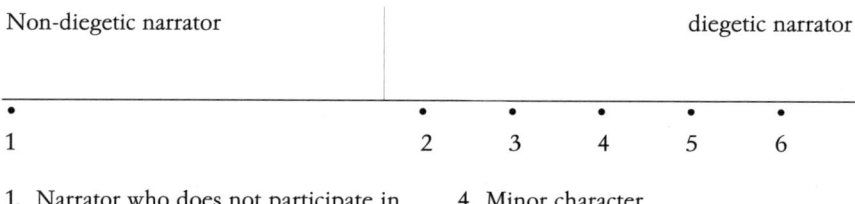

1. Narrator who does not participate in the story
2. Observer uninvolved in the story
3. Observer who participates in the story
4. Minor character
5. One of the main characters
6. Main character

Type 2: An example of an uninvolved observer is the personal narrator of the *Brothers Karamazov*. The anonymous chronicler, who reports the events that befell thirteen years previously "in our district" (Dostoevsky, BK, 1), has no diegetic significance whatsoever despite having been present in the storyworld at the time. When the author requires direct insight into the characters' consciousnesses—one need only think of Ivan Karamazov's halluci-

4. The fictive narrator

nations—he replaces the chronicler, with his limited horizons, with an omniscient and omnipresent non-diegetic narrator (see above, II.4.a).

Type 3: An example is the narrator of *The Possessed*, the chronicler Anton Lavrentyevich G-v, who relates "the very strange events that occurred in our hitherto rather unremarkable town" (Dostoevsky, P, 9). This intention presupposes the reconstruction of his own perceptions and the collection of all the hard facts he can glean from the rumors in circulation and the contradictory statements of eye-witnesses. In this, the emphasis lies more on the narrating than the narrated self. The diegetic existence of this chronicler primarily serves to provide a motivation for the difficult reconstruction of what has happened.

Type 4: A diegetic narrator whose narrated self appears as a minor character is realized in two ways in the "Bela" chapter of Mikhail Lermontov's novel *A Hero of Our Time*. In both the primary narrative of the anonymous traveler and Maksim Maksimych's secondary narrative, it is not the respective narrated self who takes center stage, but the enigmatic Pechorin, who, in this first chapter of the novel, is perceived through a twofold prism (Maksim Maksimych and the traveler).

Type 5: A narrated self as one of the main characters is encountered in Pushkin's tale "The Stationmaster." The narrating traveler as narrated self plays a somewhat dubious role in the lives of both heroes, insofar as he is "the first" twice. It is from him that Samson Vyrin, who later drinks himself to death, receives his first glass of punch (the first glass—of course—within the limits of the story), and the narrated self appears in the story as the first man who kisses Dunya.

Type 6: The narrated self as main character is present in Dostoevsky's *A Raw Youth*, in which Arkady Dolgoruky is the central character of the diegesis.

Of course, this typology cannot encompass every demonstrable or imaginable realisation of the narrated self. To which category would Karamzin's "Poor Liza," for example, be assigned? Liza's story is told by a strongly marked, subjective, personal, but simultaneously omniscient narrator capable of accessing the most private thoughts and feelings of his characters, and who was not present in the diegesis, which played out thirty years previously. At the end of the tale, however, when he presents the epilogue after Liza's death, he imparts that Erast told him "this story" a year before the latter's death. So, the narrator is present in the outermost periphery of the diegesis, only within the epilogue. The late encounter with Erast, which is supposed to justify the narrator's knowledge (which it can scarcely do), however, does not make the narrator diegetic in the context of Liza's story.

i) Narrating and narrated self

Of all types of narrated self, type 6 is probably encountered most often. The traditional quasi-autobiographical narrative creates a large temporal gap between the narrating and the narrated self. As a rule, these entities are represented as stages of a psychophysically identical figure. The paradigms for the autobiographical novel—St. Augustine's *Confessiones*, Grimmelshausen's *Simplicissimus* and, in more recent literature, Thomas Mann's *Felix Krull*— presuppose not only a temporal but also an ethical and psychological distance between an errant, sinful young person and a starkly transformed, repentant narrator, who describes the sins of his youth from the position of a pious man, of a hermit who has turned his back on the world, or of a prisoner. "I propose now to set down my past wickedness and the carnal corruptions of my soul, not for love of them but that I may love Thee, o my God." (Recordari volo transactas foeditates meas et carnales corruptiones animae meae, non quod eas amem, sed ut amem te, deus meus.) It is with these words that Augustine begins his *Confessions*.

A notable variant of the quasi-autobiographical novel is provided by Dostoevsky's *A Raw Youth*. In May of an unnamed year, the twenty-year-old Arkady Dolgoruky reports the adventures he experienced between the 19th of September and mid-December of the previous year. The many years that usually separate the narrating from the narrated self are here reduced to a few months in which the self develops. The narrator is different in many respects to his previous self, but mildly exaggerates the process of maturing that has occurred, obviously in the hope of avoiding being identified with the naiveté of the previous year. Both the nineteen-year-old narrated and the twenty-year-old narrating self undergo an unmistakable development: after the 19th of September, the youth gradually abandons his plan to become a Rothschild (development in the diegesis), and the narrator's tone, riled at first, gives way to a more relaxed way of narrating; after initial polemic against the reader, Arkady is reconciled with him (development in the exegesis). Making the self dynamic on the level of the diegesis (from the 19th of September to mid-December), the exegesis (mid-May) and in the interval (December to May) is motivated by the author's choice of an age in which one usually changes one's opinions rapidly. Significantly, Dostoevsky rejected the original plan to insert a gap of four years between experience and narration.

A distinctive feature of autobiographical narration is the tendency to a certain stylization of the previous self. This stylization is not expressed solely in the extenuation of the narrator's previous conduct, but sometimes also in a pejorative presentation of it. The psychological logic of stylizing

4. The fictive narrator

the self pejoratively was laid bare by Dostoevsky. At the end of the first chapter of *Notes from The Underground*, the narrator admits to his addressee:

> I really do wish to discover: is it really possible to be absolutely open with oneself and not be frightened of the whole truth? Incidentally, I note: Heine asserts that true autobiographies are almost impossible and that a person is bound to lie about himself. In his opinion, Rousseau, for example, undoubtedly lied about himself in his confession and even lied intentionally, through vanity. I am certain that Heine is right: I understand very well how at times out of sheer vanity it is possible to pin entire crimes on oneself, and I can also well grasp the nature of this vanity. (Dostoevsky, NU, 38–39)

Although we, as readers of a (quasi-)autobiographical narrative work, of course constantly construct the unity of the narrating with the "previous" self, the psychophysical identity of narrating and narrated selves sometimes becomes thoroughly problematic. Thus, Wolfgang Kayser (1956, 233; 1958, 209) states: "the first-person narrator of a novel is not the straightforward continuation of the narrated figure." Using the example of Thomas Mann's picaresque novel, he warns the reader against an unconditional identification of the young Krull with the old narrator. Using Herman Melville's *Moby Dick*, he demonstrates the unbridgeable gulf between the simple sailor, who appears as the narrated self, and the educated narrating self, who also reproduces the private thoughts and conversations of other people, which it would have been absolutely impossible for the sailor to access. Kayser rightly doubts the way the psychophysical unity of the narrating and narrated selves is often postulated as self-evident. In changing his view of the world, the self, represented as compact and unified, exposes himself to a certain diffusion. The narrating self can then relate to the narrated self as to a complete stranger.[36]

The psychophysical unity of the narrated and narrating selves can be called into question by the abilities of the latter. With many diegetic narrators, we observe that the narrating self goes far beyond the horizons and abilities of the narrated self, and sometimes even beyond the limits of what is possible for a human being to know. The reader is expected to accept an extreme overextension of plausible motivation in the novel *Closely Observed Trains*, by the Czech author Bohumil Hrabal. The diegetic narrator reports

---

36 Incidentally, Stanzel has written polemics against Kayser's comment throughout his career (latest 1979, 111–12). He argues vehemently for the unity of the self, with good reason, because he would otherwise have to split the "first-person narrative situation" into "authorial" and "figural," which would rob him of his triadic rosary. At another point in the same publication (1979; tr. 1984, 213), however, he himself points to the "estrangement between the narrating and the experiencing self." So, he states that, in *Moll Flanders*, one gets the impression "that Defoe has yoked together in a single person Moll Flanders's experiencing self and the reflections of the authorial 'I', an entirely different person."

events in the course of which he himself, that is, his previous narrated self, died. The crossing of boundaries such as these demonstrates the general tendency of diegetic narrators to take on certain privileges of non-diegetic narration.

Narratology must tackle the problem of the diegetic narrator from a functional viewpoint. Narrating and narrated self should be seen as two functionally differentiated entities, as *narrator* (bearer of the *narratio*) and *actor* (bearer of the *actio*), between whom a more or less conventional psychophysical relationship is represented. From a functional viewpoint, the narrating relates to the narrated self in the same way as, in a non-diegetic work, the narrator does to a character. This correlation is illustrated in the following diagram:

	Non-diegetic narrative	*Diegetic narrative*
Narrative entity = Narrator	narrator	narrating self
Actional entity = Actor	character	narrated self

5. The fictive reader

The fictive reader (*narratee*, French *narrataire*, Russian *narratator*[37]) is the addressee of the fictive narrator, the entity to whom he directs his narration. The term *fictive reader* is not entirely accurate, since only the image of the presumed addressee is meant. It is therefore more correct to refer to the *fictive addressee*.

a) Fictive addressee and fictive recipient

The fictive reader as addressee of a secondary narrative (i.e. an inner story) seems to coincide with one of the characters of the primary narrative (the frame story). For example, the sentimental traveler in Pushkin's "The Stationmaster," to whom the abandoned titular hero tells the story of his abducted daughter Dunya and who thus functions as the secondary fictive addressee, appears to coincide with the narrated self, that is, with the actor of the primary narrative. However, the equation *fictive addressee in the secondary narrative = character in the primary narrative*, an equation that forms the

---

37 On the English term *narratee* see Prince 1971; 1985; on the French *narrataire*, Genette (1972, 226) and Prince 1973a. The dichotomy *narrateur–narrataire* (by analogy with *destinateur–destinataire*) was first used by Roland Barthes (1966, 10). In Russian, the term *narratator* has been coined for this entity (Ilyin 1996d).

5. The fictive reader

basis for many essays on this entity (cf. Genette 1972; 1983), simplifies the facts in an inadmissible way. The fictive addressee is nothing other than the schema of the narrator's expectations and presumptions and therefore cannot coincide *functionally* with the figure who, in the primary narrative, acts as the recipient of the secondary narrative, and who is concretized with particular features by the primary narrator. The addressee to whom Samson Vyrin narrates the story of his daughter does not coincide with the sentimental traveler who, as the narrated self, hears the story and, as the narrating self, reports it many years later. The addressee is a mere projection of the stationmaster and the latter cannot know about his listener's weakness for sentimental stories, nor will he have any idea about sentimentalist literature; and when he laments his "poor Dunya's" sad fate, the allusion to Karamzin's "Poor Liza" appears only within the intellectual horizons of the sentimental traveler. The fictive addressee is, as such, only ever a projection of the particular narrator.[38] To speak of a fictive recipient is meaningful only when a secondary narrator addresses himself to a recipient who appears as a reader or listener in the primary narrative. However, the secondary fictive addressee coincides with this fictive recipient (the character in the primary narrative) only *materially* and not *functionally*, since being an addressee and being a recipient are separate functions.

The relations are presented in the following diagram, using "The Stationmaster" as an example:

Level	*Narrator*	*Actor*	*Addressee*	*Recipient*
Primary narrative	Traveler as narrating self	1. Traveler as narrated self 2. Vyrin 3. Dunya (etc)	Addressee of the narrating traveler	Ø
Secondary narrative	Vyrin as narrating self	1. Vyrin as narrated self 2. Dunya (etc)	Traveler in Vyrin's imagination	Traveler as the narrated self of the primary narrative

When a narrator engages in dialogue with his counterpart, it is important to distinguish whether his interlocutor is merely imagined or whether he exists as an independent, autonomous character in an overarching story. Only in the second case, when the counterpart possesses autonomy and alterity, is it a true dialogue. In the former instance, we are dealing with a staged *dialogic monologue* (see below, II.5.e).

---

38 This is why I cannot agree with the distinction, made by Alice Jedličková (1993), between the "fictive" and "projected" addressee.

b)   Fictive and abstract reader

The fictive reader had already been described by Polish narratology before the advent of French Structuralism. Maria Jasińska (1965, 215–51) distinguished between the "real" and the "epic" reader, whereby the latter corresponds to the fictive reader. The distinction between abstract and fictive reader was anticipated by Michał Głowiński (1967), when he contrasted a "recipient in the wider sense" with a "recipient in the narrow sense." In her five-level model of roles in literary communication, Aleksandra Okopień-Sławińska (1971, 125) associates the "author" with the "concrete reader," the "transmitter of the work" with the "recipient of the work" (identified with the "ideal reader") and the narrator with the "addressee of the narrative."

Even in theoretical work, we can observe not only a confusion of the fictive and the abstract reader, but also a programmatic renunciation of this distinction. As mentioned above (p. 54), Genette (1972, 267) identifies the "extradiegetic narratee" with the "virtual" or "implied" reader, something that Genette even considers a welcome economy in Ockham's sense. Bal (1977a, 17) even calls the distinction between abstract and fictive reader "semiotically insignificant" and Paducheva (1996, 216), with reference to Toolan (1988), declares that there is no need for a doubling of this sort: "In the communicative situation of the narrative, the narrator's addressee is not a representative of the reader, but the reader himself." This is certainly an inadmissible and unhelpful simplification.

Naturally, the nearer the fictive narrator to the abstract author from an axiological perspective, the more difficult it is to clearly separate the ideological positions of the fictive and the abstract reader. Nonetheless, the difference between the abstract reader as presumed addressee (or the ideal recipient) of the *author* and the fictive reader as the addressee of the *narrator* remains in force. The border between the fictive world, to which the fictive reader belongs, and reality, to which, despite all virtuality, the abstract reader belongs, cannot be crossed—unless in some narrative paradox.

There is another essential difference to be considered between the fictive reader and the abstract reader as ideal recipient. Works with a disposition to function predominantly esthetically require a reading that realizes this disposition; that is, they create an ideal recipient who adopts an esthetic mindset. In this mindset, the reader will not only react to the work in an everyday way, but also observe its fabric and structure and—aside from his or her ethical or ideological reaction to the story s/he is being told— appreciate the interplay of factors contributing to the work's esthetic value. An esthetic mindset can naturally also be suggested to the fictive reader, if, for instance, the narrator sees himself as an artist and ascribes esthetic value to the narrative. To the extent, however, that the narrator is dissociated

5. The fictive reader

from the author in this regard, his fictive addressee will also be different from the author's ideal recipient in the mindset he brings to the narrative.

The abstract reader is often compared to a "role" into which the concrete reader could or should slip. But the abstract reader, as the presumed addressee or desired recipient, is not, in most cases, created as acting, but as watching or listening to the communication occurring between the fictive entities narrator and addressee (or recipient). Lets us look, for example, at the words with which Rudy Panko, the narrator of the forewords to Nikolay Gogol's *Village Evenings near Dikanka*, bids farewell to his fictive reader:

> If I recall right, I promised to put one of my own stories in this book. And it's true, I was going to do so, but then I found that I would need at least three books this size for one of my stories. I thought I might print it separately, but I changed my mind. Because I know what you're like: you'd only laugh at me, old man that I am. No, I won't stand for that! Farewell! We won't meet again for a long time, maybe never. What of it? After all, little do you care. Give it a year or two and none of you will ever remember or spare a thought for old Ginger Panko, the bee-keeper. (Gogol, VE, 95)

The role of this snooty, insensitive person who laughs at the old narrator and leaves him without regret is one which the concrete reader will not want to take on and, moreover, is neither suggested nor designed for the abstract reader. As we know, Gogol wrote for a public that had developed a taste for the "Little Russian" and appreciated folk tales highly, as well as the *skaz* style associated with them.

c) Explicit and implicit representation of the fictive reader

The fictive reader, just like the fictive narrator, can be represented in two ways, explicitly and implicitly.

Explicit representation occurs with the help of pronouns and grammatical forms such as the second person, or with well-known forms of address such as "gentle reader" etc.[39] The image of the reader created in this way can be equipped with more or less concrete features. Let us take Pushkin's novel in verse *Eugene Onegin* as an example. When the narrator, who assumes various identities, appears as the author, his addressee becomes an expert in contemporary Russian literature and an adherent of Pushkin:

> Friends of Lyudmila and Ruslan!
> The hero of my novel,
> without preambles, forthwith,
> I'd like to have you meet.
> (I, 2, V. 5–8; Pushkin, EO, 96)

---

39 Variants of the reader addressed in this way are investigated by Paul Goetsch (1983).

The hero, narrator and fictive reader are connected by the topos of Petersburg:

> Onegin, a good pal of mine,
> was born upon the Neva's banks,
> where maybe you were born,
> or used to shine, my reader!
> There formerly I too promenaded—
> but harmful is the North to me.
> (I, 2, V. 9–14; Pushkin, EO, 96)

The presence of the fictive reader is activated by the anticipation of questions:

> But what about Onegin? By the way, brothers!
> I beg your patience:
> his daily occupations
> in detail I'll describe to you
> (IV, 37, V. 1–4; Pushkin, EO, 192)

The *implicit* representation of the fictive reader operates with the same indexical signs as the representation of the narrator and is equally based on unintentional self-expression. In general, the representation of the fictive reader is built up on the representation of the narrator, insofar as the former is an attribute of the latter (similar to how the image of the abstract reader belongs to the characteristics of the abstract author; see above, p. 51).[40] The markedness of the fictive reader depends to a decisive degree on the markedness of the narrator: the more marked the narrator, the more likely that he will evoke an image of the counterpart he addresses. However the presence of a marked narrator does not automatically imply the presence of an addressee manifest to the same degree.

In principle, every narrative creates a fictive reader (just as every text creates an abstract reader as assumed addressee or ideal recipient), since the indexical signs that point to his existence, no matter how weak they may become, can never disappear completely.[41]

One of the characteristics of the narrator reflected in the text is, as already implied, his relation to the addressee. Two operations that character-

---

[40] In his influential work, Gerald Prince (1973a) discusses the "signaux du narrataire," insofar as they go beyond the "degré zéro du narrataire." This zero status was the object of such fierce criticism (cf. Prince 1985), that Prince 1982 eventually renounced it. On the other hand, Prince (1985, 300) dismisses as "trivial" another valid argument: that the supposed "signaux du narrataire" could just as well be seen as the "characteristics of the narrator" (Pratt 1982, 212).

[41] By saying this, I mean to correct my previous thesis (Schmid 1973, 29; 1986, 308), which said that a fictive reader could be completely absent from a narrative text, a thesis that has attracted much criticism, e.g. from Roland Harweg (1979, 113).

5. The fictive reader

ize this relationship are relevant for the representation of the fictive reader: *appeal* and *orientation*.

Appeal is the demand, usually expressed implicitly, made on the addressee to form a particular opinion of the narrator, his narrative, the narrated world, or some of its characters. The appeal is, in itself, a mode of expressing the presence of an addressee. From its contents emerge the attitudes and opinions the narrator assumes in the addressee and those which he considers possible. The appeal function can, in principle, never reach absolute zero; it is present even in statements with a predominantly referential function, even when in a minimal form: "Know that ..." or "I just want you to know that ..."

One type of appeal is the *impression*. The narrator attempts to use it to present himself in a particular way to his counterpart, to elicit a reaction that can take on either a positive form, as admiration, or a negative one, as contempt. (An intentional negative impression is characteristic of Dostoevsky's paradoxical monologists.)

What is meant by *orientation* is the alignment of the narrator with the addressee, without which no comprehensible communication can occur. The orientation on the addressee can naturally only be reconstructed to the extent that it affects the mode of representation.

Orientation refers, first, to the *codes* and *norms* it is presumed the addressee shares, which can be linguistic, epistemological, ethical and social. The narrator need not share the norms assumed in the addressee, but he cannot but use language comprehensible to the addressee and must take into account the presumed scope of his knowledge. It is to this extent that every narrative contains implicit information about the image that the narrator has of the abilities and norms of his addressee.

Second, the orientation can consist in the anticipation of the imagined addressee's *behavior*. The narrator can imagine the addressee as a passive listener and obedient executor of his appeals, or, alternatively, as an active interlocutor who independently judges what is narrated, poses questions, expresses doubts and raises objections.

For no other author of Russian literature (and perhaps of any literature) does the fictive reader play so active a role as for Dostoevsky. In *Notes from the Underground* and "A Gentle Spirit," the narrator speaks literally every word "with a sidelong glance" (Bakhtin 1929, 96), i.e. aligned on the fictive listener. The narrator, who wants to win his listener's admiration, leaves behind unmistakable traces in the text of his appeal (especially of impression), and his orientation: he wants to present himself in a positive or negative way to the reader or listener (impression), pays attention to his counterpart's reaction (orientation), guesses his critical replies (orientation), anticipates them (impression), attempts to rebut them (impression), and clearly recognizes (orientation) that he does not succeed in doing so. This type of narrative, whose addressee is imagined as an active interlocutor, is assigned by Bakhtin, in his "metalinguistic" typology of discourse,[42] to the type "active double-voiced word" (or "word with orientation toward someone else's discourse"), i.e. a word, in which two contradictory points of meaning can be recognized simultaneously, that of the speaker and the anticipated evaluative position of the addressee. In contrast to the "passive variety of the double-voiced word," where "the other person's discourse is a completely passive tool in the hands of the author wielding it," in the active variety "the other's words actively influence the author's speech, forcing it to alter itself accordingly under their influence and initiative" (Bakhtin 1929; tr. 1984, 197).

d) Narration with a sidelong glance at the fictive reader (*A Raw Youth*)

Dostoevsky's novel *A Raw Youth* provides an example of the fictive reader exerting a strong influence on the narration. The twenty-year-old Arkady Dolgoruky, reporting his adventures of the previous year, addresses himself to a reader who is conceptualized as neither an individual nor as the bearer of an ideology. The essential feature of this imagined entity, who, for the young narrator, becomes a representative of the adult world, is mockery of the young man's immature opinions. The alignment on this reader can be seen in the *impressive* function, which is particularly noticeable in the passages in which Arkady writes about himself, about his ideas and actions. The impression's characteristic feature is the shift from a neutral representation focused on its object to a more or less agitated auto-thematization, accompanied by a certain affectation of lexis and syntax, as well as by rhetorical flourishes. Arkady wants to make an impression, to be acknowledged. It is in the impressive function that the appeal is expressed to the adult reader to take him, the youth, seriously. The appeal for recognition is manifested in verbal flourishes that palliate reality as well as in those which portray the actual situation as having been worse than it was. In this pejorative portrayal, we discover, alongside the desire to make an impression by having the courage to portray himself negatively, the diametrically opposite endeavor, something which provides the basis for the structure that Bakhtin called the "word with a loophole":

> For example, the confessional self-definition with a loophole [...] is, judging by its meaning, an ultimate word about oneself, a final definition of oneself, but in fact it is forever taking into account internally the responsive, contrary evaluation of oneself made by another. The hero who repents and condemns himself

---

42 On this typology see in English: Morson & Emerson 1990, 121–268.

5. The fictive reader

> actually wants only to provoke praise and acceptance by another. (Bakhtin 1929; tr. 1984, 233)

The attempt to influence the reader encounters, in the narrator's imagination, a counter-reaction in the addressee. This is because the narrator imagines his counterpart as someone who does not accept the way he portrays himself and who reacts to his confessions with mocking, sobering objections. It is for this reason that, in this narration, the constant orientation on the interlocutor's reaction comes into effect alongside the appeal function.

By examining the way the reader's anticipated critical replies are rebutted in Arkady's narrative, we can differentiate various forms of orientation. The orientation makes itself known in general terms in changes to the style and to the way the story is told. When Arkady writes in a more adolescent way than might be expected from an intelligent, educated twenty-year-old not entirely unpracticed in writing, when he slips into the brash, jargon-filled teenage tone characterized by stereotypes and hyperbolic statements, or when he shows off with defiantly apodictic claims, he has, as it were, looked over his shoulder at the reader and attempted, with false self-confidence, to nip all possible objections in the bud. This type of orientation is present, for instance, in Arkady's introductory remarks to his narrative:

> I cannot resist sitting down to write the history of the first steps in my career, though I might very well abstain from doing so ... I know one thing for certain: I shall never again sit down to write my autobiography even if I live to be a hundred. One must be too disgustingly in love with oneself to be able without shame to write about oneself. I can only excuse myself on the ground that I am not writing with the same object with which other people write, that is, to win the praise of my readers. [...] I am not a professional writer and don't want to be, and to drag forth into the literary market-place the inmost secrets of my soul and an artistic description of my feelings I should regard as indecent and contemptible. (Dostoevsky, RY, 1)

The orientation on the reader shapes the argument, the register, and the style. There are also moments when Arkady directly addresses his imaginary interlocutor. The revolt against his own immaturity often suddenly switches to an irritated attack on the imaginary reader, whom Arkady imagines as mocking him relentlessly:

> My "idea" is—to become a Rothschild. I invite the reader to keep calm and not to excite himself. (Dostoevsky, RY, 74)

As he reaches the final exposition of this "idea," the vulnerability of which he knows all too well, Arkady turns to the reader and exclaims:

> Gentlemen, can it be that even the smallest independence of mind is so distasteful to you? (Dostoevsky, RY, 87–88)

As he sets out his "idea," Arkady anticipates the reader's expected explanations for its emergence, and rebuts them decisively. He believes that he can protect himself against the reader's understanding—and, for him, humiliating—smile at his adolescent plans, with a gloomy portrayal of himself, which he is, in turn, forced to soften under the influence of possible objections:

> No, it was not being illegitimate, [...] not my sorrowful childhood, it was not revenge, nor the desire to protest, that was at the bottom of my idea; my character alone was responsible for everything. At twelve years old, I believe, that is almost at the dawn of real consciousness, I began to dislike my fellow creatures. It was not that I disliked them exactly, but that their presence weighed upon me. I was sometimes in my moments of purest sincerity quite sad that [...] I'm mistrustful, sullen and reserved. [...] Yes, I am a gloomy person; I'm always shutting myself up. (Dostoevsky, RY, 82)

The more explicitly the young man formulates the reader's expected reactions, the closer the narrative comes to an open, dramatic dialogue:

> I have suddenly realized that if I had a single reader he would certainly be laughing at me as a most ridiculous raw youth, still stupidly innocent, putting himself forward to discuss and criticize what he knows nothing about. It is true that I know nothing about it, though I recognize that not at all with pride, for I know how stupid such inexperience is in a great dolt of twenty; only I would tell such a gentleman that he knows nothing about it himself, and I will prove it to him. (Dostoevsky, RY, 7)

In some places, the reader's anticipated replies come through in independent direct speech (of which Arkady naturally remains the creator). The narrative monologue then breaks down, as it were, into autonomous speeches, which react to each other in a dialogic way:

> "We have heard that; it's nothing new," people will tell me. Every "vater," in Germany repeats this to his children, and meanwhile your Rothschild [...] is unique while there are millions of such "vaters." I should answer: "You assert that you've heard it, but you've heard nothing." (Dostoevsky, RY, 74)

When Arkady arrives at a point from which, as a result of his shameful admissions, there can be no honourable retreat from his opponent's perceptive replies, he reaches for a device beloved of Dostoevsky's confessional narrators: the paradoxical denial of the existence of the reader to whom this denial is addressed:

> Let me tell the reader, he will perhaps be horrified at the candor of my confession, and in the simplicity of his heart will wonder how the author could help blushing: but my answer is that I'm not writing for publication, and I may not have a reader for ten years, and by that time everything will be so thoroughly past, settled and defined that there will be no need to blush. And so, if I sometimes in my autobiography appeal to my reader it is simply a form of expression. My reader is an imaginary figure. (Dostoevsky, RY, 81–82)

5. The fictive reader 87

e) Dialogic narrative monologue

In *Notes from the Underground* and "A Gentle Spirit," Dostoevsky created an oral variant of the narration with a sidelong glance at the listener. In the first, philosophical part of the *Notes*, this narrative type takes on a form that the Polish literary scholar Michał Głowiński (1963) calls "narrative as spoken monologue." This form developed in European prose in the 1950s following the lead of existentialism and the philosophy of the absurd. In Western Europe, the model for this narrative construction (ideologically colored dispute of a speaker who pours scorn on both himself and the world with a listener who defends the present world order) was provided by Albert Camus' *The Fall*. This work, which had a profound influence on post-war Polish literature, is, in turn, indebted to Dostoevsky's *Notes*, and the allusions to it are unmistakeable.

The "spoken monologue" is, according to Głowiński's definition, an oral narrative monologue which differentiates itself from the traditional type of narrative through the following features: (1) dialogic situation, in which the addressed counterpart influences the narrative; (2) connection of *skaz*-elements with rhetoric; (3) relocation of the thematic emphasis from what is narrated to the narration itself. This type is different from *skaz* narrative in (1) its ideological themes; (2) the intellectualism of the argumentation; (3) the inclusion of rhetorical elements.

"A Gentle Spirit" and the second part of the *Notes* do not quite conform to this type, as they are lacking the ideological themes and the intellectual argumentation. Taking these two works of Dostoevsky's as a starting point, I would like to present a type of narrative defined structurally rather than thematically, which I will call *dialogic narrative monologue*. This type is defined by the three features implied in its name:

1. *Dialogic*: The narrator addresses himself to a listener whom he imagines as reacting actively. The narration develops in the tension between the conflicting evaluative positions of the narrator and the addressee, which occasionally takes the form of an open dialogue.

2. *Monologue*: The dialogicity is only staged and does not transcend the limits of the narrator's consciousness. There is no real interlocutor present who could intervene with unforeseeable replies. The imagined interlocutor, who is, after all, a product of the narrator, possesses neither autonomy nor alterity. It is therefore a case of a quasi-dialogue, a dialogically staged variant of the monologue.

3. *Narrativity*: This dialogically constructed monologue has a narrative function. However much the narrator may look around and occupy himself with defending or accusing himself, and with responses to the listener, he is

nonetheless narrating a story and, regardless of all dialogic digressions, pursues a narrative aim.

"A Gentle Spirit" and the *Notes from the Underground* tell stories of failure. But the open and ultimately truthful narration is bound up with the dialogic functions, with the appeal and particularly with the impression. The logic is the following: as the narrator was unable to excel through noble deeds, he endeavors to make an impression with, at the very least, the candor and mercilessness of his self-analysis, with the fearless anticipation of perceptive objections.

Dostoevsky's dialogic monologues are full of paradoxes. There is no listener, but the entire monologue is directed at one. The imagined interlocutor is not a different person, but the speaker argues with him and puts the most devastating objections in his mouth, at which point he simultaneously denies and confirms his presence:

> Of course, I myself have invented all your words. They're also from the underground. It is now forty years that I've been there listening to your words through a chink. I thought them up myself, you see that's all there was to think up. It's no wonder they've been learnt by heart and have adopted a literary form...
> But surely, surely you aren't really so gullible as to imagine that I would publish all this, let alone give it to you to read? (Dostoevsky, NU, 38)

There is another paradoxical feature of Dostoevsky's dialogic narrative monologues: the absent otherness of the addressee, who remains a projection of the speaker's, is replaced by the narrating self's alterity before himself. The paradox consists in the alterity of identity, in the foreignness of the subject when facing him or herself. The self is so foreign to itself that it is more afraid of its own possibilities and abysses than it would ever fear those of another. The solipsistic dimension of the dialogicity, the relocation of the alterity from exterior to interior, is an essential characteristic of the Dostoevskyan conceptions of dialogue and subject. The alterity of the subject, the foreignness of the self, lends Dostoevsky's narrative monologues the true dialogic nature which the merely imagined status of the addressee would deny them.

III. Point of view

1. Theories of point of view, perspective, and focalization

Point of view is one of the central categories of narratology. The term, introduced by Henry James in the essay *The Art of Fiction* (1884), developed in the prefaces to his novels (James 1907/09) and systematized by Percy Lubbock, denotes "the relation in which the narrator stands to the story" (Lubbock 1921 [1957, 83]). Where the *point of view* category (however translated) is used in Romance and Slavic literary study, German study has preferred to use the largely analogous term *narrative perspective* (Erzählperspektive).[1] Since the 1980s, Gérard Genette's (1972) term *focalization* has found widespread acceptance in international narratology.

The variety of existing concepts of point of view in literary study[2] is not based primarily on differences of terminology or on different principles underlying the typologies, but rather, above all, on a divergence in the subject matter associated with the concept. One main point of difference consists in the dimensions of the phenomenon, in the question of which of the work's relations are affected and how deep the model should reach. Although the impression is given in large sections of literary study that the manifestations of point of view have been sufficiently investigated and that the remaining differences between the models are no more than an argument about nomenclature, the phenomenon has not, in reality, been adequately clarified.[3] Before a definition of point of view and an analysis of its structure are attempted, the most influential models will first be examined.

---

1 *Point of view* and *perspective*—terms which will be used synonymously—are, as a rule, taken to denote the *narrative*—or the *narrator's*— point of view or perspective. However, it must not be overlooked that every represented fictive entity in a narrative work potentially has a point of view or perspective of his or her own.
2 Cf. the overviews: Lintvelt 1981, 111–76; Markus 1985, 17–39; Bonheim 1990; Nünning 1990; Jahn 1995, 38–48; Tolmachev 1996; Tamarchenko 1999.
3 Still valid today is Susan Lanser's (1981, 13) judgement that the implications of point of view are, contrary to the general impression, "underestimated" and "underexplored."

a) F. K. Stanzel

One important model of point of view is contained in the typology of "narrative situations" put forward by the Austrian Anglist Franz K. Stanzel for more than fifty years. Stanzel's triad of "authorial," "figural," and "first-person narrative situation" still enjoys great popularity today, not only in German-speaking countries. This typology has been used as the basis for countless analyses and anyone drawing up a new theory of perspective has, as a rule, done so by engaging with Stanzel's "typological circle." Admittedly, Stanzel's system encountered criticism almost immediately (as mentioned above in section II.4). The most problematic aspect of the theory throughout all its versions is the central concept of the "narrative situation".[4] Differing dichotomies are brought together in this category. In the version from 1979 (tr. 1984), the latest version, Stanzel models the category of narrative situations on the basis of three oppositions:

(1) The opposition *person*: "identity vs. non-identity of the realms of existence of the narrator and the fictional characters (first- and third-person reference)";
(2) The opposition *perspective*: "internal vs. external perspective";
(3) The opposition *mode*: "teller-character vs. reflector-character."

Stanzel (in the version from 1979) defines the three narrative situations with the respective dominance of one part of the three oppositions: the first-person narrative situation is characterized by the "identity of the realm where the narrator and his point of view are located with that realm in which the characters are at home" (1979; tr. 1984, 111); in the authorial situation, the external perspective dominates, and, in the figural narrative situation, it is the mode of the reflector that does so. Thus, each of the three oppositions contributes to the triad of narrative situations only once and then with only one of its two parts. The combination of three binary oppositions should, however, produce six types. It must be noted here that Stanzel did not sufficiently distinguish between the categories of "perspective" and "mode." So he states "that there evidently exists a close correspondence between internal perspective and the mode dominated by a reflector-character, on the one hand, and between external perspective and the mode dominated by a teller-character, on the other" (1979; tr. 1984, 141). Obviously fascinated by the idea of a triadic structure in the narrative and narratological

---

4 Stanzel's theory ultimately could not profit from being embedded in the context of current discourses and from the totalization of its triadic structure, as Stanzel attempted in the 1979 variant. The supposed modernization and systematization served only to obscure the underlying approach. The wide dissemination of Stanzel's concepts is on the basis of the early variants of the theory (1955; 1964).

world, he doggedly clings to the triple set of oppositions and narrative situations, which he uses as the basis for his labyrinthine typological circle. It was clearly the weak foundation of the triad that prompted Cohn (1981, 176) and Genette (1983; tr. 1988, 116) to reject Stanzel's differentiation between "perspective" and "mode" as superfluous, where Cohn wanted to discard the former, perspective, and Genette the latter, mode (which denotes a different category in Stanzel's system than French *mode* does in Genette's). If "perspective" and "mode" coincide, the entire system is reduced to the two oppositions that formed the basis of Stanzel's work in 1955 and 1964: (1) "identity vs. non-identity of the realms of existence," (2) "authorial vs. figural." However, a typology built on two binary oppositions does not produce three comparable narrative situations, but rather four clearly defined types (cf. Schmid 1973, 27-28; Cohn 1981, 179; Genette 1983; tr. 1988, 119). First-person narrative then disintegrates, as does third-person narrative, into two variants, the "authorial" and the "figural," in which this last opposition does not describe any kind of complex "narrative situations," but only the two possibilities of perspective. Stanzel's terms "authorial" and "figural," in this sense, have long been used in the analysis of narrative texts.

b) G. Genette and M. Bal

According to Genette (1972; tr. 1980, 185-94), the mistake underlying Stanzel's typology, as well as almost all other work on narrative perspective, is the failure to distinguish between "mood" ("regulation of narrative information" 1972; tr. 1980, 162) and "voice," i.e. the following questions are confused: "Who sees?" (more accurately: "who is the character whose point of view orients the narrative perspective?") and "Who speaks?" ("Who is the narrator?"). Under *mood*, Genette distinguishes the two essential factors in the regulation of information as (1) *distance* (with which the Platonic opposition of *diegesis* and *mimesis*, and its modern equivalent, *telling* vs. *showing*, are rendered) and (2) *perspective*. For Genette, perspective is "the second mode of regulating information, arising from the choice (or not) of a restrictive 'point of view'" (1972; tr. 1980, 185-86). With this reductive conception, Genette falls back on the typology of "visions" erected by Jean Pouillon (1946) and renewed by Tzvetan Todorov (1966, 141-42) with the term *aspects du récit*. In order to avoid the visual connotations of the terms *vision*, *field* and *point of view*, Genette prefers to call the phenomenon, described by Pouillon and Todorov, *focalization*.[5] For this term (which evokes associations no less visual than the rejected alternatives), he draws on the category *focus*

---

5   On focalization, cf. the overviews: Rimmon 1976; Bal 1977b; Angelet/Herman 1987, 183-93; Kablitz 1988; Ilyin 1996e.

of narration, introduced by Brooks and Warren (1943). Genette (1983; tr. 1988, 74) defines *focalization* as "restriction of 'field'," "a selection of narrative information with respect to what was traditionally called *omniscience*." Following in the footsteps of the triadic typologies of his predecessors, Genette (1972; tr. 1980, 189–94) distinguishes three levels of *focalization*:[6]

Pouillon	Todorov	Genette
vision from behind	narrator > character	*zero focalization:* "the narrator knows more than the characters or, more exactly, says more than any of the characters knows"; "what English-language criticism calls the narrative with omniscient narrator"
vision with	narrator = character	*internal focalization:* "the narrator says only what a given character knows"; "the narrative with 'point of view' after Lubbock"
vision from without	narrator < character	*external focalization:* "the narrator says less than the character knows"; "'objective' or 'behaviorist' narrative"

Despite Genette's best efforts to achieve clarity of definition, three features of the narrator are confused in his triad: (1) "knowledge," (2) capability for accessing the characters' consciousnesses, (3) perspective. With regard to the third feature, which is what interests us here, the three levels of focalization correspond to the following forms of perspective:

(1) "Zero focalization": the perspective of an omniscient narrator is predominant.

(2) "Internal focalization": the narration is oriented on the perspective of a narrated character.

(3) "External focalization": the narration is dominated by the perspective of a narrator who possesses no capability for accessing the characters' consciousnesses (or does not communicate it).

---

6 The recourse to traditional typologies which are merely re-formulated determines that Genette's theory has little innovative thinking to offer in the field of perspective. Nonetheless, it has, perhaps by riding the coattails of the more productive parts of *Discours du récit*, become extraordinarily popular and today has the status of a standard model.

Genette's triad of focalization has already been criticized in various ways. Alongside the mixing of separate attributes belonging to the narrator, the following aspects have also proven problematic:

1. Genette reduces the complex phenomenon of point of view, which manifests itself in many different facets, to a single feature, the mere restriction of knowledge. The price for the supposed gain in the concept's clarity is the unhelpful narrowing of its application.

2. It remains unclear what is meant by "knowledge," whether knowledge of the world in general, knowledge about the action, its circumstances and history, or knowledge of what is occurring inside the protagonist in a given moment.

3. Point of view cannot be described with "knowledge" alone, no matter how it is defined, as there is no direct link from it to the perception that, after all, forms the pre-requisite for point of view or perspective (Kablitz 1988, 243; cf. already Jost 1983, 196). Or does "knowing" mean nothing more than "seeing"? Does more or less "knowledge" mean merely lesser or greater "restriction of the field"? If that were accurate, the term "knowledge" would be misleading, at the very least. But nor can point of view be adequately described with only "seeing."

4. Genette's concept of "zero focalization" admits the possibility of narration without point of view. A construct of this sort seems largely meaningless, since point of view is implied in all narration.[7] Even an omniscient narrator, whose field of view, in Genette's sense, is not in the least restricted, still narrates with a particular perspective.

5. Mieke Bal (1977a, 28) rightly points out that the triad is only homogenous insofar as the narrator's knowledge decreases with each of the three consecutive types.[8] She notes that the concept of focalization is, however, used in different senses and that Genette's lacking or inexplicit definition of this term serves to create confusion. External focalization is distinguished from the other two not by perspective but by a reversal of functions. In type 2, the person is the *subject* of the focalization and the object is what s/he perceives; whereas, in type 3, the perceiving person is him or herself the object of focalization, a term which then loses its original meaning: "In the second type, the 'focalized' character *sees*; in the third, s/he does not see but

---

[7] Marjet Berendsen (1984, 141) rightly points out that the notion of zero focalization is a "*contradictio in terminis* since any text fragment contains focalization. Therefore, this notion is completely redundant."

[8] On criticism of the inconsistency of Genette's triad of focalizations, cf. also Nünning 1990, 257-58.

is *seen*. It is not a case of difference between the 'seeing' entities, but between the objects of that vision."[9]

An important role in the dissemination of Genette's theory was played by Mieke Bal herself, as she presented, criticized and modified it in Dutch, French and English. From these modifications emerged what was fundamentally a new theory, which developed Genette's terminology—often with differing contents—and about which Genette (1983) was not particularly enthusiastic.

Bal (1985, 104) defines "focalization" (a term she retains on entirely pragmatic grounds, because of the terms that can be derived from it, such as *focalizer, to focalize*) as "the relationship between the 'vision,' the agent that sees, and that which is seen." To the great dissatisfaction of Genette (1983; tr. 1988, 72-78), Bal postulated a separate subject for focalization, the *focalizer*, which she placed between the narrator and the character, and to which she attributed activity of its own:

> Each entity [the narrator, the focalizer, and the actor] realizes the transition from one plane to another: the actor, using the action as material in making the *histoire*; the focalizer, who selects the actions and chooses the angle from which they are presented, in making the *récit*, while the narrator turns the *récit* into *parole*: s/he makes the narrative text. (Bal 1977a, 32 f.)

Bal even placed an addressee opposite the focalizer, the *spectateur implicite* (1977a, 33; 1977b, 116), and added an independent communication level for the two entities. Alongside the subject and the addressee of the focalization, she also introduced an object, *the focalized* (1977a, 33), a function that could be fulfilled by a narrated character or by the surrounding world. W. J. M. Bronzwaer (1981) convincingly turned against this kind of "emancipation" of the focalizer and the endowment of focalization with a communicative function. According to Genette (1983; tr. 1988, 73), only a narrative can be *focalized* and only a narrator can *focalize*. The autonomizing of focalization as an independent communicative act with a subject, object and addressee is certainly a problematic facet of Mieke Bal's early theory, as published in French.

---

9   The difference between subject and object status of the character was used as the basis for a typology by Pierre Vitoux (1982), in which a distinction is made between an "objective" and "subjective" focalization (cf. also Angelet/Herman 1987, 182-93). Genette (1983; tr. 1988, 72-78) reacted to Bal's justified objection about the ambiguity of his focalization concept, which means, on one hand, concentration on a character and also, on the other, narration from his or her point of view, with a counterattack. The terms Bal derives, such as "focalized character" cannot be reconciled with his approach. Although Genette's criticism of Bal's terms is justified (cf. also below), this counterattack in no way relieves him from the inconsistencies in his theory noted by Bal.

1. Theories of point of view, perspective, and focalization

Fortunately, the idea of a special activity on the part of the focalizer, as well as that of a separate addressee for focalization, is dropped in *Narratology* (Bal 1985). The term *focalizer* is still encountered, but it is defined much more carefully and in a way that is not oriented on any entities or on communication: "the point from which the elements are viewed" (1985, 104). This point is found either in one of the actional characters (*internal focalization*) or in an "anonymous agent, situated outside the fabula" (*external focalization*). With that, focalization denotes a dichotomy of possible perspectives, which are no longer essentially different from the traditional dichotomy *internal* vs. *external point of view*.

c) B. A. Uspensky, J. Lintvelt, and Sh. Rimmon

A decisive contribution to the modeling of point of view was made by the Russian philologist and semiotician Boris Uspensky in his book *Poetics of Composition* (1970). Soon translated into French, English and German and regularly discussed in Russia[10] and the West,[11] the book had a great impact on international narratology.[12] Influenced by Russian formalism and drawing on the work of Viktor Vinogradov and Grigory Gukovsky, as well as Mikhail Bakhtin and Valentin Voloshinov, Uspensky advocated the investigation of perspective with a model that included other "representational arts" such as painting and film alongside literature. With that, Uspensky not only filled a gap in Russian narrative research, in which the problems of point of view had been conspicuously absent, but also gave a decisive impulse to Western theory, which had always paid particular attention to the phenomenon of perspectivization. The innovation of *Poetics of Composition* consists, above all, in the delineation of a stratified model of perspective, i.e. a model that allows for different levels of the manifestation of point of view. In contrast to traditional models, which, as a rule, regarded point of view on only one level, Uspensky distinguished four *planes*, on which point of view is manifested:

(1) The *evaluative* or *ideological* plane, on which the evaluative position or *ideological point of view* appears;

---

10 The official reception in the Soviet Union of this first volume in the series "Semiotic Studies in the Theory of Art" was, as expected, somewhat frosty (one has to wonder at the fact that it could be published at all). Worth reading are, however, the discussions by Segal 1970; Gurvich 1971; Khanpira 1971.
11 Cf. especially Drozda 1971; Schmid 1971; Żółkiewski1971; 1972; de Valk 1972; Mathauserová 1972; Todorov 1972; Foster 1972; Shukman 1972; Steiner 1976; Lintvelt 1981, 167–76.
12 Cf. for instance the work by Lintvelt 1981; Rimmon 1983.

(2) The *phraseological* plane;
(3) The *spatial* and *temporal* plane;
(4) The plane of *psychology*.

On each of these planes, says Uspensky, the "author" can present the happenings from two separate positions,[13] either from his own position, *external* to the happenings, or from an *internal* position, i.e. from the point of view of one or more of the represented characters. The distinction between the two standpoints forms a fundamental opposition, which Uspensky employs on all four planes.

By applying the opposition *external* vs. *internal* to the four planes, Uspensky does, however, reach some debatable results, because he switches the contents of the two terms. "Where the author reproduces foreign or irregular speech naturalistically," he takes—according to Uspensky—"a deliberately external point of view in respect to the person described." However, in instances where the writer concentrates "not on the particularities of speech, but on its essence" and where he accordingly "translates the idiosyncratic features of speech into a neutral phraseology," Uspensky sees internal point of view (1970; tr. 1973, 52). This is tantamount to a swapping of the intensions of inner and outer, or substituting for the oppositions of *standpoints* an opposition of *foreign or outer perception* and *self- or inner perception*. On the phraseological plane, the exact reproduction of a character's speech should sensibly be attributed not to the external but to the internal point of view.

On the psychological level, the problem, well known from other typologies, of the ambivalence of the internal vs. external opposition rears its head. In Uspensky's definition and examples, the expression "internal point of view on the psychological plane" has two different meanings (but not explicitly): (1) the representation of the world through the eyes or the prism of one or more represented characters (here, consciousness is the *subject* of perception), (2) the representation of a character's consciousness from the standpoint of a narrator, who is capable of accessing it (consciousness is here the *object* of perception).

The distinction between the planes is made more difficult, as Uspensky explicitly notes, by the fact that they do not exist entirely independently of one another, but sometimes overlap. So, evaluation can be expressed by phraseological means, and also by the temporal position of the narrator, similar to the way in which the psychological standpoint can also be realized through phraseology.

---

13 By "author," Uspensky usually means the narrator. As is usual in a Russian context, Uspensky refers to a "narrator" only in the case of a narrative entity clearly profiled as a person.

1. Theories of point of view, perspective, and focalization

Particularly interesting are Uspensky's observations on the "interrelations of points of view on different levels." The standpoints tend to coincide on all the different planes, i.e. on all four planes, the narration orients itself on either only the external or only the internal standpoint. But this concurrence does not necessarily occur. It is thoroughly possible for the standpoint to be external on some planes and internal on others. It is precisely this non-concurrence that justifies the stratification of the standpoint into four planes and, indeed, makes it essential.

The demonstration on classic Russian works of the non-concurrence of the ideological and spatial-temporal plane, on the one hand, and the psychological and phraseological planes, on the other, is the centerpiece of Uspensky's work, and many reviewers see this analysis as his great contribution. However, the lack of semantic clarification and the inconsistent treatment of the outer-inner dichotomy serve to cast doubt on many of his conclusions. So, for example, the ironic quotation of a character's speech by the narrator is not simply a case of the "non-concurrence of the ideological and the phraseological planes," as Uspensky (1970; tr. 1973, 103) has it. Insofar as the position of the character is revealed in the quoted speech, word for word reproduction of it is bound up with an orientation on the inner standpoint, on the ideological plane. However, insofar as this speech contains additional accentuation alien to the speaking figure, on a higher communication level, i.e. the narrator's text, this can be seen as external ideological position. In this way, we obtain a doubled evaluative standpoint, one which is *primarily internal* and *secondarily external*, and which takes the primary standpoint as its base. By not paraphrasing the character's speech, and by rendering it word for word with all its idiosyncrasies, the narrator adopts an internal standpoint to it, and simultaneously signals through the context that he, the narrator, evaluates the reproduced speech differently to the speaking character, i.e. adopts a contradictory ideological standpoint. Therefore, the irony is not based simply on an external standpoint on the evaluative plane, but on the simultaneous presence and interference of two evaluative positions, one internal and one external.

Uspensky's analysis of examples of the non-concurrence of ideological and psychological, or of spatial-temporal and psychological standpoints, suffers from the ambivalence described above, that of the expression *internal point of view on the plane of psychology*. When the narrator of the *Brothers Karamazov* describes old Fyodor Karamazov "from within," he does not necessarily adopt an internal psychological viewpoint. It is thoroughly possible for a narrator to have complete access to the internal condition of a protagonist and nonetheless describe him or her from an external standpoint. Here, Uspensky confuses access to a character's consciousness with perspective. An internal point of view, in the sense of perspective, would require that the world be perceived through the eyes of Fyodor Karamazov. It would therefore only be correct to talk about an internal point of view in the representation of a protagonist's internal condition, if the narrator portrayed the self-perception of this character, that is, the perception of innermost thoughts and feelings by the protagonist him or herself. This technique is, however, not applied to Fyodor Karamazov, who never becomes a reflector.

An actual non-concurrence of viewpoints is, however, encountered when the narrator describes the world from the spatial-temporal standpoint of the character (internal standpoint), but does not portray his or her perception, adopting rather an external standpoint on the psychological plane. As an example, Uspensky (1970; tr. 1973, 107) adduces the description of Captain Lebyadkin's room in Dostoevsky's *The Possessed*. The room, as Uspensky says, is described from the spatial standpoint of Stavrogin, which the narrator has already followed before, but is not seen "through the eyes" of Stavrogin (i.e. with his unique selection of elements from the "setting"), but rather as it would have been perceived by an attentive observer from Stavrogin's spatial-temporal standpoint.

Regardless of some inconsistent and problematic analyses, particularly with regard to the opposition of internal and external, Uspensky's model represented a decisive advance insofar as it portrayed perspective as a phenomenon existing on multiple planes. His theory provided the impetus for the elaboration of other stratified models

The Dutch Romance studies scholar Jaap Lintvelt (1981, 39) has also suggested a model consisting of four planes, but defines these differently to Uspensky. Lintvelt distinguishes: (1) a *plan perceptif-psychique*, (2) a *plan temporel*, (3) a *plan spatial*, and (4) a *plan verbal*. However, Lintvelt locates the phenomenon of *narrative perspective* only on the first plane, the *plan perceptif-psychique*. For him, the three other levels are no longer those of point of view, but, more generally, of *narrative categories*. It is in this way that he modifies Uspensky's stratified model. Like Genette before him, who recognizes only the former of *mood* and *voice* as a category of the phenomenon of perspective, Lintvelt excludes the level of linguistic realization of the discourse from the facts of perspective. And what remains, for Lintvelt, of Uspensky's "evaluation" or "ideology"? It appears to him, as he expresses it, not to be isolatable, but rather to result from the four named planes.

The Israeli scholar Shlomit Rimmon-Kenan (1983, 71–85) takes on Genette's term *focalization* but broadens its purely visual sense to include "cognitive, emotive and ideological orientation." Encouraged by Uspensky, she distinguishes three *facets of focalization*: (1) the *perceptual facet*, which is determined by space and time, (2) the *psychological facet*, for which the "cognitive and the emotive orientation of the focalizer towards the focalized" are determining components, (3) the *ideological facet*. Following Uspensky, Rimmon-Kenan examines the "interrelations among the various facets" and concedes the possibility that the facets may "belong to different, even clashing focalizers." But where, in her model, is Uspensky's "phraseological plane"? Apparently with the intention of avoiding conflict with Genette's distinction between "voice" ("Who speaks?") and "mood" ("Who sees?"), Rimmon-Kenan excludes language from the domain of point of view or perspective and does not grant it the status of a facet of its own, but only that of a complementary "verbal indicator of focalization" (1983, 82).

2. A model of narrative point of view

What could and should "narrative point of view" mean in a narratological sense? Point of view is defined here as *the complex, formed by internal and external factors, of conditions for the comprehension and representation of happenings*. This definition will be explained in the following three steps.

a) The happenings as the object of point of view

We will begin with the last term in the definition, the happenings. In contrast to most models of narrative operations, which allow the existence of a story without point of view, it will be assumed here that point of view is not applied to a story already constituted, but to the happenings that form its basis. Without point of view, there is no story. A story is only constituted at all when the amorphous, continuous happenings are subjected to a selecting and hierarchizing viewpoint. One of the premises of this study is that every representation of reality implies a point of view or perspective in the acts of selection, naming and evaluation of its elements.

The constitutive role that perspective plays in a story also applies to factual narration. It is impossible to describe a real incident without selecting a limited number of the fundamentally infinite mass of elements and characteristics that could be ascribed to it. The difference between factual and fictional narration consists in that the happenings in the former are real and, in the latter, exist only as the implication of the fictive story.

b) Comprehension and representation

In the definition of point of view suggested above, two acts are distinguished: the *comprehension* and the *representation* of happenings. This distinction is necessary because a narrator can represent a happening differently from how he comprehends or has comprehended it. In such cases of non-concurrence of comprehension and representation, the narrator does not render what and how he perceived, but rather reproduces the perception of one or more narrated characters. This type of non-concurrence of comprehension and representation, which is characteristic of fictional narration, and which is encountered by way of exception in factual narration, is a feature of the figural narration which has become a central mode of representing reality in European literature since the era of sentimentalism.

Comprehension and representation are different acts in narration. This distinction is, as a rule, not made or not given due attention in the popular models of perspective. The distinction, introduced by Genette, between *mood* ("Who sees?") and *voice* ("Who speaks?") has points of contact with the dichotomy of comprehension and representation, but is not identical with it and, incidentally, is not consistently executed by Genette. He is hindered by the identification of the "extradiegetic" narrator with the author (see above), something which excludes the possibility of independent comprehension (in the fictive, represented world) from the outset, for this kind of narrator. For Genette, *vision* is the privilege of the characters. It is for that reason that he can postulate the existence of such a thing as "zero focalization."

c) The parameters of point of view

It was assumed above that comprehension and representation are conditioned by *external and internal factors*. These factors are assigned to a variety of parameters, aspects and facets, in each of which the phenomenon of point of view manifests itself in a distinct way. In order to differentiate the parameters of point of view, in which distinct factors of comprehension and representation can occur, we will conduct a thought experiment. Let us imagine some witnesses to a car accident who are supposed to make statements in court about the happenings as they comprehended them. Each witness will possibly present an independent version of what happened, i.e. tell his or her own story of the accident. Even with the witnesses' greatest attempts at objectivity, their statements may well contradict one another and not only because they remember what happened with varying degrees of clarity. The divergence of the statements already exists in the specific individual perception of the happenings, i.e. on a differing selection of the facts and on a distinct weighting of the circumstances.

1. Spatial point of view

If the witnesses have perceived the happenings differently, that could have been determined primarily by their *spatial* point of view. According to their

2. A model of narrative point of view

spatial position relative to the accident, and depending on their angle of vision, the witnesses will have perceived differing facets of reality and used them as elements in their stories. One witness may have seen that one of those involved signaled before the accident, a detail that necessarily escaped another witness because of his or her position. Spatial perspective is constituted by the location from which the happenings are perceived, with the restrictions of the field of vision that result from this standpoint. The concept of spatial point of view is the only one of the terms that express a reference of comprehension and representation to a subject that fulfils the intension of *point of view* or *perspective* in the actual, original sense of the word. All other uses of the term *point of view* are more or less metaphorical.

2. Ideological point of view

What the witnesses perceive can also diverge when they all take up an identical spatial standpoint and have an identical field of vision. The difference in comprehension of the happenings can namely be down to a difference in *ideological* viewpoints. The ideological perspective encompasses various factors that determine the subjective relationship of the observer to an occurrence: knowledge, way of thinking, evaluative position and intellectual horizons. Depending on these factors, observers will each focus on different components of the happenings and construct differing stories as a result. In this way, comprehension is shaped by *knowledge*. A young man with excellent knowledge of cars and traffic laws will comprehend other details of a traffic accident than an old woman who has never driven a car. Comprehension is, of course, also influenced by *evaluative positions*. Two young people who have identical knowledge of cars and traffic laws, but hold different opinions on traffic politics, will, as a result of their different evaluative positions, comprehend different facets of the same accident and perceive differently the involvement of pedestrians, cyclists and drivers in the accident.

The differing perceptions of one and the same occurrence by the various witnesses as a result of differences in their interests and evaluative positions is vividly illustrated in the short story "The Poet" by the Czech author Karel Čapek, from the cycle *Stories from a Pocket*. One night in Prague, a car driver injures a pedestrian in a hit and run accident. From the questioning of the witnesses, it becomes clear that they all perceived entirely different things, but also that none of them can provide the car's license plate number. The policeman who rushed to help the victim did not pay attention to the car. The engineering student concentrated entirely on the noise of the engine and immediately noted that it was a four-stroke internal combustion engine, but did not see the license plate and cannot even state the color or shape of the car. Incidentally, he knows nothing about makes of car. And his friend, the poet, who was also a witness, can only make statements about the "atmosphere" of the street at night with the injured victim of the accident lying on the asphalt. He did, however, compose a poem immediately after the accident. From the images it contains, "swan's neck, female breast, resounding drums," it proves possible to reconstruct the subconsciously registered license plate number: it contains the digits 235.

The isolation of a distinct ideological perspective might meet with objections. Not that ideology could be seen as irrelevant to perspective, no; problems arise from the fact that it is also involved in other facets of perspective. It is for this reason that Lintvelt (1981, 168), opposing Uspensky, drew attention to the fact that his plane of "evaluation" or "ideology" could not be isolated from the others. In his own model, he attempts to do without the ideological plane, since, he argues, it is already partially contained in the other planes. It is true that evaluation or ideology can be implied in the other aspects of perspective. However, it can also appear independent of other facets, in the form of direct, explicit evaluation. It is for this reason that the separation of an independent ideological perspective appears both meaningful and necessary.

3. Temporal point of view

If the witnesses in our thought experiment make their statements at different points in time, then the *temporal* point of view comes into play. Temporal perspective denotes the interval between the original comprehension and the later acts of comprehension and representation. "Comprehension" does not mean only the initial impression but also its later processing and interpretation. So, it is not only the gap between the (initial) comprehension and representation that is relevant to temporal perspective, but also the intervals between the various phases of processing and interpretation.

What are the consequences of a displacement of the standpoint on the temporal axis? Whereas a spatial displacement can be bound up with a change to the field of perception, a temporal displacement can result in changes to both knowledge and evaluation. With temporal distance from the happenings, knowledge of its causes and effects can be extended and that can lead to a changed evaluation of the happenings. A witness who was not familiar with cars and traffic laws at the time of her initial statement, but who has since increased her knowledge of them, can reassess earlier impressions and assign new meaning to certain details of the occurrence that she had perceived but not been able to interpret properly. With a lengthened temporal interval between the initial comprehension (or a later interpretation of the first impression) and its rendering, however, the witness's knowledge can also dwindle, if the witness forgets particular facts in the passage of time (as usually happens with those elements that are not firmly integrated into the perceived story).

The question of to what extent the separation of a distinct parameter is justified also presents itself for temporal point of view. This is because time is not relevant to perspective in and of itself, but only as the bearer of changes to knowledge and evaluation. But it is precisely because of this function that the question of whether temporal interval is a factor that influences comprehension and representation can be answered only in the affirmative.

4. Linguistic point of view

Witnesses can use a range of different linguistic registers in their statements. In the rendering of what they comprehended, they can use expressions and intonations that correspond to their knowledge and evaluation, their internal condition at the time, or also forms of expression in which a changed internal condition or altered knowledge and evaluation are revealed. This choice manifests the *linguistic* point of view. The term *linguistic point of view* is, of course, highly metaphorical. This is where the tendency towards figurative word usage, dominant in theories of perspective, reaches its zenith. Nevertheless, that is no reason to exclude language from the facts of perspective, as happens in many theories (e.g. explicitly in Rimmon-Kenan 1983, 82). Particularly relevant to point of view are the linguistic subsections lexis, syntax and expression; morphology less so (unless one regards cases of incorrect grammar as an intentionally included feature serving the characterization of the narrator's or character's discourse).

Linguistic point of view attains a special significance for non-diegetic narrators. They face the decision of whether to render an occurrence in their own language or in the language of one of the narrated characters (or that of a milieu). The difference between fictional and factual narration does not have a significant role to play here. In any everyday non-diegetic narrative situation, the narrator has to decide whether to narrate in his or her own language or with the terms and style of an involved third person.

The division of linguistic from ideological point of view is sometimes problematic. The various appellations for Napoleon in *War and Peace* ("Buonaparte"—"Bonaparte"—"Napoleon"—"l'empereur Napoléon"), which Uspensky (1970; tr. 1973, 27–32) adduces as an example of the "point of view on the phraseological plane," do not differ only linguistically, but also in their evaluative position. There are, however, lexical and syntactical techniques in which the evaluative position is far less strongly expressed, as is often the case with *naming*. That in itself is a reason to distinguish between ideological and linguistic perspective.

In our thought experiment, we did not relate linguistic point of view to the comprehension of an occurrence, but to its representation (statements in court). However, the language parameter is also relevant to perception, because we perceive reality in categories and terms taken from the semantic system of a particular language. Fictional literature, at least, takes as its starting point that a protagonist who perceives an event articulates his or her impression in speech, even if it is only internal. On that is based the rendering of what a character perceives in a direct interior discourse. The language is not added by the narrator who passes on the perception, but is already extant in the act of perception itself, before it is rendered. In this way, linguistic point of view is also relevant to the comprehension of an occurrence.

5. Perceptual point of view

The most important factor that determines the perception of an occurrence, and is often actually identified with point of view or perspective, is the prism through which the occurrence is perceived. It is at the perceptual point of view that questions such as the following are aimed: "Through whose eyes does the narrator look at the world?" or "Who is responsible for the selection of these, and not other, elements of the happenings for use in the story?"

In factual texts, the narrator renders merely his or her own perception, whereby s/he can, however, choose between the comprehension of his or her earlier, narrated self and his or her present, narrating self. In contrast, the narrator of a fictional text can take on an alien perceptual perspective, i.e. represent the world through the prism of a character.

The representation of the world as perceived by a character assumes the narrator's capability for accessing the consciousness of the character. The reverse is certainly not valid: access to the character's consciousness is also thoroughly possible in cases when the narrator does not narrate through the prism of the character. The narrator can describe a character's consciousness without taking on his or her perceptual perspective. Fyodor Karamazov is, as we have seen, described "internally," but absolutely not through the prism of his own perception. Access to a character's interior and the taking on of the character's perceptual perspective, no matter how often they are mixed in theories of perspective (as indicated above), are two entirely separate things. In the first case, the character or, more specifically, his or her consciousness, is the *object* of the narrator's perception; in the second, it is the *subject* or the prism of perception through which the narrator sees the narrated world.

Perceptual point of view often coincides with spatial point of view, but that is not necessarily the case. The narrator can take on a character's spatial position without perceiving the world through his or her eyes. The description of Captain Lebyadkin's room in Dostoevsky's *The Possessed*, as referred to by Uspensky (1970; tr. 1973, 107) can again serve as an example (cf. above p. 98). What is described is what Stavrogin could have perceived, but it

2. A model of narrative point of view

is not described through his prism. The selection of details does not correspond to his unique perception.

Description from a character's perceptual perspective is often marked by this character's evaluation and style. But this coincidence is not obligatory: in the parameters of perception, evaluation and language, the perspective need not be oriented on one and the same entity.

The thought experiment with the witnesses' statements about a traffic accident has yielded five parameters of perspective. If one were to place these parameters in order according not to their significance in the experiment but to their relevance for the constitution of point of view in literary work, the following sequence would result: (1) perception, (2) ideology, (3) space, (4) time, (5) language.

d) Narratorial and figural point of view

The narrator has two basic possibilities for how to represent an occurrence.[14] S/he can narrate from his or her own, *narratorial*, point of view or take on a *figural* standpoint, i.e. narrate from the perspective of one or more of the narrated characters.[15] From this arises a simple, binary opposition of points of view. The binary quality results from the fact that a narrative work can represent, in one and the same section of text, two perceiving, evaluating, speaking and actional entities, two centers for the generation of meaning: the narrator and the character. There is no third possibility. That is why there is no place in the model presented here for a "neutral" perspective, which is allowed for in a range of theories (Stanzel 1955[16]; Petersen 1977, 187-92; Lintvelt 1981, 38-39[17]; Broich 1983[18]), nor for "zero focalization" as postulated by Genette.

---

[14] Kristin Morrison (1961) has already drawn attention to the fact that, in the work of H. James and P. Lubbock, perspective is oriented on two separate entities, on one hand to the narrator ("speaker of the narrative words"), and, on the other, to the perceiving character, the reflector, ("knower of the narrative story") (cf. Stanzel 1979; tr. 1984, 9; Martinez/Scheffel 1999, 63).

[15] Dorrit Cohn (1978, 145-61; 1981, 179-80) calls the two perspectives, to the extent that they appear in third-person narrative and following Stanzel, *authorial* and *figural*; in first-person narrative, for which Stanzel refused to the last to recognize the existence of two possible perspectives, *dissonant* and *consonant*. In this book, the concept *authorial* refers not to the narrator but to the author. Therefore, a distinction is made here between *authorial*, *narratorial* and *figural*.

[16] In later works, Stanzel (1964; 1979) did without the concept of the "neutral narrative situation."

[17] Lintvelt accepts a *type narratif neutre* only for "heterodiegetic" narration.

In the opposition *narratorial* vs. *figural perspective*, the second element is marked. That means: if the perspective is not figural (and the opposition of the points of view is not entirely neutralized), it is seen as narratorial. Thus, perspective is narratorial not only when the narration bears traces of comprehension and representation by an individual narrator, but also when the narration appears "objective" or contains only slight traces of reality being refracted through some kind of prism. This is because the narrator is always present in the narrative work as a giver of meaning, even if only through the selection of elements.

The model proposed here differs from the majority of point-of-view typologies in that the presence of the narrator in the story (as well as his or her competence, access to characters' consciousnesses, markedness and subjectivity) is viewed as a phenomenon belonging not to point of view, but to the typology of the narrator.

Narratorial and figural perspectives appear in both non-diegetic and diegetic narration. If one combines the two binary oppositions *narratorial* vs. *figural* and *non-diegetic* vs. *diegetic*, four types arise which actually do all appear in real texts:

Type of narrator Point of view	non-diegetic	diegetic
narratorial	1	2
figural	3	4

Type 1: A non-diegetic narrator narrates in a narratorial fashion. An example of this is provided by *Anna Karenina*, in which the narrator, who does not appear in the storyworld, presents the happenings, with a few exceptions, from his own perspective.

---

18   To strengthen the necessity of a third, "neutral" type of perspective, Ulrich Broich (1983, 136) refers to texts in free indirect discourse, "which are simultaneously mediated by a narrator as well as by a reflector." But the perspective in that case is not "neutral," but hybrid, mixed, both narratorial and figural. Therefore, the necessity or acceptability of a category of neutral perspective cannot be justified with the structure of free indirect discourse. The opposition of narratorial and figural perspective can be *neutralized* with regard to certain features in a given segment of a text (see below). The neutralization of opposition does not, however, produce a third, "neutral" type of perspective.

Type 2: A narrator who appears in the story as the narrated self narrates from the perspective of the "present," i.e. the narrating self. This type is present in Dostoevsky's short story "A Gentle Spirit," for example, in which the pawnbroker's probing into his past is influenced by the undeniable fact that his wife's corpse is lying on the table, she having thrown herself from a window a few minutes earlier.

Type 3: A non-diegetic narrator takes on the standpoint of a character who functions as a reflector. Dostoevsky's *Eternal Husband* is an example of this (see above, II.4.c).

Type 4: A diegetic narrator reports his or her experiences from the perspective of the "earlier" narrated self. That is the perspective that dominates in Dostoevsky's *A Raw Youth*. Arkady Dolgoruky describes his life in the previous year "with the characteristics of the time"; in any given moment, he discloses only what he knew as the narrated self, and evaluates people as well as events from the standpoint of his earlier self.

e) Point of view in diegetic narrative ("The Shot")

If the narrator places his or her accentuation on the words that express the character's evaluation, this statement becomes "double-voiced" (Bakhtin). For the non-diegetic narrator, the double-voiced rendering of figural evaluation has already been demonstrated on the example of the *Eternal Husband* (II.4.c). In this section, the double-voicedness of figural narration will be examined in the diegetic variant, using the example of Pushkin's tale "The Shot." This example will prove again that it is both meaningful and necessary to distinguish between narratorial and figural perspective in diegetic narration.

The primary narrator of "The Shot" reports two encounters, one with each of the duelists, and, in the process, reproduces Silvio's narrative of the first part of the duel and the count's narrative of the second part. The stories of both encounters are told double-voiced, with both the figural evaluation of the narrated self and the narratorial accentuation of the narrating self. The simultaneous effect of figural and narratorial perspective gains further in complexity because the self, which encompasses both functional entities, is represented as a dynamic figure. The narrator develops in contrast to Silvio, the static, romantic hero. The young man leaves military service and swaps the noisy, carefree life of the garrison for a lonely life as the owner of a dilapidated estate. The change in living conditions is accompanied by the sobering and maturing of the young man. While he found himself under the influence of the romantic Silvio in the first chapter, he is significantly cooler when talking about him in the second chapter, in which the action takes place five years later. Tellingly, Silvio only crosses his mind as a result of a conversation with the count, and then merely as a prosaic example of a diligently practicing marksman. The romantic aura that surrounded Silvio in the first chapter has dissipated for the estate-owner. The narrated self of the second chapter has overcome the romance that fascinated him in the first.

Of interest to us in this context is how the perspectivization and the correlation of the narrated and narrating selves are constructed in the first part of the tale. The perspective of the narrated self dominates, i.e. the reader perceives Silvio and his strange behavior according to the perception and evaluation of the young narrated self, who is initially fascinated by Silvio, then disappointed, and finally honored by the trust of his older friend. But there are noticeable accentuations in the text that bring the sober standpoint of the narrating self to bear. In this way, two voices, two evaluative positions, interfere. The perception and evaluation of the naive youngster who has succumbed to the fascination of romantic stereotypes are countermanded by the views of the mature narrator. In the process, the narrating self's accentuation is marked merely by the signs of a certain reservation, a relativization, a distancing.

There follow a few examples of how the evaluation of the romantically inclined narrated self (marked by simple underlining) is relativized by signals placed by the narrating self (dotted underlining):

> Endowed with a romantic imagination by nature, I had been his greatest admirer before the incident, for the life of this man was an enigma, and he himself had appeared to me as the hero of some mysterious story. (Pushkin, Prose, 67; transl. slightly revised)

The narrated self would hardly have mentioned his "romantic imagination," nor connected the "mysterious story" with the somewhat detracting indefinite pronoun "some," and certainly not used the verb "to appear," which emphasizes the subjectivity of his perception at the time.

> We supposed that some hapless victim of his terrifying skill lay on his conscience. I must remark that we never dreamed of suspecting anything in him that resembled timidity. There are people whose mere appearance precludes such suspicion. (Pushkin, Prose, 66)

This comment implies that the thought the narrator would never have even dreamed at the time now does not seem alien to him. And the word "appearance," which precludes any suspicion of timidity, can now be understood as a reference to Silvio's romantic poses.

The description of Silvio's romantic demonism contains a modal signal that casts doubt on the perception and evaluation of the young narrated self:

> His grim pallor, his flashing eyes, and the dense smoke issuing from his mouth lent him a truly diabolic appearance. (Pushkin, Prose, 69)

2. A model of narrative point of view

The narrating self places the emphasis on the "appearance" corresponding to the "appearance" that precludes any suspicion of timidity.

This section was intended to demonstrate that narratorial and figural point of view must also be distinguished in diegetic narration. Using Pushkin's "The Shot," it was also examined how the dominant figural perspective, i.e. the evaluation of the narrated self, is superimposed with the accentuation of the narrating self.

f) Narratorial and figural manifestations in the five parameters of point of view

How do narratorial and figural points of view manifest themselves in the five parameters?

1. Perceptual point of view

If the narrated world is perceived through the eyes of a character, according to the symptoms of the text, it is a case of figural point of view. However, if no indications can be found for the refraction of the world through the prism of one or more characters, then the perceptual perspective will be regarded as narratorial, no matter how marked and subjective the narrator is.

One example of a manifestly figural point of view in the parameter of perception is the portrayal, in *War and Peace*, of the unexpected reunion of Pierre Bezukhov and Natasha Rostova in Moscow after the end of its occupation by Napoleon, at the home of Princess Marya Bolkonskaya:

> In a low-pitched room, lighted by a single candle, he found the princess, and someone with her in a black dress. Pierre recollected that the princess had always had lady-companions of some sort with her, but who those companions were, and what they were like, he did not remember. 'That is one of her companions,' he thought, glancing at the lady in the black dress. (Tolstoy, WaP, 1047)

The selection of the thematic elements indicates Pierre's perspective. In his perception, there are three objects: (1) the "low-pitched room, lighted by a single candle," (2) "the princess," (3) "someone with her in a black dress." Since Pierre does not recognize this woman, she is introduced with a single characteristic: "in a black dress." It is only after a second, closer look at the not yet recognized Natasha that Pierre perceives a second characteristic: her alert and friendly eyes.

Figural perspective in terms of perception is, as a rule, accompanied by figurality in the other parameters as well, particularly in evaluation and language. This means that figural perception is usually also ideologically and linguistically oriented on the character. Thus, in Dostoevsky's *The Double*, the narrative of the misdeeds of the crafty "twin" (who exists only in the protagonist's perception) is presented almost throughout in the style of Golyadkin's speech and with the evaluation typical of him:

> As soon as Mr. Golyadkin junior noticed that his opponent [...] might actually be driven to attack him, he promptly and in the most shameless way hastened to be beforehand with his victim. Patting him two or three times on the cheek, tickling him two or three times, playing with him for a few seconds in this way while his victim stood rigid and beside himself with fury to the no little diversion of the young men standing round, Mr. Golyadkin junior ended with a most revolting shamelessness by giving Mr. Golyadkin senior a poke in his rather prominent stomach [...] (Dostoevsky, D, 208)

However, figural perception is not necessarily attended by figural speech and evaluation. The less the figural perception is accompanied by figural speech and evaluation, the harder it is for the reader to identify. The question of whether perceptual perspective is oriented on the narrator or on one of the characters can sometimes become a riddle. Let us examine a central scene in *Anna Karenina*, in which it is not immediately recognizable who appears as the seeing, thinking, feeling entity. It deals with the situation after the fulfillment of what Vronsky had fervently wished for and what had appeared to Anna as a dream never to be realized:

> She felt so sinful, so guilty, that nothing was left her but to humiliate herself and beg forgiveness; and as now there was no one in her life but him, to him she addressed her prayer for forgiveness. Looking at him, she had a physical sense of her humiliation, and she could say nothing more. *He felt what a murderer must feel when he sees the body he has robbed of life. That body, robbed by him of life, was their love, the first stage of their love.* There was something awful and revolting in the memory of what had been bought at this fearful price of shame. Shame at their spiritual nakedness crushed her and infected him. But in spite of all the murderer's horror before the body of his victim, he must hack it to pieces, hide the body, must use what he has gained by his murder.
> *And with fury, as it were with passion, the murderer falls on the body and drags it and hacks at it*; so he covered her face and shoulders with kisses. She held his hand, and did not stir. "Yes, these kisses—that is what has been bought by this shame. Yes, and one hand, which will always be mine—the hand of my accomplice." (Tolstoy, AK, 158–59. Italics mine—*W. Sch.*)

Who is comparing the lover with a murderer? It might initially appear that Vronsky experiences it in this way. It does after all expressly state that "He felt what a murderer must feel." But would the cavalry captain really experience the fulfillment of that "which had been for almost a whole year the one absorbing desire of [his] life" (ibid.) in terms of a murder? The narratorial rendering of Vronsky's feelings is also improbable. Vronsky's feelings must be different. Naturally, what also comes into consideration is a comparison made by the narrator in his own name, behind the backs of the characters, as it were, i.e. a purely narratorial commentary or even an authorial one, one which refers back to the author. These kinds of narratorial—and ultimately authorial—comments are encountered relatively often in Tolstoy's work. Nonetheless, the formation of this passage suggests a different way of reading it. If one considers that Anna's sentiments and interior monologue are presented around the italicized segments, one can certainly reach the conclusion that the comparison of the furious lover with a murderer is drawn by none other than Anna herself. Such an association would be strongly motivated within her consciousness, psychologically as well as compositionally. This is because the image of the sliced up corpse can be interpreted as a reflection of the "horrible death" suffered by the railwayman at her first encounter with Vronsky. The words that she overheard from two passers-by at the time must have engraved themselves deeply in her consciousness:

> "What a horrible death!" said a gentleman passing by. "They say he was cut in two pieces." (Tolstoy, AK, 71)

Anna is severely shaken and interprets the accident as an "evil omen" (ibid.). From this moment on, the heroine becomes the bearer of the fatal image of the sliced up corpse, which she associates with Vronsky. She superimposes this image onto her romantic encounter with Vronsky and carries it within herself until her destiny has been fulfilled under the slicing wheels of the train. Shortly before her suicide, she remembers the railwayman who was run over and realizes what she has to do. With this concatenation of motifs, her death under the wheels of the train appears as the fulfillment of a schema of her fatal expectations, which had formed as early as during the first encounter with Vronsky. Insofar as the key scene after the act of love, quoted above, is presented from a figural perspective oriented on Anna, the author indicates to us that the heroine is the engineer of her own fate.

2. Ideological point of view

In the ideology, the narrative text can give form to the evaluative position of either the narrator or a character. As an example of figural ideological point of view, we will examine the start of Chekhov's story "The Student." The first sentences, in which the narrator "sees" and speaks, are, nonetheless, interspersed with what are clearly figural evaluations (emphasized here with italics):

> At first the weather was *fine* and still. The thrushes were calling, and in the swamps close by *something alive* droned pitifully with a sound like blowing into an empty bottle. A snipe flew by, and the shot aimed at it rang out *with a gay, resounding note* in the spring air. But when it began to get dark in the forest a cold, *penetrating* wind blew *inappropriately* from the east, and everything sank in-

to silence. Needles of ice stretched across the pools, and it felt *cheerless, remote, and lonely* in the forest. There was a whiff of winter. (Chekhov, S, 106)

Before introducing the protagonist, the narrator already describes the world from the hero's ideological perspective, without, however, employing lexical or syntactic features that would indicate him.

By contrast, the beginning of Thomas Mann's novel *Royal Highness* also thematizes the weather but with an evaluation that, in the wider context, proves itself to be narratorial (here in italics):

> The scene is the Albrechtstrasse, the main artery of the capital, which runs from Albrechtplatz and the Old Schloss to the barracks of the Fusiliers of the Guard. The time is noon on an *ordinary* week-day; the season of the year *does not matter*. The weather is fair to moderate. It is not raining, but the sky is not clear; it is a uniform light grey, *uninteresting* and *sombre*, and the street lies in a *dull* and *sober* light which *robs it of all mystery, all individuality*. (Mann, RH, XI)

3. Spatial point of view

The figural point of view on the spatial plane is indicated by the orientation of the narration on a particular spatial position taken up by a character. This position defines the character's field of vision and allows him or her to perceive only certain aspects of the happenings. The clearest signal of figural spatial perspective is the use of deictic adverbs of place referring to the location of the character, such as *here, there, right, left* etc. An example is provided by Lion Feuchtwanger's historical novel *Josephus*. Josef Ben Matthias (who will later be called Flavius Josephus) is in Rome for the first time, but can already roughly find his way around:

> He knew that the place *just in front of him* was the cattle market, and that the Circus Maximus was *to the right*, and that *over there* on the Palatine and behind it, where there were such crowds of people, the Emperor was building his new house, and that the street *to the left* led to the Forum, and that the Palatine and the Forum were the heart of the world. (Feuchtwanger, Josephus, 3–4)

Narratorial spatial perspective is, depending on the spatial competence of the narrating entity, bound up with either the narrowly defined position of a human being or with Olympic omnipresence. If the spatial position is not marked and the view of the spaces in which the happenings occur is not restricted, then the spatial perspective is certainly narratorial.

4. Temporal point of view

On the temporal plane, the figural point of view is manifested in the binding of the narration to the present of one of the characters. The orientation on the temporal position of a character shows itself most clearly in deictic adverbs of time, such as *now, today, yesterday, tomorrow* etc., which only become meaningful in reference to a particular temporal zero point, the character's present. It is thoroughly possible for deictic adverbs of present and

2. A model of narrative point of view

future to be connected with verbs in the past tense. In the Western, particularly German, discussions on the "epic preterite" and its detemporalization (see above, I.2.c), an important role is played by quotations in which deictic adverbs of present or future (dotted underlining in the following examples) are connected with verbs in the preterite (double underlining).

1) Adverbs of future:

> But in the morning she had to trim the tree. Tomorrow was Christmas. (Alice Berend: *The Bridegrooms of Babette Bomberling*)[19]
>
> [...] and of course he was coming to her party to-night. (Virginia Woolf: *Mrs. Dalloway*)

2) Adverbs of present:

> Still today, when she closed her eyes, she saw before her the expression on his face. (Thomas Mann: *Lotte in Weimar*)

Connections of this sort are also entirely usual in Russian:

> [...] до завтра было еще далеко (Dostoevsky, PSS, XIII, 241)
>
> [...] there was plenty of time to decide before to-morrow (Dostoevsky, RY, 293)
>
> The pistol and the dagger and the peasant's coat were ready, Napoleon was making his entry to-morrow (въезжал завтра; Tolstoy, WaP, 856; transl. revised; C. Garnett replaces the deictic *to-morrow* by the anaphoric *on the morrow*)

The narratorial perspective in the parameter of time is that correlated with the temporal position of the narrative act. In the narratorial statements, anaphoric adverbs are used instead of deictic ones to denote a point in time in the story, i.e. expressions such as *in that moment, on that day, on the previous day, on the morrow* etc., which refer to a point in time already fixed in the text and do not rely on the definition of a character's present.

An ideologically revealing switch of figural and narratorial temporal perspective is staged by the speaker in Dostoevsky's story "A Gentle Spirit." Here, deictic and anaphoric usages are connected, in reverse, with narratorial and figural perspective:

> That was yesterday evening—and—the following morning...
> In the morning? Madman! why, that morning was today, just now, only just now!
> Listen and try to understand [...] (Dostoevsky, GS, 318; transl. slightly revised)

At first, the diegetic speaker reports from the narratorial perspective, i.e. from the temporal standpoint of the narrative act (the deictic *yesterday evening* refers to the present of the narration). Going over to the report of the following day in the same sentence, the speaker places himself in the tem-

---

19   The examples from Berend, Woolf and Mann are quoted from Hamburger (1957; tr. 1973, 72).

poral position of the narrated self, using not a deictic but an anaphoric statement: *the following morning*. Why does the speaker undertake this change of perspective? Why does he see his "today" as the *following morning* of the narrated self? It is clear that he shies away from the horrifying present in which his wife is laid out on the table, and prefers to dwell in the past before the catastrophe. Taking on a figural position is intended to suppress an insight that becomes unavoidable when the past flows into the present, when the narrated self melts into the narrating self. Despite grasping the identity of the narrated moment (*the following morning*) with the moment of narration, and judging his forgetting of the present (*Madman!*), the speaker still does not reach an admission of guilt, but rather attempts to pull the listener, the imaginary judge, into his apologia (*Listen and try to understand*).

One and the same event can be comprehended in various moments of the narrated story by one character, for example when a character remembers what s/he has experienced and attempts to understand it. The narrator can mention one and the same event in various moments of the narrative act. In both cases, the shift on the temporal axis will be bound up with a change in comprehension, determined by a change in knowledge and—as a consequence—in the respectively accepted norms.

Figural temporal point of view manifests itself, as demonstrated above, in the tight binding of the narration to the character's present. Also characteristic is the coupling of the narration to the perception and experience of this character. The latter connection is expressed, for instance, in a strong detailing of what is narrated (i.e. in the dominance of "expansion" over "compression", see below V.3.e) and in the chronological presentation of events. A consistent figural perspective means the complete reproduction of the events or, more accurately, of their perception by the character in the particular chronology provided by the story. Permutations of the elements against the chronological order (called "anachronies" by Genette 1972) are, in principle, only possible in the figural perspective insofar as they are motivated by acts of consciousness (remembering something from the past or anticipation of something in the future) on the part of the character. An authentic and not merely hypothetical anticipation of later occurrences (which Genette calls "prolepsis") cannot be figurally justified in a realistic storyworld. By contrast, narratorial temporal perspective allows total freedom in dealing with time. The narrator can switch between temporal planes at will and anticipate future developments without coming into conflict with the rules of realistic motivation.

5. Linguistic point of view

The narrator can render the events in his or her own language or also in the language of one of the characters. This alternative also applies to diegetic narrators. They have the choice between their present and past language. The difference between the two languages of one self in varying temporal situations can be significant, in the lexis as well as in the syntax and expression function. Dostoevsky's *A Raw Youth*, in which the interval between experience and narration amounts to only a few months, nonetheless shows clear differences in the nomenclature, syntax and expressiveness used by the narrated and narrating selves.

Figural linguistic point of view can be demonstrated in Dostoevsky's *The Double*. Almost all the way through the work, the narrator takes on the language of the protagonist, Mr. Golyadkin, even when the perceptual perspective is not that of the character, as in the following quotation. The narrator then reproduces the language of the protagonist, not only in its lexis, in the solemn, pathetic, sometimes archaic vocabulary, but also in its syntax, which is, on the one hand, interspersed with the expressions of the chancery, pretentious phrases and pseudo-poetical stylings, and, on the other, shows a certain linguistic inadequacy in the stereotypical repetition of expressions and a colloquial, defective sentence structure, which, in its ellipses and aposiopeses comes close to aphasia. In the quotation, the narrator, who had initially eulogized Berendeyev's ball in dramatic language riddled with rhetorical devices, describes Golyadkin's situation:

> Let us rather return to Mr. Golyadkin, the true and only hero of my very truthful tale. The fact is that he found himself now in a very strange position, to say the least of it. He was also here, gentlemen—that is, not at the dance, but almost at the dance; he was all right, though; he could take care of himself, yet at this moment he was a little astray; he was standing at that moment, strange to say— on the landing of the back stairs to Olsufy Ivanovich's flat. But it was all right, his standing there; he was quite well. He was standing in a corner, huddled in a place which was not very warm, though it was dark, partly hidden by a huge cupboard and an old screen, in the midst of rubbish, litter, and odds and ends of all sorts, concealing himself for the time being and watching the course of proceedings as a disinterested spectator. He was only looking on now, gentlemen; he, too, gentlemen, might go in, of course: why should he not go in? He had only to take one step and he would go in, and would go in very adroitly. (Dostoevsky, D, 164)[20]

---

20 The English translation by Constance Garnett tellingly places some of the figural expressions in quotation marks, which are removed here.

g) Compact and diffuse points of view

The narrator's choice of narratorial or figural perspective often turns out to be the same in respect of all five parameters, i.e. the point of view is consistently narratorial or figural. A point of view which rests on the same choice of one of the two possibilities in all five parameters will be called *compact*. The coincidence of choices regarding the five parameters, resulting in a compact point of view, is displayed in the following diagrams:

Compact narratorial point of view

	Perception	Ideology	Space	Time	Language
Narratorial	x	x	x	x	x
Figural					

Compact narratorial point of view

	Perception	Ideology	Space	Time	Language
Narratorial					
Figural	x	x	x	x	x

However, it is also common for the perspective to be *diffuse*. This is the case when the choices for point of view turn out differently on different planes. A distribution of perspective onto the two entities could be observed in the examples given above. In the extract from "The Student" (p. 111), only the ideological perspective was oriented on the character. In the other parameters, the perspective was, by contrast, narratorial. This distribution of point of view choices is illustrated in the following diagram:

Diffuse point of view
(on the example of the extract from "The Student")

	Perception	Ideology	Space	Time	Language
Narratorial	x		x	x	x
Figural		x			

This picture can require modification, when the opposition of narratorial and figural perspective is neutralized in one parameter (or simultaneously in more than one), either because there are no indications whatsoever or because they can be related to either entity. When, for instance, the opposition of languages in neutralized in a work, the following schema results (in which the other parameters have not been filled in):

2. A model of narrative point of view   117

Neutralization of the opposition of languages

	Perception	Ideology	Space	Time	Language
Narratorial					x
Figural					x

This kind of neutralization can also refer to each of the other parameters and, in the most extreme case, to all of them simultaneously. In that case, the diagram would look like this:

Total neutralization of oppositions
between narratorial and figural points of view

	Perception	Ideology	Space	Time	Language
Narratorial	x	x	x	x	x
Figural	x	x	x	x	x

h) On the methods of analysis: three central questions

In textual analysis, it is time-consuming and not always productive to go through all five parameters of point of view, not least because it is not unusual for there to be no indicators (so that some parameters are not represented at all) or because there is a partial or total neutralization of the opposition between narratorial and figural points of view. For the analysis of shorter sections of text, therefore, a simplified process is to be recommended, which can be extended as required. This method envisages three central questions that concern the fundamental acts of narration: (1) the *selection*, (3) the *evaluation*, (3) the *naming* of elements. These are the acts that correspond to the parameters (1) *perception*, (2) *ideology* and (3) *language*:

1. Who is responsible for the selection of elements in the given textual section? To which entity does the author devolve the act of selecting the elements contained in the story: the narrator or the character? If the selection of narrative units corresponds to the horizon of the character, the question must be asked whether these units are the *actual* contents of the character's consciousness or whether the narrator is merely rendering them according to the character's *modes* of comprehension and thought.

2. Which is the *evaluating* entity in the relevant section?

3. Whose *language* (lexis, syntax, expression) shapes the section?

IV. Narrator's text and characters' text

1. The two components of the narrative text

a) Narrator's discourse and characters' discourse

As early as Plato, it was recognized that the text in a narrative literary work is made up of two components. In *The Republic* (392–94), Plato calls the epic a mixed genre, encompassing both "pure narration" (*diegesis*) and also "imitation" (*mimesis*) of the characters' speeches.[1] Whereas the poet speaks through *diegesis* in the dithyrambs and through *mimesis* in drama, the two modes of representation are mixed in the epic: when reproducing the persons' speeches, the poet speaks in the same way as in drama and, between those speeches, as in the dithyrambs, i.e. as himself.

We will take as our starting point that the *narrative text* is made up of two components, the *narrator's discourse* and the *characters' discourse*. Whereas the narrator's discourse is produced only in the act of narration, the characters' discourse is represented as having existed before the act of narration, and as being merely reproduced in the performance of that act.

b) The characters' discourse in the narrative text

The narrator's discourse and characters' discourse are unified by the narrator to form the *narrative text*. The characters' discourse appears as quotation in the discourse of the narrator, who selects it. The fundamental subordination of the characters' discourse was already indicated by Plato: in the reproduction of the heroes' speeches in the Iliad, Homer "never leads us to suppose that he is anyone else" (*Republic*, 393a). The autonomy of the characters' discourse is, according to Plato, illusory; in reality, the speaking entity in the characters' discourse is still the poet (we would say: the narrator).

The inclusion of the characters' discourse in the narrative text means that it is not necessarily reproduced authentically. The narrator, the creator of the narrative text, can modify the characters' discourse in a particular way, which becomes apparent when he, as can occasionally be observed in

---

1 As noted above (1.2.a), the Platonic concept of *mimesis* means 'imitation' (in contrast to the Aristotelian concept). It must also be emphasized that *diegesis* does not, for Plato, denote the represented world, as in modern narratology, but rather 'pure narration.'

1. The two components of the narrative text

Dostoevsky's works, reproduces one and the same discourse twice, but with different expressions or with different accentuations by the character. In a narrative that holds strictly to the perspective of a subjective and linguistically distinctive narrator, the characters' discourse can be stylistically resprayed, as it were, bringing it closer to the narrator's linguistic horizons. This kind of assimilation is characteristic for the narrative form known in Russian as *skaz* (a term that has found its way via the Russian formalists into the literary study of Western countries, see below, IV.2.b–d). In *skaz*, the ability of the non-professional narrator to authentically reproduce someone else's discourse, particularly discourse from another social milieu, is manifestly deficient. This reveals itself, for instance, in the inadequate reproduction of elaborate or official speech, when the inept narrator attempts to imitate the language unfamiliar to him (on which the comic effect of many *skaz* works is based).

Even when a narrator capable of authentic reproduction of someone else's speech reproduces the characters' discourse trustworthily with regard to its content, and strives for the strict imitation of the axiological and stylistic features of the discourse, as well as its expression, the mere selection of individual sections from the continuum of the character's speech and thoughts, and the non-selection of others, lends the reproduction a certain narratoriality.

In any case, the segments of a character's discourse in the narrative text experience a functional overdetermination, insofar as they express figural contents on the one hand, and, on the other, carry out the doubled task of characterizing that figure and furthering the narration. This means that words intended by the speaking person as communication also serve the narrator, in their reproduction, as means of both characterizing that figure and representing the story.

In general, one can say that the narrator, by quoting the characters' words (or thoughts), employs the characters' discourse for his own ends. The characters' discourse takes on a narrative role, replacing the narrator's discourse. In section II.2.f, it was demonstrated that the narrator, when he reproduces the characters' discourse, uses the figural signifiers and signifieds, and their interdependence, as signifiers that, together with other signifiers, express his narratorial signifieds. That is why all attempts to exclude direct discourse and dialogue from the narrative text and from the field of narratology are mistaken. Proponents of this approach cannot rely on Plato's distinction between *diegesis* as "pure narration" and *mimesis* as the imitation of the characters' discourse, since Plato himself asks the rhetorical question: "And a narrative [*diegesis*] it remains both in the speeches which the poet recites from time to time and in the intermediate passages?" (*Republic*, 393c).

c) Narrator's discourse and narrator's text, characters' discourse and characters' text

Since the beginnings of modern narration in the 18th century, it has been possible to observe that the narrator's discourse does not correspond to the pure, unmixed text of the narrator, but is rather interspersed with features characteristic of the characters' discourse. We must, therefore, introduce a further distinction between the two components that are mixed in the narrator's discourse in modern prose, often in ways that can hardly be disentangled. We call the two components, in their unmixed, pure form, *narrator's text* and *characters' text*. As a rule, the characters' text is portrayed as being fully mimetically represented in the characters' discourse. That is, the rules of fiction envisage that the reader considers the characters' discourse the authentic reproduction of the unmixed characters' text. However, we have seen that the character's speech need not reproduce the character's text entirely mimetically. The narrator can add a narratorial element to the pure character's text, either unintentionally, out of a lack of ability to reproduce someone else's speech authentically, or intentionally, with a particular purpose. In the notebooks for *A Raw Youth*, Dostoevsky repeatedly expressed the sense that the young narrator would not be able to authentically reproduce the concrete form of the adults' discourse along with all its characteristics. And the narrator himself then also often admits that he is reproducing someone else's speech only to the extent that he understood it and that he can remember it.

Since the beginning of modern prose, the difference between narrator's discourse and narrator's text has tended to be larger than that between characters' discourse and characters' text. In modern prose, the characters' discourse results from a complex mixture of features indicating the narrator's text or the character's text.[2] With the increasing *figuralization* of narration, i.e. the increasing orientation of the narration on the perspective of the figure, the elements of the narrator's text recede. In extreme cases of figuralization, the narrator's text is only present in the narrator's discourse in certain grammatical characteristics, whereas, in all other features, from the selection of themes to the linguistic form, it is the characters' text that is realized.

At this point, one might ask why the two components of narrative text are called *texts* and differentiated from the *discourses*. In our use of the term, *text* is distinguished from *discourse* in that it contains the subject sphere of the entity in question, its perceptual, ideological and linguistic point of view in pure, uncontaminated form. This pure, genotypic form, in which the nar-

---

2   On this mixture, characteristic of modern prose, cf. as a basis, the work of Lubomír Doležel 1958; 1960; 1973a; 1993.

1. The two components of the narrative text

rator's text and the character's text must be conceived, is, of course, an abstraction of the phenotypic form in which the discourse that can be directly observed exists. A second difference concerns the extension of the term *text* in the two compounds. *Text* is here taken to mean the complex of all exterior and interior speech, thoughts and perception of both entities, narrator and character. The interference of the two texts, which will be the central concern of this chapter, is not limited to words or statements, but rather pertains to the entire complexes of the two entities' acts of perception and ascription of meaning, including their own ideologies and evaluative positions. That is why the concept of the text used here encompasses, alongside the already linguistically manifested speeches, exterior as well as interior, the acts that remain in the status of thoughts, perception or only of evaluation.[3] The relationships between the terms introduced here are clarified in the following diagram:

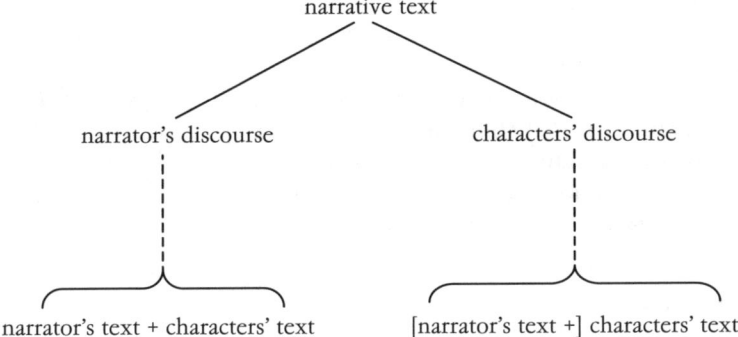

Explanation

The narrative text is constituted (as symbolized by solid lines) of the narrator's discourse and the characters' discourse. In the narrator's discourse are manifested (dashed line) the narrator's text and the characters' text, in varying mixtures in modern prose. The characters' discourse is portrayed as the unmixed manifestation of the characters' text, but it is also entirely possible for it to contain features of the narrator's text. (The comparatively seldom appearance of narratorial revision of the character's discourse is accommodated by the bracketing of *narrator's text*.)

---

3   In this preference for the term *text*, I am following Doležel (1958). However, there is an essential difference between Doležel's and my terms "narrator's text" and "characters' text"; see below.

2. Ornamental prose and *skaz*

Before examining the interference of narrator's text and characters' text more closely, I will discuss two specific stylizations of the narrative text that were cultivated in the literature of the 19th and 20th centuries, especially in the keenly experimental prose of Russian modernism and avant-garde between 1890 and 1930: *ornamental prose* and *skaz*. Comparable forms can also be found in other literatures, both Slavic and Western, but in no other European literature do they appear to play so great a role as in the Russian.

Using Natalya Kozhevnikova's (1971, 115–17) words, it is possible to say that Russian narrative art between 1890 and 1930 is distinguished by the dominance of two "hypertrophies" striving in opposite directions, a "hypertrophy of the literary," manifested in ornamental prose, and a "hypertrophy of characterization," on which *skaz* is based.[4] Whereas the first "hypertrophy" implies a poetization of the narrative text (in both its elements, narrator's discourse and characters' discourse) and is associated with a weakening of the expression function of both the narrator's text and the characters' text, the second hypertrophy manifests itself in a stylization of the narrative text according to the non-literary forms of colloquial speech, as well as in the presentation of verbal communication and the strengthening of the expressivity of the narrative text, which reveals a non-professional narrator, whose thoughts, values and speech can become more important than the story which he is in the process of narrating.

a) Ornamental prose

The problematic term *ornamental prose*,[5] which has, however, become conventional and is now generally accepted, denotes the result of an overdetermination of the narrative text with such specifically poetic techniques as paradigmatization, rhythmization, the creation of thematic and formal

---

4 The Russian term *kharakternost* used by Kozhevnikova means, in this context, the orientation of the narrative text on the narrative subject, i.e. the function that Karl Bühler termed "profession" (*Kundgabe*; 1918/20) or "expression" (*Ausdruck*; 1934).

5 Alternative, more appropriate, terms have not been able to assert themselves. The following are examples: "poetic prose" or "purely esthetic prose" (Zhirmunsky 1921), "poetized prose" (Tynyanov 1922, 132), "lyrical prose" (N. Kozhevnikova 1971, 97), "dynamic prose" (Struve 1951; Oulanoff 1966, 53) or "non-classic prose" (N. Kozhevnikova 1976). On the systematic and historical description of ornamental prose cf.: Shklovsky 1924; Oulanoff 1966, 53–71; Carden 1976; Browning 1979; Levin 1981. The most convincing descriptions are given by N. Kozhevnikova 1971; 1976; Jensen 1984; Szilárd 1986. On *ornamental narration*, a narrativized variant of ornamental prose, cf. Schmid 1992a.

2. Ornamental prose and *skaz*

equivalence, i.e. with the dominance of non-temporal over temporal links (cf. above I.1.h).

Realism and its picture of the world, shaped by empirical sciences, find their expression in the hegemony of the fictional-narrative, of "narrative art" (*Erzählkunst*). By contrast, post-realist modernism has a tendency towards the generalization of the principle constitutive of poetry, the imaginative-poetic, which is realized in "verbal art" (*Wortkunst*).[6] And just as, in realist writing, the laws of narrative prose spread onto poetry, including its non-narrative genres, so, in modernist writing, do the constructive techniques of poetry spread onto the field of narrative prose.

In itself demonstrable in all eras, the traces of ornamental prose accumulate in epochs in which the genre system is dominated by the poetic and the (neo-)mythical thinking underpinning it. Whereas the prose of Russian realism orients itself on the ideal of *narrative art*, the prose of post-realism realizes the other type, *verbal art*.

In English literature, the forms of ornamental prose can be found, for instance, in D. H. Lawrence's novels *The Rainbow* (1915) and *Women in Love* (1920). A high water mark for the poetization of narrative prose is Virginia Woolf's *The Waves* (1931). The poetization becomes particularly clear in the italicized interludes between the interior monologues:

> The sun had not yet risen. The sea was indistinguishable from the sky, except that the sea was slightly creased as if a cloth had wrinkles in it. Gradually as the sky whitened a dark line lay on the horizon dividing the sea from the sky and the grey cloth became barred with thick strokes moving, one after another, beneath the surface, following each other, pursuing each other, perpetually.
> (Woolf, W, 3)

In German literature, the high point of this type of prose, which in German studies is called "lyrical," "poetical," or "rhythmical," coincides with the epoch of symbolism, in which the genre system was dominated by the poetic.

---

6 The symbolist and then formalist concept *verbal art* is contrasted by Hansen-Löve (1978; 1982; 1983; 1984) with the antonym *narrative art*, reconstructed from the thinking of the formalists, and is developed by him into a fertile dichotomy that, as a fundamental opposition, is more accurate than traditional, superficial pairings such as *verse* vs. *prose* or *lyric* vs. *epic* in describing the two hemispheres of the literary world (cf. Schmid 2008a). *Verbal art* is in no way limited to verse or even to lyric, but also appears in prose genres, as can *narrative art* be realized in verse genres. In this respect, the dichotomy *verbal art* vs. *narrative art* covers different ground to *poetry* vs. *prose* not just in its contents but also in its scope. We are dealing with verbal art wherever—in line with Roman Jakobson's famous definition of "poetic function" (1960)—the principle of the paradigm, namely that of equivalence, also comes into effect in the syntagma and overlays its causal-temporal sequentiality. Whereas in non-perspectivized verbal art the archaic, mythic-unconscious imagination unfolds, modern *fiction* is assigned to the perspectivized and stylistically fanned out discourse of narrative art, in which the conscious thought of a reflecting self is assumed.

Ornamental traces are borne particularly by the prose poetry of lyricists such as Stefan George, Hugo von Hofmannsthal and Rainer Maria Rilke. A paradigmatic example of German ornamental prose is Rainer Maria Rilke's *The Lay of Love and Death of Cornet Christopher Rilke*:

> Ein Tag durch den Tross. Flüche, Farben, Lachen –: davon blendet das Land. Kommen bunte Buben gelaufen. Raufen und Rufen. Kommen Dirnen mit purpurnen Hüten im flutenden Haar. Winken. Kommen Knechte, schwarzeisern wie wandernde Nacht. Packen die Dirnen heiß, dass ihnen die Kleider zerreißen. Drücken sie an den Trommelrand. Und von der wilderen Gegenwehr hastiger Hände werden die Trommeln wach, wie im Traum poltern sie, poltern–.
> [...] Rast! Gast sein einmal. Nicht immer selbst seine Wünsche bewirten mit kärglicher Kost. Nicht immer feindlich nach allem fassen; einmal sich alles geschehen lassen und wissen: was geschieht, ist gut. (Rilke, Weise, 144–47)

The following translation reproduces the ornamental element well:

> A day full of baggage and curses, colors and laughter that drown the whole country. Boisterous boys come running, brawling and bawling. Wenches come winking with purple hats in their flowing hair. Soldiers come iron-dark as the wandering night, seizing the women with lust and tearing their clothes, pressing them hard against the edge of the drums. And the drums leap to life awakened by violent resistance of passionate hands, and as in a dream they rattle and roll—. [...] Rest! For once to be a guest. No longer to feed on meager fare. No longer to snatch greedily. For once to let everything come and know: all that happens is good. (Rilke, Lay, 43–55)

This text in "verse-infected prose," as Rilke later disparagingly called it, is an extreme case of poetic stylization of a narrative text, with its dense instrumentation of sounds, in which rhythmization, alliteration, assonance and paronomasias play a large part, a case that is perceived as lying on the border of preciousness, of the stylistically questionable. In Russian prose, which distinguishes itself through a greater linguistic sensuality, however, such intensive ornamentalism shaped a wide current of texts between 1890 and 1930. Many of the later "socialist realists" also paid homage to ornamentalism in their earlier work, in the 1920s.

In the Rilke text, one can observe the aperspectivism of ornamental prose and the weakening of the expression function. Although large parts of the narrative text take the form of the interior monologue, directly linked to the consciousness, in which the narrator's discourse reproduces the perceptions and evaluations of the figural reflector, the ascription of text segments to the narratorial or figural perspective is only barely relevant. This is because the opposition of narrator's text and characters' text is, when at all present, only weakly marked, since overdetermining ornamentalization largely negates the function of ideological and linguistic expression of narrating and speaking subjects in both texts. The narrative text directs the attention entirely onto the poetic element, which organizes both its two components in the same way. And this element is not the expression of realistic, objective thinking, but rather realizes the poetic mode of thought. It lends the text the suggestivity characteristic of mythical speech.

Because of its poeticity, the ornamental element is an artistic icon of myth, whereby poetic and mythical thinking are assumed to be isomorphic. The underlying feature that makes ornamental prose homologous with mythical thinking is the tendency to abolish the non-motivation of signs valid in realism. The word, which, in the realistic approach to language, is only a fundamentally arbitrary symbol determined by convention, tends to become, in ornamentalism as well as in mythical thinking, an icon, an image of its meaning. The iconicity that poetry brings to the prose transformed by it corresponds to the law of magical speaking in myth. There is no mediative convention between name and thing, at heart not even a relationship of reference or representation. The name does not *mean* the thing, it *is* the thing. "The separation of the ideal from the real, [the] distinction between a world of immediate reality and a world of mediate signification, this opposition of 'image' and 'object,' is alien to it," as Ernst Cassirer (1925; tr. 1971, 38) characterizes mythical thought: "Where we see mere 'representation,' myth [...] sees real identity." The myth's pre-semiotic approach to language and the mythical identification of word and thing are displayed in ornamental prose in both the narrative text's tendency to iconicity, in the affinity for realizing tropes, for taking images literally, and for the unfolding of literally understood meanings.[7]

The characteristic iconicity of ornamental prose consists in the tendency to *co-occurrence* or *isotopism* between the orders of discourse and story. Therefore, the assumption of a thematic relevance for various formal relationships is relevant for ornamental prose. This means: every equivalence of the *signantia* suggests an analogous or contrasting equivalence of the *signata*. The general tendency is for every formal ordering on the level of discourse to be ascribed to a thematic ordering in the story. Paronomasia becomes the basic form, a sound repetition that produces an occasional relationship of meaning between words that, in themselves, have neither a genetic, etymological nor semantic connection. It is in paronomasia that the law of mythical thinking formulated by Cassirer comes into effect (1925; tr. 1971, 67), according to which "every perceptible similarity is an immediate expression of an identity of *essence*." The tendency to iconicity, indeed to the reification of all signs, ultimately leads to a relaxation of the border, strictly drawn in narrative art, between words and things, between discourse and story. Ornamental prose forms crossing points between the two levels, whose opposi-

---

7   On the verbal art device of "unfolding" of tropes, semantic figures and proverbs in texts, cf. Hansen-Löve 1982. This technique is already characteristic of Pushkin's verbal-artistic *Belkin Tales* (cf. Schmid 1991, 96–99 et passim).

tions (expression and content, external and internal, arbitrary and essential) are abolished and which appear equally relevant: metamorphoses of pure sound patterns into characters and objects (the best examples of this are provided by the prose of Andrey Bely, particularly the novel *Petersburg*) and the narrative unfolding of verbal figure to sujet motifs (Pushkin's *The Tales of Belkin* contains rich material for this).

The iterativity of the mythical world view corresponds in ornamental prose to the repetition of sound as well as thematic motifs. As the iteration of entire motifs, it produces the system of leitmotifs; as the repetition of single features, it produces equivalence.[8] The system of leitmotifs and the equivalences overlay both the text's linguistic system, where they lead to rhythmization and assonance, and the thematic sequence of the story, onto the temporal progression of which they lay a network of non-temporal concatenation. Where a story is no longer being told, as is the case in purely ornamental prose (e.g. Andrey Bely's *Symphonies*), the techniques of iteration remain the only factors of the text's cohesion, the decisive bearers of thematic coherence and the crucial semantic operators.[9]

The poetization of prose inevitably leads to weakening of its narrativity. This weakening can go so far that an eventful story is not formed at all, so the text merely denotes fragments of a plot, the interrelation between which is no longer narrative-syntagmatic, but only poetic-paradigmatic, produced in line with principles of association, similarity and contrast.

It is certainly true that ornamental prose does not attain great semantic *complexity* in the total dissolution of its narrative substratum, but rather there where the paradigmatization encounters the successful resistance of an eventful narrative. The interference of verbal art and narrative art leads to a deepening of meaning. When poetic techniques constructively reshape the narrative, the two text types' possibilities of meaning enrich each other on their mutual determining and relativization. On the one hand, the poetic links that, as it were, draw a net over the narrative substratum, make new aspects and relationships visible among the narrated situations, characters and plots, while, on the other, the archaic, imaginative thinking of verbal art, where it is integrated into a fictional-narrative context, is subordinated to refraction through perspective and to psychological motivation.

---

8   On the role of thematic and formal equivalences in narrative prose and on the combined effect of temporal and non-temporal links, see above, 1.1.h. More exhaustively: Schmid 1992a, 29–71. On the semantic functions of equivalence also Schmid 1977.

9   Cf. N. Kozhevnikova (1976, 57): "With a sufficiently developed sujet, the leitmotifs exist, as it were, parallel to the sujet; with a weakened sujet, the system of leitmotifs replaces the sujet, compensates for its absence." To that should be added that the iterative techniques (to which, alongside the leitmotifs, formal and thematic equivalences also belong) do not exist only "parallel" to the unfolded sujet, but can also focus, profile and modulate the temporal links.

2. Ornamental prose and *skaz*

In Russian literature, Chekhov's stories, which are before the threshold to the modernist hypertrophy of poetization, provide examples of the highly complex interference between the poetic and the narrative ways of creating semantic interrelationships; as do the works of Isaak Babel and Yevgeny Zamyatin after this threshold has been crossed.[10]

Chekhov's ornamentalizing narration even occasionally gives the impression that the connection between the thematic units is not determined only by the happenings being narrated, but are also steered by the phonic arrangements of the text. This technique specific to verbal art can be seen at one point in "Rothschild's Fiddle," which will, as an exception, be quoted in transcribed Russian for comprehension of the phonic links. The Russian coffin-maker Yakov Ivanov, nicknamed Bronze, a coarse man, whose thoughts center exclusively on the losses made by his business, but who is also an excellent violinist prevented from supplementing his income by playing in the Jewish orchestra only by his hatred of Jews, sits dying on the doorstep of his hut and, while thinking about his "life so full of waste and losses," plays an entirely new "sorrowful and touching" lay on his violin, which brings tears to his, the crude coffin maker's, eyes:

> I chem krépche on dúmal, tem pechál'nee péla skrípka. Skrípnula shchekoldá raz-drugój, i v kalítke pokazálsja Rotshil'd. (Chekhov, PSS, VIII, 304–05)
>
> And the more he thought the more sorrowfully sang his violin. The latch clicked and Rothschild came in through the garden gate. (Chekhov, S, 105)

The first sentence brings the violin's mournful singing into not only a thematic but also a phonic relationship with Yakov's thinking: *krepche* ("the more") appears in *skripka* ("fiddle") and *pechal'nee* ("more sorrowfully"), separated into its phonetic constituent parts. Sensitized by this isotopism of thematic and phonic relationships, the reader will read the second sentence, as well as its connection to the one preceding it, attentively. The words at the join of the sentences, *skripka* ("fiddle") and *skripnula* ("clicked"), which—basically combinable—here nonetheless denote the *agens* and *actio* of two totally different actions, form a paronomasia. This, in turn, suggests a more than coincidental relationship between these actions. The phonic arrangement of the discourse thus founds a nexus of actions, something not performed by the story itself. Naturally, the pre-condition for this is that the reader projects the principle of equivalence from the phonic level to that of the storyline. That is, however, demanded by the tendency to iconicity in ornamental narration. If *skripnula* ("clicked") sounds like a verbal echo of *skripka* ("fiddle") in the discourse, then the repeated creaking of the door's hinges, which announces the fearfully hesitating Rothschild, appears in the

---

10 Cf. my analyses of Chekhov's tales, of Babel's "Crossing the Zbruch" and Zamyatin's "The Flood" in Schmid 1992a, 135–77; Schmid 1998, 213–344.

story as the echo of the mournfully singing violin in the storyline. One can go even further: Rothschild's appearance is motivated both through the story and through the discourse. And it is justified in the story in two ways: Rothschild is supposed to carry out the task assigned by the orchestra leader, namely inviting Yakov to play at a wedding, but he also seems to follow the sound of the violin. And the phonic ornament of the discourse suggests the following: Rothschild, who is metonymically represented by the clicking (*skripnula*) latch, is also summoned by the sound of the word (*skripka*—"fiddle") that metonymically denotes the new thoughts of Yakov Ivanov as he plays his violin on death's threshold (cf. for details Schmid 1992c).

Before and after the blooming of hypertrophic ornamentalization, hybrid, ornamental-narrative prose generates structures that turn the apsychological and non-perspectivized world view of myth into narrative, and subordinate it to perspectivization and psychological motivation. It is not unusual for modernism to make use of the isomorphism between mythic-poetic thinking and ontogenetic as well as phylogenetic antiquity, on one hand, and the activity of the unconscious, on the other; an isomorphism that belongs to the cultural understanding of the epoch. The associative enrichment of meaning typical of narrative art and the fictional embedding of verbal art offer highly complex possibilities for indirect representation of the person and his or her inner world. These possibilities are used, above all, by the prose of Russian modernism, which uses the hybridization of verbal art and narrative art for the modeling of a complex, simultaneously archaic and modern image of man. A model text is, for instance, Yevgeny Zamyatin's "The Cave." In this dystopian narrative written in 1920, a year of famine and hardship, a settlement is described, which stands on the spot where Petersburg was "centuries ago":

> Glaciers, mammoths, wastes. Black nocturnal cliffs, somehow resembling houses; in the cliffs, caves. And no one knows who trumpets at night on the stony path between the cliffs, who blows up white snow-dust, sniffing out the path. Perhaps it is a grey-trunked mammoth, perhaps the wind. Or is the wind itself the icy roar of the king of mammoths? One thing is clear: it is winter. And you must clench your teeth as tightly as you can, to keep them from chattering; and you must split wood with a stone axe; and every night you must carry your fire from cave to cave, deeper and deeper. And you must wrap yourself into shaggy animal hides, more and more of them. (Zamyatin, Cave, 140)

2. Ornamental prose and *skaz*

b) The *skaz*: definitions

Although *skaz* has enjoyed particular interest ever since the work of the Russian formalists (who thought of it as a form of *defamiliarization*), there is still no consensus today on what is meant by the term and what phenomena should sensibly be ascribed to it. In Russian narrative theory, there is hardly another term with such an ambiguous meaning and such an indistinct scope.

It is not unusual for *skaz* to be seen as a form related to ornamental prose or even one that can be subsumed within it. That is justified insofar as both stylizations, although their deviation away from reference-oriented narration is in different directions, similarly lead to a heightened perceptibility of the narrative text. The overlarge extension of the concept of ornamental prose resulting from this approach has led to the emergence of a need for more specific definitions. In the authoritative *Short Encyclopedia of Literature*, Alexander Chudakov and Marietta Chudakova (1971) define *skaz* in the following way:

> [*Skaz*] is a particular type of narration, constituted as narration by a (concretely named or implicit) figure dissociated from the author, and which distinguishes itself though an idiosyncratic style of expression.

According to this, still quite broad, definition, *skaz* coincides with the narrative mode of an entity sufficiently dissociated from the author. This definition covers even narrative texts such as the *Brothers Karamazov*, whose narrator, although he appears in some parts as a relatively chatty chronicler and allows himself all kinds of stylistic ineptitudes, logical inconsistencies and superfluous digressions, narrates competently in others and that even with access to the deepest secrets of the characters. Hardly anyone would want to classify this narrative mode as *skaz*. Anyone who would, would be faced not only with the fluctuation of the narrating entity, the lack of consistency in the execution of the subjective narrative mode, but also with the intellectual horizon and narrative abilities, which one cannot deny the personal narrator, for all his weaknesses.

The overly general definition in the *Short Encyclopedia of Literature* is followed by a certain restriction of the features:

> [...] in *skaz*, the constant perceptibility of a "non-professional" narrative mode comes to the fore, which builds on wording which is "foreign" and often unacceptable to the author. The orientation on the devices of oral narration serves only as a means of placing the narrator's discourse in opposition to both the "author's" words and also, more generally, the literary systems valid to the time.

Alongside the idiosyncratic way of speaking and the dissociation of the narrator from the author, Chudakov and Chudakova stress a third feature, dialogicity:

> The structure of *skaz* is directed at a reader imagined as an interlocutor, to whom the narrator, as it were, directly addresses his words with a lively intonation.

This feature, taken by itself, also proves inadequately discriminating. Active alignment on the fictive reader also characterizes, for instance, the dialogic narrative monologue in Dostoevsky's *Notes from the Underground*. However, the intellectualism and rhetoric dominating in this monologue, as well as its philosophical and psychological themes, cannot be reconciled with the generally held conception of *skaz*.

In *Poetics of Skaz* (Mushchenko, Skobelev, Kroychik 1978, 34), the narrative mode of *skaz* is defined very specifically:

> [*Skaz*] is a double-voiced narration that brings the author and the narrator into a certain correlation, stylized in the orally presented and theatrically improvised monologue of someone who assumes a sympathetic audience, and who is either directly connected with the democratic milieu or oriented on it.

In this definition, various features are connected with each other, which, individually or as a group, have been favored since the beginning of research into *skaz*.

c) The *skaz*: history of research (B. Eikhenbaum, Yu. Tynyanov, V. Vinogradov, M. Bakhtin)

The discussion was opened with Boris Eikhenbaum's "The Illusion of Skaz" (1918), one of the key essays of early formalism. Here, *skaz* is regarded above all as the emancipation of verbal art from the "literariness, which is not always valuable for the verbal artist," as a means of introducing into literature the word as "a living, dynamic act which is formed by voice, articulation, and intonation and is also accompanied by gestures and mimicry" (Eikhenbaum 1918; tr. 1978, 233). In the subsequent essay "How Gogol's 'Overcoat' is Made," Eikhenbaum (1919) underlines the shift of the center of gravity from the plot (which in Gogol's *skaz* is reduced to a minimum) to the devices, which make the language as such "perceptible." In this essay, Eikhenbaum distinguishes two types of *skaz*: (1) "that which narrates" and (2) "that which reproduces" (1919; tr. 1974, 269). The first type refers to *skaz motivated* by the narrator and his language and ideology, and which characterizes him. The second type consists of "devices of verbal mimicry and verbal gesture, in the form of specially devised comic articulations, word-plays based on sounds, capricious arrangements of syntax and so on" (ibid.). "The *skaz* here becomes a kind of play-acting" (270), in which the narrator appears as merely the wearer of linguistic masks. In his essay on the "Overcoat," with its montage-structure and ornamental stylization, Eikhenbaum is interested in only the second type. By contrast, in the later work on Leskov (1925; tr. 1975, 214), he defines *skaz* as a "form of narrative prose which, in vocabulary, syntax, and choice of speech rhythms, displays an orientation toward the narrator's oral speech," and here explicitly excludes from *skaz* all narrative forms "which have a declamatory character or the character of 'poetic prose' and which at the same time are not oriented toward telling, but toward oratorical speech or lyrical monologue." With this definition, he restricts *skaz* to the first, characterizing, perspectivized type. Nevertheless, he does concede the existence of such paradoxical forms as "ornamental *skaz*," which preserves "traces of a folkloric foundation and of *skaz* intonation" but where there is actually "no narrator as such" (1925; tr. 1975, 221). At heart, however, *skaz* does not interest Eikhenbaum as a specific narrative and narratorial phenomenon, but as a "demonstration" of the more general principle of verbal art:

> *Skaz* in itself is not important; what is important is the *orientation toward the word, toward intonation, toward voice*, be it even in written transformation. This is the natural and indispensable basis of narrative prose. [...] We are starting in large measure from the beginning, as it were; and herein lies the historical strength of our time. We perceive many things differently, including the word. Our relationship toward the word has become more concrete, more sensitive, more physiological. [...] We want to hear it and feel it—as a thing. Thus "literature" is returning to "diction," and narration to story telling. (Eikhenbaum 1925; tr. 1975, 223; italics in the original)

Yury Tynyanov (1924b, 160–61) also distinguishes variants of *skaz* in the literature of his time: (1) the older, humorous *skaz*, which goes back to Nikolay Leskov and was cultivated by Mikhail Zoshchenko, (2) the "Remizov-*skaz*," a "lyrical, almost poetical" variant. In the same way as Eikhenbaum, Tynyanov sees the function of *skaz*, in one variant as in the other, as making the word perceptible, but he places his emphasis slightly differently, insofar as he stresses the role of the reader:

> *Skaz* makes the word physiologically perceptible. The entire narrative becomes a monologue and the reader enters into the narration, starts to intone, to gesticulate, to smile. He does not read *skaz*, he plays it. Skaz introduces into prose not the hero, but the reader. (Tynyanov 1924b, 160)

In his essay "The Problem of Skaz in Stylistics," which balanced the discussion, Viktor Vinogradov (1925) calls it inadequate to define the technique with orientation on oral or colloquial speech, since *skaz* was also possible without any kind of orientation on these types of language:

> *Skaz* is a self-willed literary, artistic orientation toward an oral monologue of the narrative type; it is an artistic imitation of monological speech which contains a narrative plot and is constructed, as it were, as if it were being directly spoken. (Vinogradov 1925; tr. 1978, 244)

Similarly to Eikhenbaum and Tynyanov, Vinogradov (1925; tr. 1978, 248–49) distinguishes two types of *skaz*: (1) *skaz* that is bound to a character, and (2) "authorial *skaz*," "preceding from the author's 'I'." Whereas, in the first, "the illusion of an everyday situation is created," "the amplitude of lexical oscillations grows narrow" and "the stylistic motion leads a secluded life within the narrow confines of a linguistic consciousness that is dominated by the conditions of the social mode of life that is to be presented," the second type, the author's *skaz* is "free":

> The writer's 'I' is not a name but a pronoun. Consequently, one can conceal under it whatever one wants to. It is able to conceal forms of speech appropriated from constructions of various bookish genres and from *skaz*-dialectal elements. An integral psychology is also a superfluous burden for the writer. The writer's broad right to transform has always been acknowledged. In the literary masquerade the writer can freely change stylistic masks within a single artistic work. (Vinogradov 1925; tr. 1978, 249)

Eikhenbaum's conception of *skaz* as an orientation toward oral speech is also contradicted by Mikhail Bakhtin, who places new emphases, while focusing only on the "narrating" type (in Eikhenbaum's terminology):

> [Eikhenbaum] completely fails to take into account the fact that in the majority of cases *skaz* is above all an orientation toward *someone else's speech*, and only then, as a consequence, toward oral speech. [...] It seems to us that in most cases *skaz* is introduced precisely for the sake of *someone else's voice*, a voice socially distinct, carrying with it precisely those points of view and evaluations necessary to the author. (Bakhtin 1929; tr. 1984, 191–92; italics in the original)

Someone else's speech is, for Bakhtin, above all the bearer of a different evaluative position. If, however, the orientation on someone else's speech is elevated to a basic feature of *skaz*, phenomena will be ascribed to it that could not be reconciled with it according to a traditional understanding. To these belongs, for example, the intellectual, oratorical speech that closely addresses the listener's evaluative position, as is the case, for instance, in Dostoevsky's *Notes from the Underground*. Natalya Kozhevnikova (1971, 100) is right to state that, in Bakhtin's conception, "*skaz* disappears as an independent narrative form."

d) Characterizing and ornamental *skaz*

In the following sections, a new definition of *skaz* and a systematization of its variants will be attempted, based on the positions discussed. It will be asked pragmatically: which narrative forms and semantic-stylistic phenomena can meaningfully be subsumed into the concept of *skaz*, so that it, on the one hand, retains its differentiating function for textual analysis, and, on the other, is not counter-intuitive? The aim of this definition consists in putting together a catalog of differentiating features, which, taken as a whole, secure a general identifiability of the phenomenon.

Following tradition, it appears sensible to distinguish two basic types of *skaz*:

(1) *Characterizing skaz*, which is motivated by the narrator and realizes his linguistic-ideological perspective.

(2) *Ornamental skaz*, which does not indicate a particular personal narrator, but must be referred to an entire spectrum of heterogeneous voices and masks, and which shows traces of authorial (not narratorial!) ornamentalization.

An exact description according to its features is possible solely for the first, classical type. Ornamental *skaz* can be described only against the background of characterizing *skaz*, and that only by means of the deviations resulting from the poetic reshaping of the narrative text.

e) Features of characterizing *skaz*

It seems meaningful to refer to characterizing *skaz* when the following features are present:

1. Narratoriality
Skaz should be understood as an exclusively narratorial phenomenon. It appears in the text of the narrating entity (regardless of whether this is a primary, secondary or tertiary narrator) and not in a character's text. This basic definition excludes from the domain of *skaz* all semantic-stylistic phenomena that have their origins in the text of a narrated character and are based on an "infection" of the narrator with the style of his or her protagonist (or of the narrated milieu) or on a conscious reproduction of individual features of the characters' discourse.[11]

2. Restrictedness of intellectual horizons
An obligatory feature of classical *skaz* is also the noticeable intellectual distance between the narrator and the author, i.e. the restrictedness of his or her intellectual horizons. The narrator of characterizing *skaz* is a non-professional narrator, a man (or woman) of the people, whose narrative method distinguishes itself through a certain naiveté and clumsiness. This inexperienced narrator does not control all shades of his or her discourse. The result is the tension, characteristic of *skaz*, between what the narrator

---

11 With that, the interpretation of *skaz* as a manifestation of free indirect discourse and similar techniques, as is suggested, for instance, by I. R. Titunik in his works (1963; 1977), is fundamentally rejected.

would like to say and what he actually reveals unintentionally.[12] Without the feature of the narrator as a man of the people, characterizing *skaz* loses its definition.

3. Double-voicedness

The distance between narrator and author determines a narratorial-authorial double-voicedness of the narrator's text. In it, the naive narrator and the author, who presents the former's discourse with particular semantic accentuation, express themselves simultaneously. The double-voicedness also means there is a bi-functionality in the narrator's discourse: it functions as both the representing medium and as represented discourse.

4. Orality

Oral presentation of the narrator's text has been seen as a founding feature of *skaz* since the beginning. Indeed, it is hardly meaningful to talk in terms of characterizing *skaz* if the narrator's discourse in not portrayed as being orally presented. Naturally, oral discourse does not preclude the imitation of written discourse. Many *skaz* narrators, such as Mikhail Zoshchenko's, like to use forms of expression belonging to official written discourse. However, these do then bear traces of their oral reproduction.

5. Spontaneity

Skaz should be understood as a spontaneous oral discourse and not as a prepared speech (such as an orator's address or a barrister's plea). Spontaneity means the representation of the discourse as a developing process that is not necessarily linear, consistent or goal-oriented.[13]

6. Colloquialism

The spontaneous oral discourse of a narrator who is a man of the people bears, as a rule in literary representation, the characteristics of colloquial language and often takes on features of vulgar, non-grammatical or slightly aphasic speech. On the other hand, the colloquialism in no way rules out occasional use of written style. Zoshchenko's "little man" likes to employ the Soviet idiom he has learned from newspapers and propaganda. But the use of literary or official expression is unintentionally defamiliarized in his "mouth" and receives ironic authorial accentuation.

---

12 Cf. Shklovsky's (1928, 17) observation: "*Skaz* motivates a second perception of a given thing. [...] Two levels arise: (1) That which is narrated by the person, (2) That which breaks through in his narrative, as it were, accidentally."

13 More comprehensive on the features of spontaneous discourse cf. Květa Koževniková 1970.

2. Ornamental prose and *skaz*

7. Dialogicity

The orientation of the speaker on his or her listener and his or her reactions is characteristic of *skaz*. So long as the narrator assumes a well-disposed listener from the same milieu, dialogicity does not, as a rule, create any particular tension. The speaker will, in any case, give explanations, anticipate questions and answer them. However, as soon as the *skaz*-speaker ascribes a critical stance to his public, tension will build between him or her and the addressee.

The features listed do not all have the same relevance. Orality, spontaneity, colloquialism and dialogicity are more or less strongly developed in the works traditionally classified as *skaz*. A weaker development of one does not mean the work is necessarily not *skaz*. However, the first three features should be seen as obligatory: narratoriality, restrictedness of intellectual horizons and double-voicedness. Without them, the term (characterizing) *skaz* loses its meaning.

It is not unusual for *skaz* to be oriented on a secondary narrator. In this case, the frame story is, as a rule, limited to a few short sentences that serve as an introduction to the scene of a lively narration, as is the case in, for example, Zoshchenko's short story "The Lady Aristocrat":

> Fellows, I don't like dames who wear hats. If a woman wears a hat, if her stockings are fuzzy, if she has a lap dog in her arms, or if she has a gold tooth, such a lady aristocrat, to my mind, is not a woman, but just a void.
>
> But there was a time when I felt the attractions of an aristocratic lady. When I went out walking with one and took her to the theater. It was in the theater that it all happened. There, in the theater, she unfurled her ideology to its full length. (Zoshchenko, LA, 54)

f) Ornamental *skaz*

Ornamental *skaz* is a hybrid phenomenon, based on a paradoxical mixture of the actually mutually excluding principles of characterization and poetization.[14] In contrast to characterizing *skaz*, ornamental *skaz* does not indicate a personal narrator endowed with non-professional characteristics, but rather, insofar as an expression function is at all in force, calls into being an impersonal narrating entity that appears in various roles and masks. Of the features of characterizing *skaz*, a basic oral tone, traces of colloquialism and the narrative gestures of a personal narrator can remain in ornamental *skaz*, but these traits no longer indicate the unified figure of a narrator, no longer combine to form the unity of a personality and psychology, but are oriented

---

14 This mixture is comprehensively described in the work of N. A. Kozhevnikova (especially 1994, 64–74).

on an entire spectrum of heterogeneous voices. Ornamental *skaz* is multifaceted and poly-stylistic, fluctuating between orality and literacy, colloquialism and poetry, literature and folklore.

Ornamental *skaz* combines narrativity with poeticity; to the extent, however, that the poeticity, along with non-temporal links that constitute it, supplants the story's temporal links, ornamental *skaz*, which is positioned on the border of narrative literature anyway, moves from the domain of narrative art into that of verbal art. The impersonal narrator then appears only as the intersection of heterogeneous verbal gestures, as the point at which different stylistic lines converge. In ornamental *skaz*, not only is the expression function of the text in reference to the narrator decreased, but the role of perspective is generally weakened. Insofar as characters' discourses are at all represented, they tend to remain stylistically subordinated to the homogenizing poetization and display no linguistic individuality. The opposition of narrator's text and characters' text is largely neutralized by the poetic-ornamental reshaping. It is also true of consistently characterizing *skaz* that the difference between narrator's discourse and characters' discourse is often weakened. But, in that case, it is not caused by the fundamental reduction of perspective, but rather by the fact that the narrator, limited in his or her abilities, is hardly capable of bringing other styles to life, and thus narratorially reshapes the characters' text by necessity. Whereas characterizing *skaz* is conclusively motivated by the ideological and linguistic physiognomy of the concrete speaker, ornamental *skaz* distinguishes itself through reduced, diffuse perspective, through characterological non-motivation, and the esthetic self-referentiality of the narrative text.

Ornamental *skaz* is represented by Gogol's short story "The Overcoat". The first sentence of the initial draft contained a play on sound: "In the Department of *Assessments* and *Collections*—which, however, is sometimes called the Department of *Nonsenses* and *Confections*" (Eikhenbaum 1919; tr. 1974, 276).

Etymological puns are particular favorites of Gogol's, as Eikhenbaum (ibid.) notes, and he vacillated for a long time between various surnames for his hero. In the end, he decided on Bashmachkin, a name that, according to Eikhenbaum, had the advantages over its competitors of "greater expressive power" and that it "produces a kind of phonic gesture." This name, which sounds extremely strange in Russian, is explained by the narrator in a pointedly absurd way:

> From the name alone it is already clear that it was derived from the word for shoe [in Russian *bashmak*]; but when, at what time, and in what manner it derived from 'shoe'—of this nothing is known. His father, his grandfather, and even his brother-in-law, and absolutely all the Bashmachkins wore boots,

2. Ornamental prose and *skaz*

merely having them resoled about three times a year. (Eikhenbaum 1919; tr. 1974, 277)

The illogicality of this narration does not characterize the narrator. His naiveté is not authentic, but feigned. The very abstract and diffuse narrating entity, which manifests itself in diverse rhetorical devices, plays out various linguistic and ideological roles. A distance between the subject of this ornamental *skaz*, assembled out of heterogeneous ways of speaking, who handles the language ironically and playfully, and the author, remains, of course, but is perceptible only with difficulty. This is why Vinogradov (1925) also calls this type "authorial *skaz*" (see above, p. 132). Of the clear, unambiguous authorial-narratorial double-voicedness, as distinguishes the *skaz* of Gogol's forewords to *Village Evenings near Dikanka* (cf. above, II.5.b), there is no trace.

3. The interference of narrator's text and characters' text

a) The structure of text interference

The subjectivity of the narrator's discourse, which is bound up with *skaz*, owes itself to the subjectivity of the narrator. However, there are also phenomena of subjectivity in the narrator's discourse that have a fundamentally different origin, namely that they are not traced back to the narrator, but to the character. Figural subjectivity encroaches on the narrator's discourse via the structure that will be called the *interference of narrator's text and characters' text*, or, more concisely, *text interference* (Schmid 1973, 39–79).

Text interference is a hybrid phenomenon, in which *mimesis* and *diegesis* (in the Platonic sense) are mixed, a structure that unites two functions: the reproduction of the characters' text (*mimesis*) and the actual narration (*diegesis*). The text interference, which is characteristic of narrative prose, with its two components, appears in various forms, of which the so-called *free indirect discourse* (subsequently FID) has most often been the subject of academic study.

In these forms, the interference results from the way that, in one and the same segment of the narrator's discourse, certain features refer to the narrator's text and others, in contrast, to the characters' text. As a result of the distribution of features to both texts and the expression function pointing in two directions, these texts are simultaneously realized in one and the same segment of the narrator's discourse. The simultaneous realization of narrator's text and characters' text is shown in the following diagram:

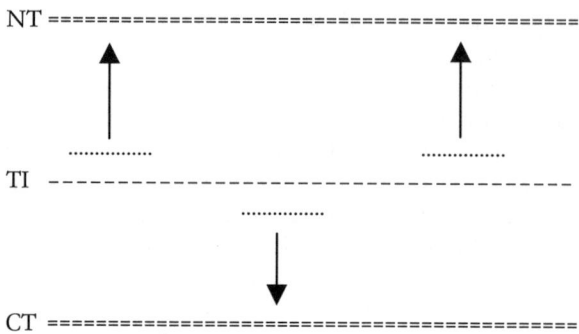

Explanation

NT = Narrator's Text. TI = Text Interference. CT = Characters' Text. Dashed Line (----) = Segment of the narrator's discourse, that refers to the NT in some individual features and to the CT in others. Dotted Line (......) = the features contained in a given segment. Doubled Dotted Line (====) = the NT or CT realized by means of these features.

Mikhail Bakhtin (1934/1935; tr. 1981, 304) has already pointed out the double-structure, which he calls a "hybrid construction," of text interference:

> What we are calling a hybrid construction is an utterance that belongs, by its grammatical (syntactic) and compositional markers, to a single speaker, but that actually contains mixed within it two utterances, two speech manners, two styles, two "languages," two semantic and axiological belief systems.

The term *text interference* draws on Valentin Voloshinov's (1929; tr. 1973, 137) concept of "speech interference," but does not coincide with it in terms of what is denoted. As a prime example of speech interference, Voloshinov quotes an extract from Dostoevsky's tale "A Nasty Story":

> Once in winter, on a cold and frosty evening—very late evening, rather, it being already the twelfth hour—three *extremely distinguished* gentlemen were sitting in a *comfortable*, even sumptuously appointed, room inside a *handsome* two-story house on Petersburg Island and were occupied in *weighty* and *superlative* talk on an *extremely remarkable* topic. All three gentlemen were officials of the rank of general. They were seated around a small table, each in a *handsome* upholstered chair, and during pauses in the conversation they *comfortably* sipped champagne. (Quotation according to Voloshinov 1929; tr. 1973, 135; his italics)

Voloshinov remarks that the "colorless, banal, insipid epithets," which are italicized in his quotation, originated in the consciousness of the generals and received ironic and mocking accentuation in the context of the narration.

Each of these colorless, banal, insipid epithets is an arena in which *two* intonations, *two* points of view, *two* speech acts converge and clash. [...] Thus almost every word in the narrative (as concerns its expressivity, its emotional coloring, its accentual position in the phrase) figures simultaneously in two intersecting contexts, two speech acts: in the speech of the author-narrator (ironic and mocking) and the speech of the hero (who is far removed from irony). [...] We have here a classic instance of a linguistic phenomenon almost never studied—the phenomenon of *speech interference*. (Voloshinov 1929; tr. 1973, 135-37)

Voloshinov's concept of "speech interference" assumes an ideological double-accentuation of the two discourses. In contrast, text interference is present even when the features of a segment refer to the two texts simultaneously. A definite difference in the evaluative position of the two texts realized is not necessary for text interference. The total ideological agreement of the two texts is also possible as a borderline case. So, the concept of text interference used here is wider in scope than Voloshinov's "speech interference" and does not automatically imply those agonal structures that Bakhtin and Voloshinov place underneath "double-voiced" structures such as interference and dialogicity.[15]

b) The opposition of the texts and their features

The analysis of text interference based on a catalog of features in which narrator's text and characters' text can differ goes back to the work of Lubomír Doležel (1958; 1960; 1965; 1967; 1973a; 1993). But the premises and methods of analysis suggested here are essentially different from Doležel's approach. Doležel takes as his starting point the fixed opposition of the "objective" text of the narrator and the "subjective" text of the character. According to Doležel (1993, 12), the narrator's text exercises an exclusively "representational function" (in the sense of Bühler's language function, 1934) and is characterized by exclusive alignment on the represented object. As Doležel also points out, the expression and appeal functions, i.e. the activation of the relation between text and speaker, or listener, are annulled in the narrator's text. Any subjectivity, i.e. any actualization of the relation of the text to speaker or listener, is seen by Doležel (1960) as a "stylistic technique," which takes away the fundamental feature of the narrator's text, namely its objectivity.[16] It is clear that this kind of rigid and circularly justi-

---

15 On the difference between Voloshinov's "speech interference" and my text interference, and on the concentration of Bakhtin and Voloshinov on agonal text structures cf. Schmid 1989b.
16 We find a similar idealization in Elena Paducheva (1996, 336-37), who defines "traditional narration" as "narration in the third-person," containing no deixis, "expressivity" or "dialogicity."

fied idealization is neither methodologically helpful nor historically demonstrable. In his organon model of language, on which Doležel draws, Bühler knew better than to allow for the exclusive effect of one function, that of "representation," and the annulment of the two others, "expression" and "appeal."[17] The objective narration postulated by Doležel is a construct, an ideal type realized only in certain cases, when literature is reacting to a preceding hypertrophic subjectivization (cf. Holý 2000). But there is no justification for elevating a borderline case to the status of the standard form.

Instead of constructing an absolute opposition of idealized texts, we will assume that both texts are endowed to the same extent with the traits of objective object-orientation and subjective listener-orientation, and can exercise the expression function to the same extent. That the narrator's text is not necessarily less subjective than the characters' text is sufficiently demonstrated in all European literatures from sentimentalism all the way through to realism.

But why does Doležel assume a fixed opposition of texts, and why does he postulate as the standard form an absolutely objective narrator's text that is hardly ever encountered in the reality of literature? It is presumably as a result of the need for methodological simplification, the desire to transfer the system of distinctive features, appropriate in phonology, to textual phenomena. This system is intended to simplify the identification of segments of the narrator's discourse as oriented on either the narrator or the character. If subjectivity can be seen as a distinctive feature of the characters' text, then every appearance of subjective traits in the narrator's discourse leads to the conclusion that the character's text is present. However, if one concedes that subjectivity, or the appearance of the expression and appeal functions, in themselves, are not distinctive, insofar as they can appear in the narrator's text as well as in the characters' text, then Doležel's method proves unsuitable for the analysis of text interference.

In the following, a catalog of features will be compiled, in which it is *possible* for the narrator's text (henceforth: NT) and the characters' text (CT) to differ. This catalog does not assume a certain type of texts or their absolute opposition, but rather starts from the empirical fact that the texts can have very different profiles in different works. For this reason, it is, as a catalog of possible differing features, applicable to every concrete work.

Naturally, this catalog of features corresponds to the catalog of parameters distinguished for perspective:

---

17 The characters' text is also idealized by Doležel when he attributes to it an absolute subjectivity, i.e. strong activation of the relationships of the text with speaker and listener. However, it is thoroughly possible for a subjective narrator to represent an objective, entirely factually speaking character.

3. The interference of narrator's text and characters' text

Parameters of perspective	Features for the differentiation of NT and CT
Perception	Thematic
Ideology	Ideological
Space	Grammatical
Time	Grammatical
Language	Stylistic

The grammatical and stylistic features need further differentiation. As a result, we obtain the following catalog of features:

1. Thematic features
NT and CT can differ in the *selection* of what is thematized and in characteristic themes.

2. Ideological features
NT and CT can differ in the *evaluation* of individual thematic units and in their general *evaluative position*.

3. Grammatical features of person
NT and CT can differ in the use of *grammatical person, pronouns* and *verb forms*. In order to describe the characters in the storyworld, the non-diegetic narrator uses the pronouns and verb forms of the third person exclusively. In the CT, the system of three grammatical persons is used: the speaking entity is described with the first person, the character addressed with the second person and a character under discussion is referred to with the third person.

4. Grammatical features of tense
NT and CT can differ in the use of tense. As a rule, three tiers of tense (present, past, future) are used in the CT. In the NT, as a rule, the epic preterite or the historical present (functioning as an equivalent) are used to describe the action in the storyworld. (In statements that refer not to the diegesis but to the exegesis, that is, in comments, auto-thematization, reader's apostrophes and so on, the narrator can, of course, use all three tenses.)

5. Grammatical features of the orientation system
NT and CT can use different orientation systems to describe space and time. The use of chronotopic deictic forms that are oriented on the character's "Origo of the Here-Now-I system" (see above, I.2.b) is characteristic of the CT, e.g. *today, yesterday, tomorrow, here, there, right, left*. In the NT, the deictic terms are replaced with anaphoric orientation terms, such as *on that day, that*

same morning, the day before, on the day after the events described, in the same place, to the right of the hero, i.e. expressions that orient themselves on statements already made in the text, but that do not presuppose a knowledge of the character's Origo.[18]

6. Features of language function

NT and CT can be characterized by different language functions (representation, expression, appeal).

7. Stylistic features of the lexis

NT and CT can be characterized by the use of different names for one and the same object (*Alexander Ivanovich* vs. *Sasha*; *horse* vs. *steed*) and by differing lexical repertoires in general, whereby the narrator's text is not necessarily literary or stylistically neutral, the characters' text not necessarily colloquial.

8. Stylistic features of the syntax

NT and CT can be characterized by differing syntactical patterns.

Doležel (1960) distinguishes five primary distinctive features and assumes the following constant opposition of the "narratorial plane" and the "figural plane":

(1) "Formal" features: CT contains all three grammatical persons and all three tenses; NT contains only one (third) grammatical person and only one tense (the preterite). (2) "Functional-situative" features: CT uses both (a) the expression and appeal language functions and (b) deixis; none of these features appear in the NT. (3) "Semantic" features: whereas, in the CT, certain means are used to express the subjective semantic aspect, the semantic aspect is not expressed in the NT. (4) "Stylistic" features: the stylistic specification of the CT on the basis of colloquial style is contrasted with the stylistically unspecified NT. (5) "Graphic" features: the statements of the CT are graphically marked; those of the NT are not.

Missing from Doležel's model are the thematic features, which prove to be extremely relevant in textual analysis, and often decisive in the classification of a segment. The graphic features do not belong in this series: they are not features of the CT itself, but features of its presentation in the narrative text. In contrast to Doležel, I do not assume that the NT, in the "formal," "functional-situative," "semantic," and "stylistic" features, is always objective or neutral, nor that the CT is always subjectively marked.

---

18   A comprehensive examination of deictic and anaphoric reference in the representation of speech and thought, particularly in FID, can be found in Fludernik 1993a, 110–46.

3. The interference of narrator's text and characters' text

c) The pure texts and the neutralization of oppositions

If, in a given segment of narrative text, all the features mentioned are represented and all the possible oppositions of NT and CT are realized, the following diagram of the distribution of those features is produced for the pure, unmixed texts:

Narrator's text

	1. Theme	2. Evaluation	3. Person	4. Tense	5. Orientation syst.	6. Lang. function	7. Lexis	8. Syntax
NT	x	x	x	x	x	x	x	x
CT								

Characters' text

	1. Theme	2. Evaluation	3. Person	4. Tense	5. Orientation syst.	6. Lang. function	7. Lexis	8. Syntax
NT								
CT	x	x	x	x	x	x	x	x

However, the pure texts are often not realized in the reality of literature, since the opposition of the texts can be partially *neutralized*. (This neutralization is represented in the diagram by an *x* for both NT and CT.[19]) Neutralization of the opposition of NT and CT takes place in two instances:

(1) If certain features do not appear at all in a given segment (which applies most frequently to the features of grammatical person and the orientation system).
(2) If NT and CT coincide in one of the features.

The coincidence of NT and CT in one feature takes place when the two texts are identical in respect of that feature. So, the grammatical past used by the CT can coincide with the NT's epic preterite. The opposition of texts is then neutralized, in respect of the time feature, in all preterite forms that describe the character's past. The narration can naturally make use of the historical present. In that case, the neutralization applies to all segments that

---

19 In order to avoid misunderstandings, it should be noted that the concept of *neutralization* used here denotes a different structure to that in Doležel (1965), where the concept refers to our text interference.

describe the character's present.[20] In non-diegetic narration, the opposition of NT and CT is neutralized in all segments in which a third person is reported on (i.e. not the character speaking or spoken to): in both the NT and the CT, the character discussed then appears in the grammatical third person.

In the cases just mentioned, the neutralization is *local*, i.e. it refers only to single segments of the narrative text. This kind of local neutralization is also possible regarding the features 1, 2, 5, 6, 7, and 8. So, for instance, it is possible to refer the lexis in particular statements of the narrator's discourse to both the NT and the CT, and, in others, to only one of the two.

Regarding the features 1, 2, 6, 7, and 8, the opposition of NT and CT can be neutralized in the entire narrative text. That is then a case of *global* neutralization. This applies most frequently to the features lexis and syntax. If the narrator and the character are, for example, endowed with the same style, which is normal in pre-realistic literature and in *skaz*, the feature lexis does not differentiate between NT and CT in the entire work.

The features 3, 4, 5, and 6 are subject to a caveat. They differentiate NT and CT only in statements that refer to the diegesis, to the storyworld. In the narrator's comments, i.e. in all statements that refer to the exegesis, we encounter the same traits as in the statements of the characters: first-person, present tense, deictic adverbs, expression and appeal functions. So, the well-known exclamation of the narrator in Karamzin's "Poor Liza" sounds, in the features 3, 4, 5, and 6, exactly like the statement of a character. Only the theme (1) and the evaluation (2) point to the narrator:

> Ah! I love those objects which touch my heart and force me to shed tears of tender sorrow! (Karamzin, SP, 55)

The distribution of features in this case is the following:

	1. Theme	2. Evaluation	3. Person	4. Tense	5. Orientation syst.	6. Lang. function	7. Lexis	8. Syntax
NT	x	x	x	x	x	x	x	x
CT			x	x	x	x	x	x

In diegetic narration, there are other conditions for the differentiation of NT and CT and for the neutralization of their oppositions. Insofar as the narrated character coincides with the narrator's earlier self, NT and CT are, in general, less strongly differentiated than in non-diegetic narration. (Naturally, the non-diegetic situation applies to all characters in diegetic narration except the narrated self.) When the narrated self is being reported on (when

---

20 The opposition of texts is, of course, neutralized in feature 4 (time) in all generally valid statements in the gnomic present.

3. The interference of narrator's text and characters' text   145

not, as with Caesar, described with the third-person) in diegetic narration, feature 3 (person) is completely abandoned for the differentiation of NT and CT. In lexis and syntax, the NT is not categorically distinguished from the text of the narrated self. A certain difference is, however, thoroughly possible, depending on the character's changed external and internal situation. The opposition of texts will consist primarily in their thematic and evaluative features. Their power to differentiate depends on how far the evaluative position of the narrating self has moved away from that of the narrated self. In this, the temporal interval is not decisive. In Dostoevsky's *A Raw Youth*, in which the exegesis is separated from the diegesis by only a few months, the narrating self presents itself as entirely distanced from the evaluative position of the narrated self.

d) Text interference as a transformation of the characters' text

Text interference is based on the distribution of the features of one segment of narrator's discourse to NT or CT. Text interference is in evidence even when only one feature refers to a different text than the others. One type of FID in English, German and many other languages, when all relevant features are present, is illustrated in the following diagram:

	1. Theme	2. Evaluation	3. Person	4. Tense	5. Orientation syst.	6. Lang. function	7. Lexis	8. Syntax
NT			x					
CT	x	x		x	x	x	x	x

Cases of text interference have been observed as early as in the literature of antiquity and in that of the Middle Ages. Traces are found, for instance, in Old French texts, in the Middle High German *Nibelungenlied* and in the Old Russian *Primary Chronicle*. However, these are always cases of mere grammatical abbreviation in the reproduction of speech and thought, without any particular intended effect. Text interference as a consciously and systematically employed technique, especially FID, became widespread in European literatures only after the start of the 19th century.[21] In German literature, Goethe's *Elective Affinities* (1809) is an early example (cf. Pascal 1977, 11); in English literature, Jane Austen's *Emma* (1816) is often postulated as being

---

21 On the development of FID in French literature: G. Lerch 1922; Lips 1926; Verschoor 1959; in German literature: Neuse 1980; 1990; in English literature: W. Bühler 1937; Glauser 1948; Neubert 1957; in Russian literature: Hodel 2001.

the first example of the systematic use of text interference.[22] In Russian literature, text interference as a consciously handled technique was introduced by Alexander Pushkin (cf. Voloshinov 1929; Bakhtin 1934/1935) and developed by Mikhail Lermontov, Nikolay Gogol und Ivan Goncharov. But it is in the early narratives of Dostoevsky that text interference first appears as a dominant technique applied for a clear and intended effect in the construction of the text (cf. Schmid 1973, 39–79). *The Double* (1846) provoked critical irritation and rejection because the technique underpinning it was not identified. In French literature, an analogous role was played by Gustave Flaubert, whose *Madame Bovary* (1857), with its mixed narratorial-figural presentation of the adulteress's sinful thoughts, still unusual at the time, directed the moral outrage of his contemporaries towards the author, who was thought to be speaking in his own name (cf. LaCapra 1982).

The proliferation of text interference is a consequence of the increasing figuralization of narration, i.e. the shifting of perspective from the narratorial to the figural. This figuralization sometimes gives the impression that the narrator is abdicating the narrative function to the character and, as it were, "leaving the stage." The conception of the disappearance of the narrator underlies countless models of FID, from Charles Bally (1912; 1914; 1930) through to Ann Banfield (1973; 1978a; 1978b; 1983) and Elena Paducheva (1996). Doležel's (1973a, 7) model, as discussed above, amounts to the same replacement of the narrator with the character, and envisages the transfer of the functions characteristic of the narrator, *representation* and *control*, to the character. In contrast, however, to all theories that postulate the disappearance of the narrator and his or her replacement with the character, the model suggested here will work from the assumption that the narrator, even in the "most objective" FID, fundamentally remains "on stage," i.e. that the NT, which is realized at least by feature 3 (person), is present simultaneously with the CT.

The concept of text interference implies that the characters' text, portrayed as pre-existing, is processed, narratorially transformed—even if only to a minimal extent—in the narrative text. Between pure NT and pure CT stretches a wide range of mixed forms, with more or less marked narratorial transformations and differing distributions of features to CT and NT.[23] Certain steps of this transformation are pre-determined by the language-specific modes of how the CT is reproduced, which are categorized in English (and similarly in other Indo-European languages) as *direct discourse* (subsequently DD), *indirect discourse* (ID) and *free indirect discourse*.

---

22 M. Klepper (2004, 73), however, points to English narrative works of the 1790s, which already make use of text interference.
23 For a scale from the purely diegetic to the purely mimetic possibilities of speech representation comprising seven forms cf. McHale 1978.

3. The interference of narrator's text and characters' text

In the following sections, ID and FID will be treated as narratorial transformations of the direct discourse, whereby it will be assumed that direct discourse authentically reproduces the character's text (something which, as we have seen, need not always be the case in literary texts). In deciding whether to refer features to the NT or CT, we will work from the starting point of a neutral NT in the given example sentences. Without a background of this type, formed in the concrete work by the entire profile of both texts, a feature-oriented analysis is not possible.

1. Direct discourse

She asked herself, "Oh! Why do I have to pitch up to this dumb Christmas party today? After all, Christmas isn't till tomorrow!"

	1. Theme	2. Evaluation	3. Person	4. Tense	5. Orientation syst.	6. Lang. function	7. Lexis	8. Syntax
NT								
CT	x	x	x	x	x	x	x	x

2. Indirect discourse

She asked herself why she had to pitch up to this dumb Christmas party today; after all, Christmas wasn't till tomorrow.

	1. Theme	2. Evaluation	3. Person	4. Tense	5. Orientation syst.	6. Lang. function	7. Lexis	8. Syntax
NT			x	x		x		x
CT	x	x			x	x	x	

The use of the third person to describe the person speaking, the tense and the syntax all point to the NT. In respect to the remaining features, either the CT is represented or the textual opposition is neutralized.

3. Free indirect discourse

Oh! Why did she have to pitch up to this dumb Christmas party today? After all, it wasn't Christmas till tomorrow!

	1. Theme	2. Evaluation	3. Person	4. Tense	5. Orientation syst.	6. Lang. function	7. Lexis	8. Syntax
NT			x	x				
CT	x	x			x	x	x	x

In this example, the FID differs from the ID in the language function (feature 6 for CT) and syntax (feature 8 for CT).

In the forms of text interference, the following contents of the characters' text are reproduced: (1) statements, (2) thoughts, (3) perceptions and emotions, and (4) evaluative position.

In the following diagram, the correlation between (1) the contents of the reproduced CT, (2) the forms of the reproduced CT and (3) the preferred patterns of representation, is illustrated:

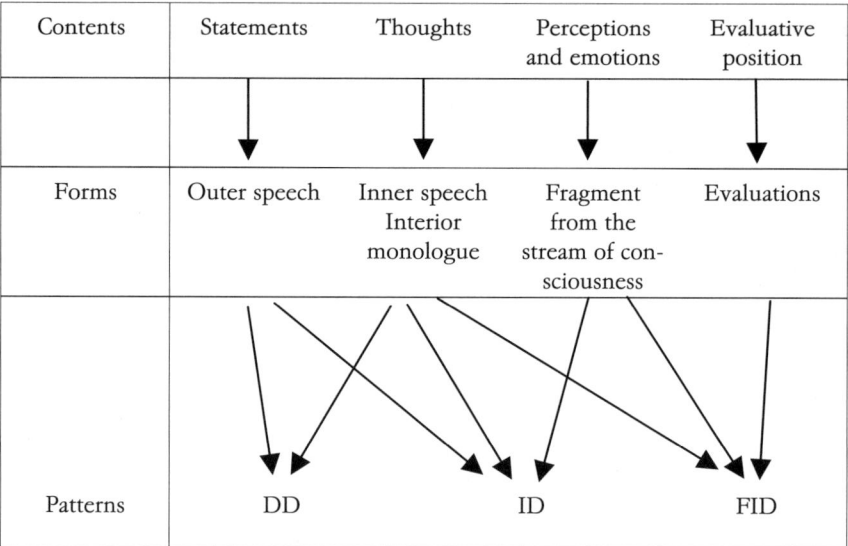

In Western literatures, FID rarely serves the reproduction of outer speech. Although there are references in the literature on FID to cases in which it is used for the representation of spoken discourse (cf. Sokolova 1968, 29–31), those are almost always examples not of the reproduction of spoken discourse itself, but rather of the *perception* of the outer speech by one of the characters (cf. Kovtunova 1955, 138).

e) Direct discourse and direct interior monologue

In DD, as can be seen in the diagram, both the character's outer and inner speech are represented. The direct mode signals authentic reproduction of the CT. There are, however, some deviations from complete representation of the CT in the DD, which will be discussed in the following.

If NT and CT do not differ in their lexical and syntactic features throughout the course of the work, that is, the opposition of the texts is neutralized in this feature, then we are dealing with a variant of the basic type of DD that can be called *de-individualized DD*. This variant is encountered in European literatures before the 19th century, although it is not consciously employed as a literary technique. Where it appears in more recent literature, as for example in modern ornamental prose, it can serve particular esthetic aims. But it has as little in common with text interference as does the basic type of DD, in which all features point to the CT.[24]

We call a longer passage of inner speech *interior monologue*. Interior monologue (which is not rarely falsely identified with FID) can be represented both in the pattern of DD and in FID. In the first scenario, we can refer to *direct interior monologue*, and, in the second, to *free indirect (interior) monologue*.

As a rule, direct interior monologue is conceptualized as a literal, authentic reproduction of a character's inner speech, a reproduction that retains not only the contents of the CT, but also all grammatical, lexical, syntactic and language function peculiarities. But direct interior monologues do not always reproduce the CT's stylistic profile. It is not rare to come across a "de-individualized" variant of the direct interior monologue, in which the syntax of the character's thoughts and reflections has been narratorially transformed. An example of this is provided by one of Pierre Bezukhov's monologues in Tolstoy's *War and Peace*:

> "Elena Vassilyevna, who has never cared for anything but her own body, and is one of the stupidest women in the world," Pierre thought, "is regarded by people as the acme of wit and refinement, and is the object of their homage. Napoleon Bonaparte was despised by every one while he was really great, and since he became a pitiful buffoon the Emperor Francis seeks to offer him his daughter in an illegal marriage. [...] My Masonic brothers swear in blood that they are ready to sacrifice all for their neighbor, but they don't give as much as one ruble to the collections for the poor [...]. We all profess the Christian law of forgiveness of sins and love for one's neighbor—the law, in honor of which we have raised forty times forty churches in Moscow—but yesterday we knouted to death a deserter; and the minister of that same law of love and forgiveness, the priest, gave the soldier the cross to kiss before his punishment."
>
> Such were Pierre's reflections, and all this universal deception recognized by all, used as he was to seeing it, was always astounding him, as though it were something new. (Tolstoy, WaP, 505)

---

24 Doležel (1960, 189; 1973a, 42–49) teases out a variety of DD, which he calls "unmarked direct discourse." It lacks any kind of separation of the character's speech from the narrative text. However, insofar as the marking cannot be seen as a feature of the CT (see above, p. 142), "unmarked direct discourse" is not a case of text interference.

Pierre Bezukhov here obviously serves as a mouthpiece for the author (from whom the narrator is hardly dissociated) and expresses an authorial truth. His interior monologue has been processed by the narrator, smoothed out and matched to the style of his narratorial discourse. In cases such as this, the characterizing function of the interior monologue is dominated by the authorial-ideological function. In this example, the traits of an associative development of the thoughts are missing, as are the features of a spontaneous production. Tellingly, the style does not change during the switch from direct interior monologue to the narrator's discourse.

As a rule, the author of *War and Peace* gives the monologues of his characters little figural freedom. But we also find interior monologues in the novel in which the processes of perception, memory and reflection are directly presented. Of this type is, for instance, the monologue in which Andrey Bolkonsky admits to himself his lust for glory:

> "Well, and then?" said the other voice again, "what then, if you do a dozen times over escape being wounded, killed, or deceived before that; well, what then?" "Why, then..." Prince Andrey answered himself, "I don't know what will come then, I can't know, and don't want to; but if I want that, if I want glory, want to be known to men, want to be loved by them, it's not my fault that I want it, that it's the only thing I care for, the only thing I live for. Yes, the only thing! I shall never say to any one, but, my God! what am I to do, if I care for nothing but glory, but men's love? [...]" (Tolstoy, WaP, 242–43)

When Tolstoy, the psychologist of everyday consciousness, describes particular mental states—dozing, feverishness, intense excitement—he uses a figural, purely "mimetic" type of interior monologue, whose associations are based not only on thematic coherence and contiguity, but also on phonic equivalence, as is the case in the following monologue, from Nikolay Rostov, a variation on the phonic motif *Na-tash-a*:

> "It must be snow—that spot: a spot—*une tache*," Rostov mused dreamily. "But that's not a *tache*... Na...tasha, my sister, her black eyes. Na...tasha (won't she be surprised when I tell her how I've seen the Emperor!) Natasha...tasha... sabretache..." [...]. "But, I say, what was I thinking? I mustn't forget. How I am going to speak to the Emperor? No, not that—that's to-morrow. Yes, yes! Natasha, attacks, tacks us,—whom? The hussars. Ah, the hussars with their moustaches... Along the Tversky boulevard rode that hussar with the moustaches, I was thinking of him too just opposite Guryev's house... Old Guryev... Ah, a fine fellow Denisov! But that's all nonsense. The great thing is that the Emperor's here now. How he looked at me and longed to say something, but he did not dare... No, it was I did not dare. But that's nonsense, and the great thing is not to forget something important I was thinking of, yes. Natasha, attacks us, yes, yes, yes. That's right." (Tolstoy, WaP, 244)

In literary study, the first instance of an interior monologue directly connected to the consciousness is often attributed to Edouard Dujardin and his

3. The interference of narrator's text and characters' text 151

novella *Les Lauriers sont coupés* (1888) or Arthur Schnitzler's *Lieutenant Gustl* (1900).[25] However, doubt was voiced as early as Gleb Struve (1954) argued that interior monologue began with Dujardin, as the latter had claimed: "le premier emploi voulu, systématique et continu du monologue intérieur date des *Lauriers sont coupés*" (Dujardin 1931, 31). Struve pointed to an earlier occurrence in the work of Leo Tolstoy: in his paper on Tolstoy's early narration, the Russian literary critic Nikolay Chernyshevsky (who later gave his own model of this technique in the novel *What Is to Be Done?* [1863]) draws attention to the interior monologue in Tolstoy's *Sebastopol Sketches* (1855). Tolstoy was, according to Struve, the first European writer to consciously and extensively use the technique that Dujardin (1931, 59) defined in the following way:

> Le monologue intérieur est, dans l'ordre de la poésie, le discours sans auditeur et non prononcé par lequel un personnage exprime sa pensée la plus intime, la plus proche de l'inconscient antérieurement à toute organisation logique, c'est à dire en son état naissant, de façon à donner l'impression „tout venant."

But priority in the use of interior monologue cannot be ascribed to Tolstoy either. As much, as nine years before the appearance of the *Sebastopol Sketches*, Dostoevsky had used an extremely figural and associative type of interior monologue, entirely corresponding to Dujardin's definition, in *The Double*. For example:

> "All right, we shall see," he thought to himself. "We shall see in due time, we'll get to the bottom of all this... Oh, Lord, have mercy upon us!" he moaned in conclusion, in quite a different voice. "And why did I invite him, to what end did I do all that? Why, I am thrusting my head into their thievish noose myself; I am tying the noose with my own hands. Oh, you fool, you fool! You can't resist babbling like some silly boy, some chancery clerk, some wretched creature of no class at all, some rag, some rotten dishclout; you're a gossip, an old woman!... Oh, all ye saints! And he wrote verses, the rogue, and expressed his love for me! How could... How can I show him the door in a polite way if he turns up again, the rogue? Of course, there are all sorts of ways and means. I can say this is how it is, my salary being so limited... Or scare him off in some way saying that, taking this and that into consideration, I am forced to make clear... that he would have to pay an equal share of the cost of board and lodging, and pay the money in advance. H'm! No, damn it all, no! That would be degrading to me. It's not quite delicate! [...] But there, even if he doesn't come, it will be a bad look-out, too! I babbled to him last night!... Oh, it's a bad look-out, a bad look-out! Oh, we're in a bad way! Oh, I'm a cursed fool, a cursed fool! You can't train yourself to behave as you ought, you can't conduct yourself reasonably. Well, what if he comes, and refuses. And God grant he may come! I should be very glad if he did come..." (Dostoevsky, D, 200–01)

---

25   Cf. lastly also the *Metzler Lexikon Literatur- und Kulturtheorie* (Nünning [ed.] 1998), s. v. "Innerer Monolog."

From the associations made by Nikolay Rostov in *War and Peace*, and from Golyadkin's dialogue with himself, it is only a small step to the *stream of consciousness*, i.e. to the technique in which the diegesis is no longer presented as a story reported by the narrator, but rather as a sequence of fleeting impressions, free association, momentary recollection and fragmentary reflections by the characters.[26]

f) Quoted figural designation

The DD sometimes appears in a reduced variant, in which merely single words in the narrative text are attributed to the CT by graphic signals. We will call this variant *quoted figural designation*. In Dostoevsky's novels, in which, as Bakhtin has shown, a struggle takes place between ideologically defined voices, we find countless examples of this technique. Leo Spitzer (1928b, 330) has already illustrated the "imitation of individual words in the narrative text," as he calls the technique, with an example from the *Brothers Karamazov*: "Starr blickte er [i.e. Dmitry Karamazov] dem 'Milchbart' in die Augen." Spitzer comments: "One sees, as it were, a beam of subjectivity, the tone of Mitya's voice, break out from the factual report" (Spitzer 1928b, 330).

The sentences quoted above (II.4.c) from Dostoevsky's *Eternal Husband* contained a range of examples for quoted figural designation. There, we are dealing with symptomatic expressions from the CT, such as "apropos of nothing" and "God knows why," which are ironically accentuated by the narrator. Quoted figural designation is also used by diegetic narrators. We find a glut of examples in Dostoevsky's *A Raw Youth*, in which it is not unusual for the narrator to condense the thinking of other people into characteristic phraseology:

> Wherever the Versilovs were [...] Makar Ivanovich never failed to send news of himself to the "family." (Dostoevsky, RY, 11)

> It was a perfect avalanche of "ideas" of the prince's [Sokolsky] which he was preparing to present to the board of directors. (Dostoevsky, RY, 22)

In this way, the narrator also distances himself from the terms that indicate the evaluative position of his earlier, narrated self:

> On that 19th of September I took one other "step." (Dostoevsky, RY, 39)

> And though my present "step" was only an *experiment* yet I had made up my mind not to take even that step till [...] I should break off with everything, hide

---

26 The concept *stream of consciousness* was introduced by the American philosopher and psychologist William James in order to characterize the erratic contents of a consciousness. A model example of this technique is the chapter "Penelope" from James Joyce's *Ulysses*.

myself in my shell, and become perfectly free. It is true that I was far from being in my "shell" [...] (Dostoevsky, RY, 39–40)

Quoted figural designation can be accompanied by indications of the source text:

[Versilov] went to the village on that occasion, "God knows why," so at least he said to me afterwards. (Dostoevsky, RY, 3)

[Makar] was "respectful in his life," to use his own surprising expression [...] (Dostoevsky, RY, 6)

Bound up with quoted figural designation, however it is realized—with or without indications of the source—there is always text interference. In those segments of the narrator's discourse, NT and CT, the quoting and the quoted text, are present simultaneously. The obvious attempt of the narrator to reproduce someone else's words as authentically as possible is, as a rule, accompanied by a certain distancing from the expressions as well as from the evaluative position of the quoted character. To this extent, double-voicedness tends to be far more developed in quoted figural designation than in DD, where it is, although possible, realized far more rarely.

In contrast to Lyudmila Sokolova (1968, 69–72), who ascribes the technique of "graphic emphasis of semantically charged words" to the category of FID, I exclude quoted figural designation from the range of FID's variants, since the graphic marking abrogates a fundamental trait of FID, the concealment of the source text.

g) Indirect representation of speech, thought, and perception

The pattern of ID, which serves not only the reproduction of statements, but also of thoughts, perceptions and emotions, consists of two parts, the introductory sentence of the reproducing entity including the *verbum dicendi, sentiendi* etc., and the reproduced text itself.

In the transformation of a DD into an ID, language-specific grammatical rules must be taken into account. For most Indo-European languages, the following rules of transformation can be seen as generally applicable:

(1) First- and second-person form oriented on the subject or addressee of the discourse tend to be replaced with third-person forms.

(2) In some languages, a change to the tense and/or mode is undertaken.

He said: "I am ill."	>	He said (that) he was ill.
Il disait: « Je suis malade ».	>	Il disait qu'il était malade.
Er sagte: „Ich bin krank".	>	Er sagte, dass er krank sei.

In Russian, by contrast, the tenses of the CT appear in the reproduced component.

| Он сказал: «Я болен». | > | Он сказал, что он болен. |
| (He said: „I am ill." | > | *He said that he is ill.) |

(3) The expressive and appellative elements of the DD have to be replaced with other means, for instance through additional qualification of the *verbum dicendi* (*He said with great excitement, that...; she asked herself in agitation why...*).

(4) Interjections and syntactic irregularities of the DD, such as ellipses, anacolutha and so on, must be smoothed out in the ID.

(5) In some languages, such as German, subordinating conjunctions require a syntactic reshaping of the reproduced discourse:

| Er sagte: „Ich bin krank". | > | Er sagte, dass er krank sei. |
| Without conjunction: | | Er sagte, er sei krank. |

In Russian, the absence of a change in tense or mode, and of syntactical inversion, means that ID differs considerably less from DD than it does in, say, English or German. This led the Russian syntax specialist Alexander Peshkovsky (1920, 466) to the conclusion that indirect reproduction was not innate to the Russian language, a conclusion that Valentin Voloshinov (1929; tr. 1973, 129) decisively refuted. In Russian, as in other languages, ID, according to Voloshinov, can, and indeed must, deal with the contents as well with the forms of the reproduced characters' text more freely than DD. For this reason, Voloshinov refers to the analytical character of this pattern ("Analysis is the heart and soul of indirect discourse") and distinguishes between two modifications, the *referent-analyzing* and the *texture-analyzing* form. In the first modification, the thematic contents and the evaluative position of the reproduced discourse are accentuated by the smoothing and neutralization of subjective-emotional forms of expression; in the second, the main component is the profiling of the "subjective and stylistic physiognomy of the message viewed as expression" (Voloshinov 1929; tr. 1973, 131).

A somewhat different typology of modifications to ID will be suggested here. It rests not on the object of the analysis, as undertaken in the process of reproducing CT, but on the reproduced discourse's proximity to, or distance from, the NT or CT.

In *narratorial indirect discourse*, the character's discourse experiences a clear transformation, which is expressed in analytical accentuation of the thematic core and in stylistic assimilation into the NT. In this form, all features except 1 (theme) and 2 (evaluation) tend to point to NT. The pattern given above (p. 147) corresponded to the *figural* variant. In the narratorial variant, the sentence could read:

3. The interference of narrator's text and characters' text

> She asked herself why she had to make an appearance at this unwanted Christmas party on that day, since, after all, it wasn't Christmas until the day after.

In the narratorial variant, the features 5 (orientation system), 6 (language function), and 7 (lexis) represent not the CT, but the NT.

Narratorial indirect discourse dominates in the work of Leo Tolstoy. An example is provided by the rendering of Boris Drubeckoy's perception and emotions:

> The son noticed how an expression of intense grief came at once into his mother's eyes, and he smiled slightly. (Tolstoy, WaP, 42)

> Boris perceived that Pierre did not know him, but did not think fit to make himself known, and without the slightest embarrassment looked him straight in the face. (Tolstoy, WaP, 45)

In *figural indirect discourse*, the narrator presents the character's discourse with all its idiosyncrasies, in its own authentic stylistic form and in its own syntactical structure. This modification is widespread in the work of Dostoevsky. We will take an example from *The Double*:

> Recognizing in a flash that he was ruined, in a sense annihilated, that he had disgraced himself and sullied his reputation, that he had been turned into ridicule and treated with contempt in the presence of spectators, that he had been treacherously insulted, by one whom he had looked on only yesterday as his greatest and most trustworthy friend, that he had been put to utter confusion, Mr Golyadkin senior rushed in pursuit of his enemy. (Dostoevsky, D, 208)

Features for CT: 5 (orientation system: *yesterday*),[27] 8 (language function: expression), 7 (lexis: hyperbolic colloquial vocabulary, oral expressions, hyperbolically high-register, overblown vocabulary) and 8 (syntax: rhetorical sequence of synonyms).

h) Autonomous indirect discourse

Figuralization can go so far that the grammatical and syntactic norms of ID are violated. In that case, a hybrid type is formed, which I will call *autonomous indirect discourse*. It arises particularly when the expressivity and syntax of the CT in a figural ID burst the syntactic restrictions of the ID, or when the ID takes on the constitutive features of DD (graphic marking, use of the first and second person).

The following quotation from *The Double* is an example of the first case, the adoption of interjections from the CT:

---

27 The English translation replaces the figural deictic *yesterday* of the Russian original with the narratorial anaphoric *the day before*.

> [Golyadkin] fancied that just now, that very minute, someone was standing near him, beside him, also leaning on the railing, and—marvelous to relate!—had even said something to him [...] (Dostoevsky, D, 174)

The second case can be documented with the following quotation from Dostoevsky's "Mr Prokharchin": the grammatical person switches from the "s/he" system of ID to the "I-you-s/he" system of DD, and this switch is marked with quotation marks:

> [...] then it could be discerned that Semyon Ivanovich seemed to be predicting that Zinovy Prokofyevich would never succeed in entering high society, and that the tailor to whom he owed money for his clothes would give him a hiding, nay, would certainly give him a hiding since the jackanapes was taking such long time to pay up, and that, finally, "You want to be a cadet in the hussars, you jackanapes, but you won't make the grade, it won't work out the way you think it will, and when the administration gets to hear of it you'll be demoted to the rank of common clerk; that's what I'm telling you, do you hear, you insolent jackanapes?" (Dostoevsky, MP, 221)

Autonomous ID often arises from the narrator's desire to reproduce the discourse of a character and all its idiosyncrasies as authentically as possible, without renouncing his or her narratorial presence. Infractions against grammatical norms should then, as a rule, be ascribed to the CT. The development of the autonomous ID from a figural ID, and the ironizing narrator's pursuit of complete reproduction of the CT within the ID both become clear in the following example from *War and Peace*:

> And immediately after that she communicated the intelligence that she had left all her clothes in Petersburg, and God knew what she would have to go about in here, and that Andrey was quite changed, and that Kitty Odintsov had married an old man, and that a suitor had turned up for Princess Marya, 'who was a suitor worth having,' but *that we would talk about that later.* (Tolstoy, WaP, 85)[28]

i) Free indirect discourse (FID): definition

The most complex manifestation of text interference is FID.[29] It differs from the other variants of text interference through the following characteristics:

---

28 I have marked the switch to the pattern of DD with italics. The translation has been revised from the original.

29 FID is in no way limited to highbrow or fictional literature, as some of its theoreticians postulate (cf. esp. Banfield 1973), but rather also appears outside fiction and, of all places, in colloquial communication. The emergence of FID in an everyday context was already stressed by Spitzer 1928b and Eugen Lerch 1928. On the role of FID in everyday communication, in parliamentary discourse and in journalism (both oral and written) cf. Pascal

3. The interference of narrator's text and characters' text

(1) In contrast to DD and ID, FID is not introduced with *verba dicendi, sentiendi* etc. and the corresponding conjunctions. That the rendered statements, thoughts, perceptions and so on belong to the CT is not marked in any way.[30]

(2) In contrast to quoted figural designation and certain forms of the autonomous ID, FID is not graphically marked.

(3) In contrast to those variants of autonomous ID that contain the forms of grammatical person corresponding to DD (I, you, s/he), in FID the characters speaking, being addressed or discussed are all described with the grammatical forms of the third person.

(4) According to the previous definitions, FID is identical with the NT. It differs from the latter in that it expresses the statements, thoughts, perceptions and so on, not of the narrator, but of a character, a reflector. In cases where the opposition of CT and NT is not complete, the features 1 (theme) and 2 (evaluation), at least, refer to the CT.

Therefore, we can define the device in the following way: *FID is a segment of the narrator's discourse that reproduces the words, thoughts, feelings, perceptions or the evaluative position of a character, whereby the reproduction of the CT is not marked, neither graphically nor by any kind of explicit indicator.*

In FID, feature 3 (person) always refers only to the NT. When the oppositions between the texts are not completely neutralized, the features 1 (theme) and 2 (evaluation), at least, are oriented on the CT. It is not unusual for the CT to be realized through other features: 5 (orientation system), 6 (language function), 7 (lexis), 8 (syntax). The more features refer to CT, the more clearly the FID sets itself apart from the surrounding narrator's discourse. But when the opposition of texts is neutralized in all features, the FID is not identifiable. In that case, it no longer distinguishes itself from the surrounding narrator's discourse.

1977, 18–19, 34, 57; McHale 1978, 282. An overview of current approaches is given by McHale 2009.

30 FID can, however, be prepared or retrospectively signaled with the transition from DD or ID, or with corresponding representation of acts of speech, thought and perception on the part of the reflector. Cf. the differentiated portrayal by Steinberg 1971, 88–106. Signaling by the context does not fully negate the ambivalence that is fundamental to FID. Even where such signals exist, an interpretation of the narrative text as the rendering of CT is required.

j) FID in German, English, French, and Russian

Our definition covers a broad spectrum of forms in which NT and CT are mixed. It would be possible to develop a differentiated typology of FID according to the presence of specific features and the representation of the two texts. In the process, one would, of course, need to take into account its respective linguistic realization. Here, we will concentrate on the classic types of FID in German (while casting a glance over the English, French and Russian forms) and base the typology solely on the treatment of tense (feature 4).

Basic type in German, English and French: tense of the NT
The basic type of FID in German distinguishes itself through a shift of tense with respect to those used in the CT (feature 4 ⇒ NT).[31] The figural present is shifted to become the narratorial epic preterite, the figural preterite to the pluperfect. To demonstrate the first shift, we will again use Alice Berend's often cited example from *Die Bräutigame der Babette Bomberling*:

> Aber am Vormittag hatte sie den Baum zu putzen. Morgen war Weihnachten.

Using sentences like these, Käte Hamburger reaches the conclusion, as already discussed above, of the detemporalization of the epic preterite and the atemporality of fiction. More appropriate seems, by contrast, the interpretation that we are dealing with a contamination of perspectives or an interference of the texts: the epic preterite refers to the narrator (time ⇒ NT), and the deictic adverb of future to the character (orientation system ⇒ CT).

In the basic type of German FID, the character's past tense is expressed with the pluperfect:

> Das Manöver gestern hatte acht Stunden gedauert. (Bruno Frank, The Days of the King; quoted from Hamburger 1957, 33)

In its ideal form (the presence of all features and no neutralization of oppositions), the basic type of German FID has the following distribution of features:[32]

---

31 The arrows used here and in the following symbolize the referential relationship.
32 In German, the explicit future with *werden* experiences special treatment. Whereas the present used as a future (Tomorrow is Christmas) undergoes a temporal shift into the preterite in FID (Tomorrow was Christmas), with the explicit future (*Wieviel wird sie verstehen?*) a shift takes place in the form *würde + infinitive* (*Wieviel würde sie verstehen?*). A similar shift applies to the English *would + infinitive* and the French *Conditionnel* (Steinberg 1971, 172-221). Cf. the example given by Hamburger (1968, 75; tr. 1973, 85) from Edzard Schaper's *Der letzte Advent*: "Das konnte einfach nicht wahr sein – wenn er nur allein an sie dachte! Aber wieviel würde sie verstehen? Würde er sie nicht schon nach den ersten drei Minuten verlieren? Und das sollte er wagen? Wer verlangte das von ihm, wer konnte es verlangen?" ("That simply could not be true—he didn't dare even think of her!

3. The interference of narrator's text and characters' text 159

	1. Theme	2. Evaluation	3. Person	4. Tense	5. Orientation syst.	6. Lang. function	7. Lexis	8. Syntax
NT			x	x				x
CT	x	x			x	x	x	

The basic type of German FID is thus relatively weakly grammatically marked: features 3 (person) and 4 (time) ⇒ NT. This makes it difficult to identify. The situation is very similar in French and English.[33] In both languages, a shift takes place, from the CT's tense to the NT's epic preterite.

The two following examples demonstrate the temporal shift in English:[34]

> And Father Conmee smiled and saluted. How <u>did</u> she do? A fine carriage she <u>had</u>. (Joyce, Ul, 208)[35]

> But instantly she was annoyed with herself for saying that. Who <u>had said</u> it? not she; she <u>had been trapped</u> into saying something she <u>did</u> not mean. (Woolf, L, 101)

In French, FID is more strongly marked, in that the tense *imparfait* takes the place of the expected *passé simple*. The two examples are taken from Gustave Flaubert's *Madame Bovary*. In the first, Léon's thoughts are rendered as he waits for Emma in the cathedral in Rouen:

> Elle <u>allait</u> <u>venir</u> tout à l'heure, charmante, agitée, épiant derrière elle les regards qui la <u>suivaient</u> [...] (Flaubert, MB, 285)

The second quotation presents Emma Bovary's hopeless deliberations during her vain attempt to raise some money:

> Elle s'étonnait, à présent, de n'avoir pas songé à lui tout d'abord; hier, il <u>avait</u> <u>donné</u> sa parole, il n'y manquerait pas [...] (Flaubert, MB, 362)[36]

But how much would she understand? Would he not already lose her after the first three minutes? And should he risk that? Who demanded that of him, who could demand that?").

33 As a basis for temporal characteristics of FID in German, English and French: Steinberg 1971, Fludernik 1993a. On the translation of FID from English, French and Russian into German cf. Kullmann (ed.) 1995.
34 Quoted from Steinberg 1971, 166.
35 This is not a case of rendering outer speech, but of the representation of her perception in the consciousness of the listeners.
36 The reference to the two passages I owe to D. Kullmann 1992, 116-17.

Variant: tense of the CT

In German, we also encounter a FID in those tenses that correspond to the CT. The passage from Lion Feuchtwanger's *Der Jüdische Krieg* quoted above (III.2.f) was an example of that. Following the quoted section comes a passage that is also kept entirely in the present (with the perfect and future):

> Er hat viel über Rom gelesen, aber es nützt ihm wenig. Der Brand vor drei Monaten hat die Stadt sehr verändert. Er hat gerade die vier Bezirke im Zentrum zerstört, über dreihundert öffentliche Gebäude, an die sechshundert Paläste und Einfamilienhäuser, mehrere tausend Mietshäuser. Es ist ein Wunder, wie viel diese Römer in der kurzen Zeit schon neu gebaut haben. Er mag sie nicht, die Römer, er hasst sie geradezu, aber das muss er ihnen lassen: Organisationstalent haben sie, sie haben ihre Technik. Technik, er denkt das fremde Wort, denkt es mehrmals, in der fremden Sprache. Er ist nicht dumm, er wird diesen Römern von ihrer Technik etwas abluchsen. (Feuchtwanger, JK, 7-8)

By contrast, the English translation of this passage—like the introduction to the novel quoted above (III.2.f)—uses the preterite:

> He had read a great deal about Rome, but that did not help him much. The fire three months before had greatly changed the city. It had destroyed the four central districts, including over three hundred public buildings, some six hundred palaces and villas, and several thousand houses. It was astonishing how much these Romans had already rebuilt in the short time since. He could not endure them, these Romans; indeed he hated them, but he was forced to admit that they had a talent for organization; they had their technique. Technique, he mused over the strange word, repeating it several times to himself in the foreign Latin tongue. He was not a dunce; he would watch these Romans and learn something of their technique. (Feuchtwanger, Josephus, 4)

At other points in the German novel, the FID corresponds to the basic type, i.e. is in the epic preterite. The tense of the FID corresponds at any one time to that of the narrator's discourse, which switches between the epic preterite and the present. In each case, the FID is only weakly dissociated from the surrounding narrator's discourse.

Two cases must be distinguished for FID in the tenses of the CT, dependent on the respective narrative tense. Where the basic tense is formed by the epic preterite and where the FID also appears in the preterite, FID is particularly marked in the present. However, when the entire story is narrated in the present, there is no alternative for the present-tense FID. This is the case, for instance, in the South African Nobel Prize laureate J. M. Coetzee's novel *The Master of Petersburg*, which is narrated in the present throughout. Here, FID in the present lacks any kind of temporal marking. The entire novel reads like the narrative unfolding of the hero's, Fyodor Dostoevsky's, inner world:

3. The interference of narrator's text and characters' text 161

> He [Dostoevsky] emerges into a crowded ante-room. How long has he been closeted with Maksimov? An hour? Longer? The bench is full, there are people lounging against the walls, people in the corridors too, where the smell of fresh paint is stifling. All talk ceases; eyes turn on him without sympathy. So many seeking justice, each with a story to tell! (Coetzee, MP, 48)

The following is valid independent of the tense of the narrator's discourse: if the FID follows the tense of the CT, then the opposition of the text in the feature time is neutralized in all general and gnomic statements. In these cases, it is no longer possible to distinguish, at least not on the basis of time, whether the narrator or the character is the author of the statement.[37]

Basic type in Russian: tense of the CT

In Russian, the basic type of FID distinguishes itself through the use of the CT's tenses (feature 4 ⇒ CT). As a result, the FID is closer to the pure CT. In the context of a narrator's discourse in the epic preterite, the effect of the CT's tense, so long as it is not a figural preterite, is relatively strong marking. Here is the ideal schema of the basic type of FID in Russian:

	1. Theme	2. Evaluation	3. Person	4. Tense	5. Orientation syst.	6. Lang. function	7. Lexis	8. Syntax
NT			x					
CT	x	x		x	x	x	x	x

The two following examples from Dostoevsky's *The Double* contain differing tense references in the CT:

The CT's present

> Это не Крестьян Иванович! Кто это? Или это он? Он! Это Крестьян Иванович, но только не прежний, это другой Крестьян Иванович. Это ужасный Крестьян Иванович!... (Dostoevsky, PSS, I, 229)

> That's not Krestyan Ivanovich! Who is it? Or is it he? It is. It is Krestyan Ivanovich, but not the old Krestyan Ivanovich, it's another Krestyan Ivanovich! It's a terrible Krestyan Ivanovich!... (Dostoevsky, D, 284)[38]

The CT's past

> Увы! он это давно уже предчувствовал! (Dostoevsky, PSS, I, 229)

> Alas! For a long while he had been haunted by a presentiment of this. (Dostoevsky, D, 284)

---

37 Leo Spitzer (1922a) adds an independent type for figural statements in the gnomic present, which he calls "pseudo-objective discourse" (cf. also Bakhtin 1934-35, 118).

38 In the English translation by Constance Garnett, these sentences appear in quotation marks, i.e. are not identified as FID.

In Russian, which has no pluperfect, the preterite is used, which coincides with the narrative tense. In such cases in Russian, the opposition of texts is neutralized in feature 4 (tense). Neutralization is, of course, also possible in the reproduction of the CT's present: if the narrator occasionally narrates in the historical or gnomic present, this tense coincides with the character's present.

Variant in Russian: tense of the NT

One variant widespread in Russian contains not the tense of the CT, but the epic preterite (feature 4 ⇒ NT). In it, the FID moves closer to the NT. This variant will be illustrated with an example taken, again, from *The Double*:

> Все было так натурално! И было отчего сокрушиться, бить такую тревогу! (Dostoevsky, PSS, I, 156)

> It was all so natural! And what a thing to break his heart over, what a thing to be so distressed about! (Dostoevsky, D, 194)

The preterite in this case does not describe the past of the character, but is rather the epic preterite, which describes the character's present. The ideal schema of this variant is the following:

	1. Theme	2. Evaluation	3. Person	4. Tense	5. Orientation syst.	6. Lang. function	7. Lexis	8. Syntax
NT			x	x				
CT	x	x			x	x	x	x

k) Free indirect perception

If the narrator reproduces the character's perception without clothing the reproduction in that character's evaluative, grammatical and stylistic forms of expression, we are dealing with a variant, which, following Willi Bühler (1937, 131, 153) and analogous to *erlebte Rede*, the German term for FID, we can call *erlebte Wahrnehmung*. Bühler's opposition of *erlebte Rede* and *erlebte Wahrnehmung* is taken up by Bernhard Fehr (1938) as *substitutionary speech* and *substitutionary perception*. Laurel Brinton (1980) terms this form *represented perception* and Alan Palmer (2004) has consistently developed the term *free indirect perception*, which we will also use. This form has been described as the "creation of images of immediate perception" (Shlykova 1962) and as the "representation of moments and sections of reality, [...] of any given phenomena of the objective exterior world from the position of an experiencing character, whereby the person's reactivity is not necessarily always precipitated in a speech act, nor even in an interior speech act" (Andryevskaya 1967, 9).

Free indirect perception is in evidence even when only feature 1 (theme) refers to the CT and all other features refer to the NT (or are neutralized).

This form appears frequently in *The Double*, where it is responsible for the narrator's pseudo-objectivity. It appears everywhere where the narrator reproduces the hallucinatory perception of the *Doppelgänger* by Golyadkin, without coloring the narration with the hero's means of expression in such a way that would make clear to the reader, just in itself, that the character is acting as a reflector:

> Again a rapidly approaching figure stood out black before him, some twenty paces away. This little figure was hastening, tripping along, hurrying nervously; the distance between them grew rapidly less. [...] The stranger did, in fact, stop ten paces from Mr Golyadkin, so that the light from the lamp-post that stood near fell full upon his whole figure—stood still, turned to Mr Golyadkin, and with impatient and anxious face waited to hear what he would say. (Dostoevsky, D, 176)

Without any conspicuous evaluative or stylistic indicators of figural perception, the narrator represents the *Doppelgänger* as he is perceived or constructed by the pathologically disturbed hero. The apparent objectivity of free indirect perception has the effect that the reader guesses the true nature of the *Doppelgänger* and the psychological motivation of the actions in the "Petersburg poem" only gradually, things he initially perceives in terms of romantic fantasy.

l)   Free indirect monologue

The interior monologue can also be reproduced in the pattern of FID. In that case, we are dealing with a *free indirect (interior) monologue*. It can be given in either the CT's tense, that is in the present tenses: present, perfect and future (feature 4 ⇒ CT), or in the epic preterite (feature 4 ⇒ NT).

The CT's tenses shape the following extract, which is taken from an interior monologue of Andrey Bolkonsky's in *War and Peace*, and which is central to the plot. This extended interior monologue is conducted first in DD, but then switches to FID and then back to DD. Part of the passages conducted in DD have already been quoted above (p. 150) as an example for the dialogic interior monologue. The central part of this monologue, given in the pattern of FID, is introduced by a narratorial representation of thought—a pattern that Dorrit Cohn (1978) terms *psycho-narration*—and gradually shifts to the figural perceptual perspective:

And he pictured the engagement, the loss of it, the concentration of the fighting at one point, and the hesitation of all the commanding officers. And then the happy moment—that Toulon he had been waiting for so long—at last comes to him. Resolutely and clearly he speaks his opinion to Kutuzov and Weierother, and the Emperors. All are struck by the justness of his view, but no one undertakes to carry it into execution, and behold, he leads the regiment, only making it a condition that no one is to interfere with his plans, and he leads his division to the critical point and wins the victory alone. [...] The disposition of the battle that ensues is all his work alone. Nominally, he is an adjutant on the staff of Kutuzov, but he does everything alone. The battle is gained by him alone. Kutuzov is replaced, he is appointed. ... (Tolstoy, WaP, 242)[39]

As an example of free indirect monologue in the epic preterite, one of Golyadkin's conversations with himself from *The Double*:

There really was a reason, however, for his being so overwhelmed. The fact is that this stranger seemed to him now somehow familiar. That would have been nothing, though. But he recognized, almost certainly recognized this man. He had often seen him, that man, had seen him some time, and very lately too; where could it have been? Surely not yesterday? But, again, that was not the chief thing that Mr Golyadkin had often seen him before; there was hardly anything special about the man; the man at first sight would not have aroused any special attention. He was just a man like any one else, a gentleman like all other gentlemen, of course, and perhaps he had some good qualities and very valuable ones too—in fact, he was a man who was quite himself. (Dostoevsky, D, 176)

It is not unusual for free indirect monologues to oscillate between the tenses of the NT and CT, as is the case in the following excerpt from Nikolay Gogol's "The Overcoat" (underlined: NT's tense; dotted underlining: CT's tense):

Then Akaky Akakievich saw that it was impossible to get along without a new overcoat, and his spirit sank utterly. How, in fact, was it to be accomplished? Where was the money to come from? He might, to be sure, depend, in part, upon his present at Christmas; but that money had long been doled out and allotted beforehand. He must have some new trousers, and pay a debt of long standing to the shoemaker [...] in a word, all his money must be spent [...]. (Gogol, O, 88)

---

39 In Tolstoy's free indirect monologues, C. Garnett often replaces the present of the original with the preterite. That is the case, for instance, in the following free indirect monologue, for Pierre Bezukhov's self-critical deliberations: "Had he not longed with his whole heart to establish a republic in Russia; then to be himself Napoleon; then to be a philosopher; and then a great strategist and the conqueror of Napoleon? [...] But instead of all that, here he was the wealthy husband of a faithless wife, a retired kammerherr, fond of dining and drinking, fond, too, as he unbuttoned his waistcoat after dinner, of indulging in a little abuse of the government..." (Tolstoy, WaP, 504)

m) FID in diegetic narration

The functional separation of the narrating self as narrator and the narrated self as actor, and the psychological and ideological dissociation of the two selves (cf. above, II.4.i), makes text interference possible also in diegetic narration, in the narration of a diegetic narrator. If, in a given statement, the features for the NT are combined with features for the CT, cases of text interference arise similar to those in non-diegetic narration. All that changes are the conditions for the neutralization of the two texts' oppositions.

Contrary to the claims of Käte Hamburger (1957; 1968) and other critics (W. Bühler 1937, 66; K. R. Meyer 1957, 25, 30), FID can also appear in diegetic narration.[40] Dorrit Cohn (1969) has provided convincing examples of this taken from German literature: the original version of Kafka's *The Castle*, Hesse's *Steppenwolf*, Schnitzler's novella "The Second," and Thomas Mann's *Felix Krull* fragment. In these cases, the FID does not reproduce the text of third persons, but rather the thoughts and perception of the earlier, narrated self.

The typology of FID is fundamentally also valid for diegetic narration. The main difference is that the opposition of NT and CT is neutralized more often than in non-diegetic narration. Feature 3 (person) is, as a rule, entirely absent in distinguishing between texts, and it is rare for the opposition between NT and CT to be strongly marked in feature 6 (lexis). Language function (feature 7) and syntax (feature 8) will form an opposition only when the narrated self finds him or herself in an exceptional psychological state. More frequently than in non-diegetic narration, the identification of FID remains reliant on features 1 (theme) and 2 (evaluation).

For example, an extract from Ivan Turgenev's tale "Asya":

> "I acted out of conscience," I insisted to myself. *Nonsense!* Was that really how I'd wanted it to end? *Am I really ready to part with her? Can I really give her up?* "Idiot! Idiot" I kept on telling myself bitterly. (Turgenev, A, 137. Italics mine — *W. Sch.*)

The section here marked in italics is clearly FID of the basic Russian type (feature 4 ⇒ CT). This assessment does, however, assume that one refers back to the thematic and evaluative symptoms. The expressive language function, often an indicator of CT, cannot play that role here, because the narrating self comes to the fore by means of expressive self-questioning.

A diegetic novel in which FID plays a prominent role is Dostoevsky's *A Raw Youth*. Arkady Dolgoruky realizes interior situations in which he found himself half a year previously. The FID portrays, in its most obvious form

---

40 Cf. already explicitly Todemann 1930, 154–55. Cf. also the discussion of the possibility of FID in diegetic narration in Gersbach-Bäschlin 1970, 21–22.

(feature 4 ⇒ CT), mainly the emotionally excited exclamations and questions of the internally agitated narrated self:

> I was immensely astonished; this piece of news was the most disturbing of all: something was wrong, something had turned up, something had happened of which I knew nothing as yet! (Dostoevsky, RY, 310)

The presence of CT is barely perceptible when the FID is rendered in the alternative type (feature 4 ⇒ NT):

> But, thank God, the letter was still in my keeping; it was still sewn up in my side pocket; I felt with my hand—it was there! So all I had to do was to get up and run away. I need not care what Lambert thought of me afterwards. Lambert was not worth of it. (Dostoevsky, RY, 517)

n) Figurally colored narration (FCN)

One type of text interference must be distinguished from FID, one which has been widespread in European and American narrative art since the end of the 19th century: the coloring of the narrative text with evaluations and terms from the CT. In Russian, where this type has played an important role since the literature of post-realism, it is called "improper authorial narration" (*nesobstvenno-avtorskoe povestvovanie*) (cf. N. A. Kozhevnikova 1971; 1994, 206–48).[41] We will call the technique *figurally colored narration* (FCN).[42]

How does FCN differ from FID? FID reproduces the text of a character in the form of narrator's discourse, with greater or lesser narratorial transformation. FCN is, by contrast, the authentic narration of the narrator, which takes on unmarked evaluations and terms from the characters' text in varying density. In FID, feature 1 (theme) refers to the CT; in FCN, by contrast, to the NT.

It is possible to distinguish two modes for the adoption of evaluations and terms from the CT. In the first mode, the figurally colored elements of the narrative text reflect the *current* contents of the character's consciousness, which, as it were, *infect* the narrator. Following Leo Spitzer (1922b), we will call this technique *contagion or infection* of the narrator's discourse by the CT. An example is provided by the beginning of Chekhov's tale "The Student," quoted above (III.2.f).

If the figurally colored elements of the narrator's discourse do not reflect the current internal situation of the figure in a given moment, but

---

[41] The term has been created as analogous to the Russian designation for FID, "improper direct discourse" (*nesobstvenno-pryamaya rech'*). For German, Johannes Holthusen (1968) has suggested the terms "erlebtes Erzählen" or "uneigentliches Erzählen."

[42] McHale (2009, 441) names the technique of figural coloring of narrative text, after a jocular proposal of Hugh Kenner's (1978), the "Uncle Charles Principle."

rather the evaluations and terms *typical* of the CT, we can refer to a *reproduction* of the CT. This technique is in evidence in the opening to Dostoevsky's tale "A Nasty Story," quoted above (p. 138). The italicized words denote evaluations that stem from the collected generals' axiology and way of thinking, despite the fact that they could not be considered the current contents of the characters' consciousnesses. Both forms, infection as well as reproduction, must be distinguished from quoted figural designation, which is separated from the narrator's discourse by means of graphic indicators.

Using the example of Chekhov's novella "The Student," one can also observe a phenomenon typical of figural narration: before the explicit appearance of a reflector character, the narration is already colored, in his or her evaluations and terms. In this way, FCN can prepare the ground for the later appearance of a reflector.[43]

In Russian literature, FCN reaches a high water mark in the later prose of Anton Chekhov. Until the first half of the 1890s, FID still dominated Chekhov's prose. From the middle of the 1890s onwards, the CT deepens its influence on the narration. The result of this development is described by Alexander Chudakov (1971, 98), using the example of "The Lady with the Dog": "The description is presented entirely in the narrator's language; nowhere does it change to reported speech [i.e. FID]. But the imprint of the characters' emotional state seems to overlay this objective recapitulation of events." The narration in Chekhov's later work gives the impression that it has been entirely immersed in the sphere of the character, although no portrayal of the current situation of the consciousness takes place.

FCN plays a special role in the Russian prose of the period before perestroika, i.e. in the years 1960–80, after it had been avoided in the 1940s and 1950s as a bourgeois-formalist technique. A key work in its renaissance was Alexander Solzhenitsyn's tale of a life in a prison camp *One Day in the Life of Ivan Denisovich* (written 1959, printed 1962):

> No sense in getting your boots wet in the morning. Even if Shukhov had dashed back to his hut he wouldn't have found another pair to change into. During eight years' imprisonment he had known various systems for allocating footwear: there'd been times when he'd gone through the winter without valenki at all, or leather boots either, and had had to make shift with bast sandals or a sort of galoshes made of scraps of motor tyres—"Chetezes" they called them, after the Chelyabinsk tractor works. Now the footwear situation seemed better... (Solzhenitsyn, OD, 14)

This excerpt is clearly not presented in FID. Neither a current interior monologue nor the recollections of the protagonist are presented; rather, it is the narrator's voice one hears, which, in the narratorial overview over the

---

43 In section V.3.d, an example of this from Chekhov's tale "Rothschild's Fiddle" is examined.

story of shoe allocation in the prison camp (feature 1 ⇒ NT), approaches as closely as possible the evaluative and linguistic horizons of the protagonist and reproduces individual stylistic traits of the CT (features 2, 7, 8 ⇒ CT).

Although FCN and FID exhibit differing structures, it is not always possible to separate them from one another in Solzhenitsyn's text. Their identification is made difficult above all in places where figural elements that correspond to the current situation of the protagonist become more frequent. As a result, the key sentences of the novel can be considered either the reproduction of a current process in the character's consciousness, summing up the day's events as he falls asleep, i.e. FID, or as the words of the narrator who, independently of the current situation in the character's consciousness, draws a balance of this day's "successes," i.e. as FCN:

> Shukhov went to sleep fully content. He'd had many strokes of luck that day: they hadn't put him in the cells; they hadn't sent the team to the settlement; he'd pinched a bowl of kasha at dinner; the team-leader had fixed the rates well; he'd built a wall and enjoyed doing it; he'd smuggled that bit of hacksaw-blade through; he'd earned something from Cezar in the evening; he'd bought that tobacco. And he hadn't fallen ill. He'd got over it. A day without a dark cloud. Almost a happy day. (Solzhenitsyn, OD, 142–43)

o) Functions of text interference

The origins of functional investigation of text interference lie in the discussion of *style indirect libre* conducted in the 1910s and 1920s in the pages of the *Germanisch-romanische Monatsschrift* between the Geneva linguist Charles Bally and his student Marguerite Lips, on the one hand, and the adherents of the Munich Vossler school on the other.[44]

Bally (1912; 1914; 1930) sees in the *style indirect libre* merely a "procédé grammatical de reproduction pure." According to Bally, this "forme linguistique" differs from the DD solely in its grammatical features (pronouns and tenses of indirect speech). As soon as the reporter lets an evaluation of his own, an ironic accentuation for instance, be recognized in the reproduced discourse, it is, for Bally, a case not of "style indirect libre," but of a "reproduction appréciée," which, as a "figure de pensée," must be kept strictly separate from the "formes linguistiques" and cannot be reconciled with the, by definition, objective "style indirect libre." Bally excludes from this all forms in which the presence of the CT is obscured. According to him, the "style indirect libre" serves exclusively the pure, objective and clear reproduction of speech and thought. Bally's objectivist conception necessarily

---

44 Comprehensive portrayal of this discussion in Vološinov 1929; tr. 1973, 141–59; cf. also Doležel 1958.

provoked contradiction from the Vossler school, who considered FID a specifically literary phenomenon. In the process, some representatives of this school tended to the other extreme. They were interested principally in the psychological capacity of FID, which they saw as being based on empathy. The essence of FID consisted, for this school of "Sprachseelenforschung," in the "empathy of the author with the creatures of his imagination" (E. Lerch 1914; G. Lerch 1922), in the direct "Erleben" of the affairs of someone else's consciousness (this is where the German term for FID, "erlebte Rede," created by Etienne Lorck 1921, originates from). With this, the Vossler school denied the possibility of a double-accented rendering of psychological processes, which was under discussion at the time. In a polemic against Werner Günther (1928, 83-91), who had described FID as a synthetic form that fused the narrator's two perspectives, the "inner view" immersing itself in the character, and the distanced "outer view," which thus combined "empathy" and "criticism" in one act, Eugen Lerch (1928, 469-71) states:

> [...] the *Erlebte Rede* signifies, in itself, solely empathy, not criticism as well [...]. Through the *Erlebte Rede*, the author can identify, at least for an instant, even with characters to whom he is in no way sympathetic or whose opinions he in no way shares [...]. The *Erlebte Rede* does not signify any criticism of what is thought or said, but rather, in contrast, a *relinquishing* of critical perspective.

The penchant of modern European and American literatures for text interference has often been explained, in the sense of the Vossler school, in that the corresponding narrative techniques allow direct insight into the characters' psychological processes (Stanzel 1955; Neubert 1957). But why, it must be asked, does this penchant orient itself on, of all things, hybrid forms in which ambiguity arises as to which entity is responsible? Why does it apply far less frequently to the forms of DD that, as a result of the unambiguousness of their attribution, are, it would seem, predestined for authentic reproduction?

The penchant for text interference cannot be explained without taking into account its hybrid character, without the fact that two texts are simultaneously present in it, the proportions of which must be reconstructed at every single moment, nor without the fact that the narrator is able to narratorially accentuate and evaluate the words, thoughts and perceptions of the character.

A step in this direction has already been taken by Lyudmila Sokolova (1968). After thorough analysis of the means by which "improper authorial discourse" is marked, she sets out which "stylistic" possibilities are available to this third pattern, alongside "author's discourse" and "character's discourse," and which advantages it has over the other two.[45] Starting from the assessment that the stylistic functions of "improper authorial discourse" result from the contamination or confrontation of the subject levels of "author" and character, Sokolova reduces the functions of this form of presentation to three possibilities: (1) "Improper authorial discourse," by reproducing the character's standpoint while retaining the author's evaluation, can demonstrate the mental development of the protagonist and reveal the essence of his or her character. (2) "Improper authorial discourse," by accentuating the author's evaluation, can be used as a compositional means of emphasizing the main ideas of the work. (3) "Improper authorial discourse," through the confrontation of the author's and the character's perspectives, can achieve particular semantic or stylistic effect: the formation of (a) a colloquial style, (b) a lively, light narrative tone in children's literature, (c) a humorous or satirical narration, (d) a historical or literary-historical stylization. In the achievement of these ends, "improper authorial discourse" is superior to "author's discourse" and "character's discourse" in that it makes it possible for the author to (1) reproduce the general contents of the character's thoughts and speech, which the character, for whatever reason, is unable to articulate, (2) reproduce contents that cannot be reconciled with the usual contents and norms of the character's DD (e.g. collective speech, blurring of boundaries between outer and inner speech), (3) achieve stylistic variety, (4) throw into relief peculiarities in the course of a dialogue, (5) accentuate certain parts of the discourse, (6) use unimportant moments of the sujet development to psychologically characterize the protagonist ("improper authorial discourse" is less conspicuous and "more economical" than characters' discourse), and (7) blur the boundaries between the character's monologic and dialogic discourse.

As comprehensive as this list of functions is, two basic functions made possible by the hybrid character of FID and of FCN are not even mentioned by Sokolova. These are *ambiguity* and *bi-textuality*.

p) Ambiguity and bi-textuality

As soon as people began to describe the phenomenon of FID, its main characteristic was stated to be *ambiguity*. Theodor Kalepky named the technique (that its "discoverer" Adolf Tobler [1887] described as the "idiosyncratic mixture of direct and indirect speech") *concealed discourse* (*verschleierte Rede*; Kalepky 1899; 1913) or *veiled discourse* (*verkleidete Rede*; Kalepky 1928) and defined it as:

---

45 Unfortunately, Sokolova refrains from separating the phenomenon, only named in general terms, into its individual manifestations, such as ID, FID, FCN etc.

> A way of portraying things in which the narrator does *not* render the thoughts and discourses of his characters in a way marking them as such, neither in "indirect" nor "direct" speech, but rather clothes them in the form that he would give his *own* thoughts, words [...] and leaves it to the reader, and indeed, without further ado, expects him, despite that, to recognize them as the thoughts and words of the character presented and to carry out the re-interpretation—as with a cipher system—correctly. (Kalepky 1913, 613)

In interpreting the technique understood in this way as the "concealment of the facts," as a formal "attempt to deceive the reader," Kalepky is aiming at—as do, following him, Spitzer (1922a) and Oskar Walzel ("game of hide-and-seek played by the narrator"; 1924, 221)—the effect resulting from its ambiguity on the reader.[46] The consequences for its reception have already been formulated by Emil Låftman in his work on what he calls *substitutional representation* (i.e. FID):

> Often, the reader can see only from the context whether the writer is speaking in his own name or in the name of his characters. [...] It is then a case of something that makes use of the reader's deductive abilities. (Låftman 1929, 165)

The ambiguity of the FID activates the reader and forces him to refer back to the context.

The forms of text interference are affected by this ambiguity to differing degrees. In quoted figural designation and all forms of ID, the presence of the other discourse is signaled graphically or with *verba dicendi*. A "concealment" of the presence of the CT is naturally not in evidence here. In the forms of ID, the concrete proportion of the CT can appear questionable. The reader must then decide which characteristics are to be attributed to NT and CT. In the types of FID in which feature 4 (time) refers to the CT, the identification of the CT is made easier by the difference in tense from the narrator's discourse. If, however, feature 4 refers to NT, it can be extremely difficult in the context of both preterite and present to identify the

---

46 Voloshinov, who gives particular attention to the interaction of "Bally's hypostasizing abstract objectivism" and the "hypostasizing individualistic subjectivism of the Vosslerites," and also comprehensively portrays Kalepky's position, praises the latter because he correctly understood the "double-faced" nature of FID, but reprimands him for his interpretation: "He incorrectly defined it. Under no conditions can we agree with Kalepky that quasi-direct discourse [i.e. FID] is 'masked' discourse and that the point of the device consists in guessing who the speaker is. No one, after all, starts off the process of understanding with abstract grammatical considerations. Therefore, it is clear to everyone from the very start that, in terms of the *sense* of what is said, it is the character speaking. Difficulties arise only for grammarians. Furthermore, our form does not at all contain an 'either/or' dilemma; its *specificum* is precisely a matter of *both* author *and* character speaking at the same time, a matter of a single linguistic construction within which the accents of two differently oriented voices are maintained." (Voloshinov 1929; tr. 1973, 144). Here we see again the preference noted above (p. 139) that Bakhtin and Voloshinov have for the agonal manifestations of "double-voicedness."

presence of the CT. An impediment to this differentiation arises in both types of FID if the opposition of NT and CT is neutralized in other features as well as time. FID can then become indistinguishable from the NT.

The least unambiguously identifiable is FCN. In many texts that contain this technique, it proves extraordinarily difficult, if not impossible, to keep separate the components of CT and NT in moments of interference. But their amalgamation facilitates the reproduction of the character's internal processes. The ambiguity of the continually changing text construction corresponds to the ambiguity of the inner life that is to be portrayed. Where direct and indirect discourse fix the character's inner processes, which are difficult to determine and not yet articulated, in an appropriately unambiguous way,[47] the ambiguity of the presence of CT in the fluctuating perspective of the narrator's discourse forms an ideal medium for the representation of the latent movements of a consciousness, a representation that counts on the cooperation of the reader.

The dispute mentioned above, on whether FID tends to serve empathy or criticism, has still not been resolved today. Elena Paducheva (1996, 360) has still taken up an unambiguous position on this controversy: she differentiates between "quotation" (by which she means *infection* and *reproduction*, the manifestations of FCN), which she distinguishes by its "double-voicedness," and the, according to her analysis, "monologic" FID, in which the voice of the character "tends to completely replace the voice the narrator." (This position corresponds to the conception of FID as a fundamentally univocal phenomenon, a position held from Bally to Banfield.) The objections to this are that, firstly, the features for NT realize the narrator and his evaluations,[48] and, secondly, that the phenomenon of simultaneous presence of two texts in one and the same statement inevitably leads to *bi-textuality*. With the development of a distance between the evaluative positions of narrator and character, this bi-textuality takes on the character of an ideological double-voicedness, a double-accentuation. One example for a sharp collision of evaluative positions takes places in "A Nasty Story," in which, according to Voloshinov's (1929; tr. 1973, 135) observations, each of the epithets "is an arena in which *two* intonations, *two* points of view, *two* speech acts converge and clash."

---

47   In his "Discourse in the Novel," Bakhtin (1934/35; tr. 1981, 319) describes FID as the best suited to rendering the interior speech of characters because "it is precisely this form that permits us to preserve the expressive structure of character's inner speech, its inability to exhaust itself in words, its flexibility, which would be absolutely impossible within the dry and logical form of indirect discourse."

48   The presence of the narrator in the grammatical features that refer to him, such as person and tense, is denied by the critics of bi-textuality (cf. Fludernik 1993a, 355).

3. The interference of narrator's text and characters' text

The double-voicedness makes the narrator's discourse axiologically doubled. Every value judgment by the character can be opposed by a narratorial evaluation position. In double-voiced FID, the narrator's implicit criticism can be directed at the ideology as well as the linguistic expressions of the CT.

In Mieke Bal's (1977a, 11) interpretation of FID, which takes up Genette's distinction between "mood" and "voice" (see above, III.1.b), a reductionism inherent to this dichotomy comes into effect. According to Bal's approach, the technique does not consist in interference between the *texts* of narrator and character (as argued by Schmid 1973, 39–79), but merely in interference between the *word* (of the narrator) and the *vision* (of the character). In this way, Bal *de facto* reduces the structure of FID to the formula "vision of the character + voice of the narrator." In this way, she simplifies the fact that, on the one hand, FID, as a rule, is realized in the lexis and syntax (i.e. in the "voice") of the character, and, on the other, that the narrator leaves traces of his or her own evaluation ("vision") on the perceptions, thoughts and words of the character. Consequently, *two* points of view and *two* voices, i.e. two *texts*, are united in FID.[49]

As has already been explained above (p. 139) in the delimitation of our text interference against Voloshinov's "speech interference," bi-textuality does not necessarily take on a double-accentuated character. In the FID of Russian romantic prose we can observe, for example, cases where there is no kind of competition between evaluations. In the FID of Chekhov's later works, no adversarial or relativizing accentuation can be detected. According to the observations of A. P. Chudakov (1971, 103), the free indirect monologues of Chekhov's later work approach the single-accentuated form that Voloshinov (1929; tr. 1973, 139) excludes from what is for him fundamentally double-voiced FID.[50] It is no coincidence that Bakhtin and Voloshinov, in their concentration on the dialogic manifestations of text interference, consistently avoided Chekhov, the master of univocal FID.

Between single-accented text interference and the double-voiced presentation that satirically portrays the contents and language of the character's speech, there is a broad spectrum of possible forms with differing evaluative relationships, which stretch from empathy to humorous accentuation, to critical irony and to destructive mockery.[51] Of course, the realization of

---

49 The unjustified criticism of my theory in Bal (1977a) is analyzed and rejected by Bronzwaer (1981, 197–200).

50 Voloshinov (1929; tr. 1973, 129) terms a representation in which the author speaks for the characters and places no accents "substituted direct discourse."

51 Portrayal of the so-called "dual-voice-hypothesis" (which already appears in the discussion of the 1920s: in Germany, with Spitzer 1922c and Günther 1928; in Russia with Bakhtin

evaluative relationships by the narrative text is not unambiguously predetermined, but is dependent on the interpretation of the changing relationship between text interference and its context. We can, however, describe certain tendencies of the forms toward certain effects. So, double-voicedness is tended towards above all by those forms in which the presence of CT is explicitly signaled, such as quoted figural designation and certain variants of autonomous indirect discourse. But double-voicedness is also widespread in FID and FCN, as is shown by the countless examples for competition between voices cited by Bakhtin and Voloshinov from a variety of literatures.

The double-voicedness of FID and FCN strengthens the difficulty of detection that arises from their ambiguity. The reader not only has the task of distinguishing the latent CT from the narrative discourse, but is also called upon to decide what evaluative standpoint the narrator is taking up on the contents and expressions of the CT.

1929 and Voloshinov 1929), synopsis of the arguments of its opponents (esp. Ann Banfield) and independent criticism in Fludernik 1993a, 338–59.

V. Narrative constitution: happenings—story—narrative—presentation of the narrative

1. "Fabula" and "sujet" in Russian formalism

a) Models of narrative constitution

Models of narrative constitution portray the narrative work as the result of a series of transformations. The work is dissected into individual constitutive tiers, and certain narrative devices are ascribed to each transformation.[1] The sequence of transformations must not in any way be understood in a temporal sense, but rather as the non-temporal unfolding of the devices that simultaneously bring the work into being. In this way, the models of narrative constitution portray neither the process of the work's production nor the process of its reception, but rather depict the ideal, non-temporal genesis of the narrative work with the help of temporal metaphors. In analogy with the transformation models of linguistics, the models could be called "generative"; factually more suitable is, however, the designation "ideal genetic models."

Why does narratology concern itself with these kinds of abstraction at all? The ideal genetic models deal less with differentiating between tiers (which are, in any case, not accessible to observation) and more with the identification of the operations that determine the transition from one tier to another. The task of the ideal genetic models thus consists in distinguishing those narrative operations that transform the source material contained in the narrative work into a narrative text accessible to observation. Consequently, the differentiation of tiers serves primarily as an aid to the analysis of the fundamental narrative devices.

The model of narrative constitution that has exercised the greatest influence on international literary study is the dichotomy *fabula* vs. *sujet*, delineated by the Russian formalists. This binary model has become very widespread in literary study and has been used as the starting point for countless narratological models (cf. Schmid 2009c). However, this dichotomy has been defined in different ways within the framework of formal-

---

1   Cf. the overview in Scheffel (2009).

ism.² In the following sections, the most important approaches will be examined.³

b) V. Shklovsky

Viktor Shklovsky did not intend to develop a narratological theory, nor even to undertake a differentiation of narrative tiers. He was interested exclusively in the *sujet*, whereby for him this concept did not, in most cases, describe a finished product, the result of transformations, but an energy, the process of artistic construction, an element of "form":

> [...] the sujet and the nature of sujet [syuzhetnost'] constitute a form no less than rhyme. (Shklovsky 1919b; tr. 1990, 46)⁴
>
> Sujet is a phenomenon of style, it is the compositional construction of the work. (Shklovsky 1928, 220)
>
> The methods and devices of sujet construction are similar to and in principle identical with the devices of, for instance, sound orchestration. Works of literature represent a *web* of sounds, movements and ideas. (Shklovsky 1919b; tr. 1990, 45; transl. revised)

Shklovsky gives the classic definition of the relationship between *fabula* and *sujet* in passing, in an essay on Sterne's *Tristram Shandy*:⁵

> The concept of *sujet* is too often confused with a description of the events in the novel, with what I'd tentatively call *fabula*. As a matter of fact, though, the

---

2   The most important meta-theoretical works are: Volek 1977; 1985; Hansen-Löve 1978, 238–63; García Landa 1998, 22–60. In Russian-language study, the anthologies in the series *Voprosy syuzhetoslozheniya* ("Questions of sujet construction"), published in Daugavpils (Latvia), in particular, are dedicated to the systematic and literary-historical investigation of the *fabula-sujet* dichotomy. Cf. esp. Tsilevich 1972; Egorov et al. 1978.

3   In sujet theory, the work of German philologists on the composition of literary texts may have had a certain influence on the Russian formalists. Those who must be named first and foremost are: Otmar Schissel von Fleschenberg, Bernhard Seuffert and Wilhelm Dibelius. The approach of using a systematic model of narrative structure, which appears as an early ideal genetic model from present perspective, can be found in W. Dibelius' (1910) *Englische Romankunst*. On the relationships between German and Russian composition theory, cf. Doležel 1973b; Hansen-Löve 1978, 264–67; Doležel 1990, 124–46. Viktor Zhirmunsky (1927) and particularly Rozaliya Shor (1927) had already referred to German composition theory in the 1920s. The latter, on whom Doležel bases much of his work, does, however, in her report on the "German formalists," tend to diminish the contribution of the very critically received Russian formal school. Cf. now Aumüller 2009, who clearly qualifies the influence of German theorists.

4   Here and in the following quotations, the English translations *plot* and *story(line)* are replaced with *sujet* and *fabula* respectively.

5   With his definition, Shklovsky placed in opposition two terms which had originally both equally described the narrated material (cf. Volek 1977, 142).

1. "Fabula" and "sujet" in Russian formalism

fabula is nothing more than material for sujet formation. In this way, the sujet of *Eugene Onegin* is not love between Eugene and Tatyana but the appropriation of that fabula in the form of digressions that interrupt the text. (Shklovsky 1921; tr. 1990, 170)

Shklovsky searched for estheticity exclusively in the acts of formation and judged as minimal the esthetic relevance of the material that was to be formed. For Shklovsky, the *sujet* as an act of formation meant a defamiliarizing deformation of the *fabula*. Art was, as the programmatic title of Shklovsky's well-known essay (1917) postulated, "device" and the devices of *sujet* construction consisted above all in the devices of parallelism, repetition, "staircase-like construction," and "slowing down," which bring about a "difficult form" and a "defamiliarization" of things. The intended effect of defamiliarization was to increase the effort and duration of perception because, Shklovsky claims, the process of perception is an end in itself in art and must be prolonged accordingly (cf. Schmid 2005c). The objects of perception were the complicating acts of formation themselves, the—as Shklovsky put it—"dancing behind the plough"[6] or the "making of a thing".[7] The substance handled in formation, the "world of emotions, of mental experiences" (Jakobson 1921, 32), became the mere "motivation" of devices, was thus degraded to the "means of justification" (Jakobson 1921, 32), and the product of this formation, the "made," the "ploughed field," was succinctly dismissed as "not important." Shklovsky repeatedly indicated that he did not think of the *sujet* as substance, neither as formed content nor as the product of the application of devices to the *fabula*; he even underlined the irrelevance of the content category for the *sujet*:

From the standpoint of sujet, there is no need for the concept of "content" in our analysis of a work of art. We may consider form in this context to be the principle underlying the construction of an object. (Shklovsky 1919b; tr. 1990, 46)

This "principle underlying the construction of an object" takes on the character of an autonomous, abstract force in Shklovsky's work. The *sujet* does not simply process existing, finished, predetermined material, following the latter's directives. In line with the "special laws of *sujet* construction still unknown to us" (1919b; tr. 1990, 18), it, by contrast, actively searches out single instances from the repertoire of eternally existing motifs, and combines

---

6   "Dance, too, is a form of walking, which is felt; more precisely, a walk that is set up in such a way that one feels it. And so, we dance behind the plough; it happens because we are ploughing, but we have no need of the ploughed field" (Shklovsky 1919a, 36). "Because we are ploughing" means "because we enjoy the feeling of ploughing."

7   "Art is a way of experiencing the making of an object; the object is not important" (Shklovsky 1917; tr. 1965, 12; transl. revised).

them.[8] Shklovsky's conception of the independent activity of the *sujet*, which is not explicated anywhere, becomes clear on the example of thematic material being introduced into folk poetry as a result of the artistic demands of devices such as "staircase-like construction" and "slowing down":

> Here we observe a phenomenon common in art: a particular form seeks to complete itself in a manner analogous to the way that words seek completion in certain sound-blurs in lyrical poetry. (Shklovsky 1919b; tr. 1910, 25)

In Shklovsky's radical conception, elements of the storyline are introduced into a work not on the basis of the real-life, ethical or philosophical content, but rather because the *sujet* construction demands them:

> The sujet constructions select fabula-situations that suit them and deform the material in the process. (Shklovsky 1928, 220)

> Certain fabula situations can be selected according to sujet principles, i.e. there can be a certain sujet construction laid out in the situations themselves, a staircase-like construction, an inversion, a circular construction. In the same way, specific types of stone have a layered structure that makes them especially well-suited to certain arrangements. (Shklovsky 1928, 220)

The laws of *sujet* construction aim at the "creation of perceptible works of art" (Shklovsky 1919a, 97). Perceptibility is, however, guaranteed by the newness of the form:

> A new form makes its appearance not in order to express a new content, but rather to replace an old form that has lost its artistic character (Shklovsky 1919b; tr. 1990, 20; transl. revised)

Insofar as Shklovsky tended towards the equation of the concept of form with the concept of the esthetically effective, he neglected not only the substance of the *fabula* but also the formed quality of the *fabula* itself. The form of the *fabula* was seen as an inherent property of the material. It did not appear as the result of artistic activity.

An overview of Shklovsky's *fabula-sujet* concept makes clear why the formalist dichotomy proves difficult to apply in practical analysis. It is not

---

[8] The extent to which compositional demands can steer even the introduction of characters is illustrated by Shklovsky with the help of a letter from Leo Tolstoy (from May 3, 1865) to a lady who asked the novelist who Andrey Bolkonsky was: "I shall endeavor to say who my Andrey is. In the battle of Austerlitz [...] it was necessary for me to kill off a brilliant young man. Later in the same novel I found that I needed old man Bolkonsky and his daughter. Since it is rather awkward to describe a character who is in no way connected with the novel, I decided to make another brilliant young man the son of old Bolkonsky. I then became interested in him and gave him a role in the unfolding of the sujet of the novel. And, feeling charitable, I had him severely wounded instead of killed. And so, my dear princess, here is my totally honest though somewhat vague explanation as to who Bolkonsky is." (Shklovsky 1919b; tr. 1990, 41–42; transl. revised)

1. "Fabula" and "sujet" in Russian formalism

only the ambiguity of the concepts,[9] but also the anti-substantialism of formalist thinking. However *fabula* was understood, the concept always meant something subordinate, whose *raison d'être* was limited to serving as a foundation for a defamiliarizing *sujet*. For the formalists, the *fabula* was important only as something to be overcome, as an order that offered resistance to the deforming new order and, in the process, ultimately only heightened the "perceptibility" of the devices that overcame this resistance. But it was not seen as an independent phenomenal fact. As soon as the devices were perceived, the reader could, in the formalists' conception, forget the material that served their manifestation.

The radical anti-substantialism of their thinking blinded the formalists to the intrinsic artistic value, the fabricated nature and the semantic content of the *fabula* that was to be transformed. It also prevented them from seeing the *fabula* and *sujet* as differently formed substances, whose incongruence—bound up with the tension resulting from it—goes beyond the mere effect of defamiliarization to precipitate new potential thematic meanings.[10]

c) M. Petrovsky

In his work on the composition of the novella, Mikhail Petrovsky[11] (1925; 1927) completely reverses the meaning of the terms taken on from Boris Eikhenbaum (1921), "fabula" and "sujet." What Eikhenbaum, following Shklovsky, called "fabula," Petrovsky calls "sujet," and what Eikhenbaum denotes as "sujet" appears in Petrovsky as "fabula":

---

9   Our reconstruction of the first *fabula-sujet* dichotomy that can be called formalist should not make us forget that Shklovsky, even in his early phase, used his key terms in no way consistently. It is not unusual for him to use especially the sujet concept in the conventional sense, as a synonym for fabula or as the description of the result of the application of devices.

10 Among the formalists in a narrow sense, Yury Tynyanov (1927a; tr. 1981, 95–96) developed his own conception of *fabula* and *sujet*. He rejects widespread definitions of *fabula* ("static pattern of relationships" and "pattern of actions") and suggests a dichotomy, which he explains in analogy with the relationship between meter and rhythm: the *fabula* is "the entire semantic (conceptual) basting of the action," the *sujet* is "the story's dynamics, composed of the interactions of all the linkages of material (including the story as a linkage of actions)—stylistic linkage, story linkage, etc." This definition certainly dissolves the classification of the two concepts. The *fabula* stands for the represented world, the *sujet* for the structure of the work. It is no longer a case of opposition, but of inclusion: the *fabula* becomes an element of the *sujet* (cf. also Todorov 1971a, 16–17; Volek 1977, 145–46).

11 M. Petrovsky did not belong to the inner circle of Russian formalists, but was rather on the periphery—just as Boris Tomashevsky, Viktor Zhirmunsky and Alexander Reformatsky, the exponents of the so-called composition theory.

> I want to use the word *sujet* in the sense of the *material* of the work of art. The sujet is, in a sense, the system of events, of actions (or a single simple or complex event), which was available to the writer in a particular form, which is, however, not yet the result of his own individual creative work. I would like to describe the *poetically* handled sujet with the term *fabula*. (Petrovsky 1925, 197; emphases in the original)

What is important here is, however, not so much that "fabula" and "sujet" change places for Petrovsky. Decisive is rather that a shift in the content of the concept—one which initially appears insignificant but is, in reality, highly distinctive—has taken place in Petrovsky's definition. Whereas Shklovsky defines his *sujet* concept mostly in terms of form or formation ("handling," "treatment"), Petrovsky uses his equivalent *fabula* concept to denote a substance, the "poetically handled material." Here we already find the shift of emphasis from *energeia* to *ergon* that became key to the entire later reception of the *fabula-sujet* dichotomy. There is also a second shift in the content of the concepts, which must be noted: the "sujet" (in Petrovsky's terms), even though it constitutes the source material for the individual creative act, is not available to the writer as amorphous material but as something that has already been formed in a certain way, as a "system of events" (in Petrovsky's Aristotelian formulation). This second shift of emphasis is then taken on in many models that seek to overcome early-formalist reductionism.

In his essay on the morphology of the novella (1927), Petrovsky places the *fabula-sujet* dichotomy (with his own reversal of the contents) in relation to the distinction between *disposition* and *composition* that originates in classical rhetoric. In the novella, Petrovsky demands that we distinguish "between the total sequence of a *sujet*'s movement and the sequence of its exposition."[12] The former is called *disposition*, the latter *composition*.[13] The *sujet* can be derived from the very text of the novella. It is not difficult for us to single it out because the sequence of the *sujet* is the causal-temporal sequence of life itself. That is why its structure (the disposition) does not have special interest for us:

---

12 In the following as above, *plot*, which is used in the English translation, will be replaced with *sujet*.

13 German composition theory worked with the dichotomy *Disposition* vs. *Komposition* during the 1910s. Rozaliya Shor refers to work by Otmar Schissel von Fleschenberg (1910) in which the composition analyst places composition as the esthetic arrangement of the contents in opposition to disposition as the logical development of the events. In a later work, Schissel also sees disposition as canonized composition, which has become characteristic of a particular genre (Shor 1927, 133). A connection arises here with formalist theory, according to which the "automated" sujet of a work or a genre can become the fabula of a new, defamiiarizing sujet.

1. "Fabula" and "sujet" in Russian formalism 181

> It is clear that the artistic structure of a novella is organically linked to its composition, with the device of exposition, i.e., the development of its sujet. (Petrovsky 1927; tr. 1987, 75)

Although Petrovsky assigns artistic priority to composition, he nonetheless, in contrast to Shklovsky, confers an independent structuredness on the material of the representation (in his terms: the *sujet*). The "sujet" is "life," but not life in its entire plenitude; it is, rather, "transformed life":

> Sujet is always a *transformation* of life, as of raw material. [...] And, above all, sujet is selection. (Petrovsky 1927; tr. 1987, 24–25)

This assessment foreshadows models that assign a selectivity to the story in contrast to the happenings to be narrated, and award it artistic status. A triad of tiers is thus indicated in Petrovsky's work: "Life"—"sujet" with its "disposition"—"fabula" with its "composition."

d) L. Vygotsky

The reductionism inherent in the formalist *fabula-sujet* dichotomy comes to light particularly in quasi-formalist textual analyses in which the formalists' categories are adapted without being guided by a genuine formalist interest, capable of compensating for all reductions.

One revealing catalyst that exposes the reductionism of the formalist *fabula-sujet* dichotomy is the exemplary analysis of Ivan Bunin's novella "Gentle Breath" undertaken by the Russian psychologist and psycho-linguist Lev Vygotsky in his book *Psychology of Art*. In the book, the psychologist addresses the question of how artworks from different genres elicit distinct mental reactions.

The theoretical discussion that precedes the analysis of Bunin's novella criticizes and modifies the premises of formalism.[14] Particularly interesting for our purposes is that Vygotsky widens the extension of the form concept and of artistic activity to the constitution of the *fabula*, and underlines the intrinsic value of the material in the psychological effect of the artwork. Just like Petrovsky, Vygotsky emphasizes that the *fabula* or "disposition" (i.e. the natural sequence of events) does not coincide with life, but is already the result of artistic treatment. Just like the composition theorist, the psychologist highlights the element of selection and underlines the artistic relevance of this act:

---

14 The relation of Vygotsky's *Psychology of Art* (whose two parts were produced between 1915 and 1922) to Russian formalism is not entirely unambiguous. Despite his explicit criticism of formalism, Vygotsky models the psychology of the esthetic reaction entirely in the terminology of formalism.

For the sake of our argument we proceeded from a comparison between disposition and composition, assuming that disposition is the natural element and composition the artificial, or art one. We did not mention, however, that disposition in itself, that is, the choice of the facts to be treated, is already a creative act. (Vygotsky 1925; tr. 1971, 158–59)

Nonetheless, Vygotsky's analysis—obviously under the spell of the formalist model—remains characteristically insufficient.[15] Vygotsky ascribes the esthetic effect of the novella to the "conflict between content and form," to Schiller's destruction of the content by form: "the artist achieves his effect by means of the form, which destroys the content." For him the "content" or "material" is the "fabula,"[16] that is, the pre-literary happenings, "the events and characters of everyday life, or the relationships between human beings—in brief, all that existed prior to the story." "Form" for Vygotsky is—in Shklovsky's sense—the "arrangement of this material in accordance with the laws of artistic construction" (1925; tr. 1971, 145). According to Vygotsky, the esthetic effect of Bunin's novella is based on the tension between the diverging structures of material and story. While the "structure of the material" (which is equated with the "disposition," the "anatomy," and the "static scheme of construction") contains the events in their "natural sequence," the "structure of the story" (the "composition," the "physiology," the "dynamic scheme") places them in an artificial sequence. The rearrangement of the material's parts—and this is Vygotsky's decisive argument—changes the emotional effect of the material, the significance and the meaning of the story. (Even though Vygotsky also refers to auxiliary devices, "the language [the author] uses, the tone, the mood, his choice of words, his construction of sentences" etc., he reduces the effect of the *sujet* practically to rearrangement.) According to Vygotsky's analysis, the events themselves in Bunin's novella cause a gloomy impression; the material, taken in itself, embodies the meaning "troubles of life." As a whole, the narrative conveys, according to Vygotsky's interpretation, the precisely opposite effect: "the feeling of liberation, lightness, the crystal transparency of life, none of which can be derived from the literal events" (1925; tr. 1971, 154). In Vygotsky's interpretation, the material, which remains substantially the same, owes its radical change in tone exclusively to the rearrangement of its parts: "The events are connected in such a way that they lose their turbidity" (1925; tr. 1971, 154).

Obviously inspired by Yury Tynyanov's (1924a) reference to the semantic function of poetic construction, Vygotsky develops an approach, presented in a metaphorical way of his own, to the analysis of the semantic

---

15 Cf. the interesting articles by Alexander Zholkovsky (1992; 1994), in which Vygotsky's "brilliant" essay is criticized as "over-interpretation of an incomplete structural analysis."
16 In the English edition, this term is translated with *plot* and "sujet" with *subject*.

"doubling" that results from the simultaneous presence of *fabula* and *sujet*, an approach that he, however, does not use consistently in what follows:

> The words of a story or verse carry its meaning (the water), whereas the composition creates another meaning for the words, transposes everything onto a completely different level, and transforms the whole into wine. Thus, the banal tale of a frivolous provincial schoolgirl is transformed into the gentle breath of Bunin's short story. (1925; tr. 1971, 154–55)

In Vygotsky's analysis, there are two serious reductions predetermined by the formalist *fabula-sujet* conception:

1. The "material" is functionally subordinated to the "form." The qualities of the material and their emotional effect function only as the medial substratum on which the final formal qualities are built. Vygotsky thereby leads his theoretical recognition of the intrinsic value of the material in analysis *ad absurdum*. The final impression of the novella is, for him, merely the static result of the formation of the material, the "gentleness" to which the novella's title refers, but not—as his dialectical premises would lead us to expect—the result of the simultaneous presence of *fabula* and *sujet*, the dissonance of turbidity of content und transparency of form, the complex unity of conflicting impressions and effects. Nor did Vygotsky ultimately acknowledge the perception of "form as flow (that is, change), as the correlation of subordinating, constructive factor and the subordinated one," which was postulated in a later part of the book (1925; tr. 1971, 220), drawing on Tynyanov (1924a, 40).

2. Vygotsky blatantly overestimates the relevance of composition to the work's meaning. The cathartic liberation from the oppressive effect of the narrated existential moments in Bunin's novella results less from rearrangement than from the artistic organization of the *fabula* itself. The *fabula* already exhibits an organization that wrenches the "troubles of life" out of direct orientation on the life of the perceiving subject while giving the dolorous events a lighter tone, admittedly without removing the tragic base note. In this work, the device of *fabula* organization that has this effect is the comic-coincidental arrangement of situations, characters and actions, particularly the surprising *equivalences* between the figures: (1) the *thematic* equivalences formed by the familial relations between characters, by their equal or contrasted social station and sphere, by their ideology and their behavior, (2) the *positional* equivalences given by the appearance of the characters at comparable moments in the story, (3) the *verbal* equivalences, which go back to the repetitions in and between the characters' discourses (which are, after all, part of the *fabula* and are not added for the first time in the *sujet*).

Even without analyzing Bunin's novella in detail, it is possible to determine that the dialectic of tragedy and comedy, of heaviness and lightness, is already present in the material. The *sujet* formation merely underlines the simultaneity of the conflicting emotions created in the *fabula*. As with the formalists, Vygotsky's blatant underestimation of the relevance of the *fabula* to the work's meaning is accompanied by an overestimation of the power of the *sujet*.

e) B. Tomashevsky

With his *Theory of Literature* (1925; 1928a), Boris Tomashevsky is the Russian theorist of the *fabula-sujet* dichotomy who has been most intensively read in western literary study. It must, however, be questioned whether Tomashevsky's position, which Todorov (1971a, 15) qualified as "a good deal more coherent than Shklovsky's," and which is often seen as the last "canonical" (Volek 1977, 142) word of Russian formalism on the *fabula-sujet* problem, actually still represents genuine formalist thinking. Hansen-Löve (1978, 268) rightly sees Tomashevsky's orientation on theme as the unifying principle of construction as being "in sharp contradiction" to the immanentism of the formalists. Nevertheless, Shklovsky (1928, 220) attests that Tomashevsky had taken on his, Shklovsky's, definition of the difference between *fabula* and *sujet* "almost exactly," and only refrained from naming the author of the definition in both editions because of the textbook nature of *Theory of Literature*.

Tomashevsky develops his definition from two approaches. From the fourth edition onwards (Tomashevsky 1928a), the first approach is formulated somewhat differently from in the first 1925 edition.

Let us begin by examining the first approach. The *fabula* is defined in the 1925 edition in the following way:

> Fabula is the aggregate of mutually related events reported in the work. No matter how the events were originally arranged in the work and despite their original order of introduction, in practice the fabula may be told in the actual chronological and causal order of events. (Tomashevsky 1925; tr. 1965, 66–67)[17]

The *sujet* is also vaguely defined as a reorganization of "order" and "connection":

> Sujet is distinct from fabula. Both include the same events, but in the sujet the events *are arranged* and connected according to the orderly sequence in which they were presented in the work. (Tomashevsky 1925; tr. 1965, 67; emphases in the original)

---

17   In the translation by L. T. Lemon and M. J. Reis (see also above, p. 3, footnote 4) I have replaced *story* with *fabula* and *plot* with *sujet*.

1. "Fabula" and "sujet" in Russian formalism

In the 1928 edition, the aspect of sequence for the *fabula* is replaced with that of connection:

> The theme of a work with a fabula presents a more or less unified system of events that emerge from, and are linked to, one another. The totality of the events in their reciprocal internal concatenation is what we call fabula. (Tomashevsky 1928a, 134)

In this edition, the *fabula* is thus not equated with the pre-literary material, but rather forms a certain abstraction from the continuum of events, characterized by connection.

In the 1928 edition, the definition of the *sujet* initially remains quite uncertain:

> It is not enough to invent an entertaining chain of events and limit them with a beginning and an end. These events need to be *arranged*, put into a certain order, be portrayed, by making of this fabula material a literary combination. The artistically organized arrangement of events in a work is what we call *sujet*. (Ibd.; emphases in the original)

The second approach to the definition of *fabula* and *sujet*, in both editions of *Theory of Literature*, uses the concept of the motif. Motifs are the "smallest particles of thematic material" (Tomashevsky 1925; tr. 1965, 67).

> Mutually related motifs form the thematic bonds of the work. From this point of view, the fabula is the aggregate of motifs in their logical, causal-chronological order; the sujet is the aggregate of those same motifs but having the relevance and the order which they had in the original work. The place in the work in which the reader learns of an event, whether the information is given by the author, or by a character, or by a series of indirect hints—all this is irrelevant to the fabula. But the esthetic function of the sujet is precisely this bringing of an arrangement of motifs to the attention of the reader. (Tomashevsky 1925; tr. 1965, 68)

The tendency, observed in Petrovsky's work, to view the *fabula* as something preformed is thus also visible in Tomashevsky. The production of a logical-causal connection, which is, after all, not found in reality, is, in itself, an artistic act. Tomashevsky draws the border between the pre-literary and the literary differently than Shklovsky (cf. Todorov 1971a, 17). Where the latter usually equates the *fabula* with the esthetically indifferent, pre-literary happenings, Tomashevsky, at least implicitly, assigns an artistic character to the *fabula*. Tomashevsky places the *sujet* in opposition to the *fabula* in two respects: on the one hand, it is the result of reorganization and the artistic connection of motifs of the *fabula*; on the other, it presents the artistically organized sequence of motifs from a certain perspective.

2. The overcoming of formalist reductionism

a) "Histoire" and "discours" in French structuralism

The manageable form that Tomashevsky gave the formalist *fabula-sujet* pair cannot disguise the fundamental problem inherent in the dichotomy from the beginning, namely the ambivalence of both concepts. The *fabula* concept oscillated between two meanings: (1) material in the sense of the pre-literary happenings of reality, and (2) an internally structured sequence of motifs bounded by a beginning and an end, in their logical, causal-temporal nexus. The *sujet* concept fluctuated between the meanings: (1) the energetic power of formation, and (2) the result of the application of various devices. In the second meaning, it remained unclear which devices were involved and in what substance the *sujet* was to be thought of, whether it was to be imagined as already formulated in the language of an art form (literature, film, music etc.) or as a medial structure not yet substantiated. Even the replacement of *fabula* and *sujet* with the dichotomy *récit* vs. *narration* (Barthes 1966) or *histoire* vs. *discours* (Todorov 1966)[18] only partially solved the problems thrown up by a dyadic model of narrative constitution. In the definition of their categories, the French structuralists drew on Tomashevsky's didactic, smoothed out model and referred primarily to a consciously simplified explication given in a famous footnote in the first edition of *Theory of Literature*, a didactic explanation that Tomashevsky excised from the later editions:

> In brief, the fabula is the "the action itself," the sujet, "how the reader learns of the action." (Tomashevsky 1925; tr. 1965, 67)

Clearly following Tomashevsky, Todorov states:

> On the most general level the literary work has two aspects; it is both story and discourse. It is a story in the sense that it evokes a certain reality of events that may have happened [...] But the work is at the same time discourse [...] On this level what counts is the way in which the narrator acquaints us with events rather than the events reported. (Todorov 1966; tr. 1977, 20)

Even Seymour Chatman, who attempts to "synthesize" the most prominent Russian formalist and French structuralist approaches in his book *Story and Discourse*, reformulates Tomashevsky's footnote in his basic definition:

> In simple terms, the story is the *what* in a narrative that is depicted, discourse the *how*. (Chatman 1978, 19; emphases in the original)[19]

---

18 Todorov borrowed the dichotomy *histoire* vs. *discours* from Emile Benveniste (1959), for whom, however, the terms have a different meaning.
19 Meir Sternberg 1974, 8–9, has a similar interpretation: "To put it as simply as possible, the fabula involves what happens in the work as (re)arranged in the 'objective' order of oc-

2. The overcoming of formalist reductionism

Despite the dependence on the formalist concept and despite the apparent homology with *fabula* vs. *sujet*, the dichotomy *histoire* vs. *discours* implies three essential shifts of emphasis, which contribute to a modeling of narrative constitution that is both more valid and more suitable for analysis:

1. The *histoire* is freed from the taint of being mere material, and an intrinsic artistic value is ascribed to it: "both aspects, the story and the discourse, are equally literary" (Todorov 1966; tr. 1977, 20).[20]

2. Whereas Shklovsky referred particularly to parallelism and stratification, and Petrovsky, Vygotsky, and Tomashevsky thought the most effective of the *sujet* devices was the reorganization of elements from the *fabula*, the French theorists emphasize the devices of amplification, perspectivization and verbalization.[21]

3. Whereas the *sujet* concept was imagined in categories of form or formation by the Russian formalists and the theorists close to them, the term *discours* is bound up with a substance-oriented approach. The term denotes not the sum of the devices applied (as *sujet* does by Shklovsky), but the *result* of artistic operations. In the *discours* concept, two aspects overlap:

a. The *discours* contains the *histoire* in transformed shape.

b. The *discours* has a categorically different substance to the *histoire*: it is speech, narration, text, which neither simply contains the story, nor merely reshapes it, but primarily denotes it as its signified, and represents it.

As a result, the *discours* concept is connected with two entirely different operations:

(1) the transformation of the *histoire* through the rearrangement of parts or other devices, and

(2) the manifestation of the *histoire* in a text denoting it.

The two operations can be presented in the following diagram:

---

currence, while the sujet involves what happens in the order, angle, and patterns of presentation actually encountered by the reader." Whereas Chatman's dichotomy amounts to the opposition of content and form, in Sternberg's interpretation of fabula and sujet, two co-occurring orders are confronted with one another.

20 In the rehabilitation of the *histoire*, some proponents of French structuralism certainly tend towards the opposite extreme to the one-sided favoring of the *sujet*, namely towards exclusive interest in the rules that guide the constitution of the *histoire*. For this also there is a model in the Russian theory of the 1920s: Vladimir Propp's (1928) model of actants and functions. This tendency is most conspicuous in the work on "narrative grammar" (e.g. Bremond 1964; Greimas 1967; Todorov 1969).

21 On points 1 and 2 cf. also Rimmon 1976, 36.

		⇒ Transformation	
Story (signified)	histoire	x	⇓ Manifestation in the
Text (signifier)		discours	signified

The diagram is to be understood as follows: the pre-linguistic story is transformed into a pre-linguistic x, which remains unnamed by the French theorists. The transformed *histoire* is then verbally (or pictorially, cinematically etc.) manifested. In the case of literature, the result of this manifestation is *discours*.

b) Three-tier models

In textual analysis, it becomes clear that every binary model of narrative constitution either operates with ambiguous concepts or ignores entire dimensions of the phenomenon. For instance, *fabula* has been used to denote the entire material of the happenings implicit in the narrative work as well as the story selected from it. In the *sujet* concept also—and subsequently in the French *discours*, as shown above—two completely different operations are lumped together, reorganization and verbalization. However, where ambiguity is eliminated, as in Todorov's *histoire* concept, for instance, which is defined in the sense of the second meaning of *fabula*, the primary, founding operation of narrative constitution is ignored, namely the formation of a shaped and meaningful story.

The ambiguity and shortcomings of the dichotomic concepts provided the impetus for the development of models with more than two tiers.[22]

One of the most widespread three-tier models was suggested by Gérard Genette (1972). Genette distinguishes three meanings for "narrative" (*récit*): (1) "the narrative statement, the oral or written discourse that undertakes to tell of an event or a series of events"; (2) "the succession of events, real or fictitious, that are the subjects of this discourse"; (3) "the act of narrating taken in itself" (1972; tr. 1980, 25–26). He assigns three terms to these concepts: (1) *text*, (2) *story*, and (3) *narration* (whereby *text* appears as a signifier and *story* as signified). Mieke Bal (1977a, 6) notes that Genette's third concept is located on a different tier to the other two. While *narration* denotes the process of the statement, *text* and *story* describe the product of an activity. *Narration*, according to Bal, therefore belongs in the series of activities

---

22 Cf. the overviews of the models of narrative constitution in García Landa 1998, 19–60; Martinez/Scheffel 1999, 22–26; Pier 2003.

2. The overcoming of formalist reductionism

formed by *narration, disposition* and *invention*. Thus Genette distinguishes only two tiers, namely those of Russian formalism, *fabula* and *sujet*.[23]

Bal herself suggests a slightly different triad: *texte—récit—histoire* (1977a, 4) or, in the English version, *text—story—fabula* (1985, 5-6). In her understanding, *text* is the signifier of the *story* (*récit*); the *story*, for its part, is the signifier of the *fabula* (*histoire*).

In a similar way, José Ángel García Landa (1998, 19-20) distinguishes three tiers for the analysis of a narrative text: (1) the "narrative discourse" (*discurso narrativo*), (2) the "story" (*relato*), and (3) the "action" (*acción*). By "action," he means the "sequence of narrated events." The "story" is the "representation [*representación*] of the plot, insofar as it is conveyed by narrative." And the "narrative discourse" is the "representation of the story."

An important step in the development of narrative constitution was the triad suggested by Karlheinz Stierle (1971; 1977), *Geschehen—Geschichte—Text der Geschichte*, which, however, went largely unnoticed in the international debate. In this triad, the two first tiers correspond to the formalist *fabula* concept. The "Geschehen" is the narrative material implied in the "Geschichte," which, in being transformed into a "Geschichte," expresses a particular meaning. (A similar distinction between *Geschehen* and *Geschichte* also appears in the four-tier model suggested below.) By distinguishing between meaningful *Geschichte* and the *Geschehen* implied in, and interpreted by, it, Stierle's triad interprets the tier that Shklovsky had seen as esthetically indifferent, pre-existing material differently, namely as the result of artistic operations that create meaning. However, the definition of the *Text der Geschichte* is problematic. Just like the pre-forming concept of *discours*, *Text der Geschichte* unites two heterogeneous aspects: (1) the rearrangement of the parts into an artistic shape, and (2) the manifestation of the *Geschichte* in the medium of language. Stierle himself sees that the two operations lie on different tiers of constitution, and accounts for this with a "makeshift" distinction between "translinguistic" "discours I (deep discourse)" and "discours II (surface discourse)." A correction is to be added to Stierle's double occupation of the *Text der Geschichte*, and it must be one that transposes the "makeshift" distinction between "deep discourse" and "surface discourse" into a systematic differentiation of two tiers.

The following diagram provides an overview of the two- and three-tier models discussed here. The columns contain analogous concepts, but these are not necessarily identical in every respect.

---

23   The three-tier nature of Genette's model is defended by Fludernik 1996, 334; Pier 2003, 82.

Tomashevsky 1925	fabula		sujet	
Todorov 1966	histoire		discours	
Genette 1972	histoire		récit	
Rimmon-K. 1983	story		text	
Bal 1977	histoire		récit	texte
Bal 1985	fabula		story	text
García Landa 1998	acción		relato	discurso
Stierle 1971	Geschehen	Geschichte	Text der Geschichte	

3. The four narrative tiers

a) The ideal genetic model

Comparison of the models leads to the conclusion that the dichotomy or triad of concepts must be replaced with a model with four tiers. A model of this sort must account for the bivalent meaning of the terms *fabula* and *sujet* or *histoire* and *discours*. In the following, a model of constitution of this type will be presented, which encompasses the tiers "happenings" (*Geschehen*), "story" (*Geschichte*), "narrative" (*Erzählung*) and "presentation of the narrative" (*Präsentation der Erzählung*):

1. Happenings
The happenings are the amorphous entirety of situations, characters and actions explicitly or implicitly represented, or logically implied, in the narrative work. The happenings understood in this way form a continuum that is spatially fundamentally unlimited, can be endlessly temporally extended into the past, can be infinitely divided internally, and can be concretized into infinite properties.[24] The happenings correspond to the formalist *fabula*

---

24 The happenings of a given work can theoretically be extended ever further into the past, into the inferred backstory, until the creation of the world. In the process, the greater the distance from the elements explicitly represented in the text becomes, the more the relevance of the implicit happenings decreases. The story narrated in the novel *Anna Karenina*, implies, for instance, that the eponymous heroine has enjoyed the benefits of an education and a good upbringing, although her schooldays and the upbringing by her parents, or indeed the parents themselves, are never explicitly discussed. Nonetheless, certain explicit motifs of the narrated story (the heroine's moral reactions, social conduct and literary reading matter) can make the concretization of the merely implicit meaningful (on the

3. The four narrative tiers

in Shklovsky's sense, but are not seen here as esthetically indifferent material, rather as the already esthetically relevant result of invention, the act that classical rhetoric called *inventio* or εὕρεσις.

2. Story

The story is the result of a *selection* from the happenings. It is constituted by two selection operations that transpose the infinitude of the happenings into a limited, meaningful form:

(1) The selection of certain *elements* (situations, characters and actions) from the happenings.

(2) The selection of certain *properties* from the infinite mass of characteristics that can be ascribed to the selected elements.

The story thus encompasses nothing other than the elements explicitly represented and furnished with certain characteristics in the text, the denoted and qualified situations, characters and actions. The represented circumstances are part of the story only in those characteristics that are concretized by the explicit qualifications given in the text. All exterior and interior situations, actions and properties, which we can, and often must, imagine and add to the represented circumstances, i.e. everything more or less unambiguously implied, remain either permanently or—in specific cases, examined below—temporarily in the infinitude of non-selected elements and properties. The story defined in this way corresponds to Tomashevsky's *fabula* and Todorov's *histoire*. In the terminology of classical rhetoric, the story is the result of disposition (*dispositio*, τάξις). It contains the selected elements in their *ordo naturalis*.

3. Narrative

The narrative is the result of composition, which places the elements in an *ordo artificialis*.[25]

The essential devices of composition are:

(1) The *linearization* of things occurring simultaneously in the story, forming a sequence of presentation.

(2) The *reorganization* of the segments of the story.

---

problem, see below). But the logically presupposed life stories of her parents have no relevance whatsoever to the novel and therefore do not practically belong to its happenings.

25 The theory of the artistic construction of the narrated story is missing in the system of classical rhetoric. The concept of *compositio* (συνθήκη) does not appear in classical thought as the theory of the construction of the action, but rather denotes the theory of joining together words in a sentence according to the rules of euphony, and belongs to the area of *elocutio* (λέξις).

While the first device is obligatory in verbal art forms, the second is facultative.

4. Presentation of the narrative

The presentation of the narrative is formed by the phenotypic tier (whereas the three previous tiers are genotypic tiers obtained only as abstractions), i.e. it is the only tier accessible to empirical observation. In the terminology of rhetoric, it is the result of the *elocutio* or the λέξις. Its constitutive device in the case of literary narration is verbalization, i.e. the rendering of the medial, not yet manifested, narrative in a verbal—and not, for instance, in a cinematic, mimic, dance, musical or sculptural—medium.

In the following diagram, the four tiers and their relations to the dichotomies *fabula* vs. *sujet* and *histoire* vs. *discourse* are presented (the symbol "o" denotes the elements).

3. The four narrative tiers

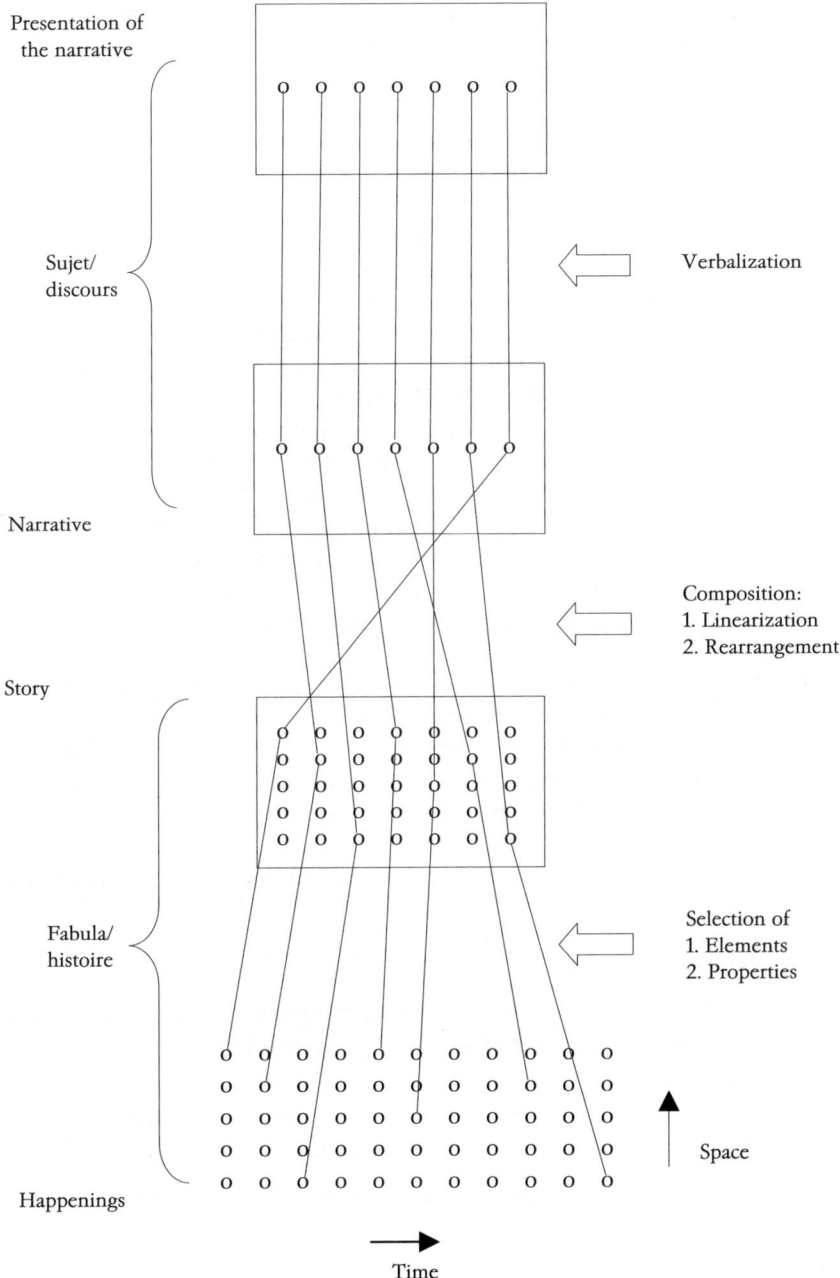

Ideal genetic model of narrative constitution

b) The location of point of view

The reader will surely miss perspectivization in the operations presented above. What position does point of view take up in narrative constitution? Let us first examine the location of point of view in some well-known models.

In the two-tier models, including in those whose first tier can be equated with our "story," perspectivization is seen as one of the operations that effect the transformation *fabula* > *sujet* or *histoire* > *discours*. Thus, Tomashevsky, as we have already seen, assigns "the bringing of an arrangement of motifs to the attention of the reader" (Tomashevsky 1925; tr. 1965, 68) and, implicitly, perspectivization, to the *sujet*. In his *Short Course of Poetics*, Tomashevsky (1928b, 87) names the decision about perspective as one of the six operations that lead from *fabula* to *sujet*. In their *Theory of Literature*, Wellek and Warren (1949, 218) give the following definition: "'Sujet' is plot as mediated through 'point of view,' 'focus of narration.'" Todorov (1966, 126) also attributes the effect of perspectivization to the "discours." Rimmon-Kenan (1976, 35) equally counts the "handling of point of view" as one of the devices that transform "récit" into "discours." And Jonathan Culler (1980, 28) postulates, for the analysis of point of view, the existence of a prior story, not yet subject to perspectivization, which he imagines as the "invariant core," as a sequence of actions, which can be represented in various ways.

In Stierle's (1971; 1977) three-tier model, perspectivization appears alongside the arrangement of temporal sequence, as well as accentuation via compression and expansion, as one of the devices that transform the "Geschichte" into the "Text der Geschichte": "in that the story becomes text, it is, first of all, bound to the perspective of a narrator and his specific narrative situation" (1977, 224). Similarly, in Mieke Bal's (1977a, 32–33) three-tier model, the *focalisation* is one of the operations that the *histoire* is subjected to before it becomes *récit*.

The concepts discussed here concur on two essential points:

(1) Perspectivization is seen as one operation among others, and is, even in models that provide more than two tiers, attributed to a single transformation.
(2) In explaining perspectivization as a transformation of the story, one implies that there is an objective, not yet perspectivized, story "in itself."

There are two objections to be made to this widespread approach:

3. The four narrative tiers

(1) A story "in itself," i.e. a story without perspective, is not possible. Nor is it helpful to postulate one in a model of constitution. Free from perspectivization are only the unlimited, amorphous happenings. Any selection of elements and their qualities, which is, after all, what initially constitutes a story, invariably presupposes a perspective.[26]

(2) Perspectivization is not one operation among others; it is the *implication* of all the other operations that were ascribed to the three transformations in the diagram outlined above. In this way, perspective is formed in the passage of the material of the happenings through the three transformations.

In the following, we will examine the three transformations in more detail and determine the role that the corresponding operations play in the formation of perspective.

c) From the happenings to the story

The narration of a story presupposes the selection of elements (situations, characters, actions) and their properties. In contrast to the happenings, which can be endlessly extended into the past and whose interior can be infinitely detailed, the story has a beginning and an end, and a certain degree of concretization.

The selection of elements and their properties in a fictional work is undertaken—in line with the rules of fiction—by the narrator. The author hands over to the narrator, as it were, the narrative material in the form of the happenings, which are the product of the author's invention, but the author him or herself does not appear in the represented world as the selecting entity. By selecting the elements of his or her story, the narrator draws a *thread* through the happenings, which connects certain elements and leaves others aside. While doing this, the narrator orientates himself on the criterion of the relevance of the elements to the story he is in the process of narrating.

The concept of the thread originated, as did the dichotomy of happenings and story, in Georg Simmel's essay "The Problem of Historical Time" (1916; tr. 1980). According to Simmel, historians must draw an "ideal line" (*ideelle Linie*) through the infinitely divisible elements of an extract from the worldwide happenings in order to create a "conceptual unit," such as the

---

26 Equally, the "real story" that is sometimes postulated in research on "everyday narration," the "story in the actual sense of the word: incidents that took place at a certain time in a certain place" (Rehbein 1980, 66), is an unhelpful construct. Extra-mental reality knows no stories, but only the unlimited continuum of happenings, which can be focused, selected and segmented in infinite ways.

Seven Years' War or the Battle of Zorndorf (Simmel 1916; tr. 1980, 139–40). The tracing of the "ideal line" presupposes a "concept" of the unit in question, which decides which "atoms" belong to it and which do not. Whereas the happenings are distinguished by "continuity," the history that is written about them is necessarily "discontinuous."

The conclusions of this philosopher apply equally to fiction. Just as the historian writes his own story about particular happenings by bringing together individual elements of an extract from continuous reality under a general term ("Seven Years' War"), so does the narrator create his own, individual story under one title, out of the happenings to be narrated.[27]

At this point, one could raise the objection that there are not actually any happenings in fictional work. This position has been adopted by, for example, Dorrit Cohn (1995, 108), who states that there is an "absolute difference" between historical and fictional narration based on the fact that fiction, in contrast to history, has no "reference level." Taking up White's concept of *emplotment* and Paul Ricœur's *mise en intrigue*, she argues that a novel is not "emplotted" but simply "plotted," and does not refer to something which could be transformed *into* an "intrigue." Against this, the argument must be presented that there certainly is a "reference level" in fiction, albeit not in the form of a preexisting historical reality, but in the mode of an implicit fictive reality. The happenings of a novel are, after all, not accessible to the reader as such, but only as a construct or, more accurately, a reconstruction formed on the basis of the narrated story. From the genetic standpoint, Cohn is completely correct. From an ideal genetic perspective, however, which will be adopted here, the fictive happenings implicit in the story form the "reference level" that logically precedes all acts of selection.

Granted, the happenings of a fictional work cannot be assigned the same status as the happenings that form the basis for the story written by a historian. Although historical happenings are also accessible only via stories, i.e. via meaning-producing reductions of continuous and infinitely detailed reality, as every "History of the Seven Years' War" is, these happenings have indeed taken place in and of themselves. This facticity and autonomy of being are lacking in literary happenings, incidentally including those instances where—as in a historical novel—the material of the literary story appears to be made up of historical occurrences. The private and also the

---

27 A comparison of the literary narrator with the historian has also been undertaken by Hayden White (1973), who describes the activity of the historian as *emplotment*. In delineating this term, White refers to the distinction between *fabula* and *sujet* taken from the Russian formalists (the latter being rendered by him in English as *plot*). Insofar as *emplotment* is based on narrative devices (cf. e.g. White 1978), White suspends the opposition of fictional and factual texts, something greeted skeptically in European narratology (cf. Nünning 1995, 129–44).

public, political happenings that provide the background for the story narrated in *War and Peace* cannot be equated with the actual historical happenings of the Napoleonic era. They are just as fictive as the story cut out of them. Although there are no real happenings underlying the author's work in fiction, and the fictive happenings are created only with the story, these happenings must be seen as an independent structural plane of the work, albeit a structural plane *in absentia*. The happenings form the material to which the selections that have brought forth the story refer. The selected nature of these elements is visible at every turn, particularly in the fragmentariness of depictions of reality (on the status of the elements not selected for the story, see below, V.3.f). When we refer to the story being "brought forth" by the selection of elements, or being "cut out" of preexisting happenings, we naturally mean neither the author's real creative acts, nor the real chronology of the work's genesis, nor even the subsequent concretization of the work by the recipient. As explained above, we use these expressions, like the temporal terms *before* and *after* in an ideal genetic sense, i.e. in the sense of an ideal genetic model of narrative constitution, which uses temporal metaphors to dissect the simultaneity of the tiers into logical-consecutive operations, in order to make the structure of the work, the devices applied in it, accessible to analysis.

Insofar as the happenings are nothing other than implicit source material for selections whose outcome forms the story, they cannot be defined in reference to the real world, but only in dependence on the story that implies them. The happenings can be endowed only with the ontological status and the pragmatic possibilities ascribed to the story itself. An answer to the questions of what ontological order determines the given narrative world, which entities can act in it, which actions are possible in principle and so on, is not given by the happenings, but by the story. In this way, the happenings are categorically entirely determined by the story that implies them.

d) Selection and point of view

The selection of elements and their properties constitutes not only a story but also the perceptual, spatial, temporal, ideological and linguistic point of view inherent in it. In purely narratorial rendering, the implicit perspective of the story is marked to a greater or lesser degree. In order to exemplify the contrast, we will examine a textual extract with the complex distribution of points of view that is characteristic of post-realist prose. It is taken from the beginning of Chekhov's tale "Rothschild's Fiddle."

It was a tiny town, worse than a village, inhabited chiefly by old people who so seldom died that it was really vexatious. Very few coffins were needed for the hospital and the jail; in a word, business was bad. (Chekhov, S, 297)

The extract presents the story's initial situation. The selection of elements (*tiny town, old people, hospital, jail, coffins, business*), their evaluation (the town is *tiny, worse than a village*; old people so *seldom* die that it is *really vexatious*; *very few coffins* are needed) and the connection of these heterogeneous elements to make a situation that expresses a certain atmosphere, that is, the selection and combination of elements, are oriented on the spatial and ideological perspective of the protagonist, the coffin-maker, Yakov Ivanov, who ekes an existence out of other people's deaths. The temporal standpoint from which the situation can be described in this way is that of the protagonist. It can be localized on the cusp between the backstory (presented later in memories) and the actual story, directly before the occurrence of the events (death of his wife Maria, Ivanov's illness) that trigger the story's mental main event, the remembering and the internal change to the crude coffin-maker. Thus, the spatial, temporal and ideological perspective of the representation is figural. However, it is not the case that a situation shaped by the elements themselves is merely figurally presented. The happenings, which are, after all, absolutely continuous and have no breaks, do not contain situations. A situation is only ever constituted in the consciousness of a latently story-forming subject, who experiences reality and reduces its complexity to a few elements. Who is the subject here? It initially appears to be Yakov who has yoked the town, the old people and the bad business together into a situation. But this situation does not exist in his consciousness, since the selected elements are not the objects of current perception or memory by Yakov, who has not yet even appeared in the story. This is not a case of free indirect discourse (FID), the more or less narratorially reshaped reproduction of the current contents of a character's consciousness, but rather of FCN, figurally colored narration by a narrator who reproduces the character's text in the selection and evaluation of the thematized elements, without the character perceiving or thinking about them at this moment in the story.[28] Although the selected elements determine the coffin-maker's general mental state and their qualification adheres entirely to Ivanov's internal sensitivities, i.e. although they fundamentally could appear in his consciousness, their selection from the myriad possible thoughts passing through his consciousness, and their combination into a situation, was undertaken by the narrator. By choosing these, and not other, elements, he draws a thread through the countless contents of Ivanov's consciousness

---

28   In section IV.3.n, this form was presented as a manifestation of interference of narrator's text and characters's text.

extant in the happenings. In this way, his ideological standpoint is also represented in the extract, in the meaning which the selected elements are given in his story. This meaning is realized primarily in the highlighting of the commercial categories that determine the coffin-maker's thoughts and feelings. It can be more concretely grasped only when the story is finished and the transformation to narrative and its presentation are complete. However, it would be incorrect to say that Yakov Ivanov's story is bound to his perspective only on a logically subsequent tier, or that it is subordinated to the intention of a subsequently added narrator. *Before* the figural perspectivization and the narratorial ascription of meaning, there is no story. It is constituted firstly from the elements that the narrator, oriented on the character's perception, has selected and combined in order to express a meaning. Of course, the author could have had the narrator narrate narratorially or be oriented on the standpoint of a different character, or made Rothschild the reflector or even the narrator of the story. However, in each of these cases, the happenings would have been filtered and organized in a different way. The circumstances presented in the sentences quoted would then not have appeared, or would have done so in an entirely different connection. It is simply not the case that the choice of a particular perspective does not affect the story, something that Tomashevsky (1925; tr. 1965, 77) appears to postulate when he concludes that, in Wilhelm Hauff's fairy tale "Caliph Stork," if the primary and secondary narrator (Caliph and the princess) had been switched, "the fabula would remain the same".

e) Compression and expansion

The story, which, in principle, cannot have a one-to-one correspondence with the happenings, as a result of their infinite divisibility, must necessarily restrict itself to a certain number of elements and leave them in a greater or lesser state of indeterminacy. While the elements in the happenings are determined in all conceivable (i.e. infinite) respects, they are only ever concretized in the story with a limited number of qualities. About Anna Karenina, for example, we are repeatedly told what colors the dress and shoes she is wearing are, and the narrator repeatedly describes her physical characteristics, the signs of a "controlled liveliness": the shining eyes, the elegant neck, the full shoulders, the small, energetic hands (incidentally, these are features she shares with Vronsky's horse Frou-Frou, an equally not quite immaculate beauty, which distinguishes itself though shining eyes, elegant legs and a simultaneously energetic and gentle expression). But regardless of the fact that even these qualities only barely concretize the heroine, many other essential traits of her character and exterior remain entirely undetermined.

For example, nothing is disclosed about her upbringing, her childhood or her parents' house.

As Roman Ingarden (1931; tr. 1973a, 246–54; 1937; tr. 1973b, 50–55) has shown, the represented objects in a literary work necessarily contain countless "places of indeterminacy" (*Unbestimmtheitsstellen*): "It is impossible to establish clearly and exhaustively the infinite multiplicity of determinacies of the individual objects portrayed in the work with a finite number of words or sentences" (Ingarden 1937; tr. 1973b, 51). Indeterminacy as an incomplete concretization of the objects is thus not an artistic device (something claimed only in the *reception* of Ingarden) but a necessary accompaniment to every linguistic representation of reality.

The relation of "narrating time" and "narrated time," which has concerned an entire generation of Germanist narrative analysts since Günther Müller's well-known essay (1948), and which Genette (1972; tr. 1980, 86–95) treats as a phenomenon of "narrative movements," ultimately boils down to a question of *the selectivity of the story with regard to the happenings*. If, for a given episode of the story, a relatively large number of elements is selected and these elements are concretized with many qualities, the representation appears *expanded* and the narration *slow*. If, however, relatively few elements and properties are selected, the representation appears *compressed* and the narration *fast*.

Compression and expansion are usually seen as "later" operations in narrative constitution.[29] In reality, they are nothing other than the implicit result of the selection of elements and qualities and are therefore "already" contained in the transformation *happenings > story*.

In the concretizing of elements and properties, which is entirely up to the narrator and has no limits in the happenings themselves, it is possible to distinguish four devices:

(1) The dissection of the change of state into ever smaller steps.

(2) The internal "division" of a situation or a character into ever more pieces.

(3) The determining of an element of the happenings (a situation, a character, an action) with an ever larger number of qualities.

(4) The external contextualization of an element of the happenings by mentioning its temporal, spatial or logical surroundings (e.g. the back-story of a character, of the location or of the causal relationships).

"As soon as" (to use a temporal metaphor) the selection of elements and properties, i.e. the formation of the story, is complete, no additional com-

---

[29] I also wrongly attributed them to the transformation of the story to the narrative at one time (Schmid 1982).

3. The four narrative tiers

pression or expansion can take place, unless via the repeated naming of one and the same element or property in the presentation of the narrative. But that is a device entirely different to the selection of a greater or lesser number of elements and qualities from the happenings.

Compression and expansion are, of course, relative terms, for which there is no objective yardstick. Any quantitative definition would be a mistake. It must only be realized that the detailing and concretization of the elements in the story fundamentally cannot achieve the all-round determinacy appertaining to the elements in the happenings. Therefore, it is necessary to reject all attempts to construct a "congruent narration" (Lämmert 1955, 83–84) or a coincidence of "story time" and (pseudo-)"time of the narrative" (Genette 1972; tr. 1980, 94). In the case of expanded representation, i.e. "slow" narration, the story, even in the most extremely descriptive passage, will never contain as many elements and properties as the internally unlimited, i.e. endlessly divisible and qualifiable happenings. When a relatively short section of the happenings corresponds to a comparatively long segment of the text, this is not necessarily a "descriptive pause," complying with Genette's (pseudo-)mathematical formula NT ∞> ST (Genette 1972; tr. 1980, 95; NT = "time of the narrative," ST = "story time"), but can rather be a result of comments oriented not on the diegesis, but the exegesis.

The relative difference between compression and expansion is depicted in the following diagram:

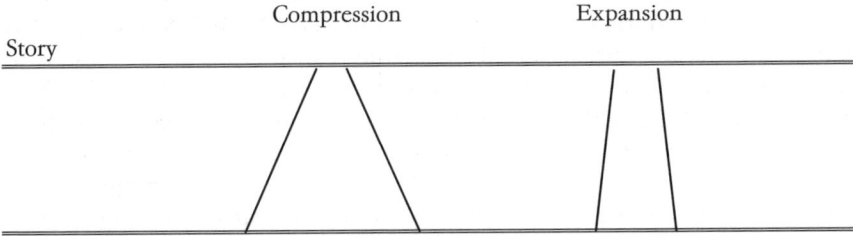

As a rule, expansion is connected with greater descriptiveness. Detailed description entails the accumulation of many facets and properties of diegetic elements. (Narration does not preclude description, as shown above in section 1.1.b, but rather requires it for the exposition of situations, characters and actions.) Expansion can also occur as a result of the dissection of one change of state into parts and phases. An example of extreme expansion of the narration is Proust's *In Search of Lost Time*, in which one single movement by the Baron de Charlus is represented across several pages and dissected into countless parts and facets.

Examples of compressed narration are provided by A. S. Pushkin's story cycle *The Tales of Belkin*. The selectivity here is of a particular type. On the one hand, it is extraordinarily sparse. The parts of the story that are not narrated, which fall between the episodes described, are denoted, at best, with such terse references as "Some years went by." Even in the comparatively comprehensively narrated episodes, only very few elements and properties are explicitly mentioned. This extremely dynamic narration hardly has space for the delays of description. Using this episodic device, Pushkin can tell entire life stories on a handful of pages. It is not for nothing that the *Tales of Belkin* have been compared with "miniature novels" (Unbegaun 1947, XV). On the other hand, the selectivity fluctuates throughout, and its oscillation does not seem to be in accord with the relevance of the motifs selected. While important parts of the happenings remain undescribed, details are concretized that initially appear to be circumstantial. For example, the four illustrations of the Parable of the Prodigal Son adorning the walls of the Russian stationmaster's humble room are comprehensively described, while the internal motives of the titular hero, in contrast, are left indeterminate.

This kind of apparently unmotivated switch between compression and expansion irritated many critics in the 19th century, such as Mikhail Katkov, who complained that the narrative in Pushkin's prose was sometimes "excessively detailed" and sometimes "excessively summary."[30] The era that was developing the representation of consciousness reacted sensitively to the absence of any concretization of the inner life. Symptomatic is the rejection of this way of narrating by the young Tolstoy (PSS 46, 187–88), who called the *Tales of Belkin* "sort of naked." It is true that the central motivations of the protagonists remain indeterminate in the five novels of the cycle. Why does Silvio in "The Shot" not shoot the count? And why does the count, a practiced shot, twice fail to hit his target from close range? Why does the upstanding heroine of "The Blizzard," Marya Gavrilovna, the virgin widow, who seems to mourn the unromantic seducer Vladimir for so long, lose all feeling of cold as soon as Burmin, her unrecognized husband, appears? Is it only a coincidence or divine providence that they fall in love without knowing that they are already married to each other? Why does the undertaker in the story of the same name invite the "Orthodox dead" (Pushkin, Prose, 90) to his house-warming party, and why, when he wakes "much gladdened" (93) from the nightmare, does he call his daughters to drink tea with him? Lastly, why does Aleksey in "The Squire's Daughter" propose marriage to the docile Akulina, although he must know about the insurmountable social barrier between him, the son of a landowner, and a poor peasant girl? This

---

30 Quotations following V. Zelinsky (ed.), *Russkaya kriticheskaya literatura o proizvedeniyakh A. S. Pushkina: Khronologicheskiy sbornik kritiko-bibliograficheskikh statey*, Moscow 1888, Vol. VII, P. 157.

kind of question is also provoked by the story that initially appears to be the least enigmatic of the five, "The Stationmaster." Why does Dunya weep throughout the journey from the station to the town when the coachman testifies "it did seem that she was going of her own free will" (Pushkin, Prose, 99)? Why does Samson Vyrin not copy his Biblical predecessor and stay at home, like the father in the Parable of the Prodigal Son, and trust to the return of his "prodigal" daughter? And why, after the reunion in Petersburg, does he abruptly give up all attempts to bring home his "lost sheep"? And—finally—why does he drink himself to death? (cf. Schmid 1991, 103–70.)

Also realized in compression and expansion is perspective, specifically the ideological standpoint, the evaluative perspective. The use of these devices depends on the significance that the narrator (and of course the author) attributes to specific episodes. In the logic of narration, expanded episodes are more important than compressed ones. The narrative relevance of actions and episodes does not, however, correspond to any extra-literary yardsticks, but is measured on how they manifest the story. This can be accompanied by a strong conflict with the reader's real-life norms. An example of how compression and expansion can realize an ideological perspective that runs counter to everyday norms is given by Chekhov's tale "Darling."

In the episodes that portray the marriages of the heroine to Kukin and Pustovalov, the happenings are compressed and expanded in a way that flagrantly contradicts our real-life ideas of relevance. While the way they get to know one another is relatively comprehensively portrayed, the proposals and marriages, events that are, after all, decisive in someone's life, are tersely communicated in a single sentence: "He [Kukin] proposed to her, and they were married"; "The match was quickly arranged, and then came the wedding" (Chekhov, S, 212, 214). From the time of the marriages, which are both dealt with in very summary fashion, primarily in the iterative mode, the narrator selects individual micro-dialogues, which initially appear insignificant to the reader, but in which the central theme of the tale becomes visible: the unreserved alignment of the literally selfless woman on the world of each of her husbands. The deaths of the husbands are also presented in laconic brevity. The telegram from the director of the opera ensemble, which communicates the news of Kukin's death in the shortest possible way—parodistically contaminating the words for "funeral" and "laughter" (*pokhorony* + *khokhot* > *khokhorony*)—does not even state the cause of death, something we never discover. Pustovalov's illness and death are also described in a single dry sentence: "He had the best doctors, but he grew worse and died after four months' illness" (Chekhov, S, 216). In this way, the narrator gives the happenings he narrates a specific accentuation through compression and expansion. The swapping of compression and expansion, or of greater and lesser selectivity, is one of the means by which the meanings of the narrative, as it appears in the narrator's horizons, are brought to light.

f) The non-selected

The reader who attempts to trace the thread constituting a story must understand both sides of selection, not only selection as position (the selection of certain elements) but also as negation, the rejection of other options. It is only against the background of the non-selected that the selected gains its identity and meaning. Experiencing a story as a meaningful whole entails inferring the *logic* of its *selectivity*. But not only that. The reader must be aware of which character has been the object of the negative selection in the work, i.e. in which *mode* the non-selected has been rejected. In selection, there are at least three modes of negation to be differentiated.

The first mode of negation is the *non-selection of elements and properties that are irrelevant to the story*. This first mode of negation leaves behind irrelevant "places of indeterminacy" (Ingarden), the concretization of which is neither necessitated nor supported by the story. Anyone who concretizes the irrelevant non-selected undertakes a reception that is not only superfluous, but also hinders the tracing of the thread, the reconstruction of the selection decisions.[31]

The second mode of negation is present when the story contains the beginnings of traditional threads that are not to be followed, because the meaning of the story is not contained in the threads indicated. Cases such as this, which demand the rejection of foreign motifs as filling for the blanks, can be found in the *Tales of Belkin*. For example, the reader who attempts to bring together the explicit motifs in "The Stationmaster" into one conclusive thread containing all details, is called upon to ignore the meanings offered by the protagonist or the narrator, and not to follow the threads that originate in Biblical, classical, sentimental or Romantic traditions. For example, it is precisely not as the innocent, seduced heroine of a sentimental tale that Dunya is to be understood, and her father proves to be neither the wise father in the Parable of the Prodigal Son, nor the Good Shepherd of John's gospel. The story of the stationmaster is constituted in a negation of the literary models that appear in the consciousness of the father and of the

---

31 However, it becomes clear only during the reception which non-selected elements are irrelevant to a story, and not in the reception by a single reader, but in the history of interpretation. In any text, constellations of motifs and allusions can be discovered, which turn an apparently irrelevant non-selected element into a highly significant one.

narrator. The non-selected elements that correspond to motifs of conventional sujets, and offer themselves for the filling of the blanks, must be rejected. For the meaningful development of the story, this second mode fundamentally demands the actualization of non-selected elements, but just not the activation of those elements suggested by the misleading allusions to conventional models.

The third mode could be called *necessarily rescinded negation*. It concerns non-selected elements that paradoxically belong to the story insofar as they form a gap in its thread. The reader must rescind the negation undertaken by the author and, in line with the indications more or less latently contained in the text, "reactivate" the non-selected elements for the story. While reading, we often perform this function, usually unintentionally, in the automatic process of inference. As a rule, we implement this filling-in of blanks consciously only when what is omitted appears in essential elements or even determines the direction of the thread. This kind of central element is often the protagonists' motivation. We can again take "The Stationmaster" as our example. In this novella, the protagonist's motives are not made explicit. The reader must reverse-engineer, as it were, the non-selection by reproducing elements that were not selected, but belong to the story. Rescindable non-selection has become characteristic of modern narrative prose. To the extent that narrative prose endows its protagonists with complex, many-sided psyches, and presents the story from the standpoint of the narrated figure, the mental processes that motivate actions and speech become a problem. The elements of the consciousness that the narrator explicitly describes are no longer able to conclusively motivate actions and speech. The reader must then infer these motivations by going beyond the explicit story and tracing certain non-selected elements of the—mental—happenings, which the narrator withholds or which are not accessible to him.

In order to avoid misunderstandings, this investigation of the relationship between happenings and story must be ended with two notes:

(1) It is not that reading is here being given the task of extrapolating the implicit happenings from the story, but rather that of understanding the logic of the story's selectivity.
(2) In narrative constitution, the happenings are not simply replaced with the story, but remain perceptible as a store of other possible choices.

g) From the story to the narrative

In the story, more than one episode can occur at the same time. Some art forms, such as narrative ballet, are able to present synchronic happenings simultaneously. Like other linear representations, literature must present what occurs simultaneously in a temporal sequence. In this way, the *linearization* of the simultaneous is a necessary device, which determines the transformation of the story into the narrative.

Linearization of simultaneously occurring strands of the happenings can be bound up with particular semantic effects. In *Anna Karenina*, for example, the fatal horse race is narrated twice, once from Vronsky's perspective (Part II, ch. 25) and once from Karenin's, though he does not watch the race itself, watching instead the reactions of his wife (Part II, ch. 28–29). Vronsky's accident and Karenin's deduction from Anna's reaction to the accident occur in one and the same moment, but they are reported in different parts of the narrative.

The second device that determines the transformation of the story into the narrative is the reorganization of the episodes away from the natural, chronological sequence, the replacement of the *ordo naturalis* with the *ordo artificialis*.

We can find this kind of rearrangement in "The Stationmaster," in which the second encounter of the narrator with the titular hero is narrated before Dunya's abduction—narrated by Samson Vyrin—which took place three years earlier.

"The Shot" contains the same device in exposed form: the story's four episodes are presented in the narrative—which has two episodes in each of its two chapters—in a doubled, symmetrical reorganization. In the story's actual chronology, the sequence of episodes is 2—1—4—3. The compositional symmetry of the four episodes does not weaken or conceal the reorganization, but, on the contrary, makes it more perceptible.

In both novellas, the reorganization is naturally motivated, i.e. determined by the fact that the inner stories are reported retrospectively in the secondary narratives of those involved. In "The Queen of Spades," we find reorganizations that are not justified in this way (i.e. through embedding) and which make comprehension of the story more difficult. The multiple rearrangement of the story's episodes and the parts of the causal sequence has the effect that information essential for the understanding of the story is withheld. So, the consequences of Germann's decision to contact the countess are narrated first, and only after that is it explained how and why Germann made this decision. Reorganization that impedes the reader's comprehension of the temporal sequence and causal relationships is a means of arousing interest in the reader and appealing to his or her ingenuity. The ambiguity of the diegetic relationship prompts the reader to immerse him or herself in this narrative world and form an image of its organization. The non-explicit exposition of characters also prepares the ground for the uncertainty of identities and relationships in this novella, whose motivation fluctuates between psychology and fantasy, and which evades a definite conclusion in favor of either of these narrative modes (cf. Schmid 1997).

Similarly to the way in which the happenings remain perceptible in the story (which is cut out of them), the story is not extinguished in the narrative. The organization of the story remains present even when re-formed by the narrative. In a narrative work, we perceive not only the narrative or the story, but also their simultaneous presence, which can be full of tensions and contradictions.

h) The composition of the narrative and point of view

The linearization of the actions occurring simultaneously in the story into a narrative sequence, which is an obligatory device in literature, and the reorganization of the sequences following one another in chronological order, which is facultative, bring the parts of the story into a meaningful sequence. In the composition of the narrative, a meaning is formed, which actualizes and modifies the potential meaning contained in the story. As a result, the evaluative position of the narrator, his or her ideological standpoint, is also constituted via the devices of composition. However, point of view is also involved in the composition in another way.

Linearization always implies a change to temporal perspective. The narrator returns from a given point on the temporal axis to an earlier point in order to narrate the events that have occurred at the same time as what has just been narrated. This switch is often accompanied by a change to the spatial perspective. For example, the narrator of *Anna Karenina* switches spatial and perceptual perspective as well as temporal perspective when switching from Vronsky's to Karenin's standpoint in the portrayal of the horse race.

Reorganization also entails the adoption of a different standpoint in the storyworld's space-time coordinate system. But this is not necessarily accompanied by a change of the reflector. Reorganization is frequently bound up with retrospective by the character who was already the reflector beforehand. When the narrator of "Rothschild's Fiddle" initially eschews any mention of the coffin-maker's past and reports the backstory only towards the end of the narrative, that is because Yakov Ivanov, whose spatial, temporal and ideological perspective is adopted by the narrator, remembers his previous, happy life only shortly before his death. If the narrator had presented Ivanov's story narratorially, we would have been told at the beginning of the narrative about the past events and situations important to the protagonist. The retrospective becomes possible because the coffin-maker, who has completely forgotten his past, is reminded by his dying wife that they once had a child. It is only now that Ivanov can (or wants to) bring to mind everything that he had forgotten or suppressed. Thus the act of remembering becomes an indication of a change to the protagonist's attitude. We learn about the backstory at precisely that moment in which Ivanov becomes capable of remembering it. In this way, the reorganization does not arise from any kind of abstract compositional ideas, but follows the logic of the protagonist's mental development.

i) From the narrative to its presentation

In the presentation of the narrative, the not yet medially manifested narrative is expressed in the specific language of an art form. In literary work, the presentation of the narrative occurs through verbalization. On this tier, the presented narrative can be connected with non-diegetic, purely exegetical textual units (evaluations, generalizations, commentaries, reflections, metanarrative comments by the narrator).

In verbalization, linguistic perspective comes into effect. When the narrator presents the narrative, s/he has the choice of various styles. S/he can use lexical units and syntactic structures that correspond to his or her own style (i.e. take up a narratorial standpoint) or—as far as his or her linguistic competence allows—align him or herself on the stylistic world of the happenings, and present the narrative in the language of one or more characters (i.e. with figural perspectivization).

Of course, the characters' (outer and inner) discourses and narratives also belong to the happenings. The constitution of the characters' discourse and of secondary narratives go through the same process of transformation as the narrative of the primary narrator. The only difference is that these discourses and secondary narratives are "already" complete "before" (to express it in temporal metaphors again) the narrator "cuts" them out of the happenings, along with the characters' perspectives realized in them, in order to narrate the story. (This means that there are no happenings free of linguistic realization, since the characters' speech acts are also part of the happenings.) However, the preexisting characters' language on the tier of the happenings need not be identical with the language presented in the narrative. It is only on this fourth tier that the characters' speech acts attain their final linguistic profile. Verbalization can be accompanied by an essential refashioning of the characters' discourses, even to the extent that they are translated into a foreign language. For example, the characters of epics speak in verse and, in novels, speech in a foreign language is usually translated into the language of the narrative text. Tolstoy's novel *War and Peace*, which reproduces the characters' French discourse entirely mimetically (with the stylistic coloring typical of Russians), is something of an exception in this regard.

3. The four narrative tiers

Whereas the reworking of the discourses spoken (or thought) in the happenings remains largely unnoticed in literature, ballet or pantomime, which express the contents of the characters' text in the language of gestures or movements, draw greater attention to the recoding that they entail.

The perspectivity of verbalization is, however, very differently marked in different literary epochs. Complete reproduction is found only in realist writing styles, which apply the mimetic principle to the styles of the characters and the narrator. In pre-realist narration, by contrast, verbalization is subject to rules of genre and literary norms, which significantly narrow the possibilities of linguistic perspective. For example, the discourses of characters and narrators in the narrative verse genres show only very slight traces of stylistic individuality. In pre-realist Russian prose novels, as well, the style of the narrator and the characters remain within the narrow borders drawn by the norms of literary language. The narrator neither gives the characters an independent linguistic existence (one need only think of the sentimentality with which Karamzin's narrator has the peasant woman speak), nor does he receive an individual stylistic physiognomy of his own. Even in the Romantic narration of Lermontov, characters and narrators cultivate the same rhetorically pointed, aphorism-rich speech. Among more modern writers, we also find those who impose restrictions on linguistic perspectivization. One need only think of the ornamental prose of Russian literature in the first third of the 20th century (see above, IV.2.a). Using devices such as rhythmization, sound instrumentation, sound repetition and paronomasia, it subordinates the narrative to a poetic organization that can be oriented on neither the narrator nor any of the characters. However, where perspectivity is reduced, one can refer to these works in terms of narrative art, which is distinguished by consistent perspectivization in all narrative operations, only with certain reservations.

Insofar as the narrator's and characters' texts are linguistically individualized, they create not only an image of the speaker, with the characteristics of origin, status, education and ideology, but can also, above and beyond that, indicate the current evaluation of the story's elements by the speaking entity. As well as this implicit evaluation, we, of course, also encounter *explicit narratorial evaluation* of elements of the story on the tier of presentation. Both evaluative acts, implicit and explicit evaluation, can refer to the diegesis but belong to the exegesis.

j) An ideal genetic model of point of view

The following diagram shows the transformations with which point of view is correlated on the various tiers of constitution:

Ideal genetic model of point of view

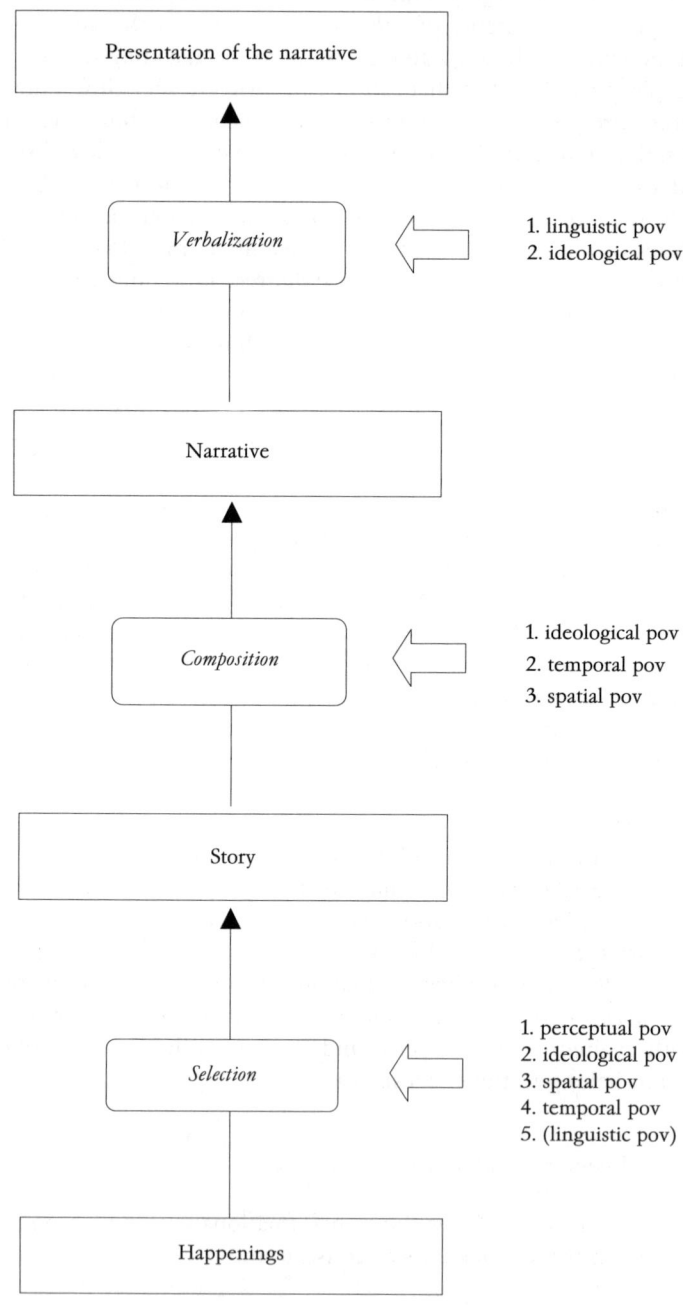

k) Discourse happenings and discourse story

The narrative text contains not only the presentation of the narrative, but also the totality of explicit evaluations, comments, generalizations, reflections and auto-thematizations on the part of the narrator. Textual units of this sort constitute not the diegesis (the storyworld), but the exegesis (the act of narration). They are not simply amplifications of the narrative, but denote or imply the *discourse story*, i.e. the story of the narrative act, in the process of which the presentation of the narrative is produced. The represented world of the narrative work thus unifies two entirely different stories:

(1) The presented narrative with the *narrated story* contained in it.
(2) The presentation itself, i.e. the *discourse story*, which underlies it.

In most works, the discourse story is only given in fragments, but there are some in which it is fully formed and even occupies center stage. This is the case in Laurence Sterne's *Life and Opinions of Tristram Shandy, Gentleman*, where the *opinions* of the exegesis overrun the *life* of the diegesis and nearly supplant it. If there are no explicit narratorial comments and no auto-thematization by the narrator, we have no discourse story at our disposal and fundamentally must, instead, postulate (fictive) *discourse happenings* (*Erzählgeschehen*, cf. Schmid 1982), without which there would be no discourse story. In these cases, no elements have been selected for the formation of the discourse story. The reader must reconstruct the *discourse happenings* from the indexical signs contained in the narrative devices. If the devices contain sufficiently clear symptoms, the mental processes guiding the narration can be extrapolated even in works apparently completely without a narrator. An extreme example of this is Alain Robbe-Grillet's *Jealousy*, in which, as a result of radical omission of the narrated self and an absence of auto-thematization of the narrating self, only the wife observed by the narrator, their mutual friend, and the precisely described objects of the external world appear in the narrative (see above, II.4.g). The selection of objects and their conspicuously repeated description, however, serve as indexical signs pointing to the non-thematized discourse happenings. The apparently impersonal, extremely objective, quasi-scientific description, complete with overly precise information about geometrical arrangement, sizes and angles, allows, at least, some conclusions as to what may be happening within the narrator.

1) The semiotic model

Ideal genetic models, as mentioned above, do not depict the actual acts of creation or reception, but rather use temporal metaphors to simulate the ideal, non-temporal genesis of the narrative work, with the aim of isolating the devices guiding narration and illuminating the relationships between them. To conclude this analysis, we will approach this model of narrative tiers from the other side, i.e. we will take the narrative text as our starting point and investigate the construction of the narrated and the discourse story by the reader. This perspective leads to a semiotic model, which depicts the correlations between signifiers and signifieds in the process of receptions.

The only tier accessible to observation is the *text of the narrative work*. All other tiers are abstractions and constructs. The text of the narrative work, as mentioned above, unifies the presentation of the narrative with the explicit evaluations, comments, generalizations, reflections and auto-thematization of the narrator, i.e. the text of the work is divided into a diegetic and an exegetic branch. The following tiers each function as signifiers for the deeper (closer to the happenings) tiers. The semiotic processes that occur here are denotation and indication, as well as the logical operation of implication.

The following diagram, in which the diegetic and exegetical branches of narrative constitution are distinguished, portrays the semiotic relationships between the tiers, and models the construction of the story and happenings, as well of the discourse story and the discourse happenings, from out of the narrative text:

3. The four narrative tiers

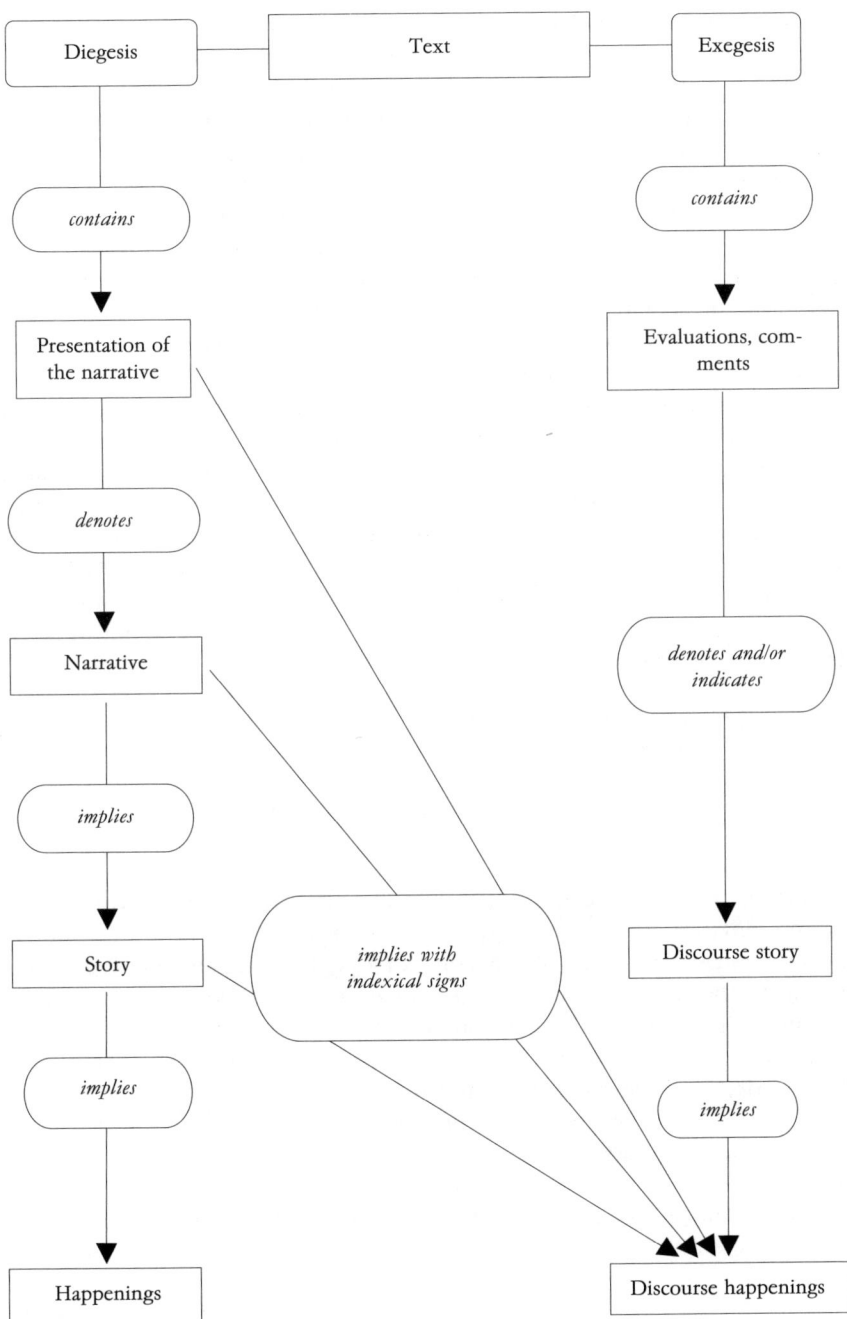

m) The correlation of the tiers in verbal art

In distinguishing between tiers, whether ideal genetic or semiotic, it must not be overlooked that they exist *simultaneously* in the work and in its reception. It has already been mentioned above that it would be wrong to imagine a complete suppression of the happenings by the story or of the story by the narrative. In the narrative work, it is much rather the case that the narrative tiers exist simultaneously and form a dynamic correlation.

This correlation appears differently in different genres and poetics. In ornamental prose, for example, which—as explained above—is not a purely stylistic, but also a structural phenomenon, the ornamentalization is not limited to the presentation of the narrative, but is manifested also on the other tiers. For an ornamental story with the qualities of verbal art, the elements of the happenings are chosen from a different standpoint than for a story that is entirely narrative art. In narrative art, it is primarily a temporal and causal relationship that binds the selected elements together, and the selection is guided by the relevance of the elements to the story to be narrated. In verbal art, by contrast, non-temporal links such as repetition, the system of leitmotifs, and equivalences also play a leading role. An element B is thus selected not only because it follows element A temporally or casually (in the diagram →), but also because it will form a thematic equivalent with a later element E (≅). The co-occurrence of temporal and non-temporal links is depicted in the following diagram:

A	→	B	→	C	→	D
		B		≅		E

The relations constituted by non-temporal connections subordinate the organizations of the three transformative tiers ([1] the linguistic syntagma of the presentation of the narrative, [2] the composition of the narrative, [3] the thematic syntagma of the story) to a poetic-ornamental overdetermination. In the presentation of the narrative, this overdetermination leads to rhythmization and sound repetition, which have authorial status and are, as a rule, not oriented on the narrative entity. In the narrative, it steers the linearization and reorganization, and it lays on top of the syntagma of the story a network of non-temporal connections, in line with the principles of similarity and contrast (cf. above 1.1.h). This means that ornamentality has an influence on the operations of selection of elements and qualities. Comparable modifications of the model of narrative constitution are necessary

3. The four narrative tiers

everywhere that perspectivized narrative art is overlaid with the devices of aperspectivized verbal art.[32]

---

32   On the modifications that ornamental prose and verbal art in general necessitate in the model of narrative transformations, cf. Schmid 2008a.

Conclusion

The aim of this book was to examine the constitutive structures of fictional narrative texts. Particular attention was paid to the categories with which Slavic (Russian, Czech, Polish) formalism and structuralism have enriched international narratology.

Concentration on literary narrative work is justified by the fact that genuine narratological theory has essentially always taken place within the framework of literary study. Narration does occur in various media and in many everyday and cultural contexts, and the investigation of verbal and non-verbal narratives does take place outside of literary study, indeed the term narratology has recently been programmatically used in the plural, but, in all these diverse narratologies, we operate with terms originating in literary study. An independent development of categories hardly exists outside literary study (with the possible exception of film theory, in which some developments are evident, particularly in the category of perspective). The mother discipline of narratology is still literary study[1]. And literature seems to still be the area that explores and exposes the manifold possibilities of narration in an exemplary way.

In order to locate the narratology presented here in the context of the current debate, the book's distinguishing arguments are summarized here:

I.1 Narrativity is seen as the constitutive feature of narration. In light of the competition from the classical position, which connects narrativity with mediacy, and the structuralist approach to narration as the representation of changes of state, a compromise solution is suggested, which includes two separate meanings for the adjective "narrative." Narrative in a wider sense are texts that represent a change of state and, consequently, a story (in the minimal form, "The king died"); narrative in a narrower sense are texts that present a story through the mediation of a narrator.

I.2 Among the changes of state, of which literature contains an inestimable number, one class, which fulfills certain conditions, is to be separated out, namely *events*. Drawing on a position suggested by Yury Lotman, who defines the condition for an event as the "crossing of a prohibition boundary," the "shifting of a persona across the borders of a semantic field," or the

---

1   This impression was confirmed by the colloquium *Narratology beyond Literary Criticism*, held by the Hamburg Research Group Narratology in 2003 (cf. Meister ed. 2005).

Conclusion

"meaningful departure from the norm," the following definition is suggested: an event is a change of state, which presupposes *reality* and *resultativity*, and fulfills the conditions of *relevance, unpredictability, persistence, irreversibility,* and *non-iterativity*.

I.3 *Eventfulness,* determined by the degree to which these criteria are fulfilled, is a gradable property of events. Events can have varying levels of eventfulness. Whereas the change of state appears objectively in the text, eventfulness is based on an attribution dependant on interpretation. To the entities confronted with a change of state—the characters, the narrator and the fictive reader, the author, the abstract reader and, of course, the concrete reader—its eventfulness can appear in an entirely different light to each.

I.4 Besides temporal connections, such as temporal and causal succession (of which a minimal definition of narratology need include only the former), it is possible also to observe, particularly in narrative texts with an "ornamental" character, non-temporal connections according to the principle of—formal and thematic—equivalence of motifs on the levels of story, narrative and the presentation of the narrative.

I.5 *Fictionality* is seen as the second distinctive feature of literary narration. The concept of fiction underlying the book is based on the Aristotelian concept of mimesis as the representation not of what has happened, but of what is possible.

I.6 In the controversy on the question of whether the specific status of literature is determined by the ontology of the represented objects or the pragmatics of the representing discourse, philosophic esthetics has clearly lost ground. The mainstream today is marked by John Searle's *pretense* conception, based on speech act theory. According to this approach, the author of a fictional text makes observations that merely have the form of observations, but are, in reality, only "pretended" observations. This approach is not shared by this book. In contrast to the currently dominant opinion, according to which fictionality is not given by the characteristics of the text, I follow K. Hamburger's conception, according to which there is a distinctive feature of fictional texts, namely the unexplained representation of another person's inner world. As E. M. Forster (1927) already noted, the formation of other people's inner worlds is specific to fictional literature.

I.7 For the fictivity of the represented world, only a yes-no decision is seen as meaningful. All types of *mixed bag* conception are rejected, in which characters, places or times can be partly real and partly fictive, or in which a text can be partly fictional and partly factual. In *War and Peace*, Napoleon is just as fictive as Natasha Rostova. Being fictive and being fictional are absolute properties.

II.1 The foundation of the model of communication levels is the thesis that the narrative work does not narrate; rather, it *represents a narration*, thereby encompassing a minimum of two levels of communication: author communication and narrative communication. The real, abstract and fictive entities of this communication are presented in a model of communication levels, with reference, *inter alia*, to Russian, Czech, and Polish theories.

II.2 In contradiction to the criticism of the author that was widespread in the 1970s and 1980s, the necessity of the *abstract author* category is defended here. In contrast to the narrator, however, the abstract author is not specifically responsible for the narrative work. Of purely semantic dimensions, he is rather a mere reconstruction, by the reader, based on the creative acts that have produced the work. The category of the abstract author is meaningful and necessary because it objectivizes the narrator and the narration.

II.3 The *abstract reader*, who is nothing other than the imagined counterpart ascribed to the abstract author by the concrete reader, appears on the one hand as the *presumed addressee* and, on the other, as the *ideal recipient*.

II.4 For the *fictive narrator*, a distinction is made between *explicit* and *implicit* representation. The latter, which is based on the expression function, is the fundamental mode, which is, in principle, always active to a greater or lesser extent, but which never entirely disappears. In this way, the postulation of a work without a narrator, or the existence of a *nonnarrator* (Chatman), is rejected. In contradiction to the widespread approach that the narrator steps off stage or blends into the author in "objective" narration, the thesis is presented that the narrator is always present in some form, even if only in the selection of characters' discourse.

II.5 Gérard Genette's complicated and, in many respects, semantically problematic typology of the narrator is placed in opposition to a simplified distinction: the triad of embedding, *extradiegetic, intradiegetic, metadiegetic*, is replaced with *primary, secondary,* and *tertiary*, and the dichotomy *homodiegetic* vs. *heterodiegetic* narrator with the opposition of *diegetic* (belonging to the storyworld) and *non-diegetic* (not appearing in the storyworld) narrator, an opposition that is identical with neither *explicit* vs. *implicit* nor *personal* vs. *impersonal*, nor any dichotomies of perspective.

II.6 The *fictive reader*, for whom the functional entities *fictive addressee* and *fictive recipient* must be distinguished, is essentially represented *implicitly*, via the operations of *appeal* and *orientation*.

III.1 The category of point of view is understood in a wide sense as *the complex, formed by internal and external factors, of conditions for the comprehension and representation of happenings*. Perspectivization is a fundamental device,

Conclusion

which is not applied to a preexisting story, as is postulated by countless models, but is already effective in the constitution of the story through the selection of elements from the happenings. Without perspective, there is no story.

III.2 Critically drawing on Boris Uspensky's four-level model, and by engaging with its derivatives (Lintvelt, Rimmon-Kenan), five parameters are distinguished for point of view: perception, ideology, space, time, language. In each of these parameters, the perspective can be *narratorial* (oriented on the narrator) or *figural* (oriented on a character). The two possibilities are valid for both diegetic and non-diegetic narration.

III.3 Perspective can be *compact*, i.e. oriented on the same entity in all five parameters, or *diffuse*, i.e. narratorial in some parameters, figural in others. It is this distribution of narratorial and figural characteristics, which increases the difficulty of reading modern prose, whose often ambiguous construction mirrors the ambiguity of the inner life.

IV.1 In this book, the phenomenon of perspective is connected with the correlation between *narrator's text* and *characters' text*, the two components of the narrative text, which appear at the text's surface in mixed form, as *narrator's* or *characters' discourse*.

IV.2 After the examination of two deviations from neutral narrative text, the poetization in *ornamental prose* and the characterizing stylization in *skaz*, for the description and typologizing of which the positions of Russian theory are applied, there follows a differentiated analysis of the basic technique of modern prose that I call interference of narrator's and characters' texts, and whose most famous manifestation is so-called *free indirect discourse* (FID). By engaging, on the one hand, with the Russian theorists Bakhtin and Voloshinov, who model FID as an agonal phenomenon, in which the narrator contests the evaluative position of the protagonist, and, on the other, with the Czech structuralist Doležel, who interprets the phenomenon solely stylistically and, for the sake of ease of analysis, presupposes ideal types of both texts, a model is suggested here that assigns the possible features for the differentiation of narrator's text and characters' text to the five different parameters of perspective. The profile of features, which contains no preliminary decisions about the relations of the texts' styles, functions as an instrument for the analysis of the parts of both texts, the neutralization of oppositions and the interference of their evaluative positions.

IV.3 The most important manifestations of text interference, such as indirect discourse, autonomous indirect discourse, free indirect discourse in all its types and variants, free indirect perception, free indirect monologue and figurally colored narration, are investigated in terms of functions, the essence of which is the creation of *ambiguity* and *bi-textuality*.

V.1 By engaging with both the dichotomy *fabula* vs. *sujet*, using which the Russian formalists (Shklovsky, Tynyanov) and the analysts close to them (Petrovsky, Tomashevsky, Vygotsky) attempted to explain the artistic character of narrative prose, and also with the French dichotomy *histoire* vs. *discours* (Todorov), including the three-tier models (Genette, Bal, García Landa, Stierle) built on it, an ideal genetic four-tier model of narrative constitution is suggested. The two ambivalent terms *fabula* and *sujet* correspond to the tiers *happenings, story, narrative* and *presentation of the narrative*. The operations that constitute the transformations between them are: (1) the *selection of elements and their properties* (with the implied *compression and expansion*), (2) *composition* (with the devices *linearization* and *reorganization*), and (3) the *manifestation* of the narrative in the medium-specific language (in literature, *verbalization*).

V.2 Perspectivization is not one device among many, nor can it be ascribed to any one of the transformations, but rather appears in all its varying facets as the implication of all three transformations. This fact is illustrated by an ideal genetic model of point of view.

V.3 In the reception of a work, a particular role is played by the elements non-selected for the story, since experiencing a story as a meaningful whole entails understanding the logic of its selectivity and determining the character of its negative selections.

V.4 Three modes are distinguished for the reader's handling of the non-selected: (1) *non-activation* of irrelevant, non-selected elements and properties, (2) *rejection* of non-selected elements that offer themselves for the filling in of places of indeterminacy, (3) the *rescinding* of negation, i.e. filling in the blanks.

V.5 The book concludes with a semiotic model that takes the empirically accessible text as its starting point and sketches the *semiotic* operations of denotation, indication and implication for the diegetic (affecting the story) and the exegetic (affecting the presentation) branches of the work, thereby tracing the perception of the narrative work, the story narrated in it, as well as the discourse story, by the reader.

Works cited

Anderegg, Johannes (1973). *Fiktion und Kommunikation. Ein Beitrag zur Theorie der Prosa*. Göttingen.
Andrievskaya, A. A. (1967). *Nesobstvenno-pryamaya rech' v khudozhestvennoy proze Lui Aragona*. Kiev.
Angelet, Christian; Herman, Jan (1987). "Narratologie." In M. Delcroix, F. Fernand (eds.). *Méthodes du texte: Introduction aux études littéraires*. Paris, 168-201.
Aumüller, Matthias (2009). "Die russische Kompositionstheorie." In W. Schmid (ed.). *Slavische Erzähltheorie. Russische und tschechische Ansätze*. Berlin/New York, 91-140.
Austin, John Langshaw (1962). *How to Do Things with Words*. Oxford.
Bakhtin, Mikhail M. (1919). "Iskusstvo i otvetstvennost'." In M. M. B. *Literaturno-kriticheskie stat'i*. Moskva 1986, 3-4.
— (1929). *Problemy tvorchestva Dostoevskogo*. In M. M. B. *Sobranie sochinenii*. Vol. 2. Moskva 2000, 5-175.
— (1934/35). "Discourse in the Novel [Slovo v romane]." In M. Bakhtin. *The Dialogic Imagination. Four Essays*. Austin 1981, 259-422.
— (1963). *Problemy poetiki Dostoevskogo*. 4th ed. Moskva 1979. Engl.: Bakhtin 1984.
— (1984). *Problems of Dostoevsky's Poetics* [Problemy poetiki Dostoevskogo]. Ed. and tr. by Caryl Emerson. Minneapolis.
— (1992). "Yazyk v khudozhestvennoy literature." In M. M. B. *Sobranie sochinenii v semi tomakh*. Vol. 5. Moskva 1996, 287-97.
— (2002a). [Excerpt from Schmid 1971]. In M. M. B. *Sobranie sochinenii v semi tomakh*. Vol. 6. Moskva, 416-18.
— (2002b). "Rabochie zapisi 60-kh — nachala 70-kh godov." In M. M. B. *Sobranie sochinenii v semi tomakh*. Vol. 6. Moskva, 371-439.
Bal, Mieke (1977a). *Narratologie. Les instances du récit. Essais sur la signification narrative dans quatre romans modernes*. Paris.
— (1977b). "Narration et focalisation. Pour une théorie des instances du récit." *Poétique* 29, 107-27.
— (1978). *De theorie van vertellen en verhalen. Inleiding in de narratologie*. 2nd ed. Muiderberg 1980. Engl.: Bal 1985.
— (1981). "Notes on Narrative Embedding." *Poetics Today* 2, 41-59.
— (1985). *Narratology: Introduction to the Theory of Narrative*. Toronto.
Balcerzan, Edward (1968). "Styl i poetyka twórczości dwujęzycznej Brunona Jasińskiego." *Z zagadnień teorii przekładu*. Wrocław, 14-16.
Bally, Charles (1912). "Le style indirect libre en français moderne." *Germanisch-romanische Monatsschrift* 4, 549-56, 597-606.
— (1914). "Figures de pensée et formes linguistiques." *Germanisch-romanische Monatsschrift* 6, 405-22, 456-70.

— (1930). "Antiphrase et style indirect libre." In N. Bøgholm et al. (eds.). *A Grammatical Miscellany Offered to Otto Jespersen on his Seventieth Birthday.* Copenhagen, 331-40.
Banfield, Ann (1973). "Narrative Style and the Grammar of Direct and Indirect Speech." *Foundations of Language* 10, 1-39.
— (1978a). "The Formal Coherence of Represented Speech and Thought." *Poetics and Theory of Literature* 3, 289-314.
— (1978b). "Where Epistemology, Style, and Grammar Meet Literary History: The Development of Represented Speech and Thought." *New Literary History* 9, 415-54.
— (1983). *Unspeakable Sentences. Narration and Representation in the Language of Fiction.* Boston/London.
Baroni, Raphaël (2009). "Tellability." In P. Hühn, J. Pier, W. Schmid, J. Schönert (eds.). *Handbook of Narratology* (= Narratologia 19). Berlin/New York, 447-54.
Barthes, Roland (1966). "Introduction à l'analyse structurale des récits." *Communications* 8, 1-27. Engl.: Barthes 2004.
— (1968). "The Death of the Author [La mort de l'auteur]." In R. B. *Image, Music, Text.* Tr. by S. Heath. London 1977, 142-48.
— (2004). "Introduction to the Structural Analysis of Narrative [Introduction à l'analyse structurale des récits]." In M. Bal (ed.). *Narrative Theory. Critical Concepts in Literary and Cultural Studies.* Vol. I. Major Issues in Narrative Theory. London/New York, 65-94.
Bartoszyński, Kazimierz (1971). "Zagadnienie komunikacji literackiej w utworach narracyjnych." In J. Sławiński (ed.). *Problemy socjologii literatury.* Wrocław.
Benveniste, Emile (1959). "Les relations de temps dans le verbe français." In E. B. *Problèmes de linguistique générale.* Paris 1966, 237-50.
Berendsen, Marjet (1984). "The Teller and the Observer: Narration and Focalization in Narrative Texts." *Style* 18, 140-58.
Bonheim, Helmut (1990). "Point of View Models." In H. B. *Literary Systematics.* London, 285-307.
Booth, Wayne C. (1961). *The Rhetoric of Fiction.* Chicago.
— (1968). "'The Rhetoric of Fiction' and the Poetics of Fictions." In M. Spilka (ed.). *Towards a Poetic of Fiction.* Bloomington/London, 77-89.
— (1979). *Critical Understanding: The Powers and Limits of Pluralism.* Chicago.
Boyd, John D. (1968). *The Function of Mimesis and its Decline.* Cambridge, MA.
Bremond, Claude (1964). "Le message narratif." *Communications* 4, 4-32.
Breuer, Horst (1998). "Typenkreise und Kreuztabellen: Modelle erzählerischer Vermittlung." *Poetica* 30, 233-49.
Brinton, Laurel (1980). "'Represented Perception': A Study in Narrative Style." *Poetics* 9, 363-81.
Broich, Ulrich (1983). "Gibt es eine 'neutrale' Erzählsituation?" *Germanisch-romanische Monatsschrift.* Neue Folge 33, 129-45.
Bronzwaer, W. J. M. (1970). *Tense in the Novel: An Investigation of Some Potentialities of Linguistic Criticism.* Groningen.

— (1978). "Implied Author, Extradiegetic Narrator and Public Reader: Gérard Genette's narratological model and the reading version of *Great Expectations.*" *Neophilologus* 62, 1-18.
— (1981). "Mieke Bal's Concept of Focalisation: A Critical Note." *Poetics Today* 2, 193-201.
Brooks, Cleanth; Warren, Robert Penn (1943). *Understanding Fiction.* New York.
Browning, Gary L. (1979). "Russian Ornamental Prose." *Slavic and East European Journal* 23, 346-52.
Brugmann, Karl (1904). *Die Demonstrativpronomina der indogermanischen Verben.* Leipzig.
Bühler, Karl (1918/20). "Kritische Musterung der neueren Theorien des Satzes." *Indogermanisches Jahrbuch* 4, 1-20.
— (1934). *Sprachtheorie. Die Darstellungsfunktion der Sprache.* Frankfurt a. M. 1978. Engl.: Bühler 1990.
— (1990). *Theory of Language. The Representational Function of Language* [Sprachtheorie. Die Darstellungsfunktion der Sprache]. Amsterdam.
Bühler, Willi (1937). *Die „Erlebte Rede" im englischen Roman. Ihre Vorstufen und ihre Ausbildung im Werke Jane Austens.* Zürich/Leipzig.
Busch, Ulrich (1962). "Erzählen, behaupten, dichten." *Wirkendes Wort* 12, 217-23.
Carden, Patricia (1976). "Ornamentalism and Modernism." In G. Gibian, H. W. Tjalsma (eds.). *Russian Modernism. Culture and Avant-Garde. 1900-1930.* Ithaca, 49-64.
Cassirer, Ernst (1925). *The Philosophy of Symbolic Forms. Vol. 2: Mythical Thought* [Philosophie der symbolischen Formen. Teil 2: Das mythische Denken]. Tr. by R. Manheim. New Haven/London 1971.
Červenka, Miroslav (1969). "Das literarische Werk als Zeichen [Literární dílo jako znak]." In M. Č. *Der Bedeutungsaufbau des literarischen Werks.* Ed. by F. Boldt and W.-D. Stempel. München 1978, 163-83.
Chatman, Seymour (1978). *Story and Discourse. Narrative Structure in Fiction and Film.* 3rd ed. Ithaca/London 1986.
— (1990). *Coming to Terms. The Rhetoric of Narrative in Fiction and Film.* Ithaca.
Chudakov, Aleksandr P. (1971). *Poetika Chekhova.* Moskva. Engl.: Chudakov 1983.
— (1983). *Chekhov's Poetics* [Poetika Chekhova]. Ann Arbor.
— (1992). "V. V. Vinogradov i ego teoriya poetiki." In A. P. Ch. *Slovo - veshch' - mir. Ot Pushkina do Tolstogo. Ocherki poetiki russkikh klassikov.* Moskva, 219-64.
—; Chudakova, Marietta O. (1971). "Skaz." In *Kratkaya literaturnaya entsiklopediya.* Vol. 6. Moskva, 876.
Cohn, Dorrit (1969). "Erlebte Rede im Ich-Roman." *Germanisch-romanische Monatsschrift.* Neue Folge 19, 305-13.
— (1978). *Transparent Minds: Narrative Modes for Presenting Consciousness in Fiction.* Princeton.
— (1981). "The Encirclement of Narrative: On Franz Stanzel's *Theorie des Erzählens.*"*Poetics Today* 2, 157-82.
— (1989). "Fictional versus Historical Lives. Borderlines and Borderline Cases." *The Journal of Narrative Technique* 19, 3-24.

— (1990). "Signposts of Fictionality. A Narratological Perspective." *Poetics Today* 11, 775-804.
— (1995). "Narratologische Kennzeichen der Fiktionalität." *Sprachkunst. Beiträge zur Literaturwissenschaft* 26, 105-12.
Crittenden, Charles (1991). *Unreality: The Metaphysics of Fictional Objects.* Ithaca.
Culler, Jonathan (1980). "Fabula and Sjuzhet in the Analysis of Narrative. Some American Discussions." *Poetics Today* 1, 27-37.
Dehne, Marianne (2006). *Der Wissensumbruch um 1800 in der russischen Lyrik* (= Slavische Literaturen 37). Frankfurt a. M.
Díaz Arenas, Ángel (1986). *Introducción y Metodología de la Instancia del Autor/Lector y del Autor/Lector abstracto-implícito.* Kassel.
Dibelius, Wilhelm (1910). *Englische Romankunst: Die Technik des englischen Romans im achtzehnten und zu Anfang des neunzehnten Jahrhunderts.* Berlin 1922.
Diengott, Nilli (1993). "Implied Author, Motivation and Theme and Their Problematic Status." *Orbis Litterarum* 48, 181-93.
Doležel, Lubomír (1958). "Polopřímá řeč v moderní české próze." *Slovo a slovesnost* 19, 20-46.
— (1960). *O stylu moderní české prózy. Výstavba textu.* Praha.
— (1965). "Neytralizatsiya protivopostavlenii v yazykovo-stilisticheskoy strukture epicheskoy prozy." In *Problemy sovremennoy filologii.* Sbornik statey k semidesyatiletiyu V. V. Vinogradova. Moskva, 116-23.
— (1967). "The Typology of the Narrator: Point of View in Fiction." In *To Honor Roman Jakobson.* Vol. 1. The Hague/Paris, 541-52.
— (1973a). *Narrative Modes in Czech Literature.* Toronto.
— (1973b). "Narrative Composition: A Link between German and Russian Poetics." In S. Bann, J. E. Bowlt (eds.). *Russian Formalism.* Edinburgh, 73-83.
— (1978). "Semantics of Narrative Motifs." In W. U. Dressler, W. Meid (eds.). *Proceedings of the Twelfth International Congress of Linguistics.* Innsbruck, 646-49.
— (1989). "Possible Worlds and Literary Fictions." In S. Allén (ed.). *Possible Worlds in Humanities, Arts and Sciences. Proceedings of Nobel Symposium* 65. Berlin/New York, 221-42.
— (1990). *Occidental Poetics. Tradition and Progress.* Lincoln.
— (1993). *Narativní způsoby v české literatuře.* Praha.
— (1998). *Heterocosmica. Fiction and Possible Worlds.* Baltimore/London.
Drozda, Miroslav (1971). "Review of Uspensky 1970." *Umjetnost riječi* 1, 83-86.
Dujardin, Edouard (1931). *Le monologue intérieur. Son apparition, ses origines, sa place dans l'œuvre de James Joyce et dans le roman contemporain.* Paris.
Dupont-Roc, Roselyne; Lallot, Jean (eds.) (1980). *Aristote: La poétique. Texte, traduction, notes.* Paris.
Easthope, Antony (1983). *Poetry as Discourse.* London.
Eco, Umberto (1979). *Lector in fabula. Die Mitarbeit der Interpretation in erzählenden Texten* [Lector in fabula. La cooperazione interpretativa nei testi narrativi]. München 1990.
Egorov, B. F.; Zaretsky, V. A.; Gushanskaya, E. M.; Taborishskaya, E. M. (1978). "Syuzhet i fabula." In *Voprosy syuzhetoslozheniya.* Sbornik statey. Vol. 5. Riga, 11-21.

Eikhenbaum, Boris (1918). "The Illusion of Skaz [Illyuziya skaza]." Tr. by M. B. Rice. *Russian Literature Triquartely* 12, Spring 1978, 233-36.
— (1919). "How Gogol's 'Overcoat' is Made [Kak sdelana 'Shinel" Gogolya]." In R. A. Maguire (ed.). *Gogol' from the Twentieth Century. Eleven Essays.* Princeton UP 1974, 269-91.
— (1921). "Probleme der Poetik Puschkins [Problemy poetiki Pushkina]." In B. E. *Aufsätze zur Theorie und Geschichte der Literatur.* Frankfurt a. M. 1965, 87-100.
— (1925). "Leskov and Contemporary Prose [Leskov i sovremennaya proza]." Tr. by M. B. Rice. *Russian Literature Triquartely* 11, Winter 1975, 211-24.
Else, Gerald F. (1957). *Aristotle's Poetics. The Argument.* Cambridge, MA.
Eng, Jan van der (1984). "Ästhetische Dominante und Fiktionalisierung. Wahrheitsanspruch und Intensivierung der Information. Autor und Leser." In J.-R. Döring-Smirnov, P. Rehder, W. Schmid (eds.). *Text – Symbol – Weltmodell. Johannes Holthusen zum 60. Geburtstag.* München, 111-30.
Evdokimova, Svetlana (1996). "Protsess khudozhestvennogo tvorchestva i avtorskii tekst." In V. M. Markovich, V. Shmid (eds.). *Avtor i tekst.* Sbornik statey. Sankt-Peterburg, 9-24.
Fehr, Bernhard (1938). "Substitutionary Narration and Description: A Chapter in Stylistics." *English Studies* 20, 97-107.
Fieguth, Rolf (1973). "Zur Rezeptionslenkung bei narrativen und dramatischen Werken." *Sprache im technischen Zeitalter* 47, 186-201.
— (1975). "Einleitung." In R. Fieguth (ed.). *Literarische Kommunikation.* Kronberg/Ts., 9-22.
— (1996). "Avtor i dramaticheskii tekst." In V. M. Markovich, W. Schmid (eds.). *Avtor i tekst.* Sbornik statey. Sankt-Peterburg, 53-83.
Fludernik, Monika (1993a). *The Fictions of Language and the Language of Fiction. The Linguistic Representation of Speech and Consciousness.* London/New York.
— (1993b). "Second Person Fiction: Narrative 'You' as Adressee and/or Protagonist." *AAA – Arbeiten aus Anglistik und Amerikanistik* 18, 217-47.
— (1994). "Second Person Narrative as a Test Case for Narratology: The Limits of Realism." *Style* 28, 445-79.
— (1996). *Towards a "Natural" Narratology.* London/New York.
Forster, Edward Morgan (1927). *Aspects of the Novel.* London 1973.
Foster, Ludmila A. (1972). "Review of Uspensky 1970." *Slavic and East European Journal* 16, 339-41.
Foucault, Michel (1969). "Qu'est-ce qu'un auteur?" In M. F. *Dits et écrits 1954-1988.* Vol. I: 1954-1969. Paris 1994, 789-821.
Frank, Joseph (1945). "Spatial Form in Modern Literature." In J. F. *The Widening Gyre: Crisis and Mastery in Modern Literature.* New Brunswick (Reprint: Bloomington 1968) 1963, 3-62.
Freise, Matthias (1993). *Michail Bachtins philosophische Ästhetik der Literatur* (= Slavische Literaturen 4). Frankfurt a. M.
— (1996). "Posle izgnaniya avtora: literaturovedenie v tupike?" In V. M. Markovich, V. Shmid (eds.). *Avtor i tekst.* Sbornik statey. Sankt-Peterburg, 25-32.
Friedemann, Käte (1910). *Die Rolle des Erzählers in der Epik.* Berlin (Reprint: Darmstadt 1965).

Friedman, Norman (1955). "Point of View in Fiction. The Development of a Critical Concept." *Publications of the Modern Language Association of America* 70, 1160-84.
Füger, Wilhelm (1972). "Zur Tiefenstruktur des Narrativen. Prolegomena zu einer generativen 'Grammatik' des Erzählens." *Poetica* 5, 268-92.
Gabriel, Gottfried (1991). *Zwischen Logik und Literatur. Erkenntnisformen von Dichtung, Philosophie und Wissenschaft.* Stuttgart.
García Landa, José Ángel (1998). *Acción, relato, discurso. Estructura de la ficción narrativa.* Salamanca.
Gebauer, Gunter; Wulf, Christoph (1992). *Mimesis. Kultur – Kunst – Gesellschaft.* Reinbek.
Genette, Gérard (1972). "Discours du récit." In G. G. *Figures III.* Paris, 67-282. Engl.: Genette 1980.
— (1980). *Narrative Discourse* [Discours du récit]. Tr. by J. E. Lewin. Oxford.
— (1983). *Nouveau discours du récit.* Paris. Engl.: Genette 1988.
— (1987). *Paratextes.* Paris.
— (1988). *Narrative discourse revisited* [Nouveau discours du récit]. Tr. by J. E. Lewin. Ithaca, NY.
— (1989). "Les actes de fiction." In G. G. *Fiction et diction.* Paris 1991, 41-63. Engl.: Genette 1993b.
— (1990). "Récit fictionnel, récit factuel." In G. G. *Fiction et diction.* Paris 1991, 65-94. Engl.: Genette 1993c.
— (1991). "Fiction et diction." In G. G. *Fiction et diction.* Paris, 11-40. Engl.: Genette 1993d.
— (1993a). *Fiction and Diction* [Fiction et diction]. Tr. by C. Porter. Ithaca.
— (1993b). "Acts of Fiction [Les actes de fiction]." In Genette 1993a, 30-53.
— (1993c). "Fictional Narrative, Factual Narrative [Récit fictionnel, récit factuel]." In Genette 1993a, 54-84.
— (1993d). "Fiction and Diction [Fiction et diction]." In Genette 1993a, 1-29.
Gersbach-Bäschlin, Annette (1970). *Reflektorischer Stil und Erzählstruktur. Studie zu den Formen der Rede- und Gedankenwiedergabe in der erzählenden Prosa von Romain Rolland und André Gide.* Bern.
Glauser, Lisa (1948). *Die erlebte Rede im englischen Roman des 19. Jahrhunderts.* Bern.
Głowiński, Michał (1963). "Narracja jako monolog wypowiedziany." In M. G. *Gry powieściowe. Szkice z teorii i historii form narracyjnych.* Warszawa 1973, 106-48.
— (1967). "Der virtuelle Empfänger in der Struktur des poetischen Werkes [Wirtualny odbiorca w strukturze utworu poetyckiego]." In R. Fieguth (ed.). *Literarische Kommunikation.* Kronberg/Ts. 1975, 93-126.
Goetsch, Paul (1983). "Leserfiguren in der Erzählkunst." *Germanisch-romanische Monatsschrift.* Neue Folge 33, 199-215.
Gogotishvili, Lyudmila A. (2002). "[Commentary on Bakhtin's workbooks]." In M. M. Bakhtin. *Sobranie sochinenii v semi tomakh.* Vol. 6. Moskva, 533-701.
Gölz, Christine (2009). "Autorkonzepte im slavischen Funktionalismus." In W. Schmid (ed.). *Slavische Erzähltheorie. Russische und tschechische Ansätze.* Berlin/New York, 187-237.
Greimas, Algirdas Julien (1967). "La structure des actants du récit. Essai d'approche générative." In A. J. G. *Du Sens. Essais sémiotiques.* Paris 1970, 249-70.

Grimm, Gunter (1977). *Rezeptionsgeschichte. Grundlegung einer Theorie.* München.
Günther, Werner (1928). *Probleme der Rededarstellung: Untersuchungen zur direkten, indirekten und „erlebten" Rede im Deutschen, Französischen und Italienischen.* Marburg.
Gurvich, Isaak A. (1971). "Zamysel i smysl issledovaniya." *Voprosy literatury* 2, 198–202.
Haard, Eric A. de (1979). "On Narration in *Vojna i mir.*" *Russian Literature* 7, 95–120.
Haller, Rudolf (1986). "Wirkliche und fiktive Gegenstände." In R. H. *Facta und Ficta. Studien zu ästhetischen Grundfragen.* Stuttgart, 57–93.
Hamburger, Käte (1951). "Zum Strukturproblem der epischen und dramatischen Dichtung." *Deutsche Vierteljahrsschrift für Literaturwissenschaft und Geistesgeschichte* 25, 1–26.
— (1953). "Das epische Präteritum." *Deutsche Vierteljahrsschrift für Literaturwissenschaft und Geistesgeschichte* 27, 329–57.
— (1955). "Die Zeitlosigkeit der Dichtung." *Deutsche Vierteljahrsschrift für Literaturwissenschaft und Geistesgeschichte* 29, 414–26.
— (1957). *Die Logik der Dichtung.* Stuttgart.
— (1968). *Die Logik der Dichtung.* 2nd rev. ed. Stuttgart. Engl.: Hamburger 1973.
— (1973). *The Logic of Literature* [Die Logik der Dichtung]. 2nd rev. ed. Tr. by M. J. Rose. Bloomington, IN.
Hansen-Löve, Aage A. (1978). *Der russische Formalismus. Methodologische Rekonstruktion seiner Entwicklung aus dem Prinzip der Verfremdung.* Wien.
— (1982). "Die 'Realisierung' und 'Entfaltung' semantischer Figuren zu Texten." *Wiener Slawistischer Almanach* 10, 197–252.
— (1983). "Intermedialität und Intertextualität. Probleme der Korrelation von Wort- und Bildkunst – Am Beispiel der russischen Moderne." In W. Schmid, W.-D. Stempel (eds.). *Dialog der Texte. Hamburger Kolloquium zur Intertextualität.* Wien, 291–360.
— (1984). "Beobachtungen zur narrativen Kurzgattung." In R. Grübel (ed.). *Russische Erzählung. Russian Short Story. Russkii rasskaz.* Amsterdam, 1–45.
— (1987) "Mythos als Wiederkehr. Ein Essay." In W. Schmid (ed.). *Mythos in der slawischen Moderne* (= Wiener Slawistischer Almanach. Sonderband 20). Wien, 9–23.
Harweg, Roland (1979). "Inhaltsentwurf, Erzählung, Inhaltswiedergabe. Zum fiktionstheoretischen Doppelstatus fiktionaler Erzählungen." In W. Frier, G. Labroisse (eds.). *Grundfragen der Textwissenschaft.* Amsterdam, 111–30.
Hempfer, Klaus W. (1977). "Zur pragmatischen Fundierung der Texttypologie." In W. Hinck (ed.). *Textsortenlehre – Gattungsgeschichte.* Heidelberg, 1–26.
— (1990). "Zu einigen Problemen der Fiktionstheorie." *Zeitschrift für französische Sprache und Literatur* 100, 109–37.
Herman, David (ed.) (1999). *Narratologies: New Perspectives on Narrative Analysis.* Columbus, OH.
Hodel, Robert (2001). *Erlebte Rede in der russischen Literatur. Vom Sentimentalismus bis zum Sozialistischen Realismus* (= Slavische Literaturen 22). Frankfurt a. M.

Hoek, Leo H. (1981). *La marque du titre. Dispositifs sémiotiques d'une pratique textuelle.* La Haye.
Holthusen, Johannes (1968). "Stilistik des 'uneigentlichen' Erzählens in der sowjetischen Gegenwartsliteratur." *Die Welt der Slaven* 13, 225-45.
Holý, Jiří (2000). "Objektivní text?" *Česká literatura* 48, 578-81.
Hoops, Wiklef (1979). "Fiktionalität als pragmatische Kategorie." *Poetica* 11, 281-317.
Horálek, Karel (1970). "Tři úvahy o struktuře epiky." *Slovo a slovesnost* 31, 125-45.
Hühn, Peter (1995). *Geschichte der englischen Lyrik.* Vol. 1. Tübingen.
— (2009). "Event and Eventfulness." In P. Hühn, J. Pier, W. Schmid, J. Schönert (eds.). *Handbook of Narratology* (= Narratologia 19). Berlin/New York, 80-97.
Ilyin, I. P. (1996a). "Narrator." In Ilyin/Tsurganova (eds.) 1996. 79-81.
— (1996b). "Depersonalizatsiya." In Ilyin/Tsurganova (eds.) 1996. 207-11.
— (1996c). "Implitsitnyi chitatel'." In Ilyin/Tsurganova (eds.) 1996. 53-54.
— (1996d). "Narratator." In Ilyin/Tsurganova (eds.) 1996. 61-63.
— (1996e). "Fokalizatsiya." In Ilyin/Tsurganova (eds.) 1996. 159-62.
—; Tsurganova, E. A. (eds.) (1996). *Sovremennoe zarubezhnoe literaturovedenie (strany Zapadnoy Evropy i SShA): kontseptsii, shkoly, terminy.* Entsiklopedicheskii spravochnik. Moskva.
Ingarden, Roman (1931). *Das literarische Kunstwerk.* Tübingen 1972. Engl.: Ingarden 1973a.
— (1937). *Vom Erkennen des literarischen Kunstwerks* [O poznawaniu dzieła literackiego]. Tübingen 1968. Engl.: Ingarden 1973b.
— (1973a). *The Literary Work of Art* [Das literarische Kunstwerk]. Tr. by G. G. Grabowicz. Evanston, IL.
— (1973b). *The Cognition of the Literary Work of Art* [O poznawaniu dzieła literackiego]. Tr. by R. A. Crowley and K. R. Olson. Evanston, IL.
Iser, Wolfgang (1972). *Der implizite Leser. Kommunikationsformen des Romans von Bunyan bis Beckett.* München. Engl.: Iser 1974.
— (1974). *The Implied Reader: Patterns of Communication in Prose Fiction from Bunyan to Beckett.* Baltimore.
— (1976). *Der Akt des Lesens. Theorie ästhetischer Wirkung.* München. Engl.: Iser 1978.
— (1978). *The Act of Reading: A Theory of Aesthetic Response.* Baltimore.
Ivanchikova, E. A. (1985). "Kategoriya 'obraza avtora' v nauchnom tvorchestve V. V. Vinogradova." *Izvestiya AN SSSR. Seriya literatury i yazyka* 44, 123-34.
Jahn, Manfred; Nünning, Ansgar (1994). "A Survey of Narratological Models." *Literatur in Wissenschaft und Unterricht* 27, 283-303.
— (1995). "Narratologie: Methoden und Modelle der Erzähltheorie." In A. Nünning (ed.). *Literaturwissenschaftliche Theorien, Modelle und Methoden. Eine Einführung.* Trier, 29-50.
Jakobson, Roman (1921). "Die neueste russische Poesie [Noveyshaya russkaya poeziya]." Russ.-Germ. in W.-D. Stempel (ed.) 1972. 18-135.
— (1960). "Linguistics and Poetics." In Th. A. Sebeok (ed.). *Style in Language.* Cambridge, MA, 350-77.
—; Pomorska, Krystyna (1980). *Dialogues.* Cambridge, MA, 1983.

James, Henry (1884). "The Art of Fiction." In H. J. *Selected Literary Criticism*. Ed. by Morris Shapira. Harmondsworth 1968, 78-96.
— (1907/09). *The Art of the Novel. Critical Prefaces*. London 1935.
Janik, Dieter (1973). *Die Kommunikationsstruktur des Erzählwerks. Ein semiologisches Modell*. Bebenhausen.
— (1985). *Literatursemiotik als Methode. Die Kommunikationsstruktur des Erzählwerks und der Zeichenwert literarischer Strukturen*. Tübingen.
Jannidis, Fotis; Lauer, Gerhard; Martinez, Matias; Winko, Simone (1999). "Rede über den Autor an die Gebildeten unter seinen Verächtern. Historische Modelle und systematische Perspektiven." In Jannidis et al. (eds.). *Rückkehr des Autors. Beiträge zur Rechtfertigung eines umstrittenen Begriffs*. Tübingen, 3-35.
— (eds.) (1999). *Rückkehr des Autors. Beiträge zur Rechtfertigung eines umstrittenen Begriffs*. Tübingen.
Jasińska, Maria (1965). *Narrator w powieści przedromantycznej (1776-1931)*. Warszawa.
Jedličková, Alice (1993). *Ke komu mluví vypravěč? Adresát v komunikační perspektivě prózy*. Praha.
Jensen, Peter Alberg (1984). "The Thing as Such: Boris Pil'njak's 'Ornamentalism.'" *Russian Literature* 16, 81-100.
Jost, François (1983). "Narration(s): en deçà et au-delà." *Communications* 38, 192-212.
Juhl, Peter D. (1980). "Life, Literature, and the Implied Author." *Deutsche Vierteljahrsschrift für Literaturwissenschaft und Geistesgeschichte* 54, 177-203.
Kablitz, Andreas (1988). "Erzählperspektive - Point of View - Focalisation. Überlegungen zu einem Konzept der Erzähltheorie." *Zeitschrift für französische Sprache und Literatur* 98, 237-55.
Kahrmann, Cordula; Reiß, Gunter; Schluchter, Manfred (1977). *Erzähltextanalyse. Eine Einführung in Grundlagen und Verfahren*. 2 Vols. Kronberg/Ts.
Kainz, Friedrich (1941). *Psychologie der Sprache*. 3rd ed. Stuttgart 1962.
Kalepky, Theodor (1899). "Zur französischen Syntax. VII. Mischung indirekter und direkter Rede. (T[obler] II, 7) oder V[erschleierte] R[ede]?" *Zeitschrift für romanische Philologie* 23, 491-513.
— (1913). "Zum 'Style indirect libre' ('Verschleierte Rede')." *Germanisch-romanische Monatsschrift* 5, 608-19.
— (1928). "Verkleidete Rede." *Neophilologus* 13, 1-4.
Kayser, Wolfgang (1956). "Das Problem des Erzählers im Roman." *German Quarterly* 29, 225-38.
— (1958). "Wer erzählt den Roman?" In Volker Klotz (ed.). *Zur Poetik des Romans*. Darmstadt 1965, 197-217.
Kenner, Hugh (1978). *Joyce's Voices*. Berkeley.
Khanpira, E. (1971). "Review of Uspensky 1970." In *Nauchnye doklady vysshey shkoly. Filologicheskie nauki* 5, 121-25.
Kindt, Tom; Müller, Hans-Harald (1999). "Der implizite Autor. Zur Explikation und Verwendung eines umstrittenen Begriffs." In F. Jannidis et al. (eds.). *Rückkehr des Autors. Beiträge zur Rechtfertigung eines umstrittenen Begriffs*. Tübingen, 273-87.
— (2006a). *The Implied Author. Concept and Controversy* (= Narratologia 9). Berlin/New York.

— (2006b). "Der implizite Autor. Zur Karriere und Kritik eines Begriffs zwischen Narratologie und Interpretationstheorie." *Archiv für Begriffsgeschichte* 48, 163-90.
— (eds.) (2003). *What is Narratology. Questions and Answers Regarding the Status of a Theory* (= Narratologia 1). Berlin/New York.
Klepper, Martin (2004). *The Discovery of Point of View. Observation and Narration in the American Novel 1790-1910.* Habil.-Schrift Hamburg.
Kohl, Stephan (1977). *Realismus: Theorie und Geschichte.* München.
Koller, Hermann (1954). *Die Mimesis in der Antike: Nachahmung. Darstellung. Ausdruck.* Bern.
Korman, Boris O. (1977). "O tselostnosti literaturnogo proizvedeniya." In B. O. K. *Izbrannye trudy po teorii i istorii literatury.* Izhevsk 1992, 119-28.
— (1981). "Tselostnost' literaturnogo proizvedeniya i eksperimental'nyi slovar' literaturovedcheskikh terminov." In B. O. K. *Izbrannye trudy po teorii i istorii literatury.* Izhevsk 1992, 172-89.
Korte, Barbara (1987). "Das Du im Erzähltext. Kommunikationsorientierte Betrachtungen zu einer vielgebrauchten Form." *Poetica* 19, 169-89.
Kovtunova, I. I. (1955). *Nesobstvenno-pryamaya rech' v yazyke russkoy literatury kontsa XVIII-pervoi poloviny XIX v.* Kandidatskaya dissertatsiya. Moskva.
Kozhevnikova, Natal'ya A. (1971). "O tipakh povestvovaniya v sovetskoy proze." In *Voprosy yazyka sovremennoy russkoy literatury.* Moskva, 97-163.
— (1976). "Iz nablyudenii nad neklassicheskoy ('ornamental'noy') prozoy." *Izvestiya AN SSSR. Seriya literatury i yazyka* 35, 55-66.
— (1994). *Tipy povestvovaniya v russkoy literature XIX-XX vv.* Moskva.
Koževniková, Květa (1970). *Spontannaya ustnaya rech' v epicheskoy proze.* Praha.
Koziol, Herbert (1956). "Episches Präteritum und historisches Präsens." *Germanisch-romanische Monatsschrift.* Neue Folge 6, 398-401.
Kristeva, Julia (1967). "Bakhtine, le mot, le dialogue et le roman." In J. K. *Semeiotiké. Recherches pour une sémanalyse.* Paris 1978, 82-112.
Kullmann, Dorothea (1992). "Systematische und historische Bemerkungen zum Style indirect libre." *Romanistische Zeitschrift für Literaturgeschichte/Cahiers d'Histoire des Littératures Romanes* 16, 113-40.
— (ed.) (1995). *Erlebte Rede und impressionistischer Stil. Europäische Erzählprosa im Vergleich mit ihren deutschen Übersetzungen.* Göttingen.
Labov, William (1972). *Language in the Inner City: Studies in the Black English Vernacular.* Philadelphia.
LaCapra, Dominick (1982). *Madame Bovary on Trial.* Ithaca.
Låftman, Emil (1929). "Stellvertretende Darstellung." *Neophilologus* 14, 161-68.
Lamarque, Peter; Olsen, Stein Haugom (1994). *Truth, Fiction, and Literature.* Oxford.
Lämmert, Eberhard (1955). *Bauformen des Erzählens.* 3rd ed. Stuttgart 1972.
Lanser, Susan S. (1981). *The Narrative Act. Point of View in Prose Fiction.* Princeton.
Leibfried, Erwin (1970). *Kritische Wissenschaft vom Text. Manipulation, Reflexion, transparente Poetologie.* Stuttgart.
Lemon, Lee T.; Reis, Marion J. (eds.) (1965). *Russian Formalist Criticism. Four Essays.* Lincoln.
Lerch, Eugen (1914). "Die stilistische Bedeutung des Imperfektums der Rede ('style indirect libre')." *Germanisch-romanische Monatsschrift* 6, 470-89.

— (1928). "Ursprung und Bedeutung der sog. 'Erlebten Rede' ('Rede als Tatsache')." *Germanisch-romanische Monatsschrift* 16, 459-78.

Lerch, Gertraud (1922). "Die uneigentlich direkte Rede." In V. Klemperer, E. Lerch (eds.). *Idealistische Neuphilologie. Festschrift für Karl Vossler zum 6. September 1922.* Heidelberg, 107-19.

Levin, V. D. (1981). "'Neklassicheskie' tipy povestvovaniya nachala XX veka v istorii russkogo literaturnogo yazyka." *Slavica Hierosolymitana* 5-6, 245-75.

Likhachev, D. S. (1971). "O teme dannoy knigi." In V. V. Vinogradov. *O teorii khudozhestvennoy rechi.* Moskva, 212-32.

Link, Hannelore (1976). *Rezeptionsforschung. Eine Einführung in Methoden und Probleme.* Stuttgart.

Lintvelt, Jaap (1979). "Les instances du texte narratif littéraire." In Ch. Grivel (ed.). *Ecriture de la religion, écriture du roman. Mélanges d'histoire de la littérature et de critique offerts à Joseph Tans.* Lille, 157-74.

— (1981). *Essai de typologie narrative. Le "point de vue". Théorie et analyse.* Paris.

Lips, Marguerite (1926). *Le style indirect libre.* Paris.

Lockemann, Wolfgang (1965). "Zur Lage der Erzählforschung." *Germanisch-romanische Monatsschrift.* Neue Folge 15, 63-84.

Lorck, Etienne (1921). *Die "Erlebte Rede." Eine sprachliche Untersuchung.* Heidelberg.

Löschnigg, Martin (1999). "Narratological Categories and the (Non-)Distinction between Factual and Fictional Narratives." In J. Pier (ed.). *Recent Trends in Narratological Research.* Tours, 31-48.

Lotman, Yury (1970). *Struktura khudozhestvennogo teksta.* Moskva. Engl.: Lotman 1977.

— (1973a). "Syuzhet v kino." In Yu. M. L. *Semiotika kino i voprosy kinoestetiki.* Tallin, 85-99. Engl.: Lotman 1976.

— (1973b). "Proiskhozhdenie syuzheta v tipologicheskom osveshchenii." In Yu. M. L. *Stat'i po tipologii kul'tury.* Part II. Tartu, 9-42.

— (1976). "Plot in Cinema." In Yu. L. *Semiotics of Cinema.* Tr. with foreword by M. Suino. Ann Arbor, 64-76.

— (1977). *The Structure of the Artistic Text.* Tr. by G. Lenhoff and R. Vroon. Ann Arbor.

Lubbock, Percy (1921). *The Craft of Fiction.* London 1957.

Markovich Vladimir (1975). "Chelovek v romanakh I. S. Turgeneva." In V. M. *Izbrannye raboty.* Sankt-Peterburg 2008, 107-206.

—; Schmid, Wolf (eds.) (1996). *Avtor i tekst. Sbornik statey.* Sankt-Peterburg.

Markus, Manfred (1985). *Point of View im Erzähltext. Eine angewandte Typologie am Beispiel der frühen amerikanischen Short Story, insbesondere Poes und Hawthornes.* Innsbruck.

Martínez, Matías (1996). *Doppelte Welten. Struktur und Sinn zweideutigen Erzählens.* Göttingen.

—; Scheffel, Michael (1999). *Einführung in die Erzähltheorie.* München.

Martínez Bonati, Félix (1980). "The Act of Writing Fiction." *New Literary History* 11, 425-34.

— (1981). *Fictive Discourse and the Structures of Literature. A Phenomenological Approach.* Ithaca/London.

Mathauserová, Světla (1972). "Review of Uspensky 1970." *Československá rusistika* 17, 41–43.
Matlaw, Ralph E. (1957). *The Brothers Karamazov – Novelistic Technique*. 's-Gravenhage.
McHale, Brian (1978). "Free Indirect Discourse: A Survey of Recent Accounts." *PTL. A Journal for Descriptive Poetics and Theory of Literature* 3, 249–87.
— (2009). "Speech Representation." In P. Hühn, J. Pier, W. Schmid, J. Schönert (eds.). *Handbook of Narratology* (= Narratologia 19). Berlin/New York, 434–46.
Meijer, Jan M. (1971). "The Author of *Brat'ja Karamazovy*." In J. van der Eng, J. M. Meijer The Brothers Karamazov *by F. M. Dostoevsky. Essays*. 's-Gravenhage, 7–46.
Meister, Jan Christoph (2003). *Computing Action. A Narratological Approach* (= Narratologia 2). Berlin/New York.
— (ed.) (2005). *Narratology beyond Literary Criticism. Mediality, Disciplinarity* (= Narratologia 6). Berlin/New York.
Meyer, Kurt Robert (1957). *Zur "erlebten Rede" im englischen Roman des zwanzigsten Jahrhunderts*. Bern.
Moenninghof, Burkhard (1996). "Paratexte." In H. L. Arnold, H. Detering (eds.). *Grundzüge der Literaturwissenschaft*. München, 349–56.
Morrison, Kristin (1961). "James's and Lubbock's Differing Points of View." *Nineteenth-Century Fiction* 16, 245–55.
Morson, Gary Saul; Emerson, Caryl (1990). "Mikhail Bakhtin. Creation of a Prosaics." Stanford UP.
Mukařovský, Jan (1937). "L'individu dans l'art." In *Deuxième congrès international d'esthétique et de la science de l'art*. Vol. I. Paris, 349–50.
— (1938). "Poetic Reference [Dénominaton poétique et la fonction esthétique de la langue]." In L. Matejka, I. R. Titunik (eds.). *Semiotics of Art: Prague School Contributions*. Cambridge, MA, 1976, 155–63.
Müller, Günther (1948). "Erzählzeit und erzählte Zeit." In *Festschrift für Paul Kluckhohn und Hermann Schneider*. Tübingen, 195–212.
Mushchenko, E. G.; Skobelev, V. P.; Kroychik, L. E. (1978). *Poetika skaza*. Voronezh.
Neschke, Ada (1980). *Die Poetik des Aristoteles. Textstruktur und Textbedeutung*. 2 Vols. Vol. 1: *Interpretationen*. Frankfurt a. M.
Neubert, Albrecht (1957). *Die Stilformen der "erlebten Rede" im neueren englischen Roman*. Halle a. d. Saale.
Neuse, Werner (1980). "Die Anfänge der 'erlebten Rede' und des 'inneren Monologs' in der deutschen Prosa des 18. Jahrhunderts." In E. R. Haymes (ed.). *Theatrum Mundi. Essays on German Drama and German Literature*. München, 1–21.
— (1990). *Geschichte der erlebten Rede und des inneren Monologs in der deutschen Prosa*. New York.
Nünning, Ansgar (1989). *Grundzüge eines kommunikationstheoretischen Modells der erzählerischen Vermittlung. Die Funktionen der Erzählinstanz in den Romanen George Eliots*. Trier.
— (1990). "'Point of view' oder 'Focalization'? Über einige Grundlagen und Kategorien konkurrierender Modelle der erzählerischen Vermittlung." *Literatur in Wissenschaft und Unterricht* 23, 249–68.

Works cited

— (1993). "Renaissance eines anthropomorphisierten Passepartouts oder Nachruf auf ein literaturkritisches Phantom? Überlegungen und Alternativen zum Konzept des 'implied author.'" *Deutsche Vierteljahrsschrift für Literaturwissenschaft und Geistesgeschichte* 67, 1-25.

— (1995). *Von historischer Fiktion zu historiographischer Metafiktion*. Vol. 1. Trier.

— (1998). "Unreliable, Compared to What: Towards a Cognitive Theory of 'Unreliable Narration': Prolegomena and Hypotheses." In W. Grünzweig, A. Solbach (eds.). *Grenzüberschreitungen. Narratologie im Kontext. Transcending Boundaries. Narratology in Context*. Tübingen, 53-73.

— (1999). "Reconceptualizing the Theory and Generic Scope of Unreliable Narration." In J. Pier (ed.). *Recent Trends in Narratological Research*. Tours, 63-84.

— (2003). "Narratology or Narratologies? Taking Stock of Recent Developments, Critique and Modest Proposals for Future Usages of the Term." In T. Kindt, H.-H. Müller (eds.). *What is Narratology. Questions and Answers Regarding the Status of a Theory* (= Narratologia 1). Berlin/New York, 239-75.

— (ed.) (1998a). *"Unreliable Narration": Studien zur Theorie und Praxis unglaubwürdigen Erzählens in der englischsprachigen Erzählliteratur*. Trier.

— (1998b). *Metzler Lexikon Literatur- und Kulturtheorie*. 2nd ed. Stuttgart/Weimar 2001.

Ohmann, Richard (1971). "Speech Acts and the Definition of Literature." *Philosophy and Rhetoric* 4, 1-19.

Okopień-Sławińska, Aleksandra (1971). "Die personalen Relationen in der literarischen Kommunikation [Relacje osobowe w literackiej komunikacji]." In R. Fieguth (ed.). *Literarische Kommunikation*, Kronberg/Ts. 1975, 127-47.

Oulanoff, Hongor (1966). *The Serapion Brothers. Theory and Practice*. 's-Gravenhage.

Paducheva, Elena V. (1996). "Semantika narrativa." In E. V. P. *Semanticheskie issledovaniya*. Moskva, 193-418.

Palmer, Alan (2004). *Fictional Minds*. Univ. of Nebraska Press 2004.

Parsons, Terence (1980). *Nonexisting Objects*. New Haven/London.

Pascal, Roy (1977). *The Dual Voice: Free Indirect Speech and Its Functioning in the Nineteenth-Century European Novel*. Manchester.

Paschen, Hans (1991). *Narrative Technik im Romanwerk von Gustavo Alvarez Gardeazabál*. Frankfurt a. M.

Pavel, Thomas G. (1986). *Fictional Worlds*. Cambridge, MA.

Peirce, Charles Sanders (1931-58). *Collected Papers*. Cambridge.

Penzkofer, Gerhard (1984). *Der Bedeutungsaufbau in den späten Erzählungen Čechovs: "Offenes" und "geschlossenes" Erzählen*. München.

Peshkovsky, Aleksandr M. (1920). *Russkii sintaksis v nauchnom osveshchenii*. Moskva.

Petersen, Jürgen H. (1977). "Kategorien des Erzählens. Zur systematischen Deskription epischer Texte." *Poetica* 9, 167-95.

Petrovsky, Mikhail A. (1925). "Morfologiya pushkinskogo 'Vystrela.'" In V. Ya. Bryusov (ed.). *Problemy poetiki*. Sbornik statey. Moskva/Leningrad, 173-204.

— (1927). "Morphology in the Novella [Morfologiya novelly]." *Essays in Poetics* 12, 1987, 22-50.

Pier, John (2003). "On the Semiotic Parameters of Discourse: A Critique of Story and Discourse." In T. Kindt, H.-H. Müller (eds.). *What is Narratology. Questions and Answers Regarding the Status of a Theory* (= Narratologia 1). Berlin/New York, 73-97.
— (2007). "After this, therefore because of this." In J. Pier, J. Á. García Landa (eds.). *Theorizing Narrativity* (= Narratologia 12). Berlin/New York, 109-40.
Polletta, Gregory T. (1984). "The Author's Place in Contemporary Narratology." In A. Mortimer (ed.). *Contemporary Approaches to Narrative*. Tübingen, 109-23.
Pouillon, Jean (1946). *Temps et roman*. Paris.
Pratt, Mary Louise (1982). "Interpretive Strategies/Strategic Interpretations: On Anglo-American Reader Response Criticism." *Boundary* 2, 201-31.
Prince, Gerald (1971). "Notes toward a Characterization of Fictional Narratees." *Genre* 4, 100-06.
— (1973a). "Introduction à l'étude du narrataire." *Poétique* 14, 178-96.
— (1973b). *A Grammar of Stories. An Introduction*. The Hague.
— (1982). *Narratology. The Form and Functioning of Narrative*. The Hague.
— (1985). "The Narratee Revisited." *Style* 19, 299-303.
— (1987). *A Dictionary of Narratology*. Lincoln/London.
— (2009). "Reader." In P. Hühn, J. Pier, W. Schmid, J. Schönert (eds.). *Handbook of Narratology* (= Narratologia 19). Berlin/New York, 398-410.
Propp, Vladimir (1928). *Morfologiya skazki*. Moskva.
Rasch, Wolfdietrich (1961). "Zur Frage des epischen Präteritums." In *Wirkendes Wort*. Sonderheft 3, 68-81.
Rehbein, Jochen (1980). "Sequentielles Erzählen – Erzählstrukturen von Immigranten bei Sozialberatungen in England." In K. Ehlich (ed.). *Erzählen im Alltag*. Frankfurt a. M., 64-108.
Renner, Karl Nikolaus (1983). *Der Findling. Eine Erzählung von H. v. Kleist und ein Film von G. Moorse. Prinzipien einer adäquaten Wiedergabe narrativer Strukturen*. München.
Ricœur, Paul (1983). *Temps et récit*. Vol. I. Paris.
Riffaterre, Michel (1990). *Fictional Truth*. Baltimore/London.
Rimmon(-Kenan), Shlomith (1976). "A Comprehensive Theory of Narrative: Genette's 'Figures III' and the Structuralist Study of Fiction." *PTL* 1, 33-62.
— (1983). *Narrative Fiction. Contemporary Poetics*. London.
Romberg, Bertil (1962). *Studies in the Narrative Technique of the First-Person Novel*. Stockholm.
Rühling, Lutz (1996). "Fiktionalität und Poetizität." In H. L. Arnold, H. Detering (eds.). *Grundzüge der Literaturwissenschaft*. München, 25-51.
Ryan, Marie-Laure (1981). "Pragmatics of Personal and Impersonal Fiction." *Poetics* 10, 517-39.
Rymar', Nikolay; Skobelev, Vladislav (1994). *Teoriya avtora i problema khudozhestvennoy deyatel'nosti*. Voronezh.
Scheffel, Michael (2009). "Narrative Constitution." In P. Hühn, J. Pier, W. Schmid, J. Schönert (eds.). *Handbook of Narratology* (= Narratologia 19). Berlin/New York, 282-94.

Works cited

Schissel von Fleschenberg, Otmar (1910). *Novellenkomposition in E. T. A. Hoffmanns Elixieren des Teufels. Ein prinzipieller Versuch.* Halle a. d. S.

Schmid, Wolf (1968). "Zur Erzähltechnik und Bewußtseinsdarstellung in Dostoevskijs 'Večnyj muž.'" *Die Welt der Slaven* 13, 294–306.

— (1971). "Review of Uspensky 1970." *Poetica* 4, 124–34.

— (1973). *Der Textaufbau in den Erzählungen Dostoevskijs.* 2nd ed. (with an afterword: "Eine Antwort an die Kritiker"). Amsterdam 1986.

— (1974a). "Review of Janik 1973." *Poetica* 6, 404–15.

— (1974b). "Zur Semantik und Ästhetik des dialogischen Erzählmonologs bei Dostoevskij." *Canadian-American Slavic Studies* 8, 381–97.

— (1977). *Der ästhetische Inhalt: Zur semantischen Funktion poetischer Verfahren.* Lisse.

— (1981). "Rasskazyvanie i rasskazyvaemoe v *Brat'yakh Karamazovykh*." In V. Sh. *Proza kak poeziya. Stat'i o povestvovanii v russkoy literature.* Sankt-Peterburg 1994, 142–50.

— (1982). "Die narrativen Ebenen 'Geschehen,' 'Geschichte,' 'Erzählung' und 'Präsentation der Erzählung.'" *Wiener Slawistischer Almanach* 9, 83–110.

— (1986). "Eine Antwort an die Kritiker." Afterword in *Der Textaufbau in den Erzählungen Dostoevskijs.* 2nd ed. Amsterdam, 299–318.

— (1989b). "Vklad Bakhtina/Voloshinova v teoriyu tekstovoy interferentsii." *Russian Literature* 26, 219–36.

— (1991). *Puškins Prosa in poetischer Lektüre. Die Erzählungen Belkins.* München. Russian transl.: Schmid 1996a.

— (1992a). *Ornamentales Erzählen in der russischen Moderne. Čechov – Babel – Zamjatin* (= Slavische Literaturen 2). Frankfurt a. M.

— (1992b). "Äquivalenzen in erzählender Prosa. Mit Beispiel aus Erzählungen Čechovs." In Schmid 1992a, 29–71.

— (1992c). "Klangwiederholungen in Čechovs Erzählprosa." In Schmid 1992a, 81–103.

— (1994). "Jak si nakouřil pan Vorel pěnovku. Událostnost v Nerudových *Povídkách malostranských*." *Česká literatura* 42, 570–83.

— (1996a). *Proza Pushkina v poeticheskom prochtenii. Povesti Belkina.* Sankt-Peterburg.

— (1996b). "Die *Brüder Karamazov* als religiöser 'nadryv' ihres Autors." In R. Fieguth (ed.). *Orthodoxien und Häresien in den slavischen Literaturen* (= Wiener Slawistischer Almanach. Sonderband 41). Wien, 25–50.

— (1997). "'Pique Dame' als poetologische Novelle." *Die Welt der Slaven* 42, 1–33.

— (1998). *Proza kak poeziya. Pushkin—Dostoevsky—Chekhov—avangard.* S.-Peterburg.

— (2003a). *Narratologiya.* Moskva. 2nd ed. 2008.

— (2003b). "Narrativity and Eventfulness." In T. Kindt, H.-H. Müller (eds.). *What is Narratology. Questions and Answers Regarding the Status of a Theory* (= Narratologia 1). Berlin/New York, 17–33.

— (2005a). *Elemente der Narratologie* (= Narratologia 8). Berlin/New York.

— (2005b). "Ereignishaftigkeit in den *Brüdern Karamasow*." *Dostoevsky Studies. The Journal of the International Dostoevsky Society.* New Series 9, 31–44.

— (2005c). "Defamiliarisation." In D. Herman, M. Jahn, M.-L. Ryan (eds.). *The Routledge Encyclopedia of Narrative Theory.* London, 98.

- (2007a). "Eventfulness as a Narratological Category." *Amsterdam International Electronic Journal for Cultural Narratology* Nº 4. http://cf.hum.uva.nl/narratology/a07_schmid.htm
- (2007b). "Textadressat." In Th. Anz (ed.). *Handbuch Literaturwissenschaft*. Vol. I. Stuttgart/Weimar, 171-81.
- (2007c). "Apogey sobytiinosti v *Brat'yakh Karamazovykh*." In S. K. Frank, S. Schahadat (eds.). *Archiv und Anfang. FS für Igor' Pavlovič Smirnov zum 65. Geburtstag* (= Wiener Slawistischer Almanach 59), 477-86.
- (2008a). "'Wortkunst' und 'Erzählkunst' im Lichte der Narratologie." In R. Grübel, W. Schmid (eds.). *Wortkunst – Erzählkunst – Bildkunst. Festschrift für Aage A. Hansen-Löve*. München, 23-37.
- (2008b). "Zum 'Autor im Text' – eine Replik auf Willem Weststeijn am Beispiel Dostoevskijs." In E. de Haard, W. Honselaar, J. Stelleman (eds.). *Literature and Beyond. Festschrift for Willem G. Weststeijn on the Occasion of his 65th Birthday*. Amsterdam, 701-12.
- (2009a). "Eventfulness and Context." In V. Ambros et al. (eds.). *Structuralism(s) Today. Paris, Prague, Tartu*. New York/Ottawa/Toronto, 101-10.
- (2009b). "Implied author." In P. Hühn, J. Pier, W. Schmid, J. Schönert (eds.). *Handbook of Narratology* (= Narratologia 19). Berlin/New York, 161-73.
- (2009c). "'Fabel' und 'Sujet.'" In W. Schmid (ed.). *Slavische Erzähltheorie. Russische und tschechische Ansätze* (= Narratologia 21). Berlin/New York, 1-45.
- (ed.) (2009a). *Russische Proto-Narratologie. Texte in kommentierten Übersetzungen* (= Narratologia 16). Berlin/New York.
- (ed.) (2009b). *Slavische Erzähltheorie. Russische und tschechische Ansätze* (= Narratologia 21). Berlin/New York.
Searle, John R. (1975). "The Logical Status of Fictional Discourse." *New Literary History* 6, 319-32.
Segal, Dimitry M. (1970). "Novoe issledovanie po strukture khudozhestvennykh form." *Dekorativnoe iskusstvo* 10, 42.
Seidler, Herbert (1952/53). "Zum Stilwert des deutschen Präteritums." *Wirkendes Wort* 3, 271-79.
Shen, Dan (2010). "Unreliability." In P. Hühn, J. C. Meister, J. Pier, W. Schmid, J. Schönert (eds.). *Living Handbook of Narratology* (in preparation).
Shipley, Joseph T. (ed.) (1943). *Dictionary of World Literature*. New York 1964.
Shklovsky, Viktor (1917). "Art as Technique [Iskusstvo kak priem]." In *Russian Formalist Criticism. Four Essays*. Tr. by L. T. Lemon, M. J. Reis. Lincoln, Univ. of Nebraska Press 1965, 5-24.
- (1919). "The Relationship between Devices of Plot Construction and General Devices of Style [Svyaz' priemov syuzhetoslozheniya s obshchimi priemami stilya]." In Shklovsky 1990, 15-51.
- (1921). "The Novel as Parody: Sterne's *Tristram Shandy* [Parodiinyi roman. *Tristram Shendi* Sterna]." In Shklovsky 1990, 147-70.
- (1924). "'Ornamental'naya proza.' Andrey Bely." In V. B. Sh. *O teorii prozy*. 2nd ed. Moskva 1929, 205-25.

— (1925). *O teorii prozy*. Moskva.
— (1928). *Material i stil' v romane L'va Tolstogo* Voyna i mir. Moskva (Reprint: The Hague 1970).
— (1929). *O teorii prozy*. 2nd ed. Moskva. Engl.: Shklovsky 1990.
— (1990). *Theory of Prose* [O teorii prozy. Transl. of the 2 nd ed. 1929]. Tr. by B. Sher. Normal, IL.
Shlykova, M. A. (1962). "Ob odnom stilisticheskom prieme." *Nauchnye doklady vysshej shkoly. Filologicheskie nauki* 4, 158–63.
Shor, Rozaliya (1927). "Formal'nyi metod na zapade. Shkola Zeyferta i 'retoricheskoe' napravlenie." *Ars Poetica* 1, 127–43.
Shukman, Ann (1972). "Review of Uspensky 1970." *The Modern Language Review* 22.6.1972, 713–16.
Simmel, Georg (1916). "The Problem of the Historical Time [Das Problem der historischen Zeit]." In G. S. *Essays on Interpretation in Social Science*. Tr. and ed. by G. Oakes. Manchester UP 1980, 127–44.
Sławiński, Janusz (1966). "O kategorii podmiotu lirycznego. Tezy referatu." In J. Trzynadlowski (ed.). *Wiersz i poezja*. Wrocław, 55–62.
— (1967). "Semantyka wypowiedzi narracyjnej." In J. S. (ed.). *W kręgu zagadnień teorii powieści*. Wrocław, 7–30.
Smith, Barbara Herrnstein (1978). *On the Margins of Discourse. The Relation of Literature to Language*. Chicago.
Sokolova, Lyudmila A. (1968). *Nesobstvenno-avtorskaya (nesobstvenno-pryamaya) rech' kak stilisticheskaya kategoriya*. Tomsk.
Sörbom, Göran (1966). *Mimesis and Art. Studies in the Origin and Early Development of an Aesthetic Vocabulary*. Uppsala.
Souriau, Etienne (1951). "La structure de l'univers filmique et le vocabulaire de la filmologie." *Revue internationale de filmologie* 2, 231–40.
Spielhagen, Friedrich (1883). *Beiträge zur Theorie und Technik des Romans*. Leipzig (Reprint: Göttingen 1967).
— (1898). *Epik und Dramatik*. Leipzig.
Spitzer, Leo (1922a). "Pseudoobjektive Motivierung bei Charles Louis Philippe." In L. S. *Stilstudien II*. München 1928, 166–207.
— (1922b). "Sprachmengung als Stilmittel und als Ausdruck der Klangphantasie." In L. S. *Stilstudien II*. 2nd ed. München 1961, 84–124.
— (1922c). *Italienische Umgangssprache*. Leipzig.
— (1928a). "Zum Stil Marcel Prousts." In L. S. *Stilstudien II*. 2nd ed. München 1961, 365–497.
— (1928b). "Zur Entstehung der sogenannten 'erlebten Rede.'" *Germanisch-romanische Monatsschrift* 16, 327–32.
Stanzel, Franz K. (1955). *Die typischen Erzählsituationen im Roman. Dargestellt an Tom Jones, Moby Dick, The Ambassadors, Ulysses u.a.* Wien. Engl.: Stanzel 1971.
— (1959). "Episches Präteritum, erlebte Rede, historisches Präsens." *Deutsche Vierteljahrsschrift für Literaturwissenschaft und Geistesgeschichte* 33, 1–12.
— (1964). *Typische Formen des Romans*. Göttingen.
— (1971). *Narrative Situations in the Novel: Tom Jones, Moby Dick, The Ambassadors, Ulysses*. Bloomington.

— (1979). *Theorie des Erzählens.* Göttingen. Engl.: Stanzel 1984.
— (1984). *Theory of Narrative.* Tr. by Ch. Goedsche. Cambridge.
Steinberg, Günter (1971). *Erlebte Rede. Ihre Eigenart und ihre Formen in neuerer deutscher, französischer und englischer Erzählliteratur.* 2 Vols. Göppingen.
Steiner, Wendy (1976). "Point of View from the Russian Point of View [= Review of Uspensky 1970]." *Dispositio. Revista Hispánica de Semiótica Literaria* 3, 315-27.
Stempel, Wolf-Dieter (1973). "Erzählung, Beschreibung und der historische Diskurs." In R. Koselleck, W.-D. Stempel (eds.). *Geschichte - Ereignis und Erzählung.* München, 325-46.
— (1978). "Zur literarischen Semiotik Miroslav Červenkas." In M. Červenka. *Der Bedeutungsaufbau des literarischen Werks.* München, VII-LIII.
— (ed.) (1972). *Texte der russischen Formalisten.* Vol. 2: *Texte zur Theorie des Verses und der poetischen Sprache.* München.
Sternberg, Meir (1974). "What is Exposition? An Essay in Temporal Delimitation." In M. S. *Expositional Modes and Temporal Ordering in Fiction.* Baltimore/London 1978, 1-34.
— (1976). "Temporal Ordering, Modes of Expositional Distribution, and Three Models of Rhetorical Control in the Narrative Text. Faulkner, Balzac and Austen." *PTL* 1, 295-316.
Stierle, Karlheinz (1971). "Geschehen, Geschichte, Text der Geschichte." In R. Koselleck, W.-D. Stempel (eds.). *Geschichte - Ereignis und Erzählung.* München 1973, 530-34.
— (1977). "Die Struktur narrativer Texte: Am Beispiel von J. P. Hebels Kalendergeschichte 'Unverhofftes Wiedersehen.'" In H. Brackert, E. Lämmert (eds.). *Funk-Kolleg Literatur 1.* Frankfurt a. M., 210-33.
Striedter, Jurij (ed.) (1969). *Texte der russischen Formalisten.* Vol. 1: *Texte zur allgemeinen Literaturtheorie und zur Theorie der Prosa.* München.
Struve, Gleb (1951). *Soviet Russian Literature 1917-1950.* Norman, OK.
— (1954). "Monologue intérieur: The Origins of the Formula and the First Statement of Its Possibilities." *Publications of the Modern Language Association of America* 69, 1101-11.
Szilárd, Léna (1986). "Ornamental'nost'/ornamentalizm." *Russian Literature* 19, 65-78.
Tamarchenko, Natan D. (1999). "Tochka zreniya." In L. V. Chernets et al. *Vvedenie v literaturovedenie. Osnovnye ponyatiya i terminy.* Moskva, 425-32.
Thürnau, Donatus (1994). *Gedichtete Versionen der Welt. Nelson Goodmans Semantik fiktionaler Literatur.* Paderborn.
Titunik, Irwin R. (1963). *The Problem of Skaz in Russian Literature.* Ph. D. Dissertation. Univ. of California.
— (1977). "The Problem of Skaz: Critique and Theory." In B. A. Stolz (ed.). *Papers in Slavic Philology.* Vol. 1. Ann Arbor, 276-301.
Titzmann, Michael (1992). "'Zeit' als strukturierende und strukturierte Kategorie in sprachlichen Texten." In W. Hömberg, M. Schmolke (eds.). *Zeit - Raum - Kommunikation.* München, 234-54.
— (2003). "Semiotische Aspekte der Literaturwissenschaft: Literatursemiotik." In R. Posner, K. Robering, Th. A. Sebeok (eds.). *Semiotik/Semiotics. Ein Handbuch zu den*

zeichentheoretischen Grundlagen von Natur und Kultur/A Handbook on the Sign-Theoretic Foundations of Nature and Culture. Vol. 3. Berlin, 3028-103.
Tobler, Adolf (1887). "Vermischte Beiträge zur französischen Grammatik." Zeitschrift für romanische Philologie 11, 433-61.
Todemann, Fritz (1930). "Die erlebte Rede im Spanischen." Romanische Forschungen 44, 103-84.
Todorov, Tzvetan (1966). "Categories of the Literary Narrative [Les catégories du récit littéraire]." Film Reader 2, 1977, 19-37.
— (1969). Grammaire du Décaméron. La Haye 1978.
— (1971a). "Some Approaches to Russian Formalism [Quelques concepts du formalisme russe]." In St. Bann, J. E. Bowlt (eds.). Russian Formalism. Edinburgh 1973, 6-19.
— (1971b). Poétique de la prose. Paris.
— (1972). "La poétique en U.R.S.S." Poétique 3, 102-15.
— (1997). "Pourquoi Jakobson et Bakhtine ne se sont jamais rencontrés." Esprit 2, 5-30.
Tolmachev, V. M. (1996). "Tochka zreniya." In I. P. Ilyin, E. A. Tsurganova (eds.) 1996. 154-57.
Tomashevsky, Boris V. (1925). Teoriya literatury. Poetika. Moskva/Leningrad (Reprint: Letchworth 1971).
— (1928a). Teoriya literatury. Poetika. 4th revised ed. Moskva/Leningrad (Reprint: New York/London 1967).
— (1928b). Kratkii kurs poetiki. Moskva/Leningrad (Reprint: Chicago 1969).
— (1965). "Thematics [Tematika]." In Russian Formalist Criticism. Four Essays. Tr. by L. T. Lemon, M. J. Reis. Lincoln, Univ. of Nebraska Press, 61-95.
Toolan, Michael J. (1988). Narrative. A Critical Linguistic Introduction. London/New York.
Tsilevich, Leonid M. (1972). "Dialektika syuzheta i fabuly." In Voprosy syuzhetoslozheniya. Sbornik statey. Vol. 2. Riga, 5-17.
Tynyanov, Yury N. (1922). "'Serapionovy brat'ya.' Al'manakh I." In Yu. N. T. Poetika. Istoriya literatury. Kino. Moskva 1977, 132-36.
— (1924a). Problema stikhotvornogo yazyka. Leningrad.
— (1924b). "Literaturnoe segodnya." In Yu. N. T. Poetika. Istoriya literatury. Kino. Moskva 1977, 150-66.
— (1927a). "On the Foundations of Cinema [Ob osnovakh kino]." In H. Eagle (ed.). Russian Formalist Film Theory. University of Michigan 1981, 81-100.
— (1927b). "On Literary Evolution [O literaturnoy evolyutsii]." In L. Matejka and K. Pomorska (eds.). Readings in Russian Poetics: Formalist and Structuralist Views. Cambridge, MA, 1971, 66-78.
Unbegaun, Boris (1947). "Introduction." In A. S. Pushkin. Tales of the Late Ivan Petrovich Belkin. Oxford, XI-XXX.
Uspensky, Boris A. (1970). Poetika kompozitsii. Struktura khudozhestvennogo teksta i tipologiya kompozitsionnoy formy. Moskva. Engl.: Uspensky 1973.
— (1973). A Poetics of Composition. The Structure of the Artistic Text and Typology of a Compositional Form [Poetika kompozitsii. Struktura khudozhestvennogo teksta i tipologiya kompozitsionnoy formy]. Tr. by V. Zavarin and S. Wittig. Berkeley.

Vaihinger, Hans (1911). *Die Philosophie des Als Ob. System der theoretischen, praktischen und religiösen Fiktionen der Menschheit auf Grund eines idealistischen Positivismus. Mit einem Anhang über Kant und Nietzsche*. Berlin.
Valk, Frans de (1972). "Review of Uspensky 1970". *Russian Literature* 2, 165-75.
Verschoor, Jan Adriaan (1959). *Etude de grammaire historique et de style sur le style direct et les styles indirects en français*. Groningue.
Vinogradov, Viktor V. (1925). "The Problem of *Skaz* in Stylistics [Problema skaza v stilistike]." Tr. by M. B. Rice. *Russian Literature Triquartely* 12, Spring 1978, 237-50.
— (1930). "O khudozhestvennoy proze." In V. V. V. *O yazyke khudozhestvennoy prozy*. Moskva 1980, 56-175.
— (1971). "Problema obraza avtora v khudozhestvennoy literature." In V. V. V. *O teorii khudozhestvennoy rechi*. Moskva, 105-211.
Vitoux, Pierre (1982). "Le jeu de la focalisation." *Poétique* 51, 354-68.
Volek, Emil (1977). "Die Begriffe 'Fabel' und 'Sujet' in der modernen Literaturwissenschaft." *Poetica* 9, 141-66.
— (1985). *Metaestructuralismo: Poética moderna, semiótica narrativa y filosofía de las ciencias sociales*. Madrid.
Voloshinov, Valentin (1929). *Marksizm i filosofiya yazyka: Osnovnye problemy sotsiologicheskogo metoda v nauke o yazyke*. Moskva 1993. Engl.: Voloshinov 1973.
— (1973). *Marxism and the Philosophy of Language* [Marksizm i filosofiya yazyka]. Tr. by L. Matejka and I. R. Titunik. New York.
Vygotsky, Lev S. (1925). *Psikhologiya iskusstva*. Moskva. Engl.: Vygotsky 1971.
— (1971). *The Psychology of Art* [Psikhologiya iskusstva]. Cambridge, MA.
Walzel, Oskar (1924). "Von 'erlebter' Rede." In O. W. *Das Wortkunstwerk. Mittel seiner Erforschung*. Leipzig 1926, 207-30.
Weidlé, Wladimir (1963). "Vom Sinn der Mimesis." *Eranos-Jahrbuch 1962* 31, 249-73.
Weimar, Klaus (1974). "Kritische Bemerkungen zur *Logik der Dichtung*." *Deutsche Vierteljahrsschrift für Literaturwissenschaft und Geistesgeschichte* 48, 10-24.
— (1997). "Diegesis." *Reallexikon der deutschen Literaturwissenschaft*. Vol. 1. Berlin, 360-63.
Weinrich, Harald (1975). "Fiktionssignale." In H. W. *Positionen der Negativität*. München, 525-26.
Wellek, René; Warren, Austin (1949). *Theory of Literature*. Harmonsworth.
Weststeijn, Willem G. (1984). "Author and Implied Author. Some Notes on the Author in the Text." In J. J. van Baak (ed.). *Signs of Friendship. To Honour A. G. F. van Holk, Slavist, Linguist, Semiotician*. Amsterdam, 553-68.
— (1991). "The Structure of Lyric Communication." *Essays in Poetics* 16, 49-69.
White, Hayden (1973). *Metahistory: The Historical Imagination in Nineteenth-Century Europe*. Baltimore.
— (1978). "The Historical Text as Literary Artifact." In H. W. *Tropics of Discourse. Essays in Cultural Criticism*. Baltimore, 81-100.
Wimsatt, William K.; Beardsley, Monroe C. (1946). "The Intentional Fallacy." In D. Newton-de Molina (ed.). *On Literary Intention*. Edinburgh 1976, 1-13.
Wolff, Erwin (1971). "Der intendierte Leser. Überlegungen und Beispiele zur Einführung eines literaturwissenschaftlichen Begriffs." *Poetica* 4, 141-66.

Zelinsky, V. (ed.) (1888). *Russkaya kriticheskaya literatura o proizvedeniyakh A. S. Pushkina: Khronologicheskii sbornik kritiko-bibliograficheskikh statey*. Moskva.

Zhirmunsky, Viktor (1921). "Die Aufgaben der Poetik [Zadachi poetiki]." Russ.-German in W.-D. Stempel (ed.). *Texte der russischen Formalisten*. Vol. 2: *Texte zur Theorie des Verses und der poetischen Sprache*. München 1972, 136–61.

— (1927). "Noveyshie techeniya istoriko-literaturnoy mysli v Germanii." In *Poetika*. Vol. 2. Leningrad 1927, 5–28.

Zholkovsky, Alexander (1992). "'Legkoe dykhanie' i 'Stantsionnyi smotritel'." Problemy kompozitsii." In B. Gasparov, R. P. Hughes, I. Paperno (eds.). *Cultural Mythologies of Russian Modernism. From the Golden Age to the Silver Age*. Berkeley, 293–314.

— (1994). "A Study in Framing: Pushkin, Bunin, Nabokov, and Theories of Stories and Discourse." In A. Z. *Text Counter Text. Rereadings in Russian Literary History*. Stanford, 88–113.

Zimmermann, Friedrich Wilhelm (1971). "Episches Präteritum, episches Ich und epische Normalform." *Poetica* 4, 306–24.

Zipfel, Frank (2001). *Fiktion, Fiktivität, Fiktionalität: Analysen zur Fiktion in der Literatur und zum Fiktionsbegriff in der Literaturwissenschaft*. Berlin.

Żółkiewski, Stefan (1971). "Review of Uspensky 1970." *Pamiętnik literacki* 62, 354–63.

— (1972). "Poétique de la composition [= Review of Uspensky 1970]." *Semiotica* 5, 206–24.

Zuckerkandl, Viktor (1958). "Mimesis." *Merkur* 12, 224–40.

Glossary and index of narratological terms

This glossary lists narratological terms which are used in a specific sense in this book. The numbers refer to the pages on which the terms are introduced or defined. Italicized numbers refer to footnotes.

Addressee = the receiver presumed or intended by the transmitter, the one to whom the transmitter sends his message, whom s/he had in mind as the presumed or desired receiver, 34, 36
  - fictive ~ = addressee of the fictive narrator, 78
  - presumed ~ = one of the two hypostases of the abstract reader, 55

Ambiguity (as a feature of text interference), 170-71

Anthropomorphism of the narrator, 60-61

Appeal = the demand, usually expressed implicitly, made on the addressee to form a particular opinion of the narrator, his or her narrative, the narrated world, or some of its characters, 83

Art
  - narrative ~ (*Erzählkunst*), 123
  - verbal ~ (*Wortkunst*), 123

Author
  - abstract ~ =
    1. the signified of all indexical signs pointing to the creator of the work, 48
    2. an anthropomorphic hypostasis of all creative acts, the personified intention of the work, 48
    3. a (re)construct(ion) of the reader's, on the basis of his or her reading of the work, 49
  - concrete ~ = the real creator of the work, 36

Authorial = pertaining to the author, 51

Bi-textuality (as a feature of text interference), 172

Change of state, 3

Characters' discourse, 118, 120

Characters' text = pure, unmixed text of the characters, 120

Colloquialism (of *skaz*), 134

Communication
  - author ~, 32-34
  - character ~, 34
  - narrative ~, 32-34

Composition of the narrative text
   1. as an indexical sign of the narrator, 58
   2. as an operation in the narrative constitution, 191

Comprehension of happenings, 99–100

Compression = a selection of a relatively small number of elements and properties for a given episode of the story, 200

Concretizing of selected elements (as indexical sign of the narrator), 58

Constitution
   – narrative ~, 175

Contagion or infection (of the narrator's discourse by the characters' text, one manifestation of figurally colored narration), 167

Context (as the basis for an assessment of the relevance and unpredictability of changes of state), 15–16

Contrast. *See* Equivalence

Co-occurrence (between the orders of discourse and story), 125

Description = representation of states, 5–6

Designation
   – quoted figural ~, 152

Dialogicity (of *skaz*), 134

Diegesis = narrated world or storyworld, 6

Diegesis (διήγησις sensu Platonis) = 'pure narration' in contrast with 'representation' (mimesis) of the hero's speech, 6, 8, *118*

Diegetic = belonging to the narrated world, 6

Discourse
   – characters' ~, 118, 120
   – direct ~, 147–49
      – de-individualized ~~, 149
   – free indirect ~ (FID), 147–48, 157
   – indirect ~ (= indirect representation of speech, thought and perception), 147–48, 153–55
      – autonomous ~~, 155–56
      – figural ~~, 155
      – narratorial ~~, 154–55
   – narrator's ~, 118, 120

Discourse happenings (*Erzählgeschehen*), 211

Discourse story (*Erzählgeschichte*), 6, 211

Disposition (*dispositio*, τάξις), 191

Distribution (of features of the narrative text to the narrator's and/or the characters' text), 137

Double-voicedness
   – of skaz, 134

Glossary and index of narratological terms

– of text interference, 173

Doxa = what is generally expected in a storyworld, 10

Elements (of a story selected from the happenings), 58

Elocutio (λέξις), 192

Equivalence (similarity and contrast) = identity of elements in reference to a particular feature and non-identity in reference to other features, 18–19
  – formal ~ = bracketing of two segments based on a common formal feature, 20
  – thematic ~ = bracketing of two segments based on a common thematic feature, 20

Evaluation of selected elements (as an indexical sign of the narrator), 58

Event = a special type of change of state that presupposes facticity and resultativity and displays five further features (relevance, unpredictability, persistence, irreversibility, non-iterativity), 8–12

Eventfulness = a scalable property of events, 9

Exegesis (ἐξήγησις) = level of narration and of the narrator's comments, explanations, reflections and meta-narrative remarks, 6, *8*

Expansion = a selection of a relatively large number of elements and properties for a given episode of the story, 200

Expression (*Ausdruck* sensu Karl Bühler), 36

Factual (as opposed to *fictional*), 22

FCN. *See* Figurally colored narration

Features for the differentiation of narrator's text and characters' text
  – ~ of language function, 142
  – grammatical ~, 141
    – ~~ of person, 141
    – ~~ of tense, 141
    – ~~ of the orientation system, 141–42
  – ideological ~, 141
  – stylistic ~ of the lexis, 142
  – stylistic ~ of the syntax, 142
  – thematic ~, 141

Fiction =
  1. the representation of a distinct, autonomous, inner-literary reality, 22
  2. (sensu Aristotelis) the artistic construction of a possible reality, 23

Fictional = a property of representations of fictive worlds, 21

Fictionality, 21

Fictive = a property of elements (time, space, situations, characters, actions) contained in the represented world of fictional works, 21, 29–32

FID. *See* Free indirect discourse

Figuralization = orientation of the narration on the point of view of the figure, 120

Happenings = the amorphous entirety of situations, characters and actions explicitly or implicitly represented, or logically implied, in the narrative work, 190

Impression = a special type of appeal: the attempt to elicit a reaction that can take on either a positive form, as admiration, or a negative one, as contempt, 83
Inclusion (of the characters' discourse in the narrative text), 118
Index (*Anzeichen, indicium*), 36–37
Individuality of the narrator, 60–61
Interference of narrator's text and characters' text, 137
Invention (*inventio* or εὕρεσις), 191
Irreversibility of a change of state (as condition of high eventfulness), 11
Isotopism (between the orders of discourse and story), 125

Knowledge (as a factor of the ideological point of view), 101

Linearization (of things occurring simultaneously in the story, forming a sequence of presentation), 191, 206
Linking
 – non-temporal ~, 18–19
 – temporal ~, 18–19

Markedness (of the narrator), 62–63
Mimesis (sensu Aristotelis) = the representation of something that is not already existent, 22–23
Mimesis (sensu Platonis) =
 1. imitation, 22
 2. representation of the hero's speech (as opposed to 'the poet's pure narration') 6, 8, 118
Mode
 – descriptive ~, 5
 – narrative ~, 5
Monologue
 – dialogic ~, 79, 102
  – ~ narrative ~, 87–88
 – free indirect ~, 163–64
  – ~~ interior ~, 149, 163–64
 – interior ~
  – direct ~, 149
   – de-individualized ~~~, 149–50
  – free indirect ~~, 149, 163–64
Narration (as opposed to *description*), 56

Glossary and index of narratological terms 247

Narration
- figurally colored ~ (FCN), 166

Narrative
1. (in the narrower sense) = denoting a change of state and representing a mediating authority (narrator) behind it, 7
2. (in the broader sense) = representing a change of state, 2, 7–8
3. as one of the four tiers of narrative constitution, the result of composition, 191

Narrativity, 1–4
- classical concept of ~, 2
- structuralist concept of ~, 2

Narratology, 1–2

Narrator
- diegetic ~ = a narrator belonging to the diegesis or narrated world (so-called "first-person narrator"), 68
- veiled ~~, 71
- fictive ~, 35, 57
- non-diegetic ~ = a narrator belonging only to the exegesis and thus not narrating about him or herself as a character in the diegesis (so-called "third-person narrator"), 68
- primary, secondary, and tertiary narrator = narrator of a frame story, an inner story, or an inner story of second degree, 67

Narrator's discourse, 118, 120

Narrator's text = pure, unmixed text of the narrator, 120

Narratoriality (of *skaz*), 133

Neutralization (of oppositions between narrator's text and characters' text), 143

Non-iterativity of a change of state (as condition of high eventfulness), 12

Non-selection (of elements and properties for the story), 204

Orality (of *skaz*), 134

Orientation = the alignment of the narrator with the addressee, 83

Ornamentalism = predominance of non-temporal linkings, 20

Parameters of point of view, 100

Perception
- free indirect ~, 162

Persistence of a change of state (as condition of high eventfulness), 11

Perspective. *See* Point of view

Poeticity (of prose), 125, 136

Point of view (perspective) = the complex (constructed of internal and external factors) of conditions for the comprehension and representation of happenings, 99
- compact ~, 116

- diffuse ~, 116
- figural ~, 105
- ideological ~, 101–02, 111–12
- linguistic ~, 103–04, 114–15
- narratorial ~, 105
- perceptual ~, 104–05, 109–11
- spatial ~, 100–01, 112
- temporal ~, 102–03, 112–14

Position
- evaluative ~, 101

Presentation of the narrative (as one of the four tiers of narrative constitution, the rendering of the narrative in a medium), 192

Profession (*Kundgabe* sensu Karl Bühler), 36

Prose
- ornamental ~, 20, 122

Reader
- abstract ~ = the image of the reader contained in the text, 52, 54, 80
- concrete ~, 36
- fictive ~ (narratee) = the addressee of the fictive narrator, 78, 80

Reality of a change of state (as requirement of an event), 9

Recipient = the factual receiver (as opposed to the addressee), 34
- fictive ~ = a character of a primary narrative (frame story) who functions as a reader or listener of a secondary narrative, 79
- ideal ~ = the projection of a reader who understands the work in a way that optimally matches its structure, and adopts the interpretive position and esthetic standpoint put forward by the work, 55

Relevance of a change of state (as condition of high eventfulness), 9–10

Reorganization (of the segments of a story), 191

Representation
- explicit and implicit ~ of the narrator, 58
- explicit and implicit ~ of the fictive reader, 81–84
- ~ of happenings, 99–100
- indirect ~ of speech, thought and perception. *See* Indirect discourse

Reproduction (of the character's text in the narrative text, one manifestation of figurally colored narration), 167

Resultativity of a change of state (as a requirement of an event), 9

Script = what the reader expects in the action on the basis of certain patterns in literature or the real world, 10

Second-person-narrative, 71

Glossary and index of narratological terms

Selection of elements
- as indexical sign of the narrator, 58
- as an operation creating a story, 191

Selection of properties (as an operation creating a story), 191

Selectivity (of the story with regard to the happenings), 200

Self
- narrated ~, 69, 76–78
- narrating ~, 69, 76–78

Sign
- indexical. *See* Index

Similarity. *See* Equivalence Situation. *See* State

Skaz, 122, 129
- characterizing ~, 133
- ornamental ~, 133

Speech interference (sensu Voloshinov), 138–39

Spontaneity (of *skaz*), 134

State = a set of properties pertaining to an agent or an external situation at a particular point in time, 2
- external ~, 2
- internal ~, 2

Story =
  1. the content of a narrative (as opposed to *discourse*), 5
     - frame ~, 67
     - inner ~, 67
  2. the result of the selection of certain elements (situations, characters and actions) and their properties from the happenings, 191

Stream of consciousness = a technique in which the diegesis is presented as a sequence of fleeting impressions, free association, momentary recollection and fragmentary reflections by the character, 152

Symptom. *See* Index

Tellability = property that makes a story worth telling, 13

Text
- characters' ~ = pure, unmixed text of the characters, 120
- descriptive ~ = text representing states, 5
- narrative ~ (as a unification of narrator's discourse and characters' discourse), 118
- narrative ~, (as opposed to descriptive text) = text representing a story, 5–6
  - mimetic ~~ = text representing a story told by a narrator, 7
- narrator's ~ = pure, unmixed text of the narrator, 120

Text interference. *See* Interference of narrator's text and characters' text

Thread (drawn through the happenings for the creation of a story), 195

Transformations
 - narrative ~, 175

Unpredictability of a change of state (as condition of high eventfulness), 10

Verbalizing (as the rendering of the narrative in a medium), 192

World
 - fictive ~, 29
 - narrated ~ = the world created by the fictive narrator, 35
 - quoted ~ = the world created by the character as a secondary narrator, 35, 68
 - represented ~ = the world created by the real author, 35

Index of authors and narratives

Italicized numbers refer to footnotes.

Abbott, Edwin A.
 Flatland. A Romance of Many Dimensions, 61
Anderegg, Johannes, *26*, 221
Andrievskaya, A. A., *163*, 221
Angelet, Christian, *94*, 221
Aristotle, *4*, *10*, 22–23, *24*, 29, *118*, 217
Augustine, St.
 Confessions (Confessiones), VI, 76
Aumüller, Matthias, *176*, 221
Austen, Jane
 Emma, 145
Austin, John Langshaw *24*, 221

Babel, Isaak E.
 "Crossing the Zbruch" (Perekhod cherez Zbruch), *127*
Bakhtin, Mikhail M., V, 38, 41–42, *48*, 56–57, 83–85, 95, 107, 132, 138–39, 146, 152, *161*, *171*, *172*, 173–74, 219, 221
Bal, Mieke, 44–45, *67*, 80, *91*, 93–95, *173*, 188–90, 194, 220–21
Balcerzan, Edward, 39, 221
Bally, Charles, 146, 168, 221–22
Banfield, Ann, 62, 146, *157*, 172, *174*, 222
Baroni, Raphaël, 13, 222
Barthes, Roland, 41, 59, *78*, 186, 222
Bartoszyński, Kazimierz, 34, 222
Beardsley, Monroe C., 41, 240
Bely, Andrey
 Petersburg (Peterburg), 126
 Symphonies, The (Simfonii), 126
Benveniste, Emile, 40, *186*, 222

Berend, Alice
 Bräutigame der Babette Bomberling, Die, 113, 158
Berendsen, Marjet, *93*, 222
Bonheim, Helmut, *89*, 222
Booth, Wayne C., 40–41, 43–44, 46, 52, *60*, 73, 222
Borges, Jorge Luis
 Shape of the Sword, The (La forma de la espada), 71
Boyd, John D., 23, 222
Bremond, Claude, *187*, 222
Breuer, Horst, 73, 222
Brinton, Laurel, 162, 222
Broich, Ulrich, 105, *106*, 222
Bronzwaer, W. J. M., 26, *43*, 44, 50, 94, *173*, 222–23
Brooks, Cleanth, 92, 223
Browning, Gary L., *122*, 223
Brugmann, Karl, *26*, 223
Bühler, Karl, *26*, 36–37, 58, *122*, 139, 140, 223
Bühler, Willi, *145*, 162, 165, 223
Bunin, Ivan A.
 "Well of Days, The" (U istoka dney), 70
 "Gentle Breath" (Legkoe dykhanie), 181–84
Busch, Ulrich, *26*, 223

Caesar Gaius Iulius
 Commentarii de Bello Gallico, 70, 145
Camus, Albert
 Fall, The (La Chute), 87
Čapek, Karel
 "Poet, The" (Básník), 101

Stories from a Pocket (Povídky z jedné kapsy), 101
Carden, Patricia, *122*, 223
Cassirer, Ernst, 125, 223
Cervantes Saavedra, Miguel de
  Dialogue of the Dogs, The (Coloquio de los perros), 60
  Exemplary Novels (Novelas ejemplares), 60
Červenka, Miroslav, 39, 53, 223
Chatman, Seymour, 7, 40, 42–43, *44*, 46, 50, 62–63, 186, *187*, 218, 223
Chekhov, Anton P., VI, 9, 56, 173
  "Betrothed, The" (Nevesta), 10, 12, 21
  "Darling" (Dushechka), 12, 21, 203–04
  "Event, An" (Sobytie), 10, 14
  "Grasshopper, The" (Poprygun'ya), 21
  "Ionych", 21
  "Lady with the Dog, The" (Dama s sobachkoy), 14, 21, 167
  "Rothschild's Fiddle" (Skripka Rotshil'da), 127–28, *167*, 207–08, 197–99
  "Student, The" (Student), 111–12, 116, 166–67
  "Teacher of Literature, The" (Uchitel' slovesnosti), 10–11
  Three Sisters, The (Tri sestry), 18
Chernyshevsky, Nikolay G.
  What Is to Be Done? (Chto delat'?), 151
Chronicle, Primary (Povest' vremennykh let), 145
Chudakov, Aleksandr P., 37, 129, 167, 173, 223
Chudakova, Marietta O., 129, 223
Coetzee, J. M.
  Master of Petersburg, The, VI, 160–61
Cohn, Dorrit, 24, *27*, 28, 73, 91, *105*, 164–65, 196, 223–24
Conan-Doyle, Arthur, 74
Crittenden, Charles, *24*, 224
Culler, Jonathan, 194, 224

Defoe, Daniel
  Moll Flanders, 77
Dehne, Marianne, 17, 224
Díaz Arenas, Angel, *34*, 224
Dibelius, Wilhelm, *176*, 224
Diengott, Nilli, 43, 224
Diomedes, 6
Doležel, Lubomír, 8, *23*, *30*, *32*, 69–70, *120*, *121*, 139–40, 142, *143*, 146, *149*, *168*, *176*, 219, 224
Dostoevsky, Fyodor M., 9, 55, 119, 138
  Brothers Karamazov, The (Brat'ya Karamazovy), 12, 17, 31, 46, *48*, 50, 59–60, 74–75, 97–98, 104, 129, 152
  Crime and Punishment (Prestuplenie i nakazanie), 17
  Double, The (Dvoynik), VI, 109–10, 115, 146, 151–52, 155–56, 161–64,
  Eternal Husband, The (Vechnyi muzh), VI, 63–64, 107, 152
  "Gentle Spirit, A" (Krotkaya), VI, 83, 87–88, 107, 113–14
  Mr Prokharchin (Gospodin Prokharchin), VI, 156
  "Nasty Story, A" (Skvernyi anekdot), 138, 167, 172
  Notes from the Underground (Zapiski iz podpol'ya), 47, 77, 83, 87–88, 130, 132
  Possessed, The (Besy), 75, 98, 104
  Raw Youth, A (Podrostok), VII, 68, 74–76, 84–86, 107, 113, 115, 120, 145, 152–53, 165–66
Drozda, Miroslav, *95*, 224
Dujardin, Edouard, 224
  Bays are Sere, The (Les Lauriers sont coupés), 150–51
Dupont-Roc, Roselyne *22*, 224

Easthope, Anthony, 40, *48*, 224
Eco, Umberto, 40, 224
Egorov, B. F., 176, 224
Eikhenbaum, Boris M., 130–32, 136–37, 179, 225
Else, Gerald F., 23, 225

Index of authors and narratives

Emerson, Caryl, *84*, 225
Eng, Jan van der, 56, 225
Evdokimova, Svetlana, *41*, 225

Fehr, Bernhard, 162, 225
Feuchtwanger, Lion
   Josephus. A Historical Romance (Der jüdische Krieg), VII, 112, 160
Fieguth, Rolf, *34*, 39, 225
Flaubert, Gustave, 40
   Madame Bovary, VII, 15, 146, 159-60
Fludernik, Monika, *71*, *142*, *159*, *172*, *174*, *189*, 225
Forster, Edward M., 2, *3*, 28, 217, 225
Foster, Ludmila A., *95*, 225
Foucault, Michel, 42, 225
Frank, Bruno
   The Days of the King (Tage des Königs), 158
Frank, Joseph, 20, 225
Freise, Matthias, *41*, *42*, 225
Friedemann, Käte, 1, 59, 225
Friedman, Norman, 62, 66, 226
Frisch, Max
   I'm not Stiller (Stiller), 27
Frol Skobeev, The Tale of (Povest' o Frole Skobeeve), 17
Füger, Wilhelm, 66, 71, 226

Gabriel, Gottfried, *21*, 226
García Landa, José Ángel, *3*, 22, *176*, *188*, 189-90, 220, 226
Garnett, Constance, 113, *115*, *161*, *164*
Gebauer, Gunter, *22*, 226
Genette, Gérard, 2, *3*, *6*, 22, 25, *26*, 27, *28*, 30, 89, 91-94, 98-100, 105, 114, 173, 188, *189*, 190, 200-01, 218, 220, 226
George, Stefan, 124
Gersbach-Bäschlin, Annette, *165*, 226
Glauser, Lisa, *145*, 226
Głowiński, Michał, 52, 53, 80, 87, 226
Gogol', Nikolay V., 130, 136, 146
   Village Evenings near Dikanka (Vechera na khutore bliz Dikan'ki), VII, 81, 137
   "The Overcoat" (Shinel'), VII, 137, 164
Gogotishvili, Lyudmila A., *48*, 57, 226
Gölz, Christine, *37*, 226
Goncharov, Ivan A., 146
Goethe, Johann Wolfgang von, 8
   Elective Affinities (Die Wahlverwandtschaften), 145
Goetsch, Paul, *81*, 226
Greimas, Algirdas Julien, *187*, 226
Grimm, Gunter, 53-54, 227
Grimmelshausen, Hans Jacob Christoffel von
   Simplicius Simplicissimus (Der abenteuerliche Simplicissimus Teutsch), 76
Gukovsky, Grigory A., 95
Günther, Werner, 169, *173*, 227
Gurvich, Isaak A., *95*, 227
Gushanskaya, E. M., 240

Haard, Eric A. de, *65*, 227
Haller, Rudolf, *32*, 227
Hamburger, Käte, 22, 23, 25-27, 29, 59, 62, 73, *113*, 158, *159*, 165, 217, 227
Hansen-Löve, Aage, 29, *123*, *125*, *176*, 184, 227
Harweg, Roland, *65*, *82*, 227
Hauff, Wilhelm
   "Caliph Stork, The" (Kalif Storch), 199
Hemingway, Ernest, 62-63
Hempfer, Klaus, 25, 42, 227
Herman, David, *VI*, 227
Herman, Jan, *91*, 221
Hesse, Hermann
   Steppenwolf (Der Steppenwolf), 165
Hodel, Robert, *145*, 227
Hoek, Leo H., *34*, 44, 228
Hoffmann, Ernst Theodor Amadeus
   Life and Opinions of Tomcat Murr, The (Die Lebensansichten des Katers Murr), 60

News of the Latest Fortunes of the Hound Berganza (Nachricht von den neuesten Schicksalen des Hundes Berganza), 60
Hofmannsthal, Hugo von, 124
Holthusen, Johannes, *166*, 228
Holý, Jiří, 140, 228
Homer
    Iliad (Ἰλιάς), 118
Hoops, Wiklef, *23*, 228
Horálek, Karel, *26*, 228
Hrabal, Bohumil
    Closely Observed Trains (Ostře sledované vlaky), 77–78
Hühn, Peter, 8, *48*, 228

Ilyin, I. P., 42, *55*, 62, *78*, 91, 228
Ingarden, Roman, 4, 30, 200, 204, 228
Iser, Wolfgang, 40, 53, 228
Ivanchikova, E. A., *37*, 228

Jahn, Manfred, 67, *89*, 228
Jakobson, Roman, V, 19–20, *123*, 177, 228
James, Henry, *8*, 62, *66*, 89, *105*, 229
James, William, *152*
Janik, Dieter, *33*, 34, 229
Jannidis, Fotis, 40, *41*, 229
Jasińska, Maria, 80, 229
Jedličková, Alice, *79*, 229
Jensen, Peter Alberg, *122*, 229
Jost, François, 93, 229
Joyce, James
    Ulysses, VII, *152*, 159
Juhl, Peter D., *41*, 229

Kablitz, Andreas, *91*, 93, 229
Kafka, Franz
    Castle, The (Das Schloss), 74, 165
    Investigations of a Dog (Forschungen eines Hundes), 60
    Report to an Academy, A (Ein Bericht für eine Akademie), 60
Kahrmann, Cordula, *34*, 229
Kainz, Friedrich, *36*, 229

Kalepky, Theodor, 170–71, 229
Karamzin, Nikolay M., VII, 209
    "Natalie, the Boyar's Daughter" (Natal'ya, boyarskaya doch'), 72
    "Poor Liza" (Bednaya Liza), 75, 79, 144
Katkov, Mikhail N., 202
Kayser, Wolfgang, 77, 229
Keller, Gottfried
    Green Henry (Der grüne Heinrich), 73
Kenner, Hugh, *166*, 229
Khanpira, E., *95*, 229
Kindt, Tom, *VI*, *40*, *41*, 229–30
Klepper, Martin, *146*, 230
Kohl, Stephan, *22*, 230
Koller, Hermann, *22*, 230
Korman, Boris O., 38, 53, 230
Korte, Barbara, *71*, 230
Kovtunova, I. I., 148, 230
Koževniková, Květa, *134*, 230
Kozhevnikova, Natal'ya A., 70, 122, *126*, 132, *135*, 166, 230
Koziol, H., *26*, 230
Kristeva, Julia, 41, 230
Kroychik, L. E., 130, 232
Kullmann, Dorothea, *159*, *160*, 230

Labov, William, *13*, 230
LaCapra, Dominick, 146, 230
Låftman, Emil, 171, 230
Lallot, Jean, *22*, 224
Lamarque, Peter, *24*, 230
Lämmert, Eberhard, 201, 230
Lanser, Susan S., *41*, 74, *89*, 230
Lauer, Gerhard, 229
Lawrence, D. H.
    Rainbow, The, 123
    Women in Love, 123
Leibfried, Erwin, 66, 73, 230
Lerch, Eugen, *157*, 169, 230
Lerch, Gertraud, *145*, 169, 231
Lermontov, Mikhail Yu., 146, 209
    Hero of Our Time, A (Geroy nashego vremeni) 47, 75

Index of authors and narratives 255

Lesage, Alain-René
  Gil Blas (L'Histoire de Gil Blas de Santillane), 74
Leskov, Nikolay S., 131
Levin, V. D., *122*, 231
Likhachev, Dimitry S., *37*, 231
Link, Hannelore, *34*, 53-54, 231
Lintvelt, Jaap, *34*, *44*, *55*, 56, *65*, 66, *89*, *95*, 98, 102, 105, 219, 231
Lips, Marguerite, *145*, 168, 231
Lockemann, Wolfgang, *26*, 231
Lorck, Etienne, *169*, 231
Löschnigg, Martin, *27*, 231
Lotman, Yury M.,V, 8, 10, 13, 216, 231
Lubbock, Percy, *8*, 62, 66, 89, *105*, 231
Lucian of Samosata
  Lucius or *The Ass* (Λούκιος ἢ ὄνος), 60
Lucius Apuleius
  Metamorphoses or *The Golden Ass* (Metamorphoses or Asinus aureus), 60
Lukios of Patrai
  Metamorphoses (Μεταμορφώσεων λόγοι), 60

Mann, Thomas
  Felix Krull (Die Bekenntnisse des Hochstaplers Felix Krull), 76-77, 165
  Royal Highness (Königliche Hoheit), VII, 112
  Lotte in Weimar: The Beloved Returns (Lotte in Weimar), 113
Markovich, Vladimir M., 17, *41*, 231
Markus, Manfred, *89*, 231
Martínez, Matías, 4, 27, *105*, *188*, 229, 231
Martínez Bonati, Félix, *24*, *25*, *30*, 231
Mathauserová, Světla, *95*, 232
Matlaw, Ralph E., *60*, 232
McHale, Brian, *146*, *157*, *166*, 232
Meijer, Jan M., *60*, 232
Meister, Jan Christoph, *VI*, *3*, *8*, *216*, 232

Melville, Herman
  Moby Dick, 77
Meyer, Kurt Robert, 165, 232
Moenninghof, Burkhard, 27, 232
Morrison, Kristin, *105*, 232
Morson, Gary Saul, *84*, 232
Mukařovský, Jan, *31*, 39, 232
Müller, Günther, 200, 232
Müller, Hans-Harald, *VI*, *40*, *41*, 43, 229-30
Mushchenko E. G., 130, 232

Nabokov, Vladimir V.
  Eye, The (Soglyadatay), 71
  King, Queen, Knave (Korol', dama, valet), 47
  Torpid Smoke (Tyazhelyi dym), VII, 70-71
Neruda, Jan
  "How Mister Vorel Broke in His Meerschaum Pipe" (Jak si pan Vorel nakouřil pěnovku), 13
Neschke, Ada B., *22*, 232
Neubert, Albrecht, *145*, 169, 232
Neuse, Werner, *145*, 232
Nibelungenlied, 145
Nünning, Ansgar, *VI*, *41*, 42-43, *61*, *67*, *89*, *93*, *151*, *196*, 228, 232-33

Ohmann, Richard, *24*, 233
Okopień-Sławińska, Aleksandra, 34, 39, 80, 233
Olsen, Stein Haugom, *24*, 233
One Thousand and One Nights, 67
Orwell, George
  Nineteen Eighty-Four, 32
Oulanoff, Hongor, *122*, 233

Paducheva, Elena V., *68*, 69, 72, 80, *139*, 146, 172, 233
Palmer, Alan, 162, 233
Parable of the Prodigal Son, 16, 202
Parsons, Terence, *32*, 233
Pascal, Roy, 145, *157*, 233
Paschen, Hans, *34*, 233
Pavel, Thomas G., *30*, *32*, 233

Peirce, Charles Sanders, 37, 233
Penzkofer, Gerhard, 65, 233
Peshkovsky, A. M., 154, 233
Petersen, Jürgen H., 26, 72-73, 105, 233
Petrov-Vodkin, Kuzma S.
  Khlynovsk (Khlynovsk. Moya povest'), 70
Petrovsky, Mikhail A., 179-81, 185, 187, 220, 233
Philippe, Charles Louis
  Bubu de Montparnasse, 64
Pier, John, 4, 188, 189, 234
Plato, 7, 8, 22, 23, 118-19, 137
Polletta, Gregory T., 41, 234
Pomorska, Krystyna, 20, 228
Pouillon, Jean, 91-92, 234
Pratt, Mary Louise, 82, 234
Prince, Gerald, 3, 5, 82, 234
Propp, Vladimir Ya., V, 18, 234
Proust, Marcel
  Search of Lost Time, In (A la recherche du temps perdu), 201
Pushkin, Alexander S., 75, 79, 146
  "Blizzard, The" (Metel'), 202
  Eugene Onegin (Evgeny Onegin), VII, 81-82, 177
  "Queen of Spades, The" (Pikovaya dama), 206-07
  "Shot, The" (Vystrel), 107-109, 202, 206
  "Squire's Daughter, The" (Baryshnya krest'yanka), 202
  "Stationmaster, The" (Stantsionnyi smotritel'), 16, 67, 78, 203-06
  Tales of Belkin, The (Povesti Belkina), 4, 125, 126, 202, 204
  "Undertaker, The" (Grobovshchik), 202

Rasch, Wolfdietrich, 26, 234
Reformatsky, Alexander, 179
Rehbein, Jochen, 195, 234
Reiß, Gunter, 34, 229
Remizov, Aleksey M., 131
Renner, Karl Nikolaus, 8, 234

Ricœur, Paul, 22, 196, 234
Riffaterre, Michel, 27, 234
Rilke, Rainer Maria
  Lay of Love and Death of Cornet Christopher Rilke, The (Die Weise von Liebe und Tod des Cornets Christoph Rilke), VII, 124
Rimmon-Kenan, Shlomit, 40, 42, 50, 43, 67, 91, 95, 98-99, 103, 187, 190, 194, 219, 234
Robbe-Grillet, Alain
  Jealousy (La Jalousie), 71, 211
Romberg, Bertil, 67, 234
Rühling, Lutz, 21, 24, 234
Ryan, Marie-Laure, 62-63, 234
Rymar', Nikolay, 37, 38, 46, 234

Schaper, Edzard
  Letzte Advent, Der, 159
Scheffel, Michael, 4, 27, 105, 175, 188, 231, 234
Schernus, Wilhelm, 61
Schiller, Friedrich von, 182
Schissel von Fleschenberg, Otmar, 176, 180, 235
Schluchter, Manfred, 34, 229
Schmid, Wolf, V, 3, 4, 6, 8, 13-14, 16-17, 20, 33, 34-37, 41, 44, 48, 50, 53, 55, 56-57, 60, 64, 73-74, 82, 91, 95, 122, 123, 125, 126, 127, 128, 137, 139, 146, 173, 175, 177, 200, 203, 207, 211, 215, 235-36
Schnitzler, Arthur
  "Lieutenant Gustl," 151
  "Second, The" (Der Sekundant), 165
Searle, John R., 22, 24-26, 27, 63 217, 236
Segal, Dimitry M., 95, 236
Seidler, Herbert, 26, 236
Seuffert, Bernhard, 176
Shipley, Joseph T., 60, 236-37
Shklovsky, Viktor B., V, 16, 122, 134, 176-79, 182, 184-85, 187, 189, 191, 220, 236
Shlykova, M. A., 162, 237
Shor, Rozaliya, 176, 180, 237

Shukman, Ann, 95, 237
Simmel, Georg, 195-96, 237
Skobelev, Vladislav, 37, 38, 46, 53, 130, 237
Sławiński, Janusz, 39, 237
Smith, Barbara Herrnstein, 24, 237
Socrates, 23
Sokolova, Lyudmila A., 148, 153, 169-70, 237
Solzhenitsyn, Alexander I.
  One Day in the Life of Ivan Denisovich (Odin den' Ivana Denisovicha), VII, 167-68
Sörbom, Göran, 22, 237
Souriau, Etienne 6, 237
Spielhagen, Friedrich, 1, 237
Spitzer, Leo, 64, 69, 152, 157, 161, 171, 173, 237
Stanzel, Franz K., 1, 2, 26, 69, 73, 169, 237-38
Steinberg, Günter, 157, 159, 238
Steiner, Wendy, 95, 238
Stempel, Wolf-Dieter, 3, 39, 238
Sternberg, Meir, 3, 186, 18, 238
Sterne, Laurence
  Life and Opinions of Tristram Shandy, Gentleman, The, 176, 211
Stierle, Karlheinz, 189, 190, 194, 220
Struve, Gleb, 122, 151
Szilárd, Léna, 122, 238

Taborishskaya, E. M., 224
Tamarchenko, Natan D., 89, 238
Thürnau, Donatus, 24, 238
Titunik, Irwin R., 133, 238
Titzmann, Michael, 3, 8, 238-39
Tobler, Adolf, 170, 239
Todemann, Fritz, 165, 239
Todorov, Tzvetan, V, 2 42, 91-92, 95, 179, 184-88, 190-91, 194, 220, 239
Tolmachev, V. M., 89, 239
Tolstoy, Leo N., 202
  Anna Karenina, VII, 17, 30, 106, 110-11, 190, 199, 206-07
  "Death of Ivan Ilyich, The" (Smert' Ivana Il'icha), 24
  "Devil, The" (D'yavol), 47
  "Father Sergius" (Otets Sergy), 47
  Kreutzer Sonata, The (Kreytserova sonata), 47
  Sebastopol Sketches (Sevastopol'skie ocherki), 151
  "Sebastopol in December" (Sevastopol' v dekabre mesyatse), VII, 72
  Strider: The Story of a Horse (Kholstomer. Istoriya loshadi), VII, 61
  War and Peace (Voyna i mir), VII, 8, 17, 28, 31, 32, 103, 109, 113, 149-52, 155-56, 163-64, 178, 197, 208, 217
Tomashevsky, Boris V., V, 6, 179, 184-87, 190-91, 194, 199, 220, 239
Toolan, Michael J., 42, 80, 239
Tsilevich, Leonid M., 176, 239
Tsurganova, E. A., 228
Turgenev, Ivan S., 17
  Asya, VII, 165
Tynyanov, Yury N., V, 46, 122, 131-32, 179, 182-83, 220, 239

Unbegaun, Boris, 202, 239
Uspensky, Boris A. V, 48, 57, 95-99, 102-04, 219, 239

Vaihinger, Hans, 22, 240
Valk, Frans de, 95, 240
Verschoor, Jan Adriaan, 145, 240
Vinogradov, Viktor V., 37, 38-39, 48, 95, 131-32, 137, 240
Vitoux, Pierre, 94, 240
Volek, Emil, 3, 176, 179, 184, 240
Voloshinov, Valentin N., V, 95, 138-39, 146, 154, 168, 171, 172-74, 219
Vygotsky, Lev S., 181-84, 187, 220, 240

Walzel, Oskar, 1, 171, 240
Warren, Robert Penn, 92, 194, 240
Weidlé, Wladimir, 22, 240
Weimar, Klaus, 6, 26, 240
Weinrich, Harald, 27, 240
Wellek, René, 194, 240

Weststeijn, Willem, *34*, 45–47, 240
White, Hayden, *196*, 240
Wimsatt, William K. 41, 240
Winko, Simone, 229
Wolff, Erwin, 53, 240
Woolf, Virginia
   Lighthouse, To the, VII, 159
   Mrs. Dalloway, 113
   Waves, The, VII, 123
Wulf, Christoph, *22*, 240

Zamyatin, Evgeny I., 127
   "Cave, The" (Peshchera), 128
   "Flood, The" (Navodnenie), *127*

Zaretsky, V. A., 240
Zholkovsky, Alexander, *182*, 241
Zhirmunsky, Viktor M., 122, 176, 179, 241
Zimmermann, Friedrich Wilhelm, *26*, 241
Zipfel, Frank, *21*, *23*, *24*, 27, *32*, 42, 241
Żółkiewski, Stefan, *95*, 241
Zoshchenko, Mikhail M., 131, 134
   "Lady Aristocrat, The" (Aristokratka), VIII, 135
Zuckerkandl, Viktor, 23, 241